HARWOOD L. CHILDS joined the faculty at Princeton University in 1931, and is currently Professor of Politics. He is also the founder, and at the present time Editor, of the *Public Opinion Quarterly*. He is a graduate of Dartmouth College and the University of Chicago, where he received his Ph.D.

The author has served on the faculties of Dartmouth, Syracuse University, the College of William and Mary, and Bucknell University. He was a Social Science Research Fellow (1931-32) and a Guggenheim Fellow (1937), both for study in Germany; Area Chief, Office of War Information, on leave from Princeton (1943-45); Visiting Professor, School of Public Administration, sponsored by the United Nations and the Brazilian Government, Rio de Janeiro (1953-54); and Visiting Professor at New York University and the University of Southern California.

A contributor to numerous scholarly publications, Professor Childs is the author of *Labor and Capital in National Politics, A Reference Guide to the Study of Public Opinion,* and *An Introduction to Public Opinion;* co-author of *Propaganda by Short Wave;* translator, and author of an introduction to *The Maze Primer;* and editor of *Propaganda and Dictatorship.*

1778

public opinion

VAN NOSTRAND POLITICAL SCIENCE SERIES

FRANKLIN L. BURDETTE, *Editor*
University of Maryland

PLISCHKE, E.—*Conduct of American Diplomacy,* 2nd Ed.

DIXON, R. G., JR., and PLISCHKE, ELMER—*American Government: Basic Documents and Materials*

LANCASTER, LANE W.—*Government in Rural America,* 2nd Ed.

JORRIN, M.—*Governments of Latin America*

PLISCHKE, ELMER—*International Relations: Basic Documents,* 2nd Ed.

LINEBARGER, P. M. A., DJANG, C., and BURKS, A. W.—*Far Eastern Governments and Politics—China and Japan,* 2nd Ed.

GOODMAN, WILLIAM—*The Two-Party System in the United States,* 3rd Ed.

SWARTZ, WILLIS G.—*American Governmental Problems,* 2nd Ed.

BAKER, BENJAMIN—*Urban Government*

DILLON, CONLEY H., LEIDEN, CARL, and STEWART, PAUL D.—*Introduction to Political Science*

ZINK, HAROLD, PENNIMAN, HOWARD R., and HATHORN, GUY B.—*American Government and Politics: National, State, and Local*

ZINK, HAROLD—*Modern Governments*

HENDEL, SAMUEL—*The Soviet Crucible: The Soviet System in Theory and Practice*

HATHORN, GUY B., PENNIMAN, HOWARD R., and FERBER, MARK—*Government and Politics in the United States,* 2nd Ed.

MADDOX, RUSSELL W., and FUQUAY, ROBERT F.—*State and Local Government*

SHARABI, H. B.—*Governments and Politics of the Middle East in the Twentieth Century*

ANDREWS, WILLIAM G.—*European Political Institutions*

SPROUT, HAROLD and MARGARET—*Foundations of International Politics*

NEEDLER, MARTIN C.—*Political Systems of Latin America*

CHILDS, HARWOOD L.—*Public Opinion: Nature, Formation, and Role*

PUBLIC OPINION:

nature, formation, and role

HARWOOD L. CHILDS

Professor of Politics, and
Editor, The Public Opinion Quarterly
Princeton University

D. VAN NOSTRAND COMPANY, INC.

PRINCETON, NEW JERSEY
Toronto • New York • London

To my family, and especially my fifteen grand-children, some of whom may also develop an interest in public opinion

D. VAN NOSTRAND COMPANY, INC.
120 Alexander Street, Princeton, New Jersey (*Principal Office*)
24 West 40 Street, New York 18, New York

D. VAN NOSTRAND COMPANY, LTD.
358, Kensington High Street, London W. 14, England

D. VAN NOSTRAND COMPANY (Canada), LTD.
25 Hollinger Road, Toronto 16, Canada

Printed in the United States of America

· PREFACE ·

THE PURPOSE of this book is threefold: to discuss the nature of public opinion; to consider the ways in which opinions are formed; and finally, to try and see as clearly as possible what the role of public opinion is and might be, particularly in the United States. After an introductory chapter, an effort is made to clarify the meaning of the term *public opinion,* to show why definitions of it differ, and to trace, somewhat summarily to be sure, the varying uses of the term over the centuries. Then follows a chapter reviewing in greater detail the significant developments in the study of public opinion during the last fifty years. Chapter 4 focuses on the problem, How does one find out what public opinion is on specific questions, and in the case of particular publics? After describing public opinion surveys and polling techniques, the question is raised, What are the opinions of publics really worth, especially those of large, mass publics? And the search for a discriminating answer is undertaken in Chapter 5.

Consideration of public opinion formation bulks large in the over-all content of the book. Chapter 6 gives a general background setting and shows how opinions are ultimately rooted in personalities, in turn the product of a dynamic, interacting process between the individual and his environment. In succeeding chapters the influence of family, church, school, of mass media, pressure groups, advertising, public relations, and government are considered, in an effort to pinpoint the discussion of opinion formation and to indicate how and to what extent these important factors mold public opinion. It will be abundantly clear that the whole process of opinion formation is frustratingly complex and obscure, but to realize this is the beginning of wisdom and a shield against impetuous assertions and foolish myths.

A final chapter is left for the basic problem of public opinion, as the author sees it; namely, the problem of how to give public opinion, in the sense of the collective opinions of the voting public in the United States, the role it should have in the social, economic, and political life of the country. All the preceding chapters contribute to this final one and assist in the search for the answer. It may not display too much enthusiasm to claim that the preservation of democracy may depend to a large extent on bringing about a redefinition of the respective roles of government and citizen, official and voter, expert and layman.

This book is the product of many years of teaching, study, discussion, and reading. It would be invidious to single out one or a few authors or students for special mention. But I do wish to acknowledge my special indebtedness to undergraduates and graduates who have taken my public opinion seminars and courses. I also wish to thank Professor Stanley Kelley for his careful reading of the manuscript and for his helpful, constructive suggestions, Mrs. Madeleine Clee for her workmanlike typing of the manuscript, and my wife who did so much to provide the household environment conducive to writing.

H.L.C.

Princeton
November 1964

· CONTENTS ·

I · Introduction

He who writes of the state, of law, or of politics, without first coming to close quarters with public opinion is simply evading the very central structure of his study.

—A. F. BENTLEY

PUBLIC OPINION is an object of widespread interest. It is venerated, feared, praised, cursed, and solicited. Politicians court it; statesmen appeal to it; philosophers extol or condemn it; merchants cater to it; military leaders fear it; sociologists analyze it; statisticians measure it; and constitution-makers try to make it sovereign. The Department of State of the United States provides top governmental officials with daily reports on the gist of public opinion within the United States and throughout the world.[1] Other government agencies have additional sources of information about public opinion of particular value to them. At the University of Michigan, Columbia, Chicago, and other institutions of higher learning, survey research organizations are diligently and continuously probing the states and trends of public opinion. The business of marketing research has grown to large proportions, and businessmen now have exceptional facilities for knowing the desires and tastes of the American people. The President of the United States, in company with group leaders generally, has his public opinion advisors. So have Brezhnev, De Gaulle, Wilson, and the political leaders of the world generally. The significance of public opinion is really the fact that a precise knowledge of the opinions of a specific group of people often is a clue to what that group is likely to do. For those who wish to lead or guide other people, knowledge of their opinions and attitudes is almost indispensable. One of the interesting things about public opinion is that it can be managed to some extent, and it is being managed on an unparalleled scale. Group leaders seek to mold, guide, lead, control, and manage opinions. Nearly everyone is both a manager and a leader as well as an object of control and leadership in matters of opinion.

The financial outlays for opinion management are tremendous. In the

1

United States alone more than 12 billion dollars are spent yearly for advertising. The political parties and others probably spent at least 200 million dollars in the 1960 Presidential and Congressional elections.[2] Other groups —business, labor, professional, religious, ethnic, and special purpose groups —spend millions of dollars every year to promote their interests. Only a few of these register in compliance with the federal lobbying law, but those that did in 1962 spent several millions merely for the purpose of influencing national legislation. The budgets of governments throughout the world reflect intense concern with problems of public opinion. The United States Information Agency has a yearly budget of well over 100 million dollars, and this is only a fraction of the amounts spent by national, state, and local government agencies to influence public opinion. It is alleged on seemingly good authority that the Soviet Union's expenditures for external propaganda alone are several times those of the United States. Similarly, in Great Britain, France, Germany, Italy, China, India, Africa, South America, and other countries, there never was a time when governments were more public opinion conscious than today.

Another salient indication of the widespread importance of public opinion is the time and money spent to survey, probe, poll, and analyze it. Nation-wide, state-wide and local polls are active throughout the United States. Never in human history has so much interest been shown in the opinions of other people, of masses and groups of all kinds and sizes. In England, Japan, Russia, France, Brazil, the nations of Africa, and other countries public opinion surveys are being conducted continually. This concern with public opinion has long been evident in academic circles, in the programs of foundations and universities, and in scholarly journals which publish an ever-mounting quota of public opinion research articles. For nearly thirty years the *Public Opinion Quarterly* has been devoting its pages exclusively to this subject. Most of the larger universities and colleges have courses specifically devoted to the study of public opinion.

REASONS FOR INCREASING EMPHASIS

There are many reasons for the increasing emphasis on public opinion. The spread of democracy and the extension of the suffrage are factors of great importance.[3] Democratic government—in the sense of widespread popular participation, majority rule, elected officials, representative assemblies, and written constitutions—developed very slowly and uncertainly until the end of the eighteenth century. The nineteenth century, however, saw rapid changes, as state after state in the United States adopted a written constitution, extended the suffrage, introduced direct primary laws, increased the number of elections and elected officials, and passed initiative and referendum laws. The proportion of the population officially taking part in public affairs has steadily increased, their responsibilities of citizenship have expanded, and the opinions of the enlarged electorate have become more and more important. By the 1830's national party organizations were convening national conventions, and organizations of workers, businessmen, and many special groups were bringing pressure to bear on government and publics alike. It has been estimated that only 5.1 per cent of the eligible voters took part in the Presidential election of 1824. Since then the proportion has grown until in 1960 it reached 60 per cent. As the voting public grew in size it became more powerful, and efforts to influence it and win its support became more intense.

A second reason for the increasing concern about public opinion has been the growth and spread of educational facilities. Winning the battle for publicly supported schools and colleges greatly expanded educational opportunities for all classes of citizens. Government appropriations for educational purposes steadily increased. Compulsory school attendance in the grades, plus laws protecting child labor, increased school attendance. The United States spends approximately 20 billion dollars yearly for public education from kindergarten through the twelfth grade. Nearly all young people of secondary school age are now attending public or private secondary schools, and almost one out of three of college age is attending institutions of higher learning. It has been estimated that approximately onefourth of the total population of the United States is directly engaged, in one way or another, with education. This growth of educational facilities tends to raise the hopes and to increase the demands of citizens. It induces a willingness, and probably a competence, to express opinions. It may encourage discontent and promote change. All in all, a better-educated body of citizens is more influential. Ideas are multiplied; hopes are expressed, intellectual unrest is stimulated; and the opinions of the masses become more vociferous, urgent, and important.

The importance of public opinion has also been enhanced because of improvements in contact and communication—in transportation, point-to-point communication, and above all, agencies of mass impression. Although most people are aware of these particular developments and take them for granted, many forget how speedily these changes have squeezed people together within countries and throughout the world. The influence of television, in any public opinion sense, has risen significantly in the last decade, since 1952 at least, when the federal communications commission discontinued the "freeze." [4] The newspaper is the oldest medium of mass communication; yet there were no daily papers in the United States until after the American Revolution, and it was not until the beginning of the twentieth century that any daily paper's circulation rose to over one million. Radio broadcasting and motion pictures, both of which seem to have already reached, if not passed, the point of greatest public opinion significance, are products of this century. In transportation, the emphasis has been on speed, until men may move from place to place at speeds faster than sound. It is difficult to think of two places on earth so distant from each other that point-to-point communication between them cannot be provided.

All of these technical improvements in communication and transportation have greatly enlarged the numerical size of publics, in the sense of groups listening to the same programs, hearing the same speaker, reading the same stories. Those who control these media have greatly enhanced their power to sway opinions; those who do not control them, have, by the same token, lost influence. Moreover, public opinion itself has become more influential as media tend to mobilize, unify, and to some extent standardize its attitudes and beliefs. Publics which can be "sold" late model cars and new detergents are also publics which may be aroused to vote for a well-publicized candidate, or approve a well-advertised legislative program.

In the fourth place, economic changes have had a profound impact on public opinion and its role in society. The growth in size of American business enterprises, as well as an increase in the number of smaller firms, has produced not only mass production but also mass consumption of goods and services. Production and consumption must, over longer periods of time at least, go hand in hand; hence, the trend toward industrial bigness, concentration, standardization, and lower unit costs, and the tremendous pressure to sell, to advertise and cajole, to push and persuade. This is not the place to amplify this point, but it is one of the elements which must be appreciated if one is to comprehend the reasons for the emphasis on public opinion today.

The increasing importance and significance of public opinion is due not only to the factors already considered but also to a fifth factor—an ever more intense struggle to win public opinion support. In the international sphere this is a competition among states, and some non-governmental groups, to align public opinion on their side. It is also a struggle between groups of states—East against West, the Soviet bloc against the non-Soviet, the Arab world against the non-Arab, the Organization of American States against the Communists. Similarly, within countries, organized groups of all kinds strive to enlist the aid of other groups and publics. Propaganda begets propaganda. As one nation or group enlarges its propaganda activities, other nations and groups in self-defense do likewise. The propaganda race can be expensive, exhausting, and possibly as absurd in the long run as an armaments race. Efforts to control or limit it have been few.[5] Some governments try to restrict campaign expenditures of political parties. In a few instances national states have signed treaties controlling or limiting international propaganda, but success has been small.

The intensity of the competition for public opinion is heightened by the stupendous stakes involved. Public opinion can make or break political and economic fortunes. Democracy and widespread suffrage have placed in the hands of the masses weapons of great power. Furthermore, the cleavages and tensions between peoples, economic crises, variations in and discrepancies among standards of living, and economic, political, and military aggrandizement all combine to help explain the intensity of the public opinion struggle.

Finally, public opinion is increasingly important because the carrying out of so many public policies necessitates the support and cooperation of large numbers of people. This is obvious in wartime when hostilities involve total populations. But in peacetime, also, public opinion support on a broad scale is needed to implement numerous public policies, domestic and foreign as well as financial and non-financial problems of desegregation, of production control, of law enforcement, of employer-employee relations, and many others. Congress may pass laws dealing with farm surpluses, desegregation, civil rights, bomb shelters, income taxes, conservation, and other matters directly affecting the behavior of millions, but if large sections of the population are opposed, enforcement of the legislation is difficult if not impossible. The Supreme Court can outlaw school segregation, but it may take decades to implement the decision in some parts of the country because of public antagonism. This problem has always been present to some extent in the United States, but not to the degree it is today. It is not enough merely to formulate, pass, and seek to enforce laws. It is necessary to win support for them.

The responsibility of government for opinion leadership has attained unprecedented proportions. Responsible government may not advisedly proceed far in advance of public opinion. This situation poses many perplexing problems. How far is government justified in going to win support for its leadership? To what extent should it censor and conceal information, distort and fabricate, engage in propaganda and stress emotional appeals? In short, to what extent do the responsibilities for opinion leadership make it necessary for government to manage opinions? [6]

This is a problem confronting all governments, authoritarian as well as democratic. The Soviet Union and Communist China have no hesitancy about using whatever means are available to manage public opinion in their countries. They censor and deceive; they control in great detail the media of communication; they jam and bar the influx of foreign intelligence; and they punish severely evidence of information leaks and deviate opinions. For authoritarians the end justifies the means, and that end is always close to 100 per cent support of government policies. Democracies, however, are usually unwilling to subordinate everything to the ends of public policy, although they come closer to this in time of war than in peacetime.

Usually, the emphasis is placed on freedom—freedom of speech, press, opinion, free enterprise, free assembly, the right of each person to form his own opinions as best he can. The presumption is that this freedom will, in the long run if not the short run, produce a truer public opinion, one that is wiser and more valid than if it were dictated by higher authority. As conditions change rapidly, as tensions local and international mount, as the shadows of war lighten and darken, the long view gives way to the short view, and even in democracies freedom of opinion is to some extent curtailed. The problems of authority and freedom are as critical and enigmatic in the areas of public opinion as in any other.

PUBLIC OPINION AND THE BRANCHES OF GOVERNMENT

It may serve to underscore further the salience of public opinion problems today if they are related more specifically to the judicial, legislative, and executive branches of government. At first glance, the courts seem to be relatively untroubled about public opinion. Their job is to decide cases, not to be concerned with public reactions to their decisions, nor to be bothered by the public views regarding the courts or legal processes. The courts enjoy, especially at the higher levels, great public prestige and confidence, probably more than either of the other branches. And this is true notwithstanding the fact that they do not have the services of press agents or specialists in public opinion management. There have been comparatively few studies of the relationships between courts and public opinion, but a few observations seem justified.[7]

(1) The prestige of the courts rises, as a rule, as one climbs the judicial ladder from justice of the peace or local municipal courts to the United States Supreme Court. The federal courts, and the Supreme Court especially, enjoy a most favorable public image, notwithstanding decisions from time to time which engender widespread protest. There are many reasons why the higher courts have this prestige: the special place occupied by the courts in the American constitutional system, the role played by lawyers both inside and outside government, the relative remoteness of the courts, especially the higher ones, from the everyday affairs of the people, and the generally high caliber of the judges themselves.

(2) The Courts, by and large, lay little emphasis upon opinion management, upon deliberate attempts to influence public opinion. At the lower levels sensational criminal trials often receive extravagant attention in the mass media, and from time to time decisions by one of the higher courts will be communicated to the public generally. As a rule, however, the day-to-day work of the courts receives little notice from the mass media and the public. Although a few judges are well-known, most remain obscured behind robes, rituals, and regalia, as well as procedures, which

emphasize the dignity, deliberative nature, and remoteness of the courts.

(3) The prestige of the closely related agencies of judicial administration and law enforcement seldom experience the degree of popular favor enjoyed by the courts. Departments of justice, Attorneys General, Bureaus of Investigation, police forces, vary considerably in their degrees of public acceptance. (The Federal Bureau of Investigation, for example, under Edgar Hoover has had a very favorable image in the eyes of a great many people.)

The press relations of the lower courts particularly have not always been salutary. Sensational press treatment of criminal trials, revelations of dishonesty, trickery, and corruption, emphasis on technicalities and procedures, preoccupation with the dramatic and unusual as well as neglect of systematic, comprehensive reporting—all tend to place the trial courts in a bad light. Many insightful observers of our judicial system have stressed the need for more public information and understanding of that system. Law enforcement and crime prevention can be furthered in no small degree through the exercise of greater care by judicial and law enforcement agencies in dealing with their public opinion problems.

The legislative branch of government is in many respects closer to the public than the other branches. Its members are elected directly by the voters, and their terms of office, at least in the lower house if there is one, are short. The question whether a legislative body should lead or reflect public opinion is usually answered by saying it should do both, and then the debate begins over the placing of emphasis. If anything, the tendency today is for legislators to turn more and more to the executive branch and to unofficial groups for policy leadership, to devote more and more time to analyzing and criticizing that leadership, and to reflect public opinion rather than lead it. It is not altogether clear just what the relationship is between public opinion and legislative policy because of the many factors which determine each. Certain it is that frequently there is a lag or sizable discrepancy between the two. The relative influence on a legislator's vote of political party, pressure group, constituency, administrative pressure, logrolling, personal bias, and the like varies greatly from measure to measure, and the role of general public opinion varies also.[8]

Students of government frequently refer to the decline of representative bodies and the ascendency of the administrative and executive.[9] There are, of course, many reasons for this: the need for quick actions, conflicts of interests within legislatures, their inability to lead, their lack of information, frequent changes in composition, and many others. Yet one important reason for declining prestige is surely poor press relations, a failure to acquaint the public in general with their problems, their activities, and their objectives. In many respects the legislature is as far removed from the

general public as the judiciary, however much attention and publicity individual senators and congressmen may obtain. In the public mind the
legislature as a democratic, representative, policy-making institution too
infrequently rises above the level of competing, self-seeking, vociferous individual members. There is no systematic, thoughtful endeavor to inform
the general public regarding the over-all legislative task. The flow of
legislative news in the press is a more or less haphazard flow of personal
notes, votes, dramatic episodes, squabbles, and rivalries. Under these circumstances the public image is necessarily a distressing one—conflict, compromise, interests, segmentation—always episodic, lacking in real meaning or significance. Publicity is left to press correspondents, to representatives of pressure groups, to publicity-seeking legislators, and to whomever
may be interested. Whatever coordination and integration of facts and
activities occur are the work of private agents, all too frequently incapable
of getting a broad perspective of the whole. Perhaps it would be futile to
try through some central information bureau of the legislature to give an
over-all picture. And yet, such a staff might be able to fill the many gaps
left by the private media. It is a curious thing that none of the proposals
for legislative reorganization in recent years have taken public opinion into
account, in the sense of recognizing its importance and its effect.[10] All
kinds of suggestions are made for improving the internal workings of legislative bodies—their procedures, control, committees, etc.—but the problem of improving the relationship between legislature and public opinion
has been largely ignored.

The effects of this negligence are readily apparent. The dim view which
prevails regarding legislators, their competence, their activities, and their
accomplishments steadily darkens. The public turns more and more to the
President and the executive branch for leadership. The activities of congressmen become clouded and hidden; private interests find their opportunities expanded; and the vision of what is and can be the public interest
fades and disappears. It may be impossible to restore legislatures to the
positions of leadership they held in the past, but it will be useless even
to try unless a closer, more meaningful rapport with public opinion is established. One man, such as the President, cannot really represent the public as well as a representative body of several hundred persons.[11] One cannot satisfactorily solve the problem of legislative demise and impotence
simply by transferring more legislative power to the President. The answer
may be found, however, in increasing the prestige of legislatures, partly by
reorganization and internal improvements but also by deliberate, planned,
thoughtful efforts to solve directly some of their external public opinion
problems. These public opinion problems will most certainly become more
acute as international tensions increase, speedier actions become necessary,
and those in executive authority find themselves obliged to act.

Of the three main branches of government the executive and administrative branch has given the most attention to public opinion, and this for several reasons. In the first place, the chief executive, be he president, governor, or mayor, is very much interested as an individual and as a party leader in carrying out certain policies. To carry them out he must maintain his own public opinion support and also win support for the measures in which he is interested. The people in his constituency seem to be looking to him more and more for leadership, and if by chance he prefers to take a more relaxed and leisurely attitude toward public policy his critics quickly multiply in cries and numbers.

Secondly, many departments and agencies are given the job of carrying out programs which require a great deal of public support. This is especially true of the Department of Agriculture, for example, where programs of crop control require a very high degree of farmer cooperation, cooperation which cannot be forced but must be won by persuasion; similarly, with many other agency responsibilities and programs, in the execution and administration of criminal laws, social security, tax administration, conservation, labor relations, and business relations. However one may react to the trend, the fact is that government is expanding its activities constantly and will continue to do so, thus affecting the daily lives of citizens more and more. Government takes at least one-fifth to four-fifths or more of people's income in taxes. It regulates an ever-increasing number of personal types of behavior. It supervises directly or indirectly what we shall learn, what we can or cannot do in our occupations, and even what we can see, read, or hear. This means that an increasing effort must be made by nearly every administrative unit of government to explain and justify what it is doing.

Thirdly, in self-protection, government agencies must answer the charges directed at them by other agencies, by legislators, by outside critics of all kinds. If a department or agency is to survive it must not only do a good and effective job but it must also let the people know that it is doing it. Most federal agencies are letting the people know or trying to within the financial and other limits prescribed by law. The information and publicity activities of agencies have expanded to some extent since World War II, although some of them seem poorly equipped even now to carry out their responsibilities to public opinion.

Government agencies, particularly the administrative ones, have grown so extensively and so rapidly that the average person cannot keep abreast and cannot acquire the minimum information required to tell him whether the government is or is not doing a good job. Within the last twenty-five years the number of federal executive employees has risen from an average in 1935 of some 780,000 to an average in 1962 of nearly 2½ million; the expenditures from less than 7 billion dollars in 1938 to nearly 88 billion in 1962. But this is only the beginning. Problems have multiplied in number and complexity. The fields of defense, health, education, welfare, agriculture, commerce and industry, transportation, mining, and manufacturing—in fact, nearly all fields—have felt the impact of scientific discoveries and technological accomplishments. Unless the government, especially through its administrative agencies, keeps the public informed in these obscure and complicated areas, the citizen will slip further and further back in his appreciation of what the government is doing, can do, and should be doing. The speed of social change is so great that more and more attention must be given by the government to informing and educating the adult population.

NOTES FOR CHAPTER 1

Epigraph. A. F. Bentley, *The Process of Government* (1908).

1. See Elder, Robert E., "The Public Studies Division of the Department of State: Public Opinion Analysts in the Formulation and Conduct of American Foreign Policy," *The Western Political Quarterly,* Vol. 10, No. 4 (December, 1957), pp. 783-92.
2. See Alexander, Herbert E., *Financing the 1960 Election* (Princeton, N. J.: Citizens' Research Foundation, 1962).
3. See Hattersley, A. N., *A Short History of Democracy* (Cambridge: Cambridge University Press, 1930); Becker, Carl L., *Modern Democracy* (New Haven: Yale University Press, 1941); Riker, W. H., *Democracy in the United States* (New York: The Macmillan Co., 1953); Frankel, Charles, *The Democratic Prospect* (New York: Harper and Row, 1962).
4. See Emery, Walter B., *Broadcasting and Government* (Lansing: Michigan State University Press, 1961). (Esp. chap. 9.) The "freeze" was a ban on the granting of new TV licenses.
5. See Martin, Leslie John, *International Propaganda: Its Legal and Diplomatic Control* (Minneapolis: University of Minnesota Press, 1958).
6. See Krock, Arthur, "Mr. Kennedy's Management of the News," *Fortune,* Vol. 67 (March, 1963), pp. 82ff.
7. See Murphy, Walter F., *Congress and the Court: A Case Study in the American Political Process* (Chicago: University of Chicago Press, 1962). (Esp. pp. 264-65.)
8. See Turner, Julius, *Party and Constituency: Pressures on Congress* (Baltimore: The Johns Hopkins University Press, 1951).
9. See Wahlke, J. C., Eulau, Heinz, Buchanan, William, and LeRoy Ferguson, *The Legislative System* (New York: John Wiley and Sons, 1962); Clapp, Charles L., *The Congressman—His Work as He Sees It* (Washington, D. C.: The Brookings Institution, 1963); Peabody, R. L. and N. W. Polsby, *New Perspectives on the House of Representatives* (Chicago: Rand McNally & Co., 1963).
10. In a news release dated January 13, 1963, Senator Clifford P. Case (R.-N. J.) announced his intention to introduce a bill creating a kind of Hoover Commission on Congressional Reorganization to deal especially with twelve specific problem areas. Public opinion was not included.

11. It is sometimes argued that the President, since he is elected by a national constituency, is better able to represent the national interest than Congress, whose members are elected by much smaller Senatorial and Congressional constituencies. However, the theory of representative government is usually based on the proposition that representative, policy-making bodies must be large enough to present a cross section of the areas, elements, views, and interests represented.

SUPPLEMENTARY READING

ALBIG, WILLIAM. *Modern Public Opinion.* New York: McGraw-Hill Book Co., 1956.

BERELSON, BERNARD, and JANOWITZ, MORRIS. *Reader in Public Opinion Communication.* Chicago: The Free Press of Glencoe, Illinois, 1953.

CHILDS, HARWOOD L. *A Reference Guide to the Study of Public Opinion.* Princeton, N. J.: Princeton University Press, 1934.

CHILDS, HARWOOD L. *An Introduction to Public Opinion.* New York: John Wiley and Sons, 1940.

CHRISTENSON, REO MILLARD, and McWILLIAMS, ROBERT O. *Voice of the People: Readings in Public Opinion and Propaganda.* New York: McGraw-Hill Book Co., 1962.

DOOB, LEONARD W. *Public Opinion and Propaganda.* New York: Henry Holt & Co., 1948.

GRAVES, WILLIAM B. *Readings in Public Opinion.* New York: D. Appleton, 1928.

IRION, FREDERICK C. *Public Opinion and Propaganda.* New York: Thomas Y. Crowell Co., 1950.

MacDOUGALL, CURTIS DANIEL. *Understanding Public Opinion.* New York: The Macmillan Co., 1952.

ODEGARD, P. H. *The American Public Mind.* New York: Columbia University Press, 1930.

OGLE, MARBURY BLADEN. *Public Opinion and Political Dynamics.* Boston: Houghton Mifflin Co., 1950.

POWELL, NORMAN JOHN. *Anatomy of Public Opinion.* New York: Prentice-Hall, Inc., 1952.

II · The Nature and History of Public Opinion

Only fools, pure theorists, or apprentices in moral philosophy fail to take public opinion into account in their political undertakings.
—JACQUES NECKER

THE TERM "public opinion" may be used to refer to any collection of individual opinions. In everyday discourse it is frequently used to designate the collective opinions of large numbers of people. In that sense it is synonymous with mass opinion. In many instances, however, it is far from clear who constitutes the "mass," whether or not reference is made to the peoples of the world, the citizens of a particular country, the man in the street, the average person, the common man, or the voting public. Vagueness in the use of the term is usually attributable to the user's failure to explain carefully what public or collection of individuals he is referring to.

PUBLICS

If one could validly assert that there was one such "public," a particular group of individuals to which the term "public opinion" always referred, the problem of definition would be much simpler, but this is not the case. It seldom happens that those who use the term have identical publics in mind. To insist that it should apply to only one public, for example a public consisting of those entitled to vote in the United States, is unacceptable and arbitrary. Vagueness may be avoided by indicating clearly the public to which the user refers.

The number of publics is legion. There are organized and unorganized publics, primary and secondary, large and small, powerful and impotent, wise and foolish, important and unimportant. Those concerned with public opinion differ greatly in the foci of their interest. Studies of public opinion include studies of the collective opinions of the electorate in the United States, Great Britain, Australia, and other countries and surveys of the opinions of businessmen, factory workers, farmers, college presidents, students in psychology courses, boys and girls, movie goers, radio and TV listeners, customers, stockholders, newspaper and magazine readers, legislators, members of the League of Women Voters, and so on. A moment's reflection will suggest the infinite variety of publics that may be studied. Theoretically, the number of possible publics is the number of groups of two or more individuals that may be selected. The word "public" and the word "group" are for all practical purposes interchangeable.

Therefore, the starting point in any discussion of public opinion should be a precise definition of the word "public." This is not to say that the word "public" is so general that it is meaningless. If the discussion is about public opinion, it is clear that such subjects as the weather, jurisprudence, naval strategy, and chemistry are not under consideration. General as it is, the term does have metes and bounds, and because the word "public" is not as precise as the term "voting public in New Jersey" there is not a valid reason for discarding it. The study of public opinion is, therefore, the study of collections of individual opinions wherever they may be found. The study is as inclusive as the study of history, economics, chemistry, meteorology, and any number of other disciplines.

OPINIONS

An opinion may be defined as an expression of attitude in words. An attitude may be said to be a person's disposition or tendency to act or react in a particular manner.[1] Psychologists tell us that, in the course of our personal development, we form certain habits of mind and behavior, certain more or less persistent ways of responding to things we read, see, hear, and experience. Without attempting to answer the questions of why we respond as we do or whether these responses are inherited or learned, the existence of such response patterns seems clear. Some people, for example, develop a distaste for cats, for spinach, or for De Gaulle. We say that they have an unfavorable attitude toward these items and that they respond in certain more or less predictable ways when they see, hear, or experience them. The attitude may be latent and unexpressed today and very active and observable tomorrow, yet it exists whether expressed or not. Knowing a person's "sets" or tendencies to react in specific ways to various types of experience, one may go far in predicting that person's behavior under given circumstances.

An individual may reveal his attitudes in many ways: by laughing, by shrugging his shoulders, by punching someone in the nose, by writing a letter to the editor, by conversing with a friend. For the sake of convenience we label expressions of attitude in the form of words as opinions. It is obvious from what has been said that words are by no means the only expressions of attitude, but are all expressions opinions? Are all verbal statements opinions, or is there a valid distinction between fact and opinion? It is much easier to illustrate the distinction than to propose an acceptable rule for making the distinction. "I think that sunset is beautiful" is clearly an expression of opinion. Obviously the statement "Lyndon B. Johnson is President of the United States" is a fact, but what about the observation that Democracy is the best form of government? The distinction between fact and opinion, truth and falsehood are questions of considerable depth, philosophically and semantically.

DIFFERENCES IN DEFINITION

Notwithstanding the simplicity of the definition of "public opinion" as any collection of individual opinions, students of the subject have preferred to employ much more intricate and involved terminology. The literature of the field is strewn with zealous attempts to find a meaningful and acceptable definition. A few examples will serve to emphasize the extent and nature of this diversity.

> Public opinion is the social judgment of a self-conscious community on a question of general import after rational public discussion.—James T. Young, *The New American Government and Its Work* (New York: The Macmillan Co., 1923), pp. 577-78.

> . . . a certain apprehension of common and fundamental interests by all members of the group. This is public opinion.—R. H. Gault, *Social Psychology* (New York: Henry Holt, 1923), pp. 176-77.

> It is rather exaggerated to pretend that there exists, at the present time, a public opinion, in the intellectual sense, outside of the elite.—J. A. Sauerwein, "The Moulders of Public Opinion," in *Public Opinion and World Politics,* ed. Quincy Wright (Chicago: University of Chicago Press; 1933), p. 29.

> Those features of the world outside which have to do with the behavior of other human beings, in so far as that behavior crosses ours, is dependent upon us, or is interesting to us, we call roughtly public affairs. The pictures inside the heads of these human beings, the pictures of themselves, of others, of their needs, purposes, and relationships are their public opinions. Those pictures which are acted upon by groups of people, or by individuals acting in the name of groups, are Public Opinion with capital letters.—Walter Lippmann, *Public Opinion* (New York: The Macmillan Co., 1922), p. 39.

> Public opinion in this discussion may simply be taken to mean those opinions held by private persons which governments find it prudent to

heed. V. O. Key, *Public Opinion and American Democracy* (New York: Alfred A. Knopf, 1961), p. 14.

Public opinion may be said to be that sentiment on any given subject which is entertained by the best informed, most intelligent, and most moral persons in the community.—W. A. MacKinnon, *On the Rise, Progress, and Present State of Public Opinion in Great Britain and Other Parts of the World* (London: Anon. 1828), p. 15.

Public opinion is not the name of a something, but a classification of a number of somethings, which on statistical arrangement in a frequency distribution present modes or frequencies that command attention and interest.—Herman C. Beyle, *Identification and Analysis of Attribute-Cluster-Blocs* (Chicago: University of Chicago Press, 1931), p. 183.

Public opinion upon any matter was conceived as the hypothetical result of an imaginary plebiscite thereon.—R. C. Binkley, "The Concept of Public Opinion in the Social Sciences," *Social Forces,* Vol. 6, pp. 389-96.

Public opinion consists of people's reactions to definitely worded statements and questions under interview conditions.—Lucien Warner, "The Reliability of Public Opinion Surveys," *The Public Opinion Quarterly,* Vol. 3 (July, 1939), p. 377.

The term public opinion is given its meaning with reference to a multi-individual situation in which individuals are expressing themselves, or can be called upon to express themselves, as favoring (or else disfavoring or opposing) some definite condition, person, or proposal of widespread importance, in such a proportion of number, intensity, and constancy, as to give rise to the probability of affecting action, directly or indirectly, toward the object concerned.—Floyd H. Allport, "Toward a Science of Public Opinion," *The Public Opinion Quarterly,* Vol. 1 (January, 1937), p. 23.

REASONS FOR DIFFERENCES IN DEFINITION

Most definitions of the concept "public opinion" attempt to restrict the meaning of the term to collections of individual opinions of a particular type, having special characteristics or attributes which, in the opinion of the author, are significant and important. Political scientists, for example, tend to restrict the meaning of the term to collections of opinions which are held by an electorate, are likely to influence public policy, are about public affairs, and represent the will of the majority. Others focus attention upon the manner in which opinions are formed, or the quality of the opinions expressed, or the intensity of the opinions, their influence, or some other attribute. It is this diversity of interest that accounts, in large measure, for the differences in definition. This is not altogether surprising, for to generalize one's own interests and activities is a natural tendency. We like to think, for example, that a word like "breakfast," or "democracy," or "justice" connotes the type of breakfast, democracy, or justice with which we are familiar. The word "man," to take another illustration, is a very general word whose meaning includes men of different races, different powers, different tastes and aspirations. To restrict the meaning of the word to men living in a particular community, possessing specific qualities of intellect, exercising a definite amount of influence would be as absurd as to attempt to circumscribe the meaning of the term "public opinion" to collections of opinions from selected persons, about a limited number of subjects, or to narrow it to opinions that we consider rational and appropriate to a fixed standard of excellence.

Differences in the definition of "public opinion," as they reflect differences in interest, are revealing. In their search for an acceptable definition, authors provide us with a list of important aspects of public opinion. Take the statement: "Public opinion may be said to be that sentiment on any given subject which is entertained by the best informed, most intelligent, and most moral persons in the community." We may not accept this as valid, in part because the opinions of a public of this nature may not be the only collection of opinions which interests us, yet the statement does suggest that a study of this type of public opinion may be valuable. Similarly, other definitions suggest the importance of studying the process of opinion formation, the extent to which the opinions of a given public are in agreement, the quality of the opinions, the influence exerted by the opinions of the public selected, the subject matter of the opinions at the forefront of a group's attention, the character of the people who hold particular opinions, and the intensity with which various types of opinions are held.

Degree of Uniformity

One important aspect of the study of public opinion of widespread interest is the extent to which a given public agrees in its opinions on a selected subject. In its simplest form this type of study by means of surveys, polls, referenda, or elections seeks to ascertain how many persons in the public favor a given measure or candidate. The results, the number of "Yeses" and "Noes," may have far-reaching implications, depending on the nature of the persons composing the public surveyed and the degree of agreement revealed. Obviously, the existence of a large majority in favor of something will have an effect on the conclusion. It should be noted, however, that the absence of agreement, or the existence of a large number of persons with no opinions, may be equally significant.

In democratic countries the principle of majority rule is generally accepted. Public policy is presumed to reflect the will of the majority. The knowledge that a majority of the voters in the country favor or do not favor this or that measure or candidate is of tremendous importance. Of course the principle of majority rule is not always applied consistently and effectively. The election or referenda procedure, the necessity to channel majority opinion through representative bodies, the devices of checks and balance, the division of powers between central and local authorities, and the absence of machinery to give continuous expression and effect to public opinion may result in minority rule at times. But majority rule is the ideal if not always the reality.

Because of the importance of a high degree of agreement in the public affairs of a state, many students, especially of government, have restricted the meaning of the term "public opinion" to those collections of individual opinions possessing a predetermined degree of agreement. The assertion is that there cannot be public opinion until or unless this degree of agreement exists. This point of view is clearly reflected in the following definitions.

> . . . a majority is not enough, and unanimity is not required, but the opinion must be such that while the minority may not share it, they feel bound, by conviction, not by fear, to accept it.—A. L. Lowell, *Public Opinion and Popular Government* (New York: Longmans, Green, 1913), pp. 15-16.

> There exists at any given time a body of beliefs, convictions, sentiments, accepted principles, or firmly rooted prejudices, which taken together, make up the public opinion of a particular era, or what we may call the reigning or predominant current of opinion (pp. 19-20); . . . the belief or conviction prevalent in a given society (p. 3); . . . speculative views held by the mass of the people (p. 3); . . . ideas entertained by the inhabitants of a country, or by the greater part thereof. (p. 4); . . . the wishes and ideas held by the majority of those citizens who have at a given moment taken an effective part in public life (p. 10).—Albert V. Dicey, *Lectures on the Relation between Law and Public Opinion in England in the Nineteenth Century* (New York: The Macmillan Co., 1905).

> . . . the coming together of the minds and feelings of the people, or a large part of the people, in common agreement on the same definite conclusions or body of conclusions.—C. C. Maxey, *The Problem of Government* (New York: Alfred A. Knopf, 1925), p. 352.

> It is the power exerted by any such view, or set of views, when held by an apparent majority of citizens.—James Bryce, *Modern Democracies* (New York: The Macmillan Co.), Vol. 1, p. 154.

> There cannot be any public opinion worthy of the name unless the great bulk of the people are agreed upon the fundamental aims and principles of government. . . . If individual opinions are not similar enough to flow together, there cannot be a public opinion.—C. W. Smith, *Public Opinion in a Democracy* (New York: Prentice-Hall, 1939), pp. 18-19.

> . . . that opinion though it be but the opinion of a single individual in which the public in question finds itself for any reason constrained to acquiesce.—G. A. Lundberg, "Public Opinion from a Behavioristic Viewpoint," *American Journal of Sociology,* Vol. 36 (Nov., 1930), pp. 387-405.

Any fairly uniform collective expression of mental or inner behavior reactions. . . . Sufficient uniformity to insure a unity of definition of the content of public opinion.—L. L. Bernard, *An Introduction to Social Psychology* (New York: Henry Holt and Company, 1926), p. 559.

All these instances attempt to narrow the meaning of the term "public opinion" to collections of individual opinions having a certain degree of agreement. However important such collections may be, especially if the degree of agreement is sufficient to have an effect on public policy, it is clearly an unsatisfactory reason to confine the meaning of public opinion in such a manner—not the least of which reasons is that within this collection the degree of agreement is far from explicit. Variations include the words:

majority	apparent majority
unanimity	great bulk of the people
predominant	fairly uniform
reigning	sufficient uniformity
greater part	common agreement
large part	views held by the mass

Process of Opinion Formation

The existence of public opinion does not depend upon the existence within the public referred to of a certain degree of agreement in the opinions expressed. Not infrequently the state of opinion evidences little or no agreement or uniformity. Knowledge of this fact may be of paramount importance. Likewise, it is probably futile to restrict the meaning of "public opinion" to collections of individual opinions formed in a particular manner; for example, after rational public discussion. The process of opinion formation, considered more fully in a subsequent chapter, is to a considerable extent a complicated and a mysterious process. However the words "rational" and "irrational" may be defined it is unlikely that students of the process of opinion formation will ever discover a method for separately identifying the rational as distinguished from the irrational opinion. In fact the existence of either type of opinion in its pure form may be questioned, and yet many writers on the subject of public opinion attempt to exclude from consideration collections of opinions formed in any other than a prescribed manner.

"Public Opinion" then is a composite expression which embraces successive phases of a dynamic social process by which competing publics attempt to adjust the political, moral, and economic framework of society to meet their changing needs.—Saul Forbes Rae, "The Concept of Public Opinion and its Measurement," (Unpublished Ph.D. thesis: London School of Economics, December, 1938), p. 161.

An opinion is a verbal reaction coming at the end of a thinking process; but there are also verbal reactions to emotional reactions, and these we do not call opinions, but rather expressions of taste, sentiment, interest, preference, and so on.—Joseph K. Folsom, *Social Psychology* (New York: Harper & Bros., 1931), p. 540.

Public opinion is the social judgment reached upon a question of general or civic import after conscious, rational public discussion.—Clyde L. King, "Public Opinion in Government," in the Introduction to W. B. Graves, *Readings in Public Opinion* (New York: Appleton, 1928), p. xxiii.

From the foregoing discussion it should be evident that we consider opinion as an individual expression. It is a group or public opinion when it has been affected by interaction in a group situation.—William Albig, *Public Opinion* (New York: McGraw-Hill Book Co., 1939), p. 210.

The most serious shortcoming to definitions of this kind is the implicit assumption that we know more about the opinion-forming process than we do. Can we, for example, identify those opinions which "embrace successive phases of a dynamic social process by which competing publics attempt to adjust the political, moral, and economic framework of society to meet their changing needs"? Do we really know that a considerable number of opinions are formed in this manner? Moreover, when does a verbal reaction come "at the end of a thinking process" and when is it merely an "emotional reaction"? Just what is meant by "conscious, rational public discussion"? How may we determine whether or not opinions have been "affected by interaction in a group situation"?

The fact of the matter is that we know all too little about the way in which opinions are formed. Even though it may seem desirable to some to restrict the meaning of "public opinion" to those opinions rationally formed, or to those that come at the conclusion of a thought process, it is virtually impossible to segregate such opinions, if there are any, and state with assurance that a given opinion is rational and that another is not. If we assume that opinions are formed in a particular manner, we may be avoiding one of the most important tasks of the student of public opinion; namely, to find out exactly how particular opinions were formed.

Quality of Opinions

It is obvious that the quality of opinions varies considerably. In ordinary discourse we distinguish and contrast expert and lay opinions, informed and uninformed, mature and immature, radical and conservative, and many other types. Whenever such distinctions are made, more or less arbitrary standards of excellence have to be assumed. Students of public opinion will differ among themselves, not only regarding the validity of the standards, but also regarding their application in particular instances. One of the perplexing problems in public opinion research is that of properly assessing the relative merits of different collections of individual opinions. Are the collective opinions of the masses as sound as those of smaller and more selected groups? On what types of questions is mass opinion particularly competent to pass judgment? These questions and many others of a similar nature frequently arise. One of the major problems in a democratic form of government is to raise the quality of mass opinion. The efforts of educators are devoted to that end.

In order that democratic government function effectively it is essential that the opinions of the masses possess a certain degree of excellence. What that degree is has never been ascertained precisely.[2] To state that the very existence of public opinion itself depends upon the existence of a specified degree of excellence is unwarranted. Foolish as the opinions of some individuals may be, their views are opinions. Impressed by the importance of the quality of opinions, some writers have attempted to restrict the meaning of the term "public opinion" to collections of individual opinions measuring up to prescribed standards of excellence.

> It is rather, as we conceive it, a certain resultant that remains over from having entertained many opinions of more or less maturity.—R. H. Gault, *Social Psychology* (New York: Henry Holt and Co., 1923), p. 177.

> Perhaps it sounds a bit harsh, but there is no such thing as a public opinion, and it requires only a moderate understanding of human nature to show that such a thing as an intelligent public opinion is not possible.— E. Jordan, *Theory of Legislation* (Indianapolis: Progress Publishing Company, 1930), p. 339.

> It is rather exaggerated to pretend that there exists at the present time, a public opinion, in the intellectual sense, outside of the elite.—J. A. Sauerwein, "The Moulders of Public Opinion" in *Public Opinion and World Politics,* ed. Quincy Wright (Chicago: University of Chicago Press), 1933, p. 29.

> [Opinions which are based on] a substantial part of the facts required for a rational decision.—A. W. Holcombe, *The Foundations of the Modern Commonwealth* (New York: Harpers, 1923), p. 36.

In each of the above definitions, an effort is made to restrict the meaning of public opinion to collections of individual opinions having a certain degree of excellence: maturity, intelligence, or rationality. To study and attempt to determine the maturity, intelligence, or rationality of a given collection of opinions may be very useful; to restrict the meaning of public opinion itself in this manner is unwarranted.

Who Holds the Opinions

As indicated earlier in this chapter the number of publics or possible collections of individual opinions is infinite. A very common practice among students of the subjects is to attempt to limit the meaning of the term "public opinion" to the opinions of a particular public which they consider important. In the illustrations which follow such publics as "the best informed, most intelligent, and most moral persons in the community," those "possessed of certain qualities," "secondary groups" as distinguished from "face-to-face groups," "interested spectators of action," "all who are giving attention in any way to the given issue," "indirect contact group," "all the people capable of thought," people reacting "to definitely worded statements and questions under interview conditions" are stressed.

Public opinion exists in a community only when the individuals of which it is composed are possessed of certain qualities which will be termed the requisites for the formation of that sentiment [p. 1]. . . . Public opinion may be said to be that sentiment on any given subject which is entertained by the best informed, most intelligent, and most moral persons in the community [p. 15].—W. A. MacKinnon, *On Public Opinion in Great Britain and Other Parts of the World* (London, Anon., 1828).

When the group involved is a public or secondary group, rather than a primary, face-to-face group, we have public opinion.—J. K. Folsom, *Social Psychology* (New York: Harper & Bros., 1931), p. 446.

Renunciation, however, is a luxury in which all men cannot indulge. They will somehow seek to control the behavior of others, if not by positive law then at least by persuasion. When men are in that posture toward events they are a public, as I am here defining the term; their opinions as to how others ought to behave are their public opinions [pp. 54-55]. . . . I have conceived of public opinion to be . . . the voice of the interested spectators of action.—Walter Lippmann, *The Phantom Public* (New York: Harcourt, Brace & Co., 1925).

. . . all who are giving attention in any way to the given issue.—E. S. Bogardus, "Public Opinion as a Social Force," *Social Forces,* Vol. 8 (Sept., 1929), p. 105.

What the members of any indirect contact group or public think or feel about anything and everything.—L. L. Bernard, *An Introduction to Social Psychology* (New York: Henry Holt and Co., 1926).

It will make for clarity if we think of the public simply as composed of all the people capable of thought in a particular area or group.—C. W. Smith, *Public Opinion in a Democracy* (New York: Prentice-Hall, Inc., 1939), p. 13.

Public opinion consists of people's reactions to definitely worded statements and questions under interview conditions.—Lucien Warner, "The Reliability of Public Opinion Surveys," *The Public Opinion Quarterly,* Vol. 3 (July, 1939), p. 377.

The unending search for *the* public goes on. Time and again a writer will conclude that he has found a public which everyone will accept as *the* public, a public which should be the primary focus of attention for all students of public opinion. Recently Professor Francis G. Wilson did this. After stating that "public opinion is the content, in terms of valuation and attitude, of the wills of those persons who compose the public" he proceeded to consider a selected list of publics which had been stressed by various political scientists and then to conclude that *the* public comprises "those persons who have the right of participation" presumably in the affairs of government.[3] He discards as unsatisfactory definitions of *the* public such as "those who are willing to abide by the decision of the majority (Lowell)," "those who are spectators, who are not judges of the merits of a question, and those who are interested chiefly in making certain rules of the game (Lippmann)," "those who can influence the conduct of government," "those upon whom the incidence of governmental action falls," "those who owe allegiance to the state (Bryce)," and "those who are willing to pay attention to the news." Inasmuch as the study of the collective opinions of not only these but many other publics may be significant, the search for *the* public seems futile.

The Subject Matter of Opinions

Efforts to confine the meaning of the term "public opinion" to collections of individual opinions about certain things, a prescribed list of topics, have also contributed to intellectual obfuscation. Not only have students of public opinion tried to find *the* public, but they have also searched for the question, or type of questions which would evidence the existence of public opinion. The following attempts are typical.

> Public opinion is judgment which is formed and entertained by those who constitute the public and is about public affairs . . . A public affair is anything which concerns the people. The public are all those affected by the problem.—John Dewey, *The Public and Its Problems* (New York: Henry Holt and Co., 1927).

> Views as to the proper solution of questions of general concern.—W. B. Graves, ed., *Readings in Public Opinion* (New York: Appleton, 1928), p. 101.

> Those features of the world outside which have to do with the behavior of other human beings, in so far as that behavior crosses ours, is dependent upon us, or is interesting to us, we call roughly public affairs. The pictures inside the heads of these human beings, the pictures of themselves, of others, of their needs, purposes, and relationships are their public opinions. Those pictures which are acted upon by groups of people or by individuals acting in the name of groups, are Public Opinion with capital letters.—Walter Lippmann, *Public Opinion* (New York: The Macmillan Co., 1922), p. 29.

> Public opinion is the social judgment of a self-conscious community on a question of general import after rational, public discussion.—James T. Young, *The New American Government and Its Work* (New York: The Macmillan Co., 1923), pp. 577-78.

> The attitudes, feelings, or ideas of the large body of the people about important public issues.—D. W. Minar, "Public Opinion in the Perspective of Political Theory," *Western Political Quarterly*, Vol. 13, No. 1 (March, 1960), p. 33.

The issue which these definitions raise is simply this: Is a collection of opinions regarding such inconsequential matters as the relative merits of different kinds of soap, tobacco, or cosmetics as much public opinion as a collection of opinions regarding "public affairs," "questions of general concern," "pictures of others, of their needs, purposes, and relationships," or "a question of general import"? To go beyond the statement that opinions are *any* verbal expression of attitude is to become involved in an interminable debate over the question of what is and what is not a question of "general import" or a "public affair." People will always differ as to the importance of topics and questions. It would seem futile to attempt to obtain agreement in the matter and to seek to restrict the meaning of the term "public opinion" to our own arbitrary conclusions.

Other Types of Emphasis

Many other aspects of any given collection of individual opinions might well be made the basis of study—aspects which cannot be validly used to circumscribe the meaning of the term "public opinion" itself. The influence of collections of individual opinions varies from group to group. The role of voters' opinions, labor opinion, business opinion, the opinions of legislators, and many other groups that might be mentioned usually exerts a far greater influence upon the community than the opinions, let us say, of children in elementary schools, housewives living in New York's East Side, and many other politically impotent groups which might be mentioned. Need opinions exert a powerful influence in order to qualify for the distinction of being labeled "public opinion"? The following writers say yes.

> Some persons think of public opinion as being merely the sum total of the political ideas and views of the people. Public opinion of this character is incapable of exerting any real influence and is unworthy of any respect.—C. C. Maxey, *The Problem of Government* (New York: Alfred A. Knopf, 1925), p. 352.
>
> An expression of dominant conviction backed by an intention to give effect to it.—J. W. Defoe, "Public Opinion as a Factor in Government," in Quincy Wright, ed., *Public Opinion and World Politics* (Chicago: University of Chicago Press, 1933), pp. 6-7.

However important such collections of opinions—opinions capable of exerting a real influence, a noticeable influence upon the life of the community, backed by an intention to give effect to it—they are by no means the only kinds of opinions. The student of public opinion does not limit his field to opinions worthy of respect, however significant they may be. An opinion is an opinion regardless of its respectability. The problem of definition must be clearly separated from the problem of evaluation.

The influence opinions exert is more or less related to the degree of intensity with which they are held. Experience shows that opinions lightly held by a large number of people frequently have less influence upon the course of human affairs than the opinions of the few when they are held intensely. Dynamic, organized minorities frequently count for more than passive, unorganized majorities. To predict the actions of a group, their electoral behavior, their fighting stamina, their overt response to events and public policies, knowledge of their opinions is not enough. One must know the intensity of those opinions. But these considerations do not justify attempts to restrict the meaning of the term "public opinion" to collections of individual opinions possessing a definite degree of intensity. Again, we discover, that the business of defining has been confused with the business of evaluating.

> The opinions of a public are not to be ascertained merely by counting heads. . . . Intensity of opinion is important.—C. W. Smith, *Public Opinion in a Democracy* (New York: Prentice-Hall, Inc., 1939), p. 18.

> In order to have public opinion there must be a coincidence of individual opinions covering a sufficient number of persons, and preferably a majority of them. Not necessarily a majority, however, for public opinion is more than a matter of numbers. The intensity of the opinions is quite as important. Public opinion is a composite of numbers and intensity.— W. B. Munro, *The Government of American Cities* (4th edition, New York: The Macmillan Co., 1931), p. 222.

Of course the statement that intensity of opinion is important is true, but opinion is opinion regardless of the degree of intensity present. The degree of agreement is also important; likewise who holds the opinions, the subject matter of the opinions, the way in which they have been formed, their quality, their influence, and many, many other aspects of any given collection of opinions are important. The attempt to define a term and at the same time to emphasize the important aspect of the subject being defined leads only to confusion.

Emphasis on Multiple Aspects

In most of the definitions cited above the authors have stressed the importance of only one aspect of various collections of individual opinions, such as agreement, content, influence, or intensity. In some instances, the definition includes more than one aspect; it restricts the meaning of the term to collections of opinions having several qualifications. Although the authors appreciate the fact that such collections of opinions can have more than one aspect, they only emphasize the impossibility of any definition including all aspects. Young's definition "Public opinion is the social judgment of a self-conscious community on a question of general import after rational public discussion" is a case in point. At least three aspects of public opinion are underlined and made to serve as restrictions: (1) who holds the opinions—"a self-conscious community"; (2) subject matter—"a question of general import"; (3) method of formation—"after rational public discussion." No importance is attached, however, to such other aspects as degree of agreement, the influence which the opinions exert, the quality of the opinions, the intensity with which they are held. One of the most inclusive definitions from this point of view is that of Professor Allport cited above:

> The term public opinion is given its meaning with reference to a multi-individual situation in which individuals are expressing themselves, or can be called upon to express themselves, as favoring or supporting (or else disfavoring or opposing) some definite condition, person, or proposal of widespread importance, in such a proportion of number, intensity, and constancy, as to give rise to the probability of affecting action, directly or indirectly, toward the object concerned.

In this definition the following aspects are used to delimit the meaning of the term "public opinion":

(1) Who? Many individuals—"multi-individual situation."
(2) Subject? "Some definite condition, person, or proposal of widespread importance."
(3) Agreement? "Such a proportion of number."
(4) Intensity? "Such a proportion of intensity."
(5) Influence? "Give rise to the probability of affecting action."

We might add a last aspect to this list: "such a proportion of constancy." This is undoubtedly an important aspect of any collection of individual opinions likely to exert an influence upon public policy or the course of human affairs. By "constancy" is meant the durability, stability, or persistence of particular opinions. Still this definition fails to include all aspects which have been emphasized by one writer or another. Francis Graham Wilson in his *A Theory of Public Opinion* (Henry Regnery, 1962), does not define public opinion precisely. He does, however, indicate several conditions of the "public opinion situation" (p. 278). "There must be a division between those who rule and those who are ruled . . . the public consists of those . . . outside the group of those who at least announce the sovereign or final decision . . . public opinion must be finally a body of opinions on political or policy decisions . . . which shares more or less in influencing decision." In other words, he seems to be primarily concerned with who holds the opinions, subject matter, and the influence of the opinions.

THE "GROUP-MIND" FALLACY

Implicit in the writings of earlier students of public opinion is the notion that public opinion is something more, or something different from, the sum of individual opinions within a group. Public opinion in this sense tends to assume a mystical character. It is something floating about, like a disembodied spirit, which has a will and a force of its own. This is all rather vague and seems to be based on the idea that, for some reason or another, you cannot find out what the public opinion of a group is simply by collecting the opinions of individuals within the group, summing them, and classifying them. One writer puts it this way:[4]

> The term "sum" seems inadequate, however, for were we to add the personal opinions of hermits or lonely exiles, our achievement would not bear the characteristics of interaction of opinions . . . And it is this complexity of interaction which differentiates public opinion from the more simple concept of aggregated personal opinions. Interdependence, interaction and influence, then, combine into a characteristic which is, for us, the sine qua non of public opinion; and public opinion then assumes the aspect of a weighted composite of personal opinions.

The objection to designating public opinion as any collection of individual opinions, that is to say, any mere summation of individual opinions, is that it fails to take account of the considerable variance of individual opinions with respect to the drive or force behind them. Merely counting opinions for and against a proposal ignores the fact that perhaps twenty negative opinions may be potentially more influential than one hundred affirmative opinions because of the persons who hold them, their position of leadership in the community, their will to act upon them. But this is only another way of saying that a given collection of individual opinions may or may not exert an influence. The principal point of this chapter is that the existence of a state of public opinion is not dependent upon the existence of a particular kind of public opinion. There are all kinds of opinions, good, bad, indifferent, opinions formed in this way and that, opinions about this and that, opinions that will exert influence and those that will not. The arithmetical or algebraic sum of the individual opinions within a given public or group is the state of public opinion in that group alone.

HISTORICAL BACKGROUND

The importance of public opinion has been recognized from earliest times in the writing of political philosophers. As Professor Paul A. Palmer has pointed out,[5] there was no explicit formulation of the term prior to the eighteenth century, and no systematic treatment prior to the nineteenth. Although Plato, Aristotle, and others writing during the early classical period did not use the expression with quite its modern meanings, they frequently referred to mass opinion and its significance. Plato questioned the competence of mass opinion, and Aristotle tried to do what some students of public opinion have tried to do since, define more precisely the sphere of its competence. The Romans, in general, held the masses in contempt, but during the medieval period such writers as Alcuin, William of Malmesbury, and later Machiavelli emphasized the importance of what we might call mass opinion. During this period the phrase *Vox populi, vox Dei* became current. Tributes to the power of mass opinion became numerous during the seventeenth and eighteenth centuries, notably in the writings of Pascal, Voltaire, Hobbes, Locke, and Hume—and even Shakespeare and William Temple.

Developments during the fifteenth century, however, profoundly affected the role of mass opinion, though their full impact was only dimly perceived for some time. The advent of printing by means of movable type, near the middle of the century, provided one means for greatly extending the scope of reading publics. The Protestant Reformation broke the monopoly of the Roman Catholic Church over the dissemination of religious ideas and marked the beginning of many competing beliefs, in matters of religion. Meanwhile the "Renaissance" had a similar liberating effect on the minds of men in the areas of economics, politics, and social life. The economic transformations which were taking place, including the rise of merchant and business classes, promoted the spread of new ideas and brought into being many new publics. Mention should also be made of the effects of the discovery of new continents and the far-flung explorations of this exciting century. The sixteenth and seventeenth centuries saw the multiplication of printing presses, books, and newspapers, the spread of new and competing ideas, and the gradual awakening of an ever wider circle of public opinions.

By the middle of the eighteenth century there was general recognition of the strength and importance of mass opinion. Perhaps the most significant thoughts on public opinion during the eighteenth century were those of Rousseau and of the French Minister of Finance, Jacques Necker. Rousseau applied the theory of popular infallibility to the state. He paid tribute to the power of public opinion and suggested that even a despotism rests on public opinion. He held that all laws, political, civil, and criminal are based upon it. Rousseau seems to have been one of the first among the important political theorists to make use of the phrase *l'opinion publique* and thus laid the basis for the further development of the concept. Although his "general will" is closely related to the idea of public opinion, he never indicated specifically the relation, nor the relation of public opinion to law. He did emphasize that public opinion could not be coerced, that government can influence morals indirectly through public opinion.

Necker was probably the first to discuss in detail the place of public opinion in statecraft, specifically the importance of public opinion in relation to public credit. In the France of his day the salon played an important role in the formation of significant public opinion. The public opinion which he considered of prime importance was that of the bourgeoisie, "an invisible power which, without treasures, without a bodyguard, and without an army gives laws to the city." Necker emphasized that the nature and force of public opinion varied according to the form and type of government and was most effective and wholesome in a limited monarchy. It is the principal safeguard against abuse of power.

The French Revolution precipitated widespread discussion of public opinion, particularly in Germany and England, discussions that were certainly in the minds of the framers of the Constitution of 1787 in the United States. In Germany, C. M. Wieland concluded that, as a consequence of the French Revolution, governments could no longer exist without respecting public opinion. The philosopher Christian Garve devoted an entire essay to public opinion, defining the term carefully and praising its competence especially on matters of general principle. Jakob Fries made an even more ambitious attempt to relate the concept to a general theory of the state and made public opinion the basis for the rule of law. Hegel, also, paid considerable attention to the matter of public opinion, and held that it is essentially contradictory to nature, deserving to be respected in part and to be despised in part, and that it is the task of the great man to find the truth in public opinion for his generation.

Jeremy Bentham was the first in the English language to treat public opinion in detail. He emphasized the importance of public opinion as a means of social control, and he regarded the free expression of public opinion as the main safeguard against despotism. He attempted to use the term precisely. He referred to it as "the moral sanction," and stressed the point that the legislator cannot ignore public opinion. As a safeguard against the abuse of power, he demanded publicity for all official acts. Public opinion constituted an integral part of his democratic theory of the state. In his *Constitutional Code* he elaborates what he calls his public opinion tribunal. He finds the most important factor in the formation and expression of public opinion to be the newspaper press.

By the end of the first quarter of the nineteenth century the concept had entered the main stream of political theory. But there existed little agreement as to the extent of the virtue and competence of public opinion. The contrasting views were clearly stated by Friedrich Ancillon in 1828. Karl Rosenkranz, W. A. R. Mackinnon, Henry Thomas Buckle, Charles Dollfus, Karl Biedermann, and J. C. Bluntschli took the side of the optimists; Friedrich Julius Stahl, David Urquhart, Sir Henry Maine, and Rudolf von Gneist, the contrary.

Some writers adopted a much more objective approach. The most detailed analysis of the subject of public opinion during the first part of the nineteenth century was that of Carl von Gersdorf in his *Über den Begriff, und das Wesen der öffentlichen Meinung* [Concerning the Concept and Nature of Public Opinion] (1846). Mention should also be made of the *Essay on the Influence of Authority in Matters of Opinion* by Sir George Cornwall Lewis (1849) and *Wesen und Werth der öffentlichen Meinung* [Nature and Value of Public Opinion] by Franz von Holtzendorff (1879). All three writers dealt with the competence of public opinion. Gersdorf also traced the history of the evolution of public opinion and defined its relation to law and to sovereignty, and both Lewis and Holtzendorff considered carefully the role of the press as a molder as well as a reflector of public opinion.

One of the most remarkable treatments of public opinion, especially in the United States, which appeared during the nineteenth century was that of the Englishman James Bryce in his classic study, *The American Commonwealth*.[6] Part IV, comprising 12 chapters, is devoted exclusively to the subject, and continues to be eminently worthwhile reading today. The chapter headings themselves suggest the range of his perspective and his grasp of the dimensions of the problem. In the first of the 12 chapters he discusses the nature of public opinion and the stages in its formation. Then follows a chapter on government by public opinion, and again he finds that there are definite stages in its development—acquiescence, conflict, popular control, directly ascertainable will. It is from this chapter that pollsters frequently quote his remarks concerning the lack of any system of weighing or measuring public opinion continuously. In the chapter on how public opinion rules in America he makes the useful point that divisions of opinion in this country are vertical rather than horizontal.

Three chapters, numbers 79, 80, and 81, are the most interesting and significant. In the first, he discusses the organs of public opinion, stating that "The more completely popular sovereignty prevails in a country, so much the more important is it that the organs of opinion should be adequate to its expression, prompt, full, and unmistakable in their utterances." He then considers at some length the role of the press, public meetings, elections, and various special organizations. In the next chapter he discusses the principal national characteristics of Americans as they mold public opinion —good nature, kindness, helpfulness; love of humor; the prevailing hopefulness; faith in the people; broad but superficial education; generally moral, decent, and religious. He notes, however, a widespread lack of reverence, a perpetual busy-ness, and a notable lack of interest in politics. Written in the 1880s, these observations are still pertinent. He also observes that Americans are a commercial people, usually thinking in terms of profit and loss; that they tend to be emotional, unsettled, changeful, and essentially conservative. Bryce's was not the first attempt to generalize about the basic elements in American public opinion, and of course he was not the last, as witness the writings of André Siegfried, Margaret Mead, and many others.

In his Chapter 81 Bryce discusses at length the role of classes as influencing public opinion and considers especially the influence of farmers, shopkeepers and small businessmen, workingmen, capitalists, and the professional classes. Then follows a chapter on local types of opinions and one on the action of public opinion. In the latter he makes a comment which will seem dated today, that "In America the profession of opinion-making and leading is the work of amateurs." He also notes that defects in our constitutional mechanism for enabling public opinion to rule promptly are in a measure covered by the expertness of Americans in using all kinds of voluntary and private agencies.

Chapters 84 and 85 of Bryce's book deal with the "tyranny of the majority" and the "fatalism of the multitude," to use his phraseology. And in the final two chapters on public opinion he analyzes the reasons why, in his judgment, public opinion in the United States has both succeeded and failed. It fails, he says, because of the difficulty of ascertaining it; because of the difficulty it faces in finding means, in contrast to expressing the ends of desired public policies; because it is slow and clumsy in grappling with large practical problems; and finally because it fills people with undue confidence. On the other hand it succeeds, in his opinion, because it tends to bring evils to light, speaks with much weight, is educative, patient, and tolerant and lacks bitterness and class divisiveness. Moreover, he finds that public opinion minimizes the need for government and laws, hinders pernicious measures, and prevents countless bad appointments. No discussion of public opinion before the twentieth century seems to make as profitable reading for Americans today as this Part IV of Volume II of Bryce's classic *American Commonwealth*. The earlier works of Alexis de Tocqueville and George Carslake Thompson are also of interest, but are narrower in scope and less relevant today.[7]

THE TWENTIETH CENTURY

The twentieth century has witnessed a tremendous spreading out of interest in public opinion. Unfortunately, this growth in interest has not always followed an orderly schedule, nor is it susceptible of rigid classification by periods. Although it may do violence to the treatment in some respects, it will be helpful to deal with the development of interest in public opinion since 1900 by decades, noting a few of the outstanding publications of each decade, some outstanding events or developments which affected the study of public opinion, and the principal foci of interest.

The first decade of this century marked the appearance of several books which signalized a new trend in thinking on public opinion—more attention to its emotional and irrational nature. Of particular significance were Gabriel Tarde's *L'Opinion et la foule* [Opinion and the Crowd] (1901) and Graham Wallas's *Human Nature in Politics* (1909). In fact, since the latter part of the nineteenth century the study of public opinion has been greatly influenced and enriched by the contributions of sociologists and social psychologists, the former much interested in it as a means of social control, the latter seeking to throw light on its formation through studies of individual and group behavior. Mention should also be made of two other studies during this first decade which are classics in the field. A. V. Dicey's *Lectures on the Relation Between Law and Public Opinion in England During the Nineteenth Century* (1905) reflected the dominant interest of many political scientists in public opinion during the nineteenth century, and in that sense was the direct descendant of such men as John Taylor (1814), John Austin (1860), Francis Lieber (1838-1859), D. G. Ritchie (1890), Esmein (1895), and W. W. Willoughby (1896). These authors as well as Dicey were interested not only in the history of public opinion but also in the specific relation of public opinion to law and to sovereignty. Since Dicey wrote, comparatively little attention has been given by students of law and political science to these questions.

A fourth book which appeared also in this decade, A. F. Bentley's *The Process of Government* (1908), stressed the role of organized groups in the opinion-forming process and gave an impetus to what became the widespread study of pressure groups in their relation to public opinion and public policy. All in all, the years 1900-1910 marked the end of dominance of the field by political writers and the beginning of a broad frontal attack on the subject by social scientists generally. During this period schools of journalism, which had sprung up throughout the country, began to study the press more systematically as a molder and reflector of public opinion. The influence of the press had been generally recognized since the end of the eighteenth century, if not before. It was also during this period that advertising and advertising agencies were coming of age, having risen to national prominence during the period of industrial expansion following the Civil War. The press agent and his brother across the tracks, the public relations counsel, emerged as colorful and significant molders of public opinion. Marketing research, in company with radio and motion pictures, was still in swaddling clothes.

On the political stage public opinion was very much in the fore. The era of the muckrakers and the trust busters was also the great age of reform, when agitation for the initiative, referendum and recall, for direct election of Senators, for the city manager form of government, for the short ballot, and for other changes that would give greater influence and power to mass opinion and popular government were sweeping the country.

It was also the heyday of the Chautauqua and Bryan oratory, a day of boundless confidence that through education, mass opinion could be raised to a standard of excellence equal to its responsibilities.

The decade 1910-20, which saw the return of the Democratic party to power in the United States and the beginning and end of World War I, was not replete with studies of public opinion, although the war itself awakened an interest in the subject of unforetold dimensions. Two books, at least, attained the stature of classics and deserve to be noted: A. L. Lowell's *Public Opinion and Popular Government* (1913) and Wilhelm Bauer's *Die öffentliche Meinung und ihre geschichtlichen Grundlagen* [Public Opinion and Its Historical Foundations] (1914). Although the years immediately preceding the outbreak of war in 1914 saw an outpouring of literature on the subject of direct legislation, except for the books mentioned few contributions of note appeared on the subject of public opinion. The war itself, with its emphasis upon government propaganda, opened the eyes of men to the new dimensions of public opinion and aroused an interest in the subject which has by no means abated to this day. It is the decade 1920-1930 to which we must turn for the real beginnings of what we may call the modern study of public opinion.

This new interest took many forms, and it opened many new vistas. The propaganda activities of the Allies and the Central Powers received considerable attention, notably in the writings of George Creel, H. D. Lasswell, J. H. Bernstorff, Georges Demartial, Hans Thimme, F. Schönemann, Campbell Stuart, and Edgar Stern-Rubarth.[8] The 1928 bibliography compiled by Kimball Young and Raymond D. Lawrence, one of the first to deal with propaganda, contained 133 pages of titles on censorship and propaganda.[9] Important contributions to the general theory of public opinion appeared in the writings of Ferdinand Tönnies, Norman Angell, A. B. Hall, Walter Lippmann, Clyde King, W. B. Graves, Peter Odegard, and E. L. Bernays. Interest in the pathology of public opinion under special conditions continued in studies by E. D. Martin and other social psychologists. Notable additions to the study of the press included the volumes by Lucy M. Salmon, Silas Bent, W. G. Bleyer, J. M. Lee, and Allan Nevins. Already the growing significance of the newer instruments of mass impression was becoming apparent and studies of the radio and motion pictures multiplied.

The propaganda activities of the wartime governments produced a host of specialists who emerged as professionals in molding public opinion under such titles as public relations counsel, publicity expert, and fund raiser. Many of them wrote on their specialities: E. L. Bernays, John C. Long, Ivy Lee, Abram Lipsky, R. W. Riis, and Ralph Casey. The general principles of advertising had been pretty well established before, but the decade of the twenties saw a tremendous growth in the literature of the subject, as well as many modifications in techniques. During this period customer surveys and reader interest studies blossomed forth in new splendor. This was also the period when *Literary Digest* polls and straw votes of other types evidenced widespread interest in "what the public thinks." [10]

Some attention had been given in previous decades to the importance of pressure groups as factors in the formation of public opinion as well as channels for the expression of public opinion, notably in the study by A. F. Bentley previously referred to and also to government revelations such as the New York insurance investigation and the congressional lobby investigation of 1913. It was the period of the twenties, however, that really came to grips with the problem. There were detailed studies of particular pressure groups such as those of the Anti-Saloon League by Odegard.[11] There were comparative studies such as those of Herring and Childs.[12] And there were the more comprehensive, theoretical analyses of A. G. Dewey, F. W. Coker, W. Y. Elliott, Herman Finer, F. E. Haynes, Helen D. Hill, E. B. Logan, Stuart Rice, and J. D. Pollock. The Federal Trade Commission issued its famous report on the public opinion activities of gas and electric light interests in 1927.[13]

The First World War stimulated a number of studies of military and civilian morale, of the psychology of leadership and other internal problems of command, and of the relationship between officers and enlisted men. The full implications of psychological warfare were apparently not perceived, or only very dimly.

This was also the decade when the new Russia was taking form, and students of public opinion were able to see how propaganda could be used not only as a weapon of war and foreign policy but also as an instrument of domestic control. The role of propaganda, or civic training as it was sometimes called, in Russia and also in Mussolini's Italy, was not unnoticed either in the United States or in Germany, where Hitler and the Nazi party were seeking to exploit the propaganda lessons learned from World War I, from Russia, from Italy, from the commercial advertising of America, and from other examples of propaganda success. In 1925 the first volume of Hitler's *Mein Kampf* appeared, followed by the second in 1927.

During the war, psychologists had been called upon to apply their newly acquired techniques of educational and intelligence testing to the task of screening soldiers for occupational and other reasons. This led to the improvement of questionnaire techniques and to the invention of machines for speedily tabulating and summarizing large quantities of data. This explains in part the growth during the twenties of widespread interest in statistical studies of public opinion and in attempts to measure opinions, and the emphasis placed upon quantitative methods. Louis L. Thurstone in psychology and Stuart Rice in the fields of statistics and politics made significant contributions.[14] Also noteworthy were the studies of C. C. Brigham, F. H. Allport and D. A. Hartman, W. B. Graves, E. S. Bogardus, G. A. Lundberg, H. T. Moore, H. F. Gosnell, and G. B. Watson.

Finally, the study of public opinion was greatly enriched by the new light being thrown on the subject of opinion formation by psychologists, social psychologists, sociologists, and anthropologists, as well as physiologists, biologists, historians, and economists. Sigmund Freud, C. G. Jung, Z. P. Pavlov, J. B. Watson, John Dewey, William Trotter, Graham Wallas, A. B. Wolfe, and William McDougall are only a few of the scholars that might be mentioned.

The decade of the thirties began with a world-wide depression and ended with world-wide strife. Both of the catastrophes had pronounced effects on the study and interest in public opinion. It was a period of extensive political, economic, and social experimentation. It saw in this country the advent of the New Deal and a tremendous growth in governmental activity, activity that needed unprecedented public support. Abroad, it witnessed the rise of Hitler to power and an onward march of Nazism and Fascism which seemed to have no bounds. Not only in Russia, Italy, and Germany, but also in Spain, Japan, Argentina, and many other countries, public opinion seemed to be well on its way toward becoming merely a tool in the hands of despots and dictators. Democracy, in the sense of rule by public opinion, seemed to be on the way out.

The years 1930-40 saw not only the development of dictatorial propaganda machines abroad but also, in the democratic countries, an increasing concern with matters of public opinion. In the United States the Blue Eagle campaign on behalf of the National Recovery Act (NRA) was only the beginning of an expanding government publicity which mushroomed throughout official agencies in Washington and over the country.[15] The new alphabetical agencies not only took on tasks which reactionaries labeled socialistic but also increased the size of their information bureaus and streamlined their press and public relations.

To counter the New Deal, business turned more and more to professional public relations agencies for support in fighting "that man in the White House" and preserving "the American Way." [16] The National Association of Manufacturers (NAM) and the Chamber of Commerce of the United States took the lead in publicity campaigns that outdistanced any experienced before. Profiting by the experience of the ill-fated NRA, propaganda methods were "decontaminated" as much as possible, and the cruder types of pressure on newspapers, schools, and other institutions avoided. Theoretical interest in public opinion continued, and at Princeton University and elsewhere graduate and undergraduate courses in the subject were introduced. Textbooks multiplied. Interest in government propaganda took various forms from objective, scholarly studies of the information problem of government, to impassioned attacks on propaganda in general and certain types of propaganda in particular. During the latter part of the decade the Institute of Propaganda Analysis was established with the help of foundation assistance and for several years sought to expose the methods of antidemocratic propagandas. In 1937 the first issue of the *Public Opinion Quarterly* appeared, the first journal to devote its pages exclusively to the growing interest in public opinion studies. The coming of age of the study of journalism was shown by the establishment of the *Journalism Quarterly* which has since covered systematically the scholarly output in the field of mass communication.

Interest in pressure groups, propaganda, communication agencies, government information and propaganda, public opinion measurement and theory, the psychology of opinion formation, and the many other aspects which were dominant during the twenties continued throughout the thirties. But several new dimensions were added. The rise of dictatorial countries abroad, the international tensions which ensued, coupled with the inauguration of international broadcasts early in the decade, focused attention as never before upon the importance of public opinion and propaganda in international relations. The Nazis, following to some extent the lead of the Russians, perceived earlier than others, perhaps, the potentialities of radio as a means for winning support of its policies abroad as well as at home. Great Britain was not far behind and soon had a powerful system of imperial and then international broadcasts. Italy, Japan, and several other countries soon entered the international competition for world-wide support.[17]

The United States lagged far behind, not so much for technical reasons as because of the lack of interest in such broadcasts on the part of commercial and advertising interests as well as the government, which did not have the authority to draft private short-wave facilities as instruments of foreign policy. Toward the end of the decade the government's interest in international propaganda increased very rapidly. At first this interest was largely negative, in the sense that the government was interested primarily in keeping American public opinion from being polluted by foreign propaganda. Finally, however, it was directed toward the use of radio and other propaganda facilities to implement the Good Neighbor policies in the Americas, and ultimately to wage psychological warfare abroad. Numerous studies here and abroad indicated the growing importance of international propaganda.[18]

The thirties also gave birth to what Stuart Chase has called one of the most important contributions of social science in the twentieth century—the public opinion poll. Newspaper and magazine polls had been conducted for more than a century, and since 1916 the *Literary Digest* poll had acquired a national, almost an international reputation. What distinguished the Gallup, Roper, and Crossley polls from preceding public opinion surveys was their alleged use of scientific methods of sampling which assured their accuracy to within a few percentage points of the public opinion sampled. These sampling methods had been used for a number of years by market researchers and were now to be applied to surveys of nation-wide opinion on political, economic, and social issues. In an historical trial of strength with the *Literary Digest* in 1936, when the old and the new type of poll both sought to predict the winner of the Presidential election, the *Digest* went down to ignominious defeat, and the Gallup type of poll reigned supreme, at least until 1948 when the "Truman poll" won a notable victory! [19]

By the end of the thirties the Gallup poll seemed to have become an institutional fixture which was having a pronounced effect upon public opinion itself. A new literature developed on the technique of sampling, and the pollsters did much to revive interest in some of the very old problems of public opinion—the competence of the masses, the role of public opinion, and similar questions affecting democracy and rule by public opinion. The Gallup poll was soon in operation in England, and thereafter spread to a number of other countries. Meanwhile, government agencies both here and abroad were making more and more use of the public opinion survey as an aid to administration.

The decade of the forties, half of which was concentrated on World War II and the other half on problems of readjustment and reconstruction, saw no diminution of interest in public opinion. Emphasis on public opinion theory gave way to emphasis on the practical application of the theories. Following a stream of studies describing the public opinion activities of the Fascist, Nazi, and Communist governments which had come forth during the thirties, there now appeared more systematic treatments of psychological warfare.[20] Students of public opinion, public relations, and propaganda analysis were mobilized in increasing numbers to man the proliferating government information and propaganda agencies. Considerable emphasis was placed upon the content analysis of communications by press, radio, motion picture, books, and other channels. Monitoring services both here and abroad kept watch over the flow of propaganda by radio. Newspaper digest services followed closely the press content throughout the world. Special studies were also made of the content of other media.

All the wartime governments employed propaganda on a hitherto unprecedented scale. Governments were more liberal in their appropriations for psychological warfare; the authoritarian states seemed to have compelled the democracies to engage in propaganda warfare; and new facilities, particularly the radio, were available. Experiments in psychological warfare took both long-range and short-range forms. By short wave, press dispatch, leaflet, and picture each government sought to bring its messages to the rest of the world. There was much experimentation in different media and in the content best calculated to produce the desired results. Organizational efficiency was vastly superior to that of the First World War, and of course the facilities were much superior. One of the most difficult problems, however, was to assess the effects of specific propagandas.

The war slowed up for a time the publication of unclassified material regarding the public opinion activities of the wartime governments. Gradually, however, this wartime experience came to light in publications by prominent participants. In this country James P. Warburg, Leonard B. Doob, C. A. H. Thomson, and Wallace Carroll published volumes describing their work on the propaganda side, whereas Samuel Stouffer and others reported their surveying activities. Francis Williams has reported on the British experience to some extent. Many gaps still exist, however, in our knowledge and understanding of the public opinion problems of government as revealed by this wartime experience.

During the last half of the decade following the war, the principal areas of interest on the part of students of public opinion seemed to be (1) public opinion surveys, as evidenced by the increase in number of government, commercial, and non-commercial agencies devoted to this work, the publications in the field, and the increasing number of courses in the subject being offered by universities and colleges; (2) psychological warfare, as shown by the emphasis placed upon this subject by our various war colleges, as well as by students of the subject; (3) mass communications, which as a field developed into an area of significant research at several institutions of higher learning. The publications of the Commission on the Freedom of the Press created quite a stir,[21] as did certain publications of the Federal Communications Commission (FCC), notably the celebrated Blue Book dealing with standards of radio broadcasting; (4) public opinion and foreign policy. The wartime use of propaganda left many countries, including the United States, facing the question, to what extent they should continue to use propaganda as an instrument of foreign policy. The Mac-Mahon report to the State Department set the general lines of policy which, as the tensions between Russia and the West become more ominous, seem to have been modified to some extent in favor of a more positive and aggressive policy;[22] (5) public relations continued to be a prominent problem of public opinion for both governmental and non-governmental institutions. Publications on the subject, which may have reached a peak during the preceding decade, still continued to appear at a lively rate.

Public opinion studies since 1950 have continued to appear quite steadily, delving ever more deeply into familiar problems, but with virtually no dramatic new discoveries. Several general works on public opinion appeared, notably those of V. O. Key, Francis Wilson, Angus Campbell,

Harold Lasswell, and Samuel Stouffer.[23] Public opinion polling and survey-ing continued to attract students, and there were numerous specialized studies of survey designs, sampling procedures, interviewing, and similar technical questions. The failure of the pollsters to predict Truman's victory in 1948 led to much soul-searching and the marked improvement of many polls. More polls began to base their sampling procedures on probability bases, and to take great care in selecting and training interviewers.

Interest in how opinions are formed continues and evokes studies of all kinds of personal as well as environmental factors. The mass media, es-pecially television, have attracted the scholarly concern of many. Attention has been directed frequently to the problems of mass media effects, espe-cially on children, and to the problem of public and social responsibility of the media.[24] Knowledge of media effects, either immediate or over a longer period, is scanty, almost trivial.[25] There has been a tendency of late to say that the effects of mass media are determined, not so much by the media, as by the personality traits of the people in the audience. Television does not cause juvenile delinquency, for example—it only activates or re-inforces a youngster already having delinquent tendencies. Moreover, so the argument runs, whatever responsibility there is for what the media do, must be shared by the public itself and the government, as well as the media proprietors.

There have been, during the last decade, many studies, primarily em-pirical, of the press and printed publications, comics, television, radio, and motion pictures. But the outpouring of sociological studies concerned with the public opinion implications of elites, mobility, status, groups of many kinds, "hidden persuaders," the organization man, personality traits, mo-tivations, character, decision-making, etc., have been much more prolific. Many of these studies have penetrated quite deeply into the opinion-form-ing process.

It is impossible to review at all satisfactorily the sweep of studies with public opinion significance. Mention should be made, however, of the suc-cession of voting studies from Michigan, Columbia, and Chicago, of presi-dential and congressional elections, as well as state and local. These are especially valuable because of the number of opinion-forming factors stud-ied, and also because of the opinion trends revealed.

Finally, mention should be made of the interest in public opinion study abroad and in the study of public opinion there. Even the undeveloped countries of Africa and Asia, as well as those of Europe and North Amer-ica, have received an increasing amount of attention by students of public opinion in recent years. Not only have the institutions for influencing opin-ion been described and analyzed, but the attitudes and opinions of the people themselves have been surveyed.

NOTES FOR CHAPTER 2

Epigraph. Jacques Necker, *Oeuvres complètes,* ed. Baron de Stael.
1. See Katz, Daniel and Floyd H. Allport, *Student Attitudes* (Syracuse, N. Y.: The Craftsman Press, 1931); Cantril, Hadley, "General and Specific Attitudes," *Psychological Monographs,* Vol. 42, No. 5 (1932); Doob, Leonard W., *Propaganda* (New York: Henry Holt & Co., 1935); and Allport, G. W., "Attitudes," chap. 17 in *A Handbook of Social Psychology,* ed. Carl Murchinson (Worcester, Mass.: Clark University Press, 1935).
2. See, however, Berelson, Bernard, "Democratic Theory and Public Opinion," *Public Opinion Quarterly,* Vol. 16 (Fall, 1952), pp. 313-30; Hyman, Herbert H. and Paul B. Sheatsley, "The Current Status of American Public Opinion," *Twenty-first Yearbook* (National Council for Social Studies, Washington, D. C.: National Education Association, 1950), pp. 11-34.
3. Wilson, Francis G., "Concepts of Public Opinion," *American Political Science Review,* Vol. 27 (June, 1933), pp. 371-91.
4. Sedman, Virginia R., "Some Interpretations of Public Opinion," *Social Forces,* Vol. 10 (March, 1932), pp. 339-42.
5. Palmer, Paul A., "The Concept of Public Opinion in Political Theory," in *Essays in History and Political Theory in Honor of Charles H. McIlwain* (Cambridge, Mass.: Harvard University Press, 1936). I have relied on this excellent survey quite extensively in reviewing early studies of public opinion.
6. Bryce, James, *The American Commonwealth,* Vol. 2, part IV (New York: The Macmillan Co., 1924).
7. DeTocqueville, Alexis, *Democracy in America,* trans. Henry Reeve, with an original preface and notes by John C. Spencer (2nd Amer. ed.; George Adlard, 1838); Thompson, George Carslake, *Public Opinion and Lord Beaconsfield* (2 vols.; London: The Macmillan Co., 1886).
8. See Lutz, Ralph Haswell, "Studies of World War Propaganda, 1914-1933," *The Journal of Modern History,* Vol. 5 (December, 1933), pp. 496-516.
9. Young, Kimball and Raymond D. Lawrence, *Bibliography on Censorship and Propaganda* (Eugene, Oregon: University of Oregon Publications, 1928).
10. See Robinson, Claude E., *Straw Votes* (New York: Columbia University Press, 1932).
11. Odegard, P. H., *Pressure Politics: The Story of the Anti-Saloon League* (New York: Columbia University Press, 1928).
12. Childs, Harwood L., *Labor and Capital in National Politics* (Columbus, Ohio: Ohio State University Press, 1930); Childs, H. L., "Pressure Groups and Propaganda," in *The American Political Scene,* ed. E. B. Logan (New York: Harper & Bros., 1936); and H. L. Childs (ed.), "Pressure Groups and Propaganda," *The Annals* of the American Academy of Political and Social Science (May, 1935). Also see Herring, E. P., *Group Representation Before Congress* (Baltimore: the Johns Hopkins Press, 1929).
13. "Efforts by Associations and Agencies of Electric and Gas Utilities to Influence Public Opinion." 70th Congress, 1st Session, Senate Document 92, Part 71 A, 1934.

14. Thurstone, L. L. and E. J. Chave, *The Measurement of Attitude* (Chicago: University of Chicago Press, 1929).
15. See McCamy, James L., *Government Publicity: Its Practice in Federal Administration* (Chicago: University of Chicago Press, 1939).
16. See Walker, S. H. and Paul Sklar, *Business Finds Its Voice* (New York: Harper & Bros., 1938).
17. See Childs, H. L. and J. B. Whitton, ed., *Propaganda by Short Wave* (Princeton: Princeton University Press, 1942).
18. There are three excellent bibliographies of items relating to propaganda, public opinion, and communication: Lasswell, H. D., Casey, R. D., and B. L. Smith, *Propaganda and Promotional Activities: An Annotated Bibliography* (Minneapolis: University of Minnesota Press, 1935); Smith, B. L., Lasswell, H. D., and R. D. Casey, *Propaganda, Communication, and Public Opinion* (Princeton: Princeton University Press, 1946); and Smith, B. L. and M. Chitra, *International Communication and Political Opinion: A Guide to the Literature* (Princeton: Princeton University Press, 1956).
19. See Mosteller, Frederick, *et al*, *The Pre-election Polls of 1948* (New York: Social Science Research Council, 1949).
20. See Farago, Ladislas, *et al.*, compilers, *German Psychological Warfare: A Critical, Annotated and Comprehensive Survey and Bibliography* (New York: Committee for National Morale, 1941).
21. See Commission on Freedom of the Press, *A Free and Responsible Press* (Chicago: University of Chicago Press, 1947).
22. MacMahon, A. W., *Memorandum on the Postwar International Information Program of the United States* (Washington, D. C.: U. S. Department of State, 1945).
23. See Key, V. O., Jr., *Public Opinion and American Democracy* (New York: Alfred A. Knopf, 1961); Wilson, Francis, *A Theory of Public Opinion* (Chicago: Henry Regnery Company, 1962); Campbell, Angus, *et al.*, *The American Voter* (New York: John Wiley and Sons, 1960.); Stouffer, Samuel, *Communism, Conformity, and Civil Liberties* (New York: Doubleday, 1955).
24. See Schramm, Wilbur, *Responsibility in Mass Communication* (New York: Harper & Bros., 1957).
25. See Klapper, Joseph T., *The Effects of Mass Communication* (Chicago: The Free Press of Glencoe, 1958).

SUPPLEMENTARY READING

ALLPORT, F. H. "Toward a Science of Public Opinion," *Public Opinion Quarterly*, Vol. 1 (Jan. 1937), pp. 7-23.
BINKLEY, R. C. "The Concept of Public Opinion in the Social Sciences," *Social Forces*, Vol. 6 (March, 1928), pp. 389-96.
BRYCE, JAMES. *The American Commonwealth*. Vol. 2, part IV. New ed.; New York: Macmillan, 1924.
CAHALAN, DON, and others. "Concepts of 'Public' and 'Public Opinion,'" *International Journal of Opinion and Attitude Research*, Vol. 1 (Dec., 1947), pp. 99-106; 2 (Fall, 1948), pp. 379-92.
CARR, L. J. "Public Opinion as a Dynamic Concept," *Sociology and Social Research*, Vol. 13 (Sept., 1928), pp. 18-30.
CHILDS, HARWOOD L. "By Public Opinion I Mean," *Public Opinion Quarterly*, Vol. 3 (April, 1939), pp. 327-36.

CHILDS, HARWOOD L. *An Introduction to the Study of Public Opinion.* New York: John Wiley and Sons, 1940. (Pp. 33-48.)

CLARK, C. D. "The Concept of the Public," *Southwest Social Science Quarterly,* Vol. 13 (March, 1933), pp. 311-21.

KEY, V. O. *Public Opinion and American Democracy.* New York: Alfred A. Knopf, 1961. (Chap. 1.)

LIPPMANN, WALTER. *Public Opinion.* Macmillan, 1922.

MINAR, DAVID W. "Public Opinion in the Perspective of Political Theory," *Western Political Quarterly,* Vol. 13 (March, 1960), pp. 31-44.

PALMER, PAUL A. "The Concept of Public Opinion in Political Theory," in *Essays in History and Political Theory in Honor of Charles H. McIlwain.* Cambridge, Mass.: Harvard University Press, 1936.

Public Opinion Quarterly, Vol. 21 (Spring, 1957), pp. 14-76.

RIESMAN, DAVID, and GLAZER, NATHAN. "The Meaning of Opinion," *Public Opinion Quarterly,* Vol. 12 (Winter, 1948-49), pp. 633-48.

SEDMAN, V. R. "Some Interpretations of Public Opinion," *Social Forces,* Vol. 10 (March, 1932), pp. 339-50.

SMITH, M. BREWSTER. "Comment on the 'Implications of Separating Opinions from Attitudes,'" *Public Opinion Quarterly,* Vol. 18 (Fall, 1954), pp. 254-70.

WIEBE, G. D. "Some Implications of Separating Opinions from Attitudes," *Public Opinion Quarterly,* Vol. 17 (Fall, 1953), pp. 328-52.

WILSON, FRANCIS G. "Concept of Public Opinion," *American Political Science Review,* Vol. 27 (June, 1933), pp. 371-91.

WILSON, FRANCIS G. *A Theory of Public Opinion.* Chicago: Henry Regnery Co., 1962.

III · Public Opinion Study and Research

It is . . . on opinion only that government is founded; and this maxim extends to the most despotic and most military governments, as well as to the most free and most popular.

—DAVID HUME

INTEREST IN public opinion seems to be of two general types: research and promotional. The research type engages a large number of scholars who are primarily interested in finding out certain things about public opinion: what the state of opinion is within a given group at a particular time, over periods of time, on a variety of subjects; how public opinion is formed, why it is what it is; what influence is exerted by selected opinion-forming factors; what the relative influence of various factors in the opinion-forming process is; who holds certain types of opinions, what their personal characteristics are, and what relationship exists between those characteristics and the opinions held. The number of aspects which challenge scholarly curiosity is almost infinite. Public opinion research of this type is largely motivated by a desire to know and by a hope that some contribution can be made to a more intelligent understanding of the subject.

The second type of interest in public opinion may be called promotional, since its end is manipulation. This interest stems from a desire to do something about public opinion: to mold, educate, or influence it. For every student of public opinion with a passion for objective research there are scores of persons eager to change public opinion, win public support for their ideas, sell their products. There is scarcely a person who is not interested in problems of the latter kind at some time or another.

The interests of promoter and scholar frequently overlap. Knowledge of states and trends of public opinion, the process of opinion formation, the relative influence of various opinion determinants, and the many other types of data revealed by scholarly research is of inestimable value to promoters. Likewise, the practical experience of those engaged in the day to day attempts to mold public opinion serves to enrich the undertakings of scholars and to test the value of their findings.

Public opinion research usually begins with the selection of a public for study. As previously indicated the choice of publics is almost unlimited. The professor is interested in the opinions of those attending his lectures, the storekeeper his customers, the radio commentator his listeners, the labor leader his trade union members, the legislator his constituents.

In the second step, the investigator selects the topics and subjects about which he desires opinions. Here, again, the interests of different investigators will vary. No one has ever undertaken to compile a complete list of such subjects. It would be as inclusive as an unabridged encyclopedia. It may happen that the student will not be interested in public opinion about any specific topic; instead, he may wish to find out what topics of opinion are on the minds of the public selected, what opinions are in the forefront of their attention.

The third step ordinarily, but not necessarily, involves the framing of a questionnaire. Questionnaires may be used to elicit opinions, but the silent observer, simply by listening, may soon discover what a person's opinions are. This technique of the public opinion listening post has not been fully employed and exploited, but it is, in some cases, a much more satisfactory method of obtaining types of opinions than the other more formal procedure.

The next step usually involves the actual collection of opinions, the filling out of the ballots, the asking of questions, or, if the listening post technique is used, the setting up of machinery for mass observation.

Then follows the task of summation and analysis. Refinements in questionnaire techniques have made possible the application of statistical methods to this process. Although, on occasion, free-answer questionnaires are employed to elicit opinions, the results of the uniform-answer type are easier to tabulate and summarize and hence, used more frequently. The simplest type of the uniform-answer questionnaire is the "Yes-No" form, which enables the investigator to summate the results very quickly, but other types of uniform-answer questionnaires, such as the ranked and scaled types, are also frequently used. The latter enables the investigator to ascertain shades of opinion and to measure degrees of favorableness and unfavorableness. Improvements in the standardization of uniform-answer types of questionnaires have facilitated the processing of data by use of tabulating machines, and these have made practicable the speedy identification of the opinions of large publics. Public opinion data lend themselves more and more to statistical treatment, and investigators can plot changes and trends in opinion, compare states of opinion between groups, and classify opinions in much the same way that other types of statistical data are treated.

From this point on the possibilities of analysis are many. Knowing states and trends in public opinion, the student may wish to study their causes or to analyze the influence of various factors which may have had a share in the opinion-forming process. In some instances significant correlations may be obtained between the opinion trends discovered and other socially significant trends. Such relationships may serve as clues to more profound observations regarding causation. Investigators may wish to study the personal characteristics of those who hold selected types of opinions, to compare and correlate these characteristics. Others may wish to appraise the quality of the opinions in terms of preconceived standards of excellence or in terms of known facts and the opinions of others.

Is it possible to predict changes in public opinion? This is, at present, extremely difficult, but not necessarily impossible. As knowledge regarding the relative influence of opinion determinants becomes more precise, and relationships between opinion trends and changes in other factors become clearer, the possibilities of a true science of public opinion become more real. Evidence shows, however, that progress in this direction is slow.

SOME BASIC PROBLEMS OF PUBLIC OPINION RESEARCH

Identification of Mass Opinion

Until quite recently it was extremely difficult, if not impossible, to ascertain speedily and accurately, states and trends of opinion within numerically large publics. To be sure, coincident with the rise of democratic institutions, governments instituted electoral procedures which made possible the expression of mass opinion on candidates for public office, and, occasionally, on questions of public policy. But elections and referenda on such a large scale were very expensive and time consuming, and they could not be used frequently. Commonly representative bodies were employed, not only to check the prejudices and passions of the multitude, but also to reflect and interpret public opinion as best they could on the basis of their own personal sources of what the public opinion was.

As late as the turn of this century, a considerable amount of public opinion research was going on with small, selected publics, such as student classes in American schools and colleges. Although the collective opinions of these small publics were not, in and of themselves, very significant from the point of view of the total society, these studies served to test the efficacy of method in eliciting, tabulating, summarizing, and analyzing public opinion. Long before the possibilities of mass opinion studies in the sense we know them today, psychologists and others had gone a long way toward perfecting relevant research techniques. Notable contributions were made by educators concerned with what is familiarly known as the science of tests and measurements.

The advent of so-called "scientific polls" during the 1930's has gone far toward solving the problem of ascertaining quickly, economically, and accurately the states and trends of public opinion on a large scale. As the advertising profession came of age, with its expenditure of huge sums of money, more precise information was desired regarding the effectiveness of their work and justification for such colossal outlays. The consequence was an expansion of marketing research to discover trends in buying habits and the relationship between such trends and advertising appropriations. Marketing research soon discovered the possibilities of sampling techniques for this purpose, and after the *Literary Digest*[1] and other periodicals had demonstrated the public's interest in information regarding the opinions of the masses on questions of public policy, advertisers and market researchers made use of their own sampling techniques to probe for such information.

The problem of identifying mass opinion is well on its way toward solution. There is no insuperable difficulty due to modern data processing techniques, so far as public opinion research is concerned, in dealing with mass publics, even with groups as inclusive as the entire electorate of a nation. This fact greatly increases the significance of the results of public opinion research, which, in the minds of many, had not been very significant when the size of the publics studied was severely limited by the absence of modern techniques. The major obstacle to mass opinion studies has been overcome, but there remain a number of minor problems which will continue to engage the attention of the student in this field: problems of interviewing technique, problems associated with the framing of questions, problems connected with the improvement of field operations. As yet those engaged in the study of mass publics have not been able to exploit many of the techniques developed in the past by students of smaller collections of opinions. The principal problem at the present time is to raise the level of methodology of studies of mass opinion up to that attained previously by students of smaller publics.

Relative Importance of Opinion Determinants

Knowledge concerning the opinion-forming process is still in a very rudimentary stage. In fact, one of the most important problems facing the student of public opinion at the present time is the problem of ascertaining precisely what role selected factors play in this process. The list of factors is virtually unlimited; they vary in their inclusiveness all the way from institutions, such as the press, the public schools, government, church denominations, and television, to narrowly restricted factors such as individual persons, or items such as a given editorial or advertisement.

Various attempts have been made to list all possible factors and to classify them. In the final analysis such a list would have to be as inclusive as our physical, biological, and cultural inheritance and environment. Conceivably anything, from climate to rationing, from topography to chewing gum may exert some influence on opinion.

There is already an abundance of literature dealing with the effect of this and that upon public opinion. Such titles as The Influence of the Press, The Influence of Detective Stories, The Influence of History Teaching, The Influence of Age and Sex, and so on, presumably tell us about the impact of each factor on public opinion. They usually prove to be more or less careful descriptions of these factors; seldom is the influence *as such* precisely indicated. This is not surprising, because we know little about the relative influence of factors in the opinion-forming process. This is a challenging area of research at the present time, and some progress is being made, as will be indicated later. The principal difficulty is the one which all science encounters: isolating factors and determining their effect under stated conditions. No elaborate research is necessary to establish the fact that *The New York Times* exerts an influence on public opinion. The question is, just how much? Books which trace in detail the history of this newspaper, describe its organization and activities, analyze its financial and editorial policies, plot its circulation, measure its reader interest fail to answer the question. Opinion formation remains the great unknown, the unexplored no-man's land of public opinion research.

Improving the Quality of Mass Opinion

Someone has said, "The great problem of public opinion is not to find out what it is, but to make it what it ought to be." In a very real sense, this is true. In spite of the stupendous progress which has been made in the field of public education, in the facilities of communication, in the offerings of libraries and laboratory, in the spread of literacy, and in the level of public discussion, the battle with ignorance, superstition, and intellectual short-sightedness has only begun. Many students of public opinion today, absorbed with the minutiae of methodology, techniques of sampling, and interviewing procedures often fail to appreciate the dimensions of their subject. If there is one motive which should spur all of those interested in public opinion research it should be to make some contribution to the solution of this problem of raising the level of public intelligence. Every researcher has a stake in the result. The efficacy of the democratic way of life depends upon it.

This is not the appropriate place to discuss and appraise systems, objectives, and achievements in the field of education and how they affect public discussion. A few observations may be hazarded to suggest the scope of the whole problem of improving the quality of mass opinion and the challenge which it presents to research. Few will deny that mass opinion is becoming more articulate and influential. Few will assert that the level of the quality and intelligence of mass opinion is as high as it should be. Few will claim that the problem is unimportant, but efforts to alleviate the situation face many obstacles. One is the pessimism which fails or refuses to see any possibilities of improvement. Another is the selfishness which regards knowledge as the vested interest of class or race or elite. Another is the insistence, the stubborn, intolerant assertion, that belief in some doctrinaire scheme of ideas must take precedence over some other, and still another is the everlasting argument over what is truth and what is intelligence.

Disregarding the extensive areas of opinion wherein "reasonable men may differ" and focusing attention exclusively upon those bodies of fact, knowledge, and information which are accepted in virtually all halls of learning—facts regarding health, history, psychology, economics, housing, human suffering and wants—one may easily find opportunities for service in raising the level of public intelligence. Whatever may be one's general philosophy of life, one's religious and political affiliations, one's esthetic tastes and predispositions—all can agree that there does exist a body of fact and information. If this knowledge were disseminated to all the masses, the level of public opinion would by definition be raised. Differences of opinion regarding the more hazy truths of life are too frequently used as the level of public opinion would by definition be raised. Differences of

Using as a standard of reference this core of "basic facts" the students of public opinion research can proceed to identify population areas in terms of their degree of ignorance. They can search for, list, and describe the principal barriers to the spread of "fact and information" in these areas, and they can try to find effective methods for removing or surmounting these barriers.

Conflicts of Opinion

Within almost any public there may exist conflicts of opinion; in families, conflicts between parents and children; in schools, between teacher and pupil; in firms, between employer and employee; in community publics, between farmers and urban dwellers; between Jews and Gentiles, Republicans and Democrats, Fascists and Communists. Why do these conflicts exist and persist? What are their causes? Are these conflicts inevitable and unavoidable? How may these conflicts be resolved amicably and satisfactorily? Here is a whole field of public opinion research which is far from being completely explored. To be sure, elaborate studies of war in all its various phases have been made. The subject of industrial relations has excited and captivated the interest of many students. Within the past few decades the study of employer-employee relations has been broadened to include the study of public relations, and the search is carried on for an understanding of the reasons for differences of opinion between publics, differences that result in hostility and sometimes violence. Likewise considerable attention has been given to interracial differences of opinion, relationships within the family, and conflicts of opinion between and among all sorts of groups and publics.

Although existing studies of this kind vary from mere descriptions and historical accounts to partisan diatribes, from personal reminiscences to thoughtful analyses, they can and frequently do throw much light on the opinion-forming process. They should not be lightly ignored by students of public opinion. Clearly enough, conflicts or differences of opinion are extolled as well as condemned. They are alleged to be evidences of the intellectual vitality of the time, and almost in the same breath they are lamented as precursors of violence. How glorious it would be if all people thought alike! Or would it? New ideas are stimulating. Without them public opinion would became stagnant, and yet new ideas are often the source of change and social revolution. It is the old conflict between conservatism and radicalism, between the desire for security and the love of adventure, between war and peace, and life and death.

It is frequently asserted that democratic government, in the sense of majority rule by public opinion, is virtually impossible without some basis of general agreement. Agreement on "fundamentals" seems to be a *sine qua non*. Possibly too much attention has been focused on conflicts of opinion, too little on areas of agreement. The problem is to find some balance in the matter, to provide the mechanism whereby groups can find a *modus vivendi* for differing in their opinions without resorting to violence. This involves the careful search for the causes of these differences, for attempts to remove the causes when they are the consequence of ignorance and lack of information, efforts to bring to the forefront of attention areas of agreement, and for the establishment of peaceful procedures of deciding issues which represent genuine conflicts of interest. Here is a rich field for public opinion studies.

The Role of Public Opinion

Mention should also be made of another problem which has been the basis of much discussion since the idea of democratic government was conceived: what is the proper role of public opinion? To what extent should the opinions of the masses be made the directing and deciding force in the determination of public policy? Extremists take the position either that the masses are wholly incapable of competent and trustworthy decisions in matters of public policy, or that their opinions are in reality God-given and hence they should govern as well as rule. Between these extremes are the views of those who would undertake to define and redefine the role of mass opinion in terms of what it should and should not be called upon to do.

Now that the application of techniques of sampling public opinion make it possible to ascertain states and trends of public opinion quickly and accurately, this problem has taken on a new significance. To answer it involves considerations which go to the very heart of the whole problem of democratic versus authoritarian government.

CONTENT CLASSIFICATION OF STUDIES FROM THE PUBLIC OPINION QUARTERLY

There are various sources of information which may be used to discover trends in public opinion study and research such as: (a) the contents of the *Public Opinion Quarterly*; (b) the programs of the American Association for Public Opinion Research; (c) lists of articles cited in periodical guides such as Public Affairs Information Service (PAIS); (d) book lists; (e) lists of doctoral dissertations; (f) contents of textbooks; (g) programs of research organizations. Most revealing are the contents of the *Quarterly*.

A survey of the contents of the *Public Opinion Quarterly*[2] since its inception twenty-eight years ago shows that the subject matter falls into several major categories as follows:

A. Public Opinion Polls
    1. Techniques
    2. Contributions
    3. Particular polls
    4. Evaluations
B. Public Opinion of Selected Groups on Specific Issues
    1. United States
        a) National
        b) State and Local
    2. Foreign Countries
    3. Special Groups
C. Influence of Selected Factors in Formation of Public Opinion
    1. In General
    2. Specifically
    3. Basic Determinants
    4. Relative Influence of Factors
D. Voting Behavior
    1. Elections
    2. Parties
    3. Candidates
    4. Determinants
    5. Prediction
E. Communication
    1. Press and Publications

      2. Radio
      3. Motion Pictures
      4. Television
      5. Other
   F. Propaganda
      1. In General
      2. Psychological Warfare
      3. USSR
      4. U. S. Government—domestic; overseas
      5. United Nations
      6. Public Relations
      7. Advertising
      8. Education
      9. Leadership
   G. Research
      1. In General
      2. Proposals
   H. Theory
      1. Definitions
      2. Models
      3. Hypotheses

Public Opinion Polls

The public opinion poll has become the indispensable tool of the student of public opinion, whether he is interested in the attitudes and opinions of selected groups, the role of selected factors in the process of opinion formation, voting behavior, communication, or propaganda. Quite naturally, therefore, much attention has been given to this tool as shown by the number and variety of articles dealing with it in the *Public Opinion Quarterly*.[3] Each step in the procedure of public opinion surveying has been subjected to careful study. Considerable attention has been given to problems of sampling and to the relative merits of quota and probability sampling.[4] Framing questionnaires has given rise to studies of question meaning and complexity, projection devices and other types of question design, pre-testing questionnaires, experiments in wording questions, and studies of question validity.

Probably no aspect of the technique of polling has been studied more carefully than the interviewer and interviewing. Numerous studies have been made of interviewer bias, depth interviewing, interviewees not at home, interviewer performance, the effect of using subquestions, group interviewing, tape recorder interviews, card-sorting interviews, and problems of translation. Attention has also been given to the organization and

administration of interviewing, to training interviewers, and to the preparation of report forms and instructions for interviewers.

During the last few years the larger nation-wide polling organizations
have been experimenting with various types of attitude scales, some of
which have been in use by psychologists for a number of years. Prior to
the thirties, national polls used rather simple, yes or no type of questions.
As funds became available, more refined and penetrating questionnaires
could be employed. Batteries of questions were asked in depth interviews
about and around specific subjects. Open-ended questions gave way in
many cases to lists of ranked, rated, or scaled statements which would
make possible the classification of opinions along an attitude or opinion
continuum. Interest in scalogram analysis and various applications of the
Thurstone scaling technique is still reflected in publications of the *Quarterly*.[5]

On the technical side of polling, mention should be made of the persistent interest in mail surveys, notwithstanding the overwhelming emphasis on the interviewing technique. The bias factor, response percentages
in general and by various categories, and the pros and cons of the mail
canvass have been subject to careful study.

Students of polling techniques have given much thought to the checking and testing of various procedures, and the validating of results as a
whole. How accurate and valid a particular survey is, is always a primary
question. *Quarterly* articles have dealt with such matters as the validity of
responses, laboratory tests of sampling techniques, coding reliability,
whether different polls give the same results, and the relationship between
survey and actual election results. Many experiments in wording questions
have helped to improve the questioning process and to give greater mean-
ingfulness and reliability to opinion data. Techniques have been developed
for detecting cheaters among interviewers and thereby reducing to some
extent the possibilities of falsification of interview returns.

The reliability of sampling procedures must rest primarily on the soundness of the logic supporting the procedures. In few instances can the results obtained from the sample be checked against results obtained from
other sampling methods, and the possibility of checking sample data with
opinion data obtainable only if the entire universe is polled is even less
likely. The logic of random or probability sampling is the real reason for
the extensive use of this method instead of the quota method. Empirical
tests of reliability are difficult if not impossible to achieve.

As indicated above, a considerable amount of space in the *Public
Opinion Quarterly* is devoted to the technique of polling. Many articles
are concerned with the contributions and uses of polls to people in varied
situations and for different purposes. Studies show the value of polls to

government officials,[6] in civil litigation, in the field of mental health, for economic forecasting, and in psychological warfare. Special articles point out how they can help public relations executives, school administrators, the press, candidates for public office, and political parties. It is obvious that a knowledge of states and trends of public opinion is extremely valuable to leaders and officials in all walks of life. Studies of the uses and contributions of polls describe and analyze the how, when, where, why, and the effects of particular uses of the polls. More and more emphasis is being placed upon studying the trends of public opinion. The trend studies are carried out by repeating surveys on the same subject matter over a period of time. These trends can be shown for the public as a whole, or for various subpublics into which the larger public can be subdivided, such as age, sex, occupational, racial, or other grouping. These time studies (time series) of opinion trends can often be correlated advantageously with other time study trends to reveal interesting and significant relationships. Studies of the contributions of polls illustrate many different uses, actual or possible; they point up areas of ignorance, predict possible types of group behavior, suggest the success or lack of success of a propaganda and promotional campaign, aid administrators in the execution of policies, serve as public relations barometers, and guide policy makers.

A third main category of *Quarterly* articles dealing with polls comprises studies or descriptions of particular polls. There have been articles dealing with the outstanding national polling organizations in the United States such as the American Institute of Public Opinion, Opinion Research Corporation, the Michigan Survey Research Center, the Crossley Poll, *Literary Digest,* Elmo Roper, and the New York *Daily News* polls. Attention has also been given to various state and local polls such as the Washington Public Opinion Laboratory, the Texas, Trenton, and other state polls, and the Reed poll.

Since polling public opinion has become a significant activity abroad, it is not surprising to find considerable interest in survey organizations operating in Great Britain, Holland, Germany, Mexico, Japan, Italy, Czechoslovakia, Switzerland, and even Ghana. Comparative studies of polling activities are valuable for many reasons. They bring to light new methods and techniques. They suggest new directions of inquiry. The states and trends in public opinion of different countries furnish keys to an understanding of the relations between countries and the bases of international tensions. The foreign offices of several countries find opinion data from other countries of value in formulating and executing policies.

The advent of nation-wide polls, and the proliferation of polling organizations at all levels, from community to international, has given rise to some apprehension as well as enthusiasm. The *Quarterly* has given space to evaluation studies of polls. These studies try to weigh the broader, social implications of this new activity.[7] Do polls serve democracy? What do editors think of polls? Have some polls been unfair to labor? What are the dangers of polls? What lessons or conclusions can be drawn from experience with pre-election polling? What do the people in the United States as a whole think of polls? How reliable are they? To what extent, if at all, are they being misused? Should polling agencies be regulated by the government? How can polls be made more responsible? These are some of the questions which authors have tried to answer in the pages of the *Quarterly*. In some cases the answers are based on empirical investigations. Often they are the product of speculation, theorizing, and deductive analysis.

Public opinion polls are not only objects of study and research, but they are also tools of research, and a large segment of public opinion research is concerned with the application of these tools. Numerous *Quarterly* articles, based on polls actually taken, report the state or trend of public opinion of particular publics in regard to particular issues. Since the number of publics is almost infinite—these publics vary in size, cohesion, organization, wealth, education, and a great many other attributes —and the subjects on which questions may be based are likewise virtually unlimited, the scope of this type of research is colossal. The opinion data collected by the American Institute of Public Opinion and several other nation-wide polling organizations in the United States and a few other countries from 1935 to 1946 fill a dictionary-size volume of nearly twelve hundred pages.[8] Of course this data represented only a fraction of the data collected by state and local organizations, academic researchers, marketing research firms, and numerous other official and unofficial agencies.

Interest in poll studies may stem from many aspects of the studies; such as methods used, the particular public questioned, the degree to which the public is unanimous in its opinion, the intensity with which the opinions are held, the probability of the public giving effect to its views, the degree of expertness and information represented by the opinions, and many other aspects. Unfortunately, many of these studies have limited value because the methods employed are in no sense novel, the public, so far as students of public opinion are concerned, is of very limited significance, there is no evidence that the public feels strongly about the questions asked, there is little likelihood that the opinions are indices of future behavior, and there is no evidence that the opinions expressed are in any sense expert or well-informed. Moreover, reviewing various collections of opinion data quickly reveals that much of the material is dated: its subject matter has limited interest and its reliability is unstable. Opinions change, and consequently, opinion surveys have a marked tendency towards obsolescence. In short, a large proportion of the public opinion surveys today and in the past may yield very little of enduring value and are comparable in that respect to last year's weather reports or stock market averages. They do have a certain historical value, however, and if they are so selected and co-ordinated as to provide the basis for significant trend lines, they can be extremely useful for correlational and predictive purposes.

Selected Groups on Specific Issues

The *Quarterly* articles dealing with the public opinion of particular groups on special issues may be conveniently classified as follows: (a) nation-wide polls in the United States, (b) state, local, and regional polls in the United States, (c) country-wide polls in foreign countries, and (d) special polls.

It will serve no useful purpose to attempt to list all the subjects on which the people in the United States have been polled during the last thirty years. World organization, foreign policy, capital punishment, World War II, party re-alignment, Russia, rationing, education, municipal services, social welfare, peace, campaign issues—these are some of the subjects on which the American people as a whole have been polled, carefully studied, and reported in the *Quarterly*.

The *Quarterly* has also reported on a number of state regional and local surveys: attitudes of the residents of Indianapolis on human fertility, what the people in the State of Washington think of Communism, public attitudes of Philadelphians regarding Franklin Delano Roosevelt, the state of public opinion regarding utilities in ten midwestern states, and popular stereotypes of Jews in the city of Denver.[9] Some of these studies are rich in suggestive hypotheses. Some employ new and experimental techniques. Some tend to support or contradict the conclusions of similar studies elsewhere. By and large, however, these studies suffer from their dated nature, the restricted nature of the publics, and above all their discreteness. They do not fit into any broad gauge research program. It is difficult to compare the specific results obtained with other studies.

Public opinion polls taken in foreign countries have an interest which is perhaps out of proportion to their intrinsic value. Polling abroad encounters many difficulties of sampling, interviewing, translating, and even framing questions largely avoided in the United States; consequently, the results have to be accepted with a great deal of caution. The surveys which have been carefully analyzed and reported in the *Quarterly* represent only a few of the hundreds, even thousands which have been taken in many foreign countries. Of this select group, the subjects covered are: public opinion in Costa Rica, public opinion in the south of Italy, Canadian views of the postwar world, Great Britain on birth control and sex, Japanese opinion on the Far East conflict, French views on anti-Semitism, opinions of French business leaders on the European Common Market, German workers' opinions regarding Russia, the opinions of Egyptian professional people.[10]

Public opinion studies continue to include surveys of student opinion, and several of these have been reported in the *Quarterly,* such as student attitudes on the Korean war, civil rights, and the Kinsey report.[11] Studies of student opinion are primarily concerned with problems of method, since student opinion as such may have very little political, social, or economic significance, if composed of publics from small classes in public opinion, sociology, or psychology.

From time to time rather special groups are studied for public opinion purposes, either to ascertain states and trends of opinion within the groups, to describe or analyze their methods of influencing public opinion, or to assess their influence on other publics or institutions. Because of the significance of pressure groups in the whole opinion-forming process, students of public opinion have paid particular attention to them. Selected groups of businessmen, ex-Communists, neighborhood residents, Korean refugees, utility employees, editors, union members, legislators, professors, and Japanese-Americans are a few of the special publics whose opinions on various subjects have been collected and analyzed.[12]

Other groups which have been studied are political extremists in Iran, people over fifty years of age, the British Labor Party, lobbies investigated by Congress, Soviet Friendship Societies, the German Wehrmacht in World War II, the American Federation of Musicians, anti-Communist mobs, veterans as a group, United States senators, church members, Indian village populations, Italian communities, military groups, the Congress of Industrial Organizations (C.I.O.), and many others.[13] Sometimes the focus of interest is the opinion or attitude of the public selected, or it may be trends of opinion within the group, the process of opinion-formation within the group, the methods used by the group to influence outsiders, or its propaganda and pressure group activity.

Influence of Selected Factors

Quite significant from the point of view of number of articles and amount of space given to them by the *Quarterly* are the studies of factors significant in the process of opinion formation. These studies all stem from efforts to find how public opinion is formed. Some of the studies list and classify as many of the important factors as possible. Some take one or a few factors and describe them in detail, to determine their specific effects in general or in special situations. Still others seek to weigh the relative influence of several factors. Attempts may be made to identify what the "so-called" basic determinants are in some public opinion situation.

The *Quarterly* has published articles on the influence of particular factors on something definite, such as the influence of previous experience on attitudes toward loyalty oaths, the influence of reference groups on children's attitudes, rumor on the stockmarket, mass media on information regarding public affairs, prosperity on political voting, pressure groups on American foreign policy, religion on voting behavior, foreign travel on business opinion, Japanese art on American opinion of Japan.[14]

These studies usually show the influence of the factor considered on the target used. The factor itself can be described with care and insight, and often the way in which it exerts its influence can be analyzed. Efforts are made to isolate the factor and measure or ascertain as precisely as possible the degree of its influence, but this is not always possible, and many of these studies conclude with lists of hypotheses and suggestions for further studies or experimentation.

Not infrequently a factor or factors will be studied without a very specific reference to any target of the influence. The assumption will be made, perhaps, that the factor or factors are significant in the public opinion process, and the emphasis will be placed on describing the factor or factors. *Quarterly* studies of this type have dealt with such factors as: the influence of stereotypes, authoritarianism, prestige suggestion, party identification, preparatory communications, expectations, magazines, women's fashions, political campaigns.[15]

Another type of factor study is the effort to find what may be called basic determinants of public opinion. Sometimes this search includes refined procedures of measuring or weighing the relative influence of several factors; more often it is based on rather arbitrary assumptions and a priori reasoning. This type of study is represented by *Quarterly* articles dealing with determinants of voting behavior, factors enhancing the effect of anti-Semitic propaganda, underlying variables of legislative roll calls, determinants of political apathy, determinants of Negro prejudice, and the bases of United States isolationism.[16]

From these discrete, isolated studies it is difficult to draw valid, broad conclusions about the opinion-forming process. Usually, the "basic determinants" vary from case to case; few attempts are made to compare the role of the same factor in different situations; and many important factors may not have been considered. How convincing these studies are depends, not so much on empirical evidence, nor on experimentation, as on the rationality and logic of the presentation and argument.

Finally, there is a type of factor study which tries to weigh the relative influence of several factors and rank, rate, or even scale them. Almost any combination of factors may be selected for this purpose. The *Quarterly* has reported on studies of the relative influence of the personality of candidates versus campaign issues, the relative role of conviction, partisanship, and knowledge in the formation of political opinions, the relationship between physical, personality, and opinion traits; the relative importance of time and events in the formation of opinion, and many others.[17] Of course, there is no limit to the number nor to the variety of factors that may be selected for purposes of comparison.

Voting Behavior

On the basis of material published in the *Quarterly* a fourth major category of public opinion studies may be discerned. These studies could logically be catalogued in one or more of the previously mentioned categories, but they justify a separate listing because they are focused on one important phenomenon—elections and voting behavior. Students of public opinion, whether they are classified as political scientists, sociologists, psychologists, economists, or statisticians, sooner or later find their research interests centering on elections, a public opinion event of obvious importance. These studies usually make use of polls, often concentrate on the opinions of selected groups on specific issues, and try to find out as much as possible about the way in which the voter's opinions are formed.[18] Over the course of the last twenty years all Presidential and Congressional elections in the United States have been subjected to close study. This is also true of many state and local elections,[19] and of national and local elections abroad. These studies deal with many aspects of the election process such as the major determinants of voting behavior (referred to before under factor studies), various types of voters and non-voters, prediction, the role of various institutions such as the press, government, pressure groups, and political parties, historical and statistical studies.

Also in this category are the various studies of election polling and prediction performance. What began as an interest in predicting the outcome of elections has developed into various related studies of polling methods, to which references were made earlier, and to factors affecting prediction accuracy, such as voter turnout and changes in attention given to voting. By far the most important concern of those engaged in commercial polling and marketing research is the improvement of polling techniques and the prediction of voter or consumer behavior.

Students have been interested in the voting behavior of subpublics as well as the voting public as a whole. There are reports on Negro voting behavior, the non-voter, labor's role, the political behavior of nationalities in the United States, the woman voter, and many other groups.[20]

In answering the question why voters vote as they do, students have explored the role of numerous factors in the political process, many of which have been mentioned earlier. Such physical attributes as age, sex, income, and place of residence have been analyzed with reference to voting behavior. The factors of party, religion, and other group affiliations have also been studied. Considerable attention has been given to the role of communication agencies, especially the mass media. Some of the newer factors studied, especially in relation to voting behavior, have been cross pressures, opinion leaders, personal contacts, friendship groups, events, machine politics, military heroes as candidates, political interest, and many others.[21] The reasons for political activity, the question whether publication of poll results does or does not have a bandwagon effect, the bases for and consequences of political apathy, the degree of political involvement of members of the electorate, migration and its impact on voting in cities —all of these aspects of the voting process have been studied and reported in the pages of the *Quarterly*.[22]

Communication Media

More attention has been given in the pages of the *Quarterly* to studies of communication media than to any other aspect of public opinion. As might be expected a large proportion of these studies relate to the mass media: press and publications, radio, motion pictures, and television. Press content, influences affecting the press, censorship, headlines, editorials, columnists, trade papers, comic strips, neighborhood papers, Catholic papers, the British press, all have been studied as well as a number of particular papers. Techniques of newspaper analysis have been appraised, as well as newspaper polls, and the use or role of newspapers in political campaigns.[23]

Several studies of radio listening and television viewing have been reported in the *Quarterly,* and radio and television broadcasts have been described and analyzed. The effects of radio and television, particularly on youth, have been appraised. Some consideration has been given to news commentators, the history of the electronic media, problems of inter-American broadcasting, tastes in programs, and the ability of listeners to recall programs.[24] In general, the formula or expression used to classify communication studies—"who communicates what, to whom, with what effect"—describes many of the studies, but consideration is also being given to "why, where, when, and for what purpose."

More attention in the *Quarterly* has been given to documentary motion pictures than to any other aspect of motion pictures. However, there are a few reports on studies of motion picture content, comic strips, cartoons, motion picture trailers, and the relationship of motion pictures to diplomacy and foreign relations.[25]

Although the *Quarterly* reports studies of television content, its use in the United States and abroad, and in political campaigns, the principal emphasis in public opinion research on television has been concerned with its effects in general and upon young people in particular.[26]

There are quite a few studies of communication media which deal with the media in general rather than from the point of view of a particular medium. Typical of this would be the studies of patterns of Soviet response to communication agencies, conditions of the effective use of communication agencies, the communications process in Israel, media habits of children, the influence of mass media on information regarding public affairs, totalitarian communications, UNESCO's mass communication's program, freedom of communication, competition among mass media, and the process of communication.[27]

Interest in communication is by no means confined to the mass media. Considerable ingenuity is shown in picking out new and significant media for examination such as congressional and White House mail, magazine fiction, basic English, specific magazines (for example, the *Hollywood Quarterly*), textbooks, songs, best sellers, letters to the editor, pageants, press conferences, and word of mouth communications, or marriage ads. Also, mention should be made of studies of short-wave listening, McGuffey readers, press agents, congressional hearings, institutional advertising, serious books, public service ads, *Izvestia,* book clubs, and space serials.[28]

In addition to studies of polls, opinions of selected groups, formation of public opinion, voting behavior, and communications, students of public opinion have displayed much interest in efforts by individuals and organizations to manage, lead, or mold public opinion. There have been studies of the information and publicity activities of world organizations such as the United Nations and UNESCO, of the USSR, the United States, and other national governments, as well as those on the state and local level. There have been studies of propaganda, public relations, advertising, press agentry, leadership, and education.

Propaganda

Since World War I, and even before, there has been widespread interest in propaganda, its methods, objectives, and effects, both from the practical and theoretical point of view. This interest may focus on the subject of propaganda in general or on its more limited types or aspects. Over the course of the last twenty-six years the *Quarterly* has published a number of studies dealing with propaganda in general: the international propaganda of the United States and the Soviet Union, the effectiveness of one-sided versus two-sided propaganda, art as national propaganda in the French Revolution, Goebbels' principles of propaganda, detecting collaboration in propaganda, foreign propaganda in the United States, propaganda analysis and the science of democracy. Of a more restricted type are such studies as the administration of Czechoslovakian propaganda, factors increasing the effect of anti-Semitic propaganda, confessions of a German propagandist, Gerald L. K. Smith's propaganda, Japanese race propaganda, German influences in southern Brazil, Chinese official publicity in the United State, propaganda by Civil War cartoonists, and the "Tai Chi" symbol in Japanese propaganda.[29]

When propaganda is used to aid military operations in wartime, either tactically or strategically, it is often referred to as psychological warfare. This term may also be applied to official propaganda in peacetime when it is used in a belligerent fashion to accomplish foreign policy aims without resort to actual war. German students of propaganda as a tool of war devoted considerable attention to psychological warfare during the nineteen thirties, and interest in the subject continues unabated. The *Quarterly* has published studies of psychological warfare in Korea, the strategies of psychological warfare, the future of psychological warfare, and other closely related studies such as Communist party broadcasts to Italy, Leninist propaganda, leaflet propaganda in World War II, Chinese handling of prisoners of war, foreign policy by propaganda leaflets, propaganda by short wave, and the like. Various aspects of the propaganda activities of the Soviet Union have received studied attention: patterns of Soviet response to media, United States and Soviet value systems, Soviet approach to international political communication, and Free Germans in Soviet psychological warfare.[30]

United States government information and propaganda activities both at home and abroad have accounted for numerous articles in the *Quarterly* such as the study of United States and Soviet propaganda mentioned above, the Voice of America, how to win neutralists, international information services in Africa, propaganda to eastern Europe, presenting America in American propaganda, the Department of State's international information program, early history of the Office of War Information, the future of American propaganda in Latin America, and the machinery for hemispheric co-operation.[31]

On the domestic front studies appearing in the *Quarterly* dealing with the information and publicity activities of the American government include a general survey of the information activities of administrative agencies, studies of the information work of the Department of Agriculture, a discussion of the question whether government agencies should use advertising, studies of censorship, and the impact of the war on information activities.[32]

Mention should also be made of a few studies of the public opinion activities of the United Nations, UNESCO, and other international organizations. The failure of the League of Nations so far as public opinion and information were concerned was analyzed. The program of UNESCO in the field of mass communications received attention, and several articles dealt with the organization and program of the United Nations division of information.[33]

The propaganda and promotional activities of public relations specialists account for extensive research interest. There have been general studies of public relations reported in the *Quarterly* dealing with such matters as problems of public relations training, personnel and ideology in public relations, the role of research in public relations, why public relations campaigns fail, public relations—a profession in search of professionals, public relations at the crossroads, buying public relations, and university courses in public relations. There are also many studies of the public relations organization, methods, problems, and effects of specific programs such as those of organized labor, the United States Army, the sugar industry, the military governments of Germany, Japan, and other occupied territories, international conferences, public utilities, TWA, the Labor Government of Great Britain, and many others.[34]

Finally, in the general category of opinion management are a few studies concerned with leadership and with education. Leadership as an object of study is by no means new, but the present tendency is to avoid general studies of leadership, and to focus attention on particular leaders and leadership situations. The significance of these studies for an understanding of the opinion-forming process is obvious. The *Quarterly* studies comprise public orientation to Franklin Delano Roosevelt, leadership selection in urban areas, techniques for the study of leadership, portrait of an American agitator, political leadership in a Midwestern city, leaders and advisers in a small town, the limits of external leadership over Negro voters, the trade-union leader, and Stresemann as a postwar leader.[35]

Very few articles have appeared in the *Quarterly* dealing with education in its relationship to public opinion. They deal for the most part in a very general way with education for citizenship in the United States. One article dealt with postwar education in enemy countries.[36] This dearth of attention to this important subject is surprising. In fact, very little attention has been given by students of public opinion to the role of the so-called basic institutions—the family, church, and school—notwithstanding their recognized importance in the over-all development and formation of public opinion.

Research

Many of the articles cited in the above categories of *Quarterly* studies deal to some extent with research as such, and often they contain suggestions for additional research. In the research proposal category are such articles as international communications research, psychological policy and total strategy, international political communications research, public opinion research in non-industrial countries, experimental approach to the study of political leadership, the obligations of pollsters to historians.[37]

Theory

From time to time a few articles of theoretical nature have appeared in the *Quarterly*. There have been discussions of such terms as opinion, attitude, democracy, and the meaning of politics in a mass society. Consideration has been given to the structure of attitudes and opinions and to the relationship of opinion and behavior. There have been a few studies of model construction, and the ideal model for controlled experiments. Other studies of a general theoretical nature deal with the group interpretation of politics, a study of elites, historic ideals operationally considered, meaning of politics in a mass society, freedom of communication, communication systems and social structure, the absorption rate of ideas, the basis of sound public opinion, on acquiring a public opinion, and public opinion in American statecraft.[38]

CONCLUSIONS

What are the main conclusions that may be drawn from this survey of trends in public opinion research insofar as they are revealed in the pages of the *Quarterly*?

(1) The primary foci of attention at the present time are public opinion polls and communication agencies.

(2) Interest in the attitudes and opinions of the electorate and in voting behavior is considerable.

(3) Studies of opinion management by governments, by organized groups, leaders, and professionals, such as public relations experts and advertisers, seem to attract less interest on the part of students of public opinion than the above categories.

(4) Theoretical and conceptual studies of public opinion have been extremely rare, and they seem to reveal little appreciation of some of the fundamental public opinion problems of today.

(5) All in all it would appear that public opinion research is overwhelmingly preoccupied with finding out what public opinion is, and with the role of communication agencies in the opinion-forming process.

(6) Much public opinion research is applied research, seeking to solve the immediate problems of public opinion pollsters, market researchers, proprietors of communication agencies, advertisers, public relations experts, and propagandists of one kind or another.

(7) What is needed at the present time is more public opinion research on the public interest rather than on private interests, toward the solution of the public opinion problems of the masses, and not merely those of private commercial interests.

(8) There is also a need for research related to significant action programs and focused on broad-gauged problems: the quality of public opinion, the role of public opinion, conflicts of opinion.

NOTES FOR CHAPTER 3

Epigraph. David Hume, *Essays and Treatises on Several Subjects,* Dublin, 1742, Vol. 1, Part 1, Essay IV, p. 29.

1. The *Literary Digest* began its nation-wide polls in 1916 and during their existence surveys were made on questions concerning the Presidential primary, the New Deal, bonus legislation, prohibition, as well as national elections. In some polls over ten million ballots were distributed. Until the Presidential election of 1936 the prestige of the *Literary Digest* poll was high.
2. In the following pages, trends in public opinion study and research are deduced mainly from the contents of the *Public Opinion Quarterly* since its inception in 1937. Other indices of trends are found in book lists, periodical indexes, research programs, and programs of professional associations.
3. No attempt is made to cite any large number of articles in the *Public Opinion Quarterly* for illustrative purposes. Only a few examples of specific types of study will be given. Moreover, in the footnote citations only the volume number and beginning page will be given, to avoid incessant repetition. As volume numbers are given annually, the year of publication can be determined by adding the volume number (less 1) to 1937 (the first year of publication).
4. See Stephan, Frederick F., "Advances in Survey Methods and Measurement Techniques," Vol. 21, p. 79.
5. Steiner, Ivan D., "Scalogram Analysis as a Tool for Selecting Poll Questions," Vol. 19, p. 415.
6. Alpert, Harry, "Opinion and Attitude Surveys in the U. S. Government," Vol. 16, p. 33.
7. *Public Opinion Quarterly,* Vol. 8, p. 461; 9:264; 10:349; 17:202.
8. *Public Opinion, 1935-1946* (Under the editorial direction of Hadley Cantril; prepared by Mildred Strunk [Princeton: Princeton University Press, 1951].)
9. *Public Opinion Quarterly,* Vol. 17, p. 496; 17:394; 15:189; 13:23; 13:93.
10. *Ibid.,* 7:242; 8:202; 8:523; 13:587; 15:76; 12:249; 20:212; 14:126; 20:277.
11. *Ibid.,* 17:171; 13:241; 12:687.
12. *Ibid.,* 20:39; 16:331; 15:229; 15:274; 14:33; 13:185; 13:5; 18:180; 8:530; 8:188.
13. *Ibid.,* 16:689; 17:391; 15:225; 14:14; 13:265; 12:280; 12:45; 12:57; 10:361; 18:5; 18:23; 18:337; 20:257; 20:270; 8:411; 5:233.
14. *Ibid.,* 11:20; 15:445; 15:461; 15:105; 14:331; 6:115; 12:377; 20:161; 20:221.
15. *Ibid.,* 17:281; 17:185; 16:77; 15:601; 15:487; 13:415; 13:520; 18:314; 14:413.
16. *Ibid.,* 14:393; 14:53; 18:191; 18:349; 9:456; 9:38.
17. *Ibid.,* 16:443; 17:171; 13:320; 15:715.
18. *Ibid.,* 27:1.
19. *Ibid.,* 12:723; 12:724; 12:726.
20. *Ibid.,* 5:267; 8:175; 8:376; 8:368; 9:79.

21. See, for example, Campbell, Angus, *et al., The Voter Decides* (Evanston, Ill.: Row, Peterson, 1954).
22. *Public Opinion Quarterly,* Vol. 15, p. 5; 18:245; 18:349; 19:206.
23. *Ibid.,* 5:463; 5:295; 18:62; 10:85; 10:518; 14:340; 15:105; 17:363; 27:515, 191, 217; 10:382; 19:5; 6:449; 7:205; 9:279; 19:31; 18:169; 15:519; 11:189; 11:558.
24. *Ibid.,* 5:210; 15:299; 13:73; 19:184; 15:421; 27:578; 19:209; 14:453.
25. *Ibid.,* 8:206; 14:554; 19:195; 9:119; 12:465; 14:443.
26. *Ibid.,* 13:223, 19:184; 19:243; 15:421; 19:79; 14:340.
27. *Ibid.,* 16:654; 17:363; 16:42; 15:445; 15:105; 14:224; 10:518; 10:85; 18:62.
28. *Ibid.,* 20:16; 5:359; 13:105; 10:201; 5:227; 11:97; 8:3; 20:5; 10:71; 11:567; 11:436; 17:91; 14:143; 15:532; 15:663; 17:297; 16:481; 5:210; 5:579; 6:221; 16:179; 16:5; 15:305; 12:209; 12:430; 12:243; 18:367.
29. *Ibid.,* 16:539; 17:311; 15:532; 14:419; 11:244; 6:351; 5:657; 13:607; 14:53; 10:216; 8:84; 7:191; 6:57; 6:10; 6:99; 5:532.
30. *Ibid.,* 15:65; 13:635; 12:5; 16:676; 15:265; 13:471; 20:321; 9:428; 5:38; 16:654; 20:314; 20:299; 14:285.
31. *Ibid.,* 16:605; 16:681; 17:7; 14:639; 11:213; 10:582; 9:283; 9:305; 6:549.
32. *Ibid.,* 11:530; 7:280; 11:221; 6:511; 6:3; 5:383.
33. *Ibid.,* 8:61; 10:518; 10:145; 12:481; 18:427.
34. *Ibid.,* 11:540; 12:697; 15:54; 11:412; 10:191; 8:551; 8:226; 5:93, 5:283; 5:275; 5:93; 7:555; 7:567; 20:308; 13:23; 13:527; 16:201; 15:189.
35. *Ibid.,* 14:262; 13:255; 12:417; 20:73; 28:83; 20:113; 9:158; 8:232.
36. *Ibid.,* 8:17.
37. *Ibid.,* 20:182; 16:149; 16:481; 16:491; 16:501; 16:527; 15:563; 14:617; 27:515; 27:526.
38. *Ibid.,* 12:653; 17:328; 18:254; 17:328; 16:333; 17:47; 15:5; 14:729; 11:507; 12:623; 8:557; 14:710; 15:567; 17:218; 16:27; 15:547; 15:5; 10:85; 19:153; 19:234; 9:140; 8:488; 6:391.

SUPPLEMENTARY READING

ALBIG, WILLIAM. "Two Decades of Opinion Study: 1936-1956," *Public Opinion Quarterly,* Vol. 21 (Spring, 1957), pp. 14-22.
ALPERT, HARRY. "Public Opinion Research as Science," *Public Opinion Quarterly,* Vol. 20 (Fall, 1956), pp. 493-500.
BERELSON, BERNARD. "The Study of Public Opinion," in *The State of the Social Sciences.* Edited by L. D. White. Chicago: University of Chicago Press, 1956.
EULAN, HEINZ, *et al.* (eds.). *Political Behavior.* Chicago: The Free Press of Glencoe, Illinois, 1956.
FESTINGER, LEON, and KATZ, DANIEL (eds.). *Research Methods in the Behavioral Sciences.* New York: Dryden Press, 1953.
HARRIS, LOUIS. "Election Polling and Research," *Public Opinion Quarterly,* Vol. 21 (Spring, 1957), pp. 108-16.
HASTINGS, PHILIP K. "The Roper Center: An International Archive of Sample Survey Data," *Public Opinion Quarterly,* Vol. 27 (Winter, 1963), pp. 590-98.
HYMAN, HERBERT H. "Toward a Theory of Public Opinion," *Public Opinion Quarterly,* Vol. 21 (Spring, 1957), pp. 54-60.
LASSWELL, HAROLD D. "The Impact of Public Opinion Research on Our Society," *Public Opinion Quarterly,* Vol. 21 (Spring, 1957), pp. 33-38.

LAZARSFELD, PAUL F. "The Obligations of the 1950 Pollster to the 1984 Historian," *Public Opinion Quarterly,* Vol. 14 (Winter, 1950-51), pp. 617-38.

LAZARSFELD, PAUL F. "Public Opinion and the Classical Tradition," *Public Opinion Quarterly,* Vol. 21 (Spring, 1957), pp. 39-52.

MEIER, N. C., and SAUNDERS, H. W. *Iowa Conference on Attitude and Opinion Research.* Iowa City: University of Iowa, 1949.

National Opinion Research Center. *Central City Conference on Public Opinion Research.* Denver: University of Denver, 1946.

SCHRAMM, WILBUR. "Twenty Years of Journalism Research," *Public Opinion Quarterly,* Vol. 22 (Spring, 1957), pp. 91-107.

STEPHAN, FREDERICK F. "Must a Researcher Tell the Truth?" *Public Opinion Quarterly,* Vol. 22 (Summer, 1958), pp. 83-90.

STOUFFER, SAMUEL A. "1665 and 1954," *Public Opinion Quarterly,* Vol. 18 (Fall, 1954), pp. 233-38.

WHITE, L. D. *The Prestige Value of Public Employment.* Chicago: University of Chicago Press, 1929.

WOODWARD, JULIAN L. "Public Opinion Research 1951-1970: A Not-Too-Reverent History," *Public Opinion Quarterly,* Vol. 15 (Fall, 1951), pp. 405-20.

IV · The Determination
of Public Opinion

Once the principle that the will of the majority honestly ascertained must prevail, has soaked into the mind and formed the habits of a nation, that nation acquires not only stability, but immense effective force.
—JAMES BRYCE

INDICES OF PUBLIC OPINION

THERE are many different ways to find out what public opinion is —ways that vary in their accuracy, completeness, precision, feasibility, and cost. With small publics each member of the group can be questioned. With large groups this is difficult, and various substitutes for a complete census must be used—indices, cues, signs, manifestations, or samples. This is not to say that complete censuses of large publics have not been attempted. William the Conqueror had his Domesday Book compiled in the eleventh century, and the United States began its decennial censuses in 1790. These surveys, however, were enumerations of persons, properties, and things, rather than opinions and attitudes. With the rise of democracies and the extension of suffrage larger and larger publics, that is, electorates, expressed candidate preferences in elections for public office. Voting was practiced in ancient and medieval times as well, but the right to vote was restricted to a relatively small number, hence a relatively small public. Not until the nineteenth century did voting publics constitute a considerable proportion of the total population, and not until the twentieth century were women allowed to vote in the United States and Great Britain.

What are the principal weaknesses of elections as devices for finding out what public opinion is? They are so cumbersome and expensive that they cannot be used frequently, issues tend to be oversimplified or confused, and the outcome seldom gives a clear mandate for public policy. A presidential election may clearly indicate the preferred candidate, but it may give only a very vague notion of the opinions of voters on specific issues. Moreover, in the United States straight party voting and non-voting, to say nothing of corruption and interest group pressures, seriously affect the accuracy and reliability of the election as a device for finding out the state of public opinion on specific public questions. As many students of government and politics have discerned, elections select officials, but they seldom settle issues. Even in those states and localities where specific measures are referred to the voters, many circumstances qualify and limit the significance of the results. In most cases, the proportion of voters actually voting on the measures is small, often less than thirty per cent; their understanding of the questions, feeble; and their opportunity to express opinions on such matters, limited, and in many states, virtually non-existent. Therefore, whether the election is concerned with candidates, issues, or both, as an attempt to canvass completely a large, inclusive public it turns out to be a rather crude index of the electorate's opinion on public issues.

Another crude index of public opinion is the newspaper press. Today some students of public opinion consider the press a good reflector of public opinion. Government officials and leaders follow newspapers closely and, in many cases, systematically. Some government agencies and business firms subscribe to newspaper clipping services. At one time the United States government supplied its top officials with the *Press Intelligence Bulletin* containing a daily digest of the content of 100 representative newspapers throughout the country. This two to three hundred page booklet was called an "opinion seismograph" since officials could easily follow trends in press opinion regarding their own and other government agencies. Today, the Public Affairs Division of the Department of State provides officials with periodic reports on press, Congressional, pressure group, and other public opinions regarding important issues of public policy, especially foreign policy.

There is no question about the importance of press opinion, be it that of newspaper editors, publishers, columnists, or reporters. There is not necessarily a correlation, however, between their opinions and those of the general public. The total impact of the newspaper through its news and advertisements, as well as its editorial matter, may not reflect public opinion at all. News stories, feature articles, comics, or even advertisements may have more influence on public opinion than obvious statements of opinion. Press opinion is, therefore, a vague expression at best, and the expression of it should be more precisely related to specific newspaper personnel—editor, columnist, reporter, etc.—whenever possible. During the 1930's a large proportion of the newspapers, particularly in their editorials, in the United States opposed the Roosevelt administration, but without telling effect,[1] as there have always been occasions when press and editorial opinions conflicted with the opinions of voters on the national, state, and local levels. As the number of daily newspapers declines; as individual cities and towns throughout the United States find that they no longer are host to several competing papers, but are dominated by one major paper; as papers become more community conscious; and as they try to serve the whole public rather than special interests, papers will tend to be less partisan, more eclectic in their viewpoints, less devoted to single causes, public policies, and crusades. It will become even more difficult than it is at present to identify newspaper opinion.

To some, the marked difference between the opinions of editors and mass opinion proves that the influence of the press is declining. This is not necessarily so. It may show merely that the influence of editorials is small, but that the impact of the news columns is large. It may well be that the crusading editorial is simply being counteracted by the front page.

There are many other indications or crude indices of public opinion in addition to elections, referenda, and the press. Television actors, soap manufacturers, politicians, and many other public personalities have their fan mail, their public critics. They watch as carefully as they can significant changes in sales, attendance at meetings, the amount of applause, voting behavior, and other evidences of public reaction. One prominent historian believes that the best index of public opinion is "the accomplished fact." [2] To find out what public opinion was one need only start with an event, a legislative act, a meeting, a battle, or any specific fact or event and then deduce what public opinion must have been. Politicians find out what the voters think by ringing doorbells, conducting canvasses, using field agents and precinct captains. Then there is the method James Bryce favored, described as follows: [3]

> The best way in which the tendencies at work in any community can be discovered and estimated is by moving freely about among all sorts and conditions of men and noting how they are affected by the news or the arguments brought from day to day to their knowledge.

Most of the crude indices mentioned are recognized and accepted as manifestations, not true indications of public opinion, with the possible exception of elections and referenda. This is also true of another index— pressure group pronouncements—although there is a tendency to think that pressure group leaders speak for larger publics than they do. Not only do such leaders fail to represent the opinions of the general public, but frequently they represent only a minority of the members of their own organization. Only a very few pressure groups ever poll their members on public policy questions[4] or provide formal, representative procedures for controlling the official expressions of opinion by their leaders. Many organizations do adopt policy resolutions at their annual meetings, but these resolutions do not necessarily control the leaders. The importance achieved by pressure groups is not for the representative nature of their pronouncements but because of the compact, cohesive, organized, political influence of their organization.

The literature of political theory is somewhat confusing regarding the function of legislative bodies. Should they reflect or lead public opinion? The idea of representation is an old one. The larger the group the more necessary it is to have smaller groups handle particular subjects. Directors direct; executive committees execute; and all kinds of committees and agencies are instituted to help formulate and execute policy. Even proponents of the purest type of direct democracy recognize this and support the idea of representative bodies. They would differ, however, among themselves and with others regarding the actual distribution of authority between the whole and the representative part of the body politic.

In the light of current public opinion sampling activities, it is interesting to note that John Stuart Mill, in his classic study of representative government, argued that a legislative assembly, selected by majority vote in single-member constituencies, would provide a trustworthy and accurate sample of electoral opinion—a true cross section of public opinion.[5] There are few today who would stress the representative nature of legislative bodies as Mill did. There have been few careful comparative studies of public and legislative opinions. Decades ago A. Lawrence Lowell and Stuart A. Rice did make such comparisons, and a few others have done so since.[6] George Gallup has frequently called attention to the gaps and lags between public and Congressional opinion and the frequency with which public opinion is ahead of Congressional action. Indeed, it seems only logical and necessary that these gaps and lags must occur. Periodic elections for two- and six-year terms; equal state representation in the Senate; over-representation of rural areas in both Houses; election of minority candidates—these and other circumstances would inevitably produce legislative bodies which were not complete and precise reflections of public opinion.

Sampling

Many developments and circumstances contributed to more precise methods of determining the states and trends of public opinion, especially the collective opinions of large publics. A comprehensive survey of English towns using sampling methods was undertaken for the first time by Bowley in 1912. Although previously a number of broad-gauged, sociological surveys in France and England had been made, none employed carefully worked out sampling methods. One of the first large-scale social surveys in the United States was the Pittsburgh Survey in 1909, directed by Paul U. Kellogg. In 1912, the Russell Sage Foundation created its department of surveys, and over the next twenty years it conducted nearly 3,000 surveys, more than 150 of which were of a general nature. Not until later, however, did survey directors pay close attention to the problem of sampling.

It is difficult, if not impossible, to list all the developments that converged to produce the Gallup-type national survey of the 1930's. Newspapers and other institutions had been taking pre-election, straw polls as far back as the early nineteenth century. Such polls, however, were usually carelessly and incompetently conducted; they depended on the voluntary co-operation of newspaper readers and paid almost no attention to the principles of statistical reporting. One of the most elaborate of the modern straw polls was that conducted by the *Literary Digest,* a venture which did much to arouse interest in nation-wide surveys. The *Digest* began its polling activities in 1916, and for twenty years it conducted nation-wide polls on the presidential primaries, the New Deal, bonus legislation, prohibition, and other issues, as well as presidential elections. Until the election of 1936, when its election predictions went astray, it was highly regarded, and its prestige showed that there was a widespread public interest in knowing what people throughout the country were thinking.

Meanwhile, business executives and advertisers were feeling the need for more accurate and efficient techniques for surveying consumer opinion. The rapid growth of national advertising during the latter part of the nineteenth century encouraged experiments to test the effectiveness of advertising and to survey consumer habits and desires. During the early years of the twentieth century a few industrial concerns were engaged in this work, and specialized marketing research agencies began to develop. Sales departments, advertising bureaus, press agents, and public opinion analysts began to appear, sometimes together under a single corporate roof or as independent, specialized enterprises. At first they were primarily interested in customer attitudes toward products and services. Then they probed deeper to find out why people bought the things they did, and ultimately they investigated popular attitudes toward much broader aspects of business operation: labor, stockholder relations, distributing policies, business leadership, and government relations. The public opinion activities of market researchers led them to devise various methods of sampling to reduce the cost of nation-wide surveys.

In general, the questions asked by newspaper polls and market researchers were simple and direct, calling for "yes" and "no" answers. The psychologists, especially those concerned with education, began to stress the importance and potentialities of the questionnaire. Their search for better methods of measuring the relative attainments of students led to the creation of many different types of tests: objective, multiple-choice, rank order, scaled, and so on. These were used for measuring intelligence, vocational aptitude, reading proficiency, and scholastic aptitude and attainment. Attitude scales were developed to ascertain shades of opinion and degrees of favor or disfavor, and standardized, uniform answer questionnaires were used to show with great precision the distribution of opinion within a group. The subject of "tests and measurements" became familiar to educators. World War I gave added impetus to psychological testing as millions of recruits had to be examined.

DEVELOPMENT OF THE NATION-WIDE POLLING ORGANIZATION

It is necessary to keep all of these developments in mind in order to understand the confluence of factors which produced the nation-wide polls. Long before the Gallup and *Fortune* polls, the *Literary Digest* and newspaper publishers discovered widespread public interest in what the masses thought about major issues of public policy. In their marketing research, businessmen and advertisers learned it was possible to canvass large publics by using sampling techniques. Psychologists and educators found that questionnaires could be devised to measure attitudes and opinions with great precision. By the mid-1930's various forms of Thurstone scales were measuring attitudes; sampling and reader interest surveys were being made; and techniques were being devised to sample radio audiences and rate radio programs. More and more newspaper columnists were appearing on the pages of the daily press, discussing public issues and public policies. In October, 1935, George Gallup's American Institute of Public Opinion (AIPO) began the publication of its poll results.

George Gallup in his Institute focused all his interest in journalism, reading interests of the public, market research, and public opinion. As an undergraduate at the University of Iowa, he had edited the university's undergraduate paper. His Ph.D. dissertation dealt with the reading habits of newspaper and magazine readers. After teaching advertising at Northwestern University, he became Director of Research for Young and Rubicam, a leading national advertising agency in New York City, where he was employed when he created the AIPO. He conceived the idea of selling a syndicated column to newspapers reporting the results of nation-wide surveys of public opinion on public policy issues.

Instead of canvassing millions as the *Literary Digest* did, he devised a sampling formula, a method for selecting a few thousand persons representing more or less precisely the total voting population in terms of age, sex, income, residence, political affiliation, and from time to time other factors. In the Presidential election of 1936 he, rather than the *Literary Digest,* correctly predicted the winner. Since then the AIPO has continued to survey public opinion on thousands of issues and hundreds of candidates. Confident of the reliability of its sampling formula (some would say over-confident), it predicted Dewey's election in 1948 far in advance of the election. This mistake almost amounted to a fiasco, but Gallup and other pollsters revised their sampling techniques, basing them more on a random, probability sample. These and other changes in the following years helped to restore at least in part the tottering image of polls in the public mind.

In July, 1935, *Fortune* magazine began publication of quarterly surveys of public opinion, using methods of sampling, interviewing and other techniques, quite similar to those of the AIPO. Archibald Crossley, whose primary interest had been marketing research and radio audience surveys, also became interested in nation-wide election polling, and he conducted voting preference surveys in 1940, 1944, and 1948.

In 1940, Professor Hadley Cantril set up his Office of Public Opinion Research (OPOR) at Princeton University, using to some extent the facilities of AIPO. He also established, with the help of Gallup and others, a library of opinion data gathered by the AIPO and a few other polling organizations. During World War II he made a number of studies of changing attitudes in the United States regarding the war, and the results of these and other studies were given to government officials. Some years after the war, Professor Cantril left Princeton University to devote himself almost exclusively to the Institute for International Social Research (IISR), which he established with financial aid from Nelson Rockefeller and others. This institute studies public opinion abroad, searching primarily for the basic reasons for change and trends.

In 1941, the National Opinion Research Center (NORC) was established as a non-profit organization in Denver, Colorado, with financial aid from the Marshall Field Foundation. The director of the Center, Harry H. Field, worked under the general supervision of a Board of Trustees composed of university, foundation, and Field Foundation members. The stated purposes of the Center were

(1) to establish the first non-profit, non-commercial organization to measure public opinion in the United States.

(2) to make available to legislators, government departments, academicians, and non-profit organizations, a staff of experts in the science of public opinion measurement, and a highly trained nation-wide corps of interviewers.

(3) to analyze and review the results of surveys made by other polling organizations.

(4) to create at the University of Denver a research center to discover, test and perfect new methods, techniques, and devices for ascertaining the status of public opinion.

(5) to provide at the University of Denver a graduate department devoted to the study of the new science of public opinion measurement.

The published reports of the Center dealt with the war in Europe, post-war problems, inflation, federal regulation, and other public issues. The untimely death of Harry Field in 1955 ultimately led to the transfer of the NORC to the University of Chicago.

Meanwhile, other universities and scholars had become more and more interested in public opinion and related subjects. Soon after his arrival in the United States in 1933 on a Rockefeller Foundation fellowship, Paul Lazarsfeld became interested in radio and radio audience research. In 1937, he was called to Columbia University where he continued to carry on radio research and in 1940 conducted, with the assistance of others, the first of a series of election voting studies in Erie County, Ohio. Since then, as Director of the Bureau of Applied Social Research, and as Chairman of the Department of Sociology, he has maintained a continuing and fruitful interest in public opinion and communications research. Many of his students and associates have been very productive as applied or theoretical researchers in the public opinion field.

During the years immediately preceding World War II, some federal government agencies became involved in public opinion surveys, notably the Department of Agriculture. Rensis Likert, who became head of the Division of Program Surveys in that department, was also director of the morale division of the United States Strategic Bombing Survey; he subsequently went to the University of Michigan to head the Survey Research Center and after 1949 was head of the Institute for Social Research there. Both of these organizations have done extensive public opinion polling and analyses for both private and governmental clients. Over the years they have devoted special attention to economic issues, health matters, as well as voting behavior, and a wide variety of social and public issues.

Today, many institutions of higher learning devote attention to public opinion in one or more of its varied aspects. Special mention should be made of the work at the Massachusetts Institute of Technology, the University of Illinois, Princeton University, Stanford University, the University of Washington, and the University of California.

In 1947, the Legislature of the State of Washington appropriated funds to establish the Washington Public Opinion Laboratory in Seattle and Pullman under the direction of Professor Stuart C. Dodd.[7] The laboratory, which is controlled jointly by the social science departments of Washington University and Washington State College, seeks to "amplify the voice of the people on current issues"; "learn how to predict and guide social behavior"; improve polling methods; and train social scientists. Any Washington citizen can suggest poll topics, and priorities are determined by a poll of the citizens themselves.

In the commercial field, especially in advertising, market research, and public relations, interest in public opinion research has steadily expanded.

Most of the agencies in this area conduct, or have conducted for them, various public opinion surveys.

The 1935-36 Study of Consumer Purchases by the WPA (Works Progress Administration) was a landmark in economic research because of the number of interviews and the variety of data collected. During World War II, with improved techniques of sampling and measuring attitudes, surveys placed more emphasis on studying economic attitudes and motives. An outstanding study of this kind was the study of why people did or did not buy war bonds, made by the Division of Program Surveys of the Department of Agriculture. Surveys of consumer finances were made yearly from 1946 by the University of Michigan Survey Research Center for the Federal Reserve Board.[8]

Specialized, commercial polling agencies abound. An early and important one was the Psychological Corporation. In 1938 Dr. Claude Robinson established the Opinion Research Corporation to supply the business community with information regarding labor attitudes, and the opinions of customers and the general public regarding products, services, corporation policies, government policies, in fact, any subject relating to business. Dr. Robinson became interested in polls as a graduate student at Columbia University and wrote his doctoral dissertation on the subject of straw polls. Before establishing his own research organization, he served for a time in Gallup's APIO.

Mention should be made, also, of the Congress of American Professions (CAP), established by Dr. Henry G. Hodges in 1940 to find out what engineers, physicians, teachers, journalists, lawyers, and other professional groups thought about public policies. Dr. Hodges believed that the opinions of such people would be superior to those of the masses and that they should be brought more forcibly to public and governmental attention. During its brief existence, the Congress probed professional opinion on such issues as aid to Britain, the Far Eastern Problem, Union of Free Peoples, and the extension of federal power. In the first survey 4,650 post-card ballots were sent to professional people, distributed on a proportional basis, in the forty-eight states and the District of Columbia. Thirty-two per cent were filled out and returned. With each ballot went a carefully organized summary of the facts and arguments pertinent to the topic. Every effort was made to give the results of each survey wide publicity. The experiment failed however, partly because of inadequate funds and partly because it did not generate much interest. The collective opinions of the voting masses often arouse much political interest, regardless of the quality of the opinions, but the opinions of special groups, however well qualified, can often be politically ignored unless they are organized, articulate, and likely to carry weight with the masses.

During and following World War II interest in public opinion surveys continued. The Department of State, through its Division of Public Affairs, followed closely the results of non-government polls and reported on them periodically to top officials of the government. The Department of Agriculture continued its survey program. The War Department, the United States Information Agency (USIA), and many other government agencies made use of the public opinion poll. According to a study by Harry Alpert there were 49 public opinion surveys conducted by federal agencies in 1950 and 1951, 20 by the Department of Agriculture, 6 by the Housing and Home Finance Agency, 5 by the Public Health Service, 3 by the Federal Reserve Board, 2 by the President's Materials Policy Commission, and 1 each by thirteen other agencies.[9]

Nevertheless, the principal users of public opinion polls continued to be market researchers, advertisers, and businessmen, although legislators, politicians, organization leaders, scholars, diplomats, and economists also used opinion surveys. Numerous regional, state, and local polling organizations appeared. The failure of the nation-wide polls in the Presidential election of 1948 dampened the enthusiasm of the pollsters for a time and led to improvements in sampling, questionnaires, interviewing, and above all to a clearer distinction in the public mind between the problems of surveying as such and those of prediction, especially predicting the outcome of elections. In subsequent election polls, strenuous efforts were made to separate the probable voters from the non-voters and to meet the problem of last minute changes by last minute polls. Not only Presidential, but Congressional, gubernatorial, legislative and other elections are now accompanied by polls of varying degrees of expertness. The so-called scientific pollsters were, and are, supplemented by others who rely less on statistical sampling than on analyzing election statistics over past years, voting trends, and carefully distributed interviews which might expose possible changes in these trends. Louis Bean, Samuel Lubell, and Louis Harris have employed various techniques for probing the minds of average voters at election time. They were perhaps less interested in predicting the quantitative distribution of the vote, than in identifying significant issues, catching important areas of dissatisfaction and change, and finding out why people held the attitudes they did.

In July, 1957, Williams College established the Roper Public Opinion Research Center, and during the next five years, 33 American survey research firms and 26 foreign public opinion organizations placed their public opinion data there, comprising nearly 2,000 studies, 15 per cent of which were made abroad.[10] The Center distributes bulletins regarding its materials and services periodically, provides copies of its data on a cost basis, and accords study facilities to serious students. The resources of the Center have been widely used by academic scholars, independent research organizations, and government agencies. During the first three years of its existence more than 250 educational institutions and more than 1,500 scholars have employed its facilities to study such public attitudes as those regarding political parties, public employment, police officials, American public education, organized labor, military policies, and many others.

It was not at all surprising that soon after World War II consideration was given to the establishment of an organization of those interested in public opinion research. At the instigation of Harry H. Field, organizer and Director of the National Opinion Research Center, then affiliated with the University of Denver, a conference was held in Central City, Colorado from July 29–31, 1946. Approximately 75 persons attended, comprising academic people interested in polling, members of commercial research agencies, and a miscellany of government researchers, journalists, and users of public opinion research. The conference decided to hold a second conference in 1947 and to further the creation of national and international public opinion research organizations. This second conference was held at Williams College in September, 1947, attended by 194 registered participants. Two associations were established at this time, the American Association for Public Opinion Research (AAPOR), and the World Congress for Public Opinion Research, later becoming the World Association for Public Opinion Research (WAPOR). At these conferences considerable attention was given to problems of technical and ethical standards, professional responsibilities and opportunities, as well as to sampling and interviewing. These two organizations have continued to meet annually; the memberships have increased; and the annual programs greatly expanded. The AAPOR Directory for 1956 listed 380 members, 55 per cent of whom were "employees of a firm organized for profit, or of a business foundation"; 28 per cent were "employees of an academic or non-profit organization, or of a non-commercial foundation; and 9 per cent were government employees.[11]

During the late 1930's, a few public opinion survey organizations were established abroad, notably the British Gallup Institute, the Australian Gallup Institute, and the French Institute of Public Opinion. During World War II, public opinion surveys were conducted in Norway, in France, in Sicily, and among German prisoners and liberated Frenchmen by the Psychological Warfare Division of the Supreme Headquarters of the Allied Expeditionary Forces (SHAEF). Interest in public opinion research abroad grew rapidly after the war, in Europe, especially in West Germany, Japan, and Latin America. In 1950 the European Society for Opinion Surveys and Market Research (ESOMAR) was established. Many international business corporations, notably the Standard Oil Company of New Jersey, became interested in public opinion activities. By 1956 Gallup had 14 survey organizations in as many different countries abroad. In 1945 Elmo C. Wilson formed International Research Associates, Inc., which by 1956 had 27 survey organizations abroad. Several of the world-wide advertising agencies also conduct or sponsor such surveys.[12]

By 1956, WAPOR had a membership of 158 from twenty countries. It had close relations with UNESCO and helped that organization with its polling activities: notably in 1948, 1951, and 1956. The 1948 study was published in 1953 as *How Nations See Each Other* by William Buchanan and Hadley Cantril.

PROBLEMS OF PUBLIC OPINION SURVEYS

Although much progress in surveying public opinion has been made during the last twenty-five years, many technical and methodological problems remain. As the committee created by the Social Science Research Council (SSRC) in 1948 discovered, errors may occur at practically every step in the survey process, especially as a result of poor questionnaires, improper sampling procedures, or interviewing shortcomings. A questionnaire which is vague, uses language not clearly understood by the respondent, is tiresome, long, wordy, emotionally charged, and replete with leading questions will not evoke satisfactory results. Pollsters use great care in formulating their questions to avoid anyone misunderstanding exactly what they mean. Often questionnaires are pre-tested in small groups more or less typical of the larger public to be polled, so that poor statements can be changed, and ambiguities removed. Nevertheless, with all the care used and with all the simplicity and clarity of expression employed, strange misunderstandings and misinterpretations sometimes occur to mar the results.[13]

Interviewing

With the best questionnaire possible there is always the problem of interviewing—of "putting the question" to the respondent. Most of the nation-wide polling agencies use personal interviewers, either full-time employees, part-time workers, or a combination of the two. These interviewers vary widely in their training for this work, in their diligence, and also in their values and honesty. The results of an interview may be greatly influenced by these factors, but the personality of the one asking questions, his or her dress, manner of speaking, color and race, general attitude, and other behavioral traits may affect the responses. Environmental circumstances may affect the outcome of the interview, such as the weather, whether the encounter is on a busy street corner or in the quiet of home or office, or whether it comes early or late in the day. In other words, no two interview situations are exactly alike and the differences may have an effect. Polling agencies do try, as a rule, to reduce these extraneous, disturbing circumstances to a minimum. They try to select and train interviewers who will facilitate rather than inhibit open, candid responses, men and women who will inspire confidence and respect, rather than suspicion and disdain.

Several methods are employed to reduce the impact of interviewer bias, such as repeating surveys with different interviewers under different interview conditions. Often the name of the respondent will be kept secret, and not infrequently a ballot box is used to emphasize still more the confidential nature of the answers. In some cases panels of the same respondents are used repeatedly. For certain purposes, open-ended questions may be used to free respondents from the rigidity of uniform, standardized questions. The interview may be short, lasting for a few minutes, or it may last for hours, when efforts are made to dig deeply into the motivations of the respondent. Sometimes group discussions are encouraged, and the responses of group members noted. There seems to be no end to the process of devising new types of interview situations. Mail ballots are still used for special types of surveys, as well as telephone and telegraph communication. Every form of questionnaire and interview has its own particular uses. The art and science of asking questions is quite as complex as that of framing the questions themselves. A question on paper may be framed quite objectively, but when asked by the interviewer, it may be so inflected or intonated as to guide the response.

Sampling Large Publics

The problem of sampling large publics is indeed one of the crucial survey problems. The idea of sampling is quite simple, and the practice is as old as the asking of questions, if not older. To sample is to select a part to represent a whole. To sample a bottle of wine one merely sips a small part of the contents. The problems of sampling become more difficult, however, as the whole becomes very large and heterogeneous. It is much more difficult to sample the people of a city than the oil in a large cistern. A good sample is one that closely resembles the whole in all its aspects. If the whole is known, as well as the distribution of its principal ingredients, then the construction of a good sample, in terms of those ingredients, is relatively easy. This was essentially the procedure of the early Gallup polls. Using census and other reliable data the distribution of the population throughout the United States in terms of age, sex, income, residence, and a few other factors was ascertained. Then a sample of a few thousand with the same distribution of factors was obtained, and its opinions polled. That a true cross section sample of the whole population in these particular respects would also truly reflect other aspects (including opinions of the whole population) was a principle assumed but not proven. Until 1948 it was believed by many of the pollsters that their "quota sample" was adequate, although they realized that they were not taking account of anywhere near all the important factors influencing the formation of opinions. In fact a few studies had shown that a true cross section in certain respects would not necessarily assure a true cross section in all.

After 1948, more and more stress was placed on random or probability sampling than on the quota method. Instead of relying on the assumption that certain factors such as age, sex, and income were the basic determinants of opinion, efforts were made to select samples by pure chance, in a purely random method. The theory was that samples so selected would, as they got larger, come closer and closer to approximating the whole. To obtain a perfectly random sample it was necessary to define the whole, to give each unit in the whole an equal chance to appear in the sample, and to hold the sampling unit the same. To obtain a purely random sample of the voting population of the United States was not easy. In fact, it was virtually impossible, since it was out of the question to give each of upwards of 100,000,000 potential voters an equal chance to appear in the sample. Even if some method could be found to do this, it would take so much time to find the individual members of the sample and question them, that poll results could not be known for weeks, perhaps months. Some more feasible, if less accurate method of sampling had to be used. Some survey agencies attempted to combine the quota and random methods. This attempt failed because the quota method was unreliable; it was almost as difficult, if not impossible, to select quotas for the sample in a purely random way, as to select the whole sample in that manner.

Another procedure designed to circumvent the obstacles to the pure random sampling of large publics is the multi-stage method. The whole public is divided into large subgroups, each of which is further subdivided, and so on until a level of very small sub-groups is reached. At each level only a sample of the subgroups is taken, until the lowest level is reached where a complete census, or a pure random sample of individuals is taken. One could start with the 50 states of the United States, select several by pure chance; in each state so selected choose a certain number of counties by pure chance, then following the same procedure select a certain number of districts, and finally precincts. In the precincts so selected the individuals to be polled would be selected in a purely random method. Since the sampling unit is changed at each level, individuals in the total voting population would not have, however, an equal chance in the final sample. Nevertheless, this is substantially the procedure followed by the Gallup poll in the 1960 Presidential elections. In "Election-Survey Procedures of the Gallup Poll," by Paul Perry, President of The Gallup Organization, Inc., and Research Director of the Gallup poll, the procedure followed was described as follows:[14]

> The sample of areas is drawn in the following manner: A systematic sample of cities and minor civil divisions is drawn from regional-city size strata with probability of selection proportional to size. Within places so drawn, for election survey purposes a selection of smaller units for which election data are available is drawn in the same manner. In cities such smaller units are usually wards. Within these units precincts are selected. The selection of the precincts proceeds in this manner: Election results for the previous national election are obtained for each precinct in the ward. One precinct is then drawn with probability of selection proportional to the precincts' total vote. Within the precinct a systematic sample of households is selected, and one adult from each household is interviewed.

Checking Accuracy

There are not many ways in which the observer can check the accuracy of poll data. Almost the only opportunity for him to do this is at election time when some polls undertake to predict the winners. Predicting or prophesying the outcome of elections by means of polls is a hazardous business. Even if the poll is one hundred per cent accurate in its estimate of voting preferences, at least two important circumstances may invalidate the prophecy: (1) turnout, and (2) opinion change. Even in Presidential elections the voter turnout seldom exceeds sixty per cent of the electorate, and in state, local, primary, and referenda elections the percentage is often much lower. Who are these non-voters? How can they be identified before the election, and their effect on the survey results deleted? Before 1948 this problem was dealt with quite casually, and often there was no real effort made to deal with the non-voter and the undecided. Since then various clues and tests have been used to screen out these elements by finding out who has voted in previous elections, who is registered and will be physically qualified to vote, who knows about the election, is interested in it, and intends to vote. Although it is impossible to predict turnout precisely, these clues and screens do eliminate from consideration a large number of non-voters formerly treated as voters.

Since people do change their minds, often at the very last minute, or finally reach a decision at that time, the Gallup and other election forecasting organizations now attempt to poll right up to the eve of the election, making extensive use of the telephone and telegraph for this purpose. In spite of these opportunities for error in prediction, as well as for surveying errors due to sampling, interviewing, and the framing of questions, the record of the Gallup poll in election forecasting since 1950 has been impressive. The deviations between the survey results and the elections are shown in the table.[15]

YEAR	ALL RESPONDENTS	THOSE REGISTERED PLAN TO REGISTER, PLAN TO VOTE	THOSE WHOSE TURN-OUT SCORE PLACED THEM IN PART OF SAMPLE CORRESPOND-ING TO EXPECTED TURNOUT PROPORTION
1950	−4.7	−3.5	−0.3
1952	−3.6	−2.6	−1.5
1954	−4.9	−3.2	−0.5
1956	+2.8	+2.6	+3.1
1958	−3.5	−2.3	−0.2
1960	−0.3	−0.5	+0.1
Mean (no signs)	3.3	2.5	1.0
Bias (signs)	−2.4	−1.6	+0.1

"In other words," says Paul Perry, "if in these elections we had been able to draw random samples of the ballots actually cast in the election booth on election day, used samples of the size employed in these six election surveys, and computed the distribution of the vote in the six elections, we could expect to have done little if any better on the average than we did using survey data." [16]

Because of the difficulties of predicting voting behavior on the basis of public opinion surveys, many pollsters, notably Elmo Roper, do not favor election polling. Gallup, however, insists, not only on the desirability, but on the necessity of such attempts to predict. He believes that the public is entitled to at least some check, however poor, on the polls.

There are virtually no public checks on the accuracy of polls on issues, since such polls do not in any sense compete with each other. Even polls on the same subject are almost never taken at the same time using the same questions. Pollsters may not use the same care in sampling, framing questions, and interviewing when they are conducting issue polls, as with candidate surveys. Often, they do use internal checks such as comparing known characteristics of the sample with known characteristics of the whole public, and, if necessary, making adjustments for divergencies. By and large, the outsider must base his confidence in polling accuracy on the performance of pre-election polls, on the internal checks reported by the pollsters themselves, and on his faith in the expertness, diligence, and integrity of the particular polling organization.

Criticism

Public opinion polls, especially those dealing with elections and public policies, have produced criticisms. In fact, they have even evoked Congressional bills designed to curb the activities of pollsters, if not abolish them entirely. On one occasion, pollsters were subjected to searching questioning by a committee of Congress. These attacks have not been as vehement in recent years as they were earlier, but even now criticism is far from being mute. Some critics contend that poll data are virtually worthless because they comprise merely the sum total of individual opinions without taking into consideration the relative competence of these individual opinions and the likelihood that they represent the views of persons or groups incapable of making them effective.[17] Moreover, it is argued, the curbstone opinions of the man in the street, as evoked by an interviewer, may evidence very little information or thought and register only a transitory, verbal reaction to the questioner. These critics are generally opposed to pure democracy in any form, and in some cases are opposed to representative democracy and even prefer forms of limited authoritarianism; they are really arguing against popular government and rule by public opinion however limited it may be.

It is undoubtedly true that many of the opinions elicited by pollsters do not reflect logical analyses based on facts or personal experience. The poll data obtained from a nation-wide survey may not only be ill-informed, but it may be quite different from the opinions of intellectual, financial, or political elites and power holders, those who "really count." But is such a collection of mass opinions worthless, especially in a country such as the United States, where nearly every adult, regardless of his intellectual, economic, or political prowess, has one vote, and only one? Mass opinion is not the only kind of opinion important in a democracy, but it is important. It may also be quite as important to poll the opinions of more select groups, such as experts, power holders, those with special competence, and those who have studied the question carefully. To criticize the pollsters by asserting that their data is worthless because they do not do all these other things is a bit unfair. It is pertinent, however, to ask how worthwhile these mass data are, for what purposes and under what conditions. It is also important to know who holds what opinions; how intensely they hold them; how stable the opinions are; how they were formed; and what are the chances that they will have an effect on official, public policy. One may even argue that democracy, in the sense of rule by public opinion, is undesirable. Yet despotic governments today very closely follow the prevailing trends in mass opinion within, as well as without, their borders, although they may have no intention of acting on them.

Critics of public opinion polls not only question the worthwhileness of the data collected, but they also bemoan the effect of the polls on elections, on representative government, and on executive leadership. It is sometimes alleged that polls influence the outcome of elections, not only by frequently reporting the comparative popularity of the candidates, but they argue even more emphatically, by comparing the standings of hopefuls during, and even before, the primary elections. It is often alleged that party bosses and conventions are influenced by the polls in their recommendations and that the voters themselves often succumb to the band-wagon effect of the publicity given to poll results. Even more serious, the critics say, has been the influence of polls on the decisions of representative bodies. Note is taken of references to public opinion in the speeches and writings of legislators, to their use of poll results to strengthen their arguments, and to the fact that many of them conduct polls themselves to ascertain public opinion trends. This obeisance, almost slavish conformity, to public opinion, is said to curtail the exercise of legislative independence of thought to such an extent as to endanger the process of policy and decision making in the United States. Not only legislators have fallen under the sway of public opinion as reported by polls, it is said, but also the executive, and perhaps the judicial branches as well. The President of the United States and his chief subordinates have their public opinion advisers and manage to "keep their ears to the ground" through the assistance of experts in public opinion. One outstanding critic, Walter Lippmann, goes so far as to claim that the subservience of government officials to public opinion, made easier by polls, is a principal explanation for the many crises of recent decades. In his noted work, *The Public Philosophy,* he takes pollsters as well as government officials to task for enthroning public opinion and letting it have the upper hand in policy making.[18]

These arguments go to the very core of the whole problem of democratic government with the question of what role public opinion should play in the formation of public policy. Should it determine the broad, general purposes of government? Should it try to direct the day-to-day affairs of government as well as define long-term goals? Or should it be deprived of any role in the formation of public policy? These are neither new, nor are they easy questions. Just how far should party officials, legislators, administrators, or judicial officers follow public opinion? When, if ever, should they depart from it? These questions will be considered at length in a subsequent chapter, but it should be emphasized at this point that criticisms of the role and place of polls in the democratic system of government cannot easily be segregated from criticisms of the democratic form of government itself. To one who believes in popular government, in government of, for, and by the people, and to one who wishes to make rule by public opinion more effective and extensive, the contributions of public opinion polls to that end will be applauded. To those opposed to democratic institutions, in the sense of rule by public opinion, polls serve to enhance the undesirable influence of this force.

Finally, there are those who stress the dangers of fraud in the use of polls. There is no question that polls are conducted with varying degrees of competence, care, and integrity. Without doubt some polls are conducted primarily for publicity, propaganda, or advertising purposes. Questions may be selected to elicit particular responses. Results may be "adjusted" or manipulated. Sometimes only favorable results are publicized, not the unwanted. In a myriad of ways polls can be used to fabricate, distort, and deceive. But it is not only the badly motivated pollsters who mislead. Even the most scrupulously honest may, through carelessness or inefficiency, obtain mistaken results. The American Association of Public Opinion Research (AAPOR) has devoted much attention to the problem of ethics and standards in the profession,[19] but control over members, to say nothing of the large number of non-members, is impossible. Each public opinion survey *must* be judged on its own merits. The integrity and competence of the survey agency must be examined very carefully. Each step in the survey must be scrutinized expertly. Even if every precaution has been taken to eliminate the possibility of error, the results must be accepted, not as one accepts a scientific truth, but with a certain degree of skeptical confidence appreciating how difficult it is to measure, much less interpret, public opinion scientifically.

The protagonists of polls are usually firm believers in democracy, in rule by public opinion, and in the desirability of making that rule increasingly more effective. George Gallup, following the lead of James Bryce, welcomes the day when it will be possible to know what the mass public is thinking on the great issues of public policy from week to week, and from day to day. Pollsters, probably much more keenly than outsiders, appreciate the difficulties they face, are quite aware of the possibilities for error, and fully realize that the motivations of all pollsters are not of the same calibre. Nevertheless, they believe in the worthwhileness of much of the data they collect. Knowledge of what mass opinion is serves as a very important check on the inflated claims of pressure groups and minority interests asserting that their views are those of the masses. In the late 1930's the nation-wide polls easily deflated the over-zealous representations of the Townsendites and Coughlinites. Similarly, erroneous claims regarding the prevalence of views of almost any kind can be exposed.

For some men, the opinion of the masses is as close an approximation as possible of what the public interest is, though others prefer to turn to ecclesiastical dignitaries, holy writs, and groups of experts of one kind or another for guidance. In any case, knowledge of the views of a public as large as the electorate of the United States is a most useful bench mark against which to evaluate the claims of what the public interest is as ascertained by individuals or smaller groups. The polls, therefore, by highlighting the views of the masses, do tend to check many uninhibited assertions of what the public interest is.

For those who believe in rule by public opinion, the most important contribution of polls is their impact on government itself. They do bring public opinion into the open and thereby make government bodies somewhat more responsible to that public opinion. Whether this is actually a blessing will be determined by one's overall attitude toward democracy. Polls have been used by a variety of official and unofficial agencies for many different purposes. They have been used to plot trends and changes in opinion as well as to ascertain static states and climates of opinion. They may reveal areas of ignorance where information and educational efforts are needed. They may be used to assess the success or failure of projects and programs. They have been used in civil litigation, in studies of mental health, economic forecasting, psychological warfare, public relations, education and school administration, and in other ways too numerous to mention. They may be used to predict, or to help to predict, individual and group behavior. In fact, new uses for poll data are being found constantly, as shown by the ever-increasing number of surveys made by business firms, other types of organized groups, government agencies, and opinion leaders.

STATISTICAL TREATMENT

Brief attention should be given to the statistical treatment of opinion data. Perhaps the most simple treatment is that given by election canvassers who merely tally the number of responses received for each candidate, or the number of affirmative and negative votes for constitutional and statutory referenda. Refinements in treatment are possible if more sophisticated questionnaires are used, such as the rated or ranked types or Thurstone or Guttman scales.[20] Considerable progress has been made in devising measures of degrees of attitude such as favor or disfavor of persons and propositions. These measures enable the investigator to obtain a clearer, more comprehensive and precise distribution of opinion within a public than would otherwise be the case. Moreover, the opinions of a group may be summarized to show averages, range, deviations, as well as comparisons and correlations of many kinds. The opinions of different publics can be compared with much precision and in great detail. In other words, accurate and valid opinion data may be treated statistically in quite the same way as data regarding wages, population, and income. To do so, however, means that the data must be standardized and made uniform in some manner. Open ended questions also are valuable, but it is difficult to treat the responses obtained statistically. The essay type of response, whether it be an answer to a College Entrance Board examination or the rambling utterances of a psychiatric patient, may be very meaningful and suggestive, even though statistical treatment is difficult.

One frequent use of collections of opinion data is to relate them to other collections: to personal traits of the respondents, to economic, political, social and other major categories of data. Very often it is possible to relate opinions to the age, sex, income, social status, place of residence, religious, and political affiliations of those holding them. Or relations between a given opinion, and other opinions and attitudes can be determined. In fact, the possibilities of comparisons and correlations seem to be virtually unlimited. Sorting and computing machines have greatly aided in this work of classifying and correlating. These breakdowns may give a useful description of the opinions of subgroups within the larger public, and they often *suggest* causal relations, if they do not prove them. Earlier classifications of the objective age–sex–income type have long since been supplemented by an infinite variety of psychological, subjective categories —extrovert-introvert, authoritarian-non-authoritarian, radical-conservative. The probing for new and more significant aspects, features, factors, whether objective or subjective, tangible or intangible, is a most promising, if never ending task.

Before leaving this discussion of the statistical treatment of opinion data, an interesting problem may be noted. Do collections of individual opinions, that is, does public opinion usually follow a normal distribution, a bell-shaped curve? It is known, for example, that in sufficiently large publics at a given age the heights and weights of individuals, and possibly their IQs, tend to have this distributive pattern, a few at either extreme, gradually increasing in number as the mean is reached. Is it reasonable to suppose that in relatively large publics the majority will usually be moderates, and a much smaller minority will be extremists to the right or left? There is no final answer, although what evidence does exist suggests wide variations in the patterns of opinion distribution, such as J-curves, bi-modals, and so on. This would seem to indicate that opinion distributions, as a rule, are not simply the chance result of the interaction of innumerable variables but that they are quite often the primary product of a few very important factors such as the efforts of organized groups, mass media content, events, personal influence, and so forth.

CHANGES IN AMERICAN CHARACTER TRAITS AS DETERMINED BY NATIONAL OPINION POLLS

Numerous attempts have been made, many of them by foreign observers, to make generalizations about the character traits of Americans.[21] It might be expected that nation-wide polls during the last twenty-five years would confirm or discountenance these findings. The principal difficulty, however, is the discrete, spasmodic, and unco-ordinated pattern of opinion-polling in the United States. Only a few polling organizations have surveyed public opinion continuously during this period; many of the questions have been asked only once or at best a few times; virtually no attempt has been made to co-ordinate the work of different polling agencies; and many of the questions have been trivial or of only local, or dated interest.

During the last twenty-five years one may observe, by a cursory examination of accumulated poll data: changes in views regarding specific things, shifts in foci of attention, some modifications of basic attitudes such as the influences affecting the formation of opinion, the competence of opinion, areas of consensus of opinion, the influence of particular opinions, methods of expression, conflicts of opinion, and intensity of opinion. It is obviously impossible to explain and illustrate all of these changes, or even many. Only a few generalizations will be hazarded.

1. There has been a decided shift in the focus of the public's attention from domestic to foreign issues raised by World War II, the Cold War, Russia, the under-developed countries, the armaments race, and space exploration. Domestic problems remain, such as those posed by racial tensions, the advent of TV, the computer, and automation generally, but interests are focused more than ever outside, rather than inside, the United States.

2. Poll results would suggest that during the last twenty-five years there have been important shifts in basic attitudes toward religion, family and sex, government and the economy, the international responsibilities of the United States, standards and values. Church membership and attendance have steadily increased, at the same time that beliefs and standards of personal behavior have been liberalized. Many doctrines and even creeds have lost their force; and there seems to be a far-reaching search, even striving, for a clearer and truer statement of religious faith. Family life and relations between the sexes have become more informal, more frank, candid and liberal. There has been a noticeable decline in the authority of the family and greater freedom and independence for women. Emphasis is still given in the United States to the virtues of laissez-faire and the free enterprise system, but the relations between government and the economy have moved rapidly, in the direction of greater government intervention— to regulate, initiate, and subsidize the economy. The isolationism of today would probably have been called internationalism twenty-five years ago. The responsibilities assumed by the United States in the Cold War, in relation to the United Nations, to under-developed areas, and to world affairs seem to be accepted in principle, if not always to the extent advocated.

3. Probably the basic processes of opinion formation are much the same today as formerly, although many new elements in the environment—television and telstars, computers and nuclear submarines, the scientific, economic, political, and social changes of the last twenty-five years—have greatly affected the detailed aspects of opinion change. The human condition biologically may remain the same, but human nature in a dynamic sense is affected so differently today by the interaction of the person and his environment that it is no longer the same.

4. The proponents of democracy in the nineteenth century believed that

through education the American public mind would gradually, but inevitably, attain a competence equal to the burgeoning tasks it would be called upon to perform. Today public and private schools, even the colleges, absorb nearly all those eligible. At the same time public affairs and public problems have increased in difficulty. Is the voting public more competent than twenty-five years ago to deal with them? Curiously, the public seems less confident today than formerly. Among leaders of opinion there is considerable divergence of opinion. Enthusiasm for direct popular rule is probably less today than during the first decade of this century. However, there is no clear indication that the majority would, if they could, take government out of the hands of the people altogether. The attitude of opinion leaders today seems far more discriminating than heretofore and far more careful to differentiate between what the voting public can and cannot do.

5. Is there greater consensus on public issues today than a quarter of a century ago? The answer is difficult. In the first place most of the opinion data collected by pollsters deals with controversial issues. Without a doubt, many queries could be posed which would reveal a high degree of agreement—fundamental questions of ends of public policy and values. The poll data in existence, however, practically always shows some disagreement and frequently sharp splits. One keen student of American government and public opinion writes of "a dualism in a moving consensus." [22] If one looks back over the party battles in the United States since 1900, it appears that earlier issues have faded from view or have been resolved, and the party struggles today are fought within a new arena of consensus. On such questions as a progressive income tax, railroad regulation, social security, crop control, support of the United Nations, and alliance with Europe a considerable degree of consensus has been achieved. Nevertheless, there are probably as many new, controversial questions remaining. Like the top, or exposed part of a floating iceberg, controversial questions are clearly visible. The submerged, larger, and perhaps most important part of the berg is not seen—these are the questions on which substantial agreement has been reached. At the same time that the number of controversial issues increases, so does the number of resolved ones.

NOTES FOR CHAPTER 4

Epigraph. James Bryce, *The American Commonwealth,* Chapter 77, Vol. 2, p. 264.

1. It was frequently asserted that at least 80 per cent of the press opposed Franklin D. Roosevelt's re-election in 1936. His overwhelming victory that year led to much soul-searching by editors and publishers. Felix Morley, *Washington Post,* November 29, 1936, sec. III, p. 2.

2. See Strayer, Joseph R., "The Historian's Concept of Public Opinion," in *Common Frontiers of the Social Sciences,* ed. Mirra Komarovsky, (Chicago, Ill.: The Free Press of Glencoe, Ill., 1957).

3. See Bryce, James, *Modern Democracies,* Vol. I (New York: The Macmillan Co., 1921), pp. 155-56.

4. A notable exception is the Chamber of Commerce of the United States which has a carefully worked out procedure for polling its members on key issues of public policy. See Childs, Harwood L., *Labor and Capital in National Politics* (Columbus: Ohio State University Press, 1930).

5. See Mill, John Stuart, *Utilitarianism, Liberty, and Representative Government.* New York: E. P. Dutton and Co., Everyman's Library ed., 1910), p. 241.

6. See Lowell, A. Lawrence, "The Influence of Party Upon Legislation in England and America," *Annual Report of the American Historical Association,* Vol. I (1910), pp. 431-542; Rice, Stuart A., *Quantitative Methods in Politics.* (New York: Alfred A. Knopf, 1928). See also Dicey, Albert V., *Lectures on the Relation between Law and Public Opinion in England in the Nineteenth Century* (London and New York: The Macmillan Co., 1905).

7. See Dodd, Stuart C., "The Washington Public Opinion Laboratory," *Public Opinion Quarterly,* Vol. 12 (Spring, 1948), pp. 118-25.

8. Katona, George, "Public Opinion and Economic Research," *Public Opinion Quarterly,* Vol. 21 (Spring, 1957), pp. 117-28.

9. Alpert, Harry, "Opinion and Attitude Surveys in the U. S. Government," *Public Opinion Quarterly,* Vol. 16 (Spring, 1952), pp. 33-41.

10. See Hastings, P. K., "The Roper Public Opinion Research Center: A Review of Its First Three Years of Operation," *Public Opinion Quarterly,* Vol. 25 (Spring, 1961), pp. 120-26.

11. See Hart, Clyde W., and Don Calahan, "The Development of AAPOR," *Public Opinion Quarterly,* Vol. 21 (Spring, 1957), pp. 165-78. The annual proceedings of AAPOR usually appear in the Winter issue of the *Quarterly.*

12. See Wilson, Elmo C., "World-Wide Development of The Public Opinion Quarterly, Vol. 21 (Spring, 1957), pp. 174-78.

13. See Payne, Stanley L., *The Art of Asking Questions* (Princeton, N. J.: Princeton University Press, 1951).

14. Perry, Paul, "Election-Survey Procedures of the Gallup Poll," *Public Opinion Quarterly,* Vol. 24 (Fall, 1960), pp. 532-33.

15. Perry, Paul, "Gallup Poll Election Survey Experience, 1950-1960," *Public Opinion Quarterly,* Vol. 26 (Summer, 1962), p. 276. According to Dr. Perry the "turnout score" used in the third column of deviations was derived "from a series of questions related to voting participation and a cutting point corresponding to the proportion of the adult population expected to vote. Those whose scale scores put them above the cutting point constitute the sample of voters for the final estimate" (P. 277).

16. *Ibid.,* p. 278.

17. See Rogers, Lindsay, *The Pollsters* (New York: Alfred A. Knopf, 1949).

18. Lippmann, Walter, *The Public Philosophy* (Boston: Little, Brown, & Co., 1955).

19. For a copy of the Code of Professional Ethics and Practices of AAPOR, see the *Public Opinion Quarterly,* Vol. 24 (Fall, 1960), pp. 529-30.

20. See Thurstone, L. L., "Attitudes Can be Measured," *American Journal*

of Sociology, Vol. 33 (Fall, 1927), pp. 529-45. Stouffer, S. A., Guttman, L., *et al., Measurement and Prediction: Studies in Social Psychology in World War II,* Vol. 4 (Princeton, N. J.: Princeton University Press, 1950).
21. For example, see Morris, Elting E. (ed.), *The American Style* (New York: Harper & Bros., 1958).
22. Key, V. O. Jr., *Politics, Parties, and Pressure Groups* (4th ed.: Thomas Y. Crowell Co., 1960), pp. 243-49.

SUPPLEMENTARY READING

ALMOND, GABRIEL A., and VERBA, SIDNEY. *The Civic Culture-Political Attitudes and Democracy in Five Nations.* Princeton, N. J.: Princeton University Press, 1963.

American Institute of Public Opinion. *The New Science of Public Opinion Measurement.* 1938.

ANDERSON, DALE. "Roper's Field Interviewing Organization," *Public Opinion Quarterly,* Vol. 16 (Summer, 1952), pp. 263-72.

BEAN, LOUIS. How to Predict Elections. New York: Alfred A. Knopf, 1948.

BERNAYS, EDWARD L. "Attitude Polls—Servants or Masters," *Public Opinion Quarterly,* Vol. 9 (Fall, 1945), pp. 264-68; Replies appear in Vol. 9 (Winter, 1945-46), pp. 403-10.

BOCKSTROM, CHARLES H. and HURSH, GERALD D. *Survey Research.* Chicago: Northwestern University Press, 1963.

BUCHANAN, WILLIAM, and CANTRIL, HADLEY. *How Nations See Each Other—A Study in Public Opinion.* Urbana: University of Illinois Press, 1953.

CANTRIL, HADLEY, and Associates. *Gauging Public Opinion.* Princeton, N. J.: Princeton University Press, 1944.

CHASE, STUART, *American Credos.* New York: Harper & Bros., 1962.

CHILDS, HARWOOD L. "Rule by Public Opinion," *Atlantic,* Vol. 157 (June, 1936), pp. 755-64.

COCHRAN, WILLIAM G. *Sampling Techniques.* 2nd edition John Wiley and Sons, 1963.

CRUM, W. L. *Straw Polls.* Cambridge, Mass.: Harvard University Press, 1928.

DEMING, W. EDWARDS. *Sample Design in Business Research.* New York: John Wiley and Sons, 1960.

ERNST, MORRIS L., and LATH, DAVID. *The People Know Best.* Washington, D. C.: Public Affairs Press, 1949.

FESTINGER, LEON, and KATZ, DANIEL (eds.). *Research Methods in the Behavioral Sciences.* New York: Dryden Press, 1952.

GALLUP, GEORGE, and RAE, SAUL FORBES. *The Pulse of Democracy.* New York: Simon and Schuster, 1940.

KEY, V. O. *Public Opinion and American Democracy.* New York: Alfred A. Knopf, 1961.

LANE, ROBERT E. *Public Opinion.* Englewood Cliffs, N. J.: Prentice-Hall, Inc., 1964.

MOSTELLER, FREDERICK, *et al. The Pre-Election Polls of 1948.* New York: Social Science Research Council, 1949.

PARTEN, MILDRED BERNICE. *Surveys, Polls, and Samples: Practical Procedures.* New York: Harper & Bros., 1950.

PAYNE, STANLEY LE BARON. *The Art of Asking Questions.* Princeton, N. J.: Princeton University Press, 1951.

PERRY, PAUL. "Election Survey Procedures of the Gallup Poll," *Public Opinion Quarterly,* Vol. 24 (Fall, 1960), pp. 531-42.

PERRY, PAUL. "Gallup Poll Election Survey Experience, 1950 to 1960," *Public Opinion Quarterly,* Vol. 26 (Summer, 1962), pp. 272-79.

The Public Opinion Quarterly, Vols. 1-27 (1937-63).

"The Public Opinion Polls: Dr. Jekyll or Mr. Hyde," *Public Opinion Quarterly,* Vol. 4 (1940), pp. 212-84; Vol. 22 (Fall, 1958), p. 3.

RANNEY, J. C. "Do the Polls Serve Democracy?" *Public Opinion Quarterly,* Vol. 10 (Winter, 1946), pp. 349-60.

RICE, STUART A. *Quantitative Methods in Politics.* New York: Alfred A. Knopf, 1928.

ROBINSON, CLAUDE EVERETT. *Straw Votes.* New York: Columbia University Press, 1932.

ROGERS, LINDSAY. *The Pollsters.* New York: Alfred A. Knopf, 1949.

ROPER, ELMO. *You and Your Leaders: Their Actions and Your Reactions, 1936-1956.* New York: William Morrow & Co., 1957.

ROWSE, A. E. "Political Polls," *Editorial Research Reports,* Vol. 11 No. 14 (Oct. 12, 1960).

STEPHAN, F. F. and McCARTHY, P. J. *Sampling Opinions.* New York: John Wiley and Sons, 1958.

STEPHAN, F. F. "Advances in Survey Methods and Measurement Techniques," *Public Opinion Quarterly,* Vol. 21 (Spring, 1957), pp. 79-90.

THURSTONE, L. L., and CHAVE, E. J. *The Measurement of Attitude.* Chicago: University of Chicago Press, 1929.

United States House Committee on Government Operations, State Department. Hearings: Public Opinion Polls, 85th Congress, 1st Sess., June 21-July 11, 1957.

WOODWARD, J. L. "Public Opinion Polls as an Aid to Democracy," *Political Science Quarterly,* Vol. 61 (June, 1946), pp. 238-46.

V · Surveys: Poll Questions and Public Competence

The opinion of a whole nation, a united and tolerably homogeneous nation, is, when at last it does express itself, the most competent authority to determine the ends of national policy.

—JAMES BRYCE

FOR MORE THAN twenty-five years polling agencies have been systematically surveying the opinions of the American voter in the United States. What do these surveys show about the competence of the people, generally, to pass on questions of public policy? Some students of public opinion, Dr. George Gallup for example, take a very optimistic view. Others, such as Walter Lippmann, are most pessimistic.[1] The answer depends to a large extent on the particular questions asked the people. All too often sweeping generalizations are made regarding the quality of public opinion without taking into account the many different types of questions asked by the pollsters, and consequently the relative worth of the answers.

CLASSIFICATION OF POLL QUESTIONS

Most people would agree that the American voter is more capable of answering some types of questions than others. Difficulties arise, however, when precise differentiations are attempted. Dogmatism is definitely out of place. It may contribute to clearer thinking about the whole problem to try and classify the types of questions according to the public's competence to answer them, even though very subjective and personal criteria are used. The word public in this chapter and elsewhere in this volume usually refers to the American electorate, the voters generally, unless otherwise indicated.

Some help in this task may be derived from the few attempts made in the past to draw a discriminating line between questions which are, and which are not for the general voting public. One distinction often made is between ends and means; this argument concludes that the general public is more competent to determine the ends of public policy, than the specific means for attaining those ends. Other distinctions frequently made on areas in which the public has special competence are those between technical and non-technical questions, financial and non-financial measures, general legislative principles and specific statutes, and those issues within or without the personal and everyday experience of people generally. Some have claimed that the man in the street is better able to judge men than measures, parties than issues. One distinction often stressed is the greater competence of the public to assess the results of policies and actions, than to evaluate new proposals, to give vent to grievances rather than to invent remedies. Some have held that the public is more competent to decide questions "involving apparent harmony or contradiction with settled conviction," such as great moral issues, to judge methods of deciding questions than the questions themselves, to pass on questions which have been discussed extensively.[2]

With these distinctions in mind let us now consider the fourteen categories of questions the Gallup organization asked in 1962 for the purpose of determining which of them are likely to yield more rather than less competent answers from the American voter. It should be noted at this point that there may be other reasons for asking questions than to obtain the most competent answers. The pollster may want to ascertain the nature and extent of ignorance regarding certain matters, the psychological obstacles to certain policies, trends in public expectations, desires, and expectations, kinds of information and instruction needed, or the degree of public acceptance for men and measures. The basic question, however, is whether there are any types of questions which yield answers from the public so substantively wise and competent that they should influence public policy directly.

Dr. Gallup's 1962 polls suggest that the questions asked may be typed as follows.

1. Questions regarding *persons*—candidates for office, public officials, labor leaders, prominent men and women—asking for preferences, appraisals, and the like.
2. Questions of *fact* regarding almost anything from personal habits to historical dates and technical information.
3. Questions calling for an appraisal of the *results* of public policies, governmental actions, trends, institutional developments.
4. Questions regarding *proposed* legislation, governmental action, suggested remedies for social, economic, and political problems.

5. Questions calling for the appraisal of *institutions* such as the family, church, schools, press, and trade unions.
6. Questions asking for *predictions* of, or expectations regarding forthcoming events, developments, governmental actions, etc.
7. Questions regarding the *relative* importance of things such as campaign issues and personal problems—ends and goals.
8. *Ethical* questions regarding fairness, justice, and rightness.
9. *Information* questions.
10. What to *do* questions.
11. Questions regarding the *reasons* for things.
12. Questions regarding the *meaning* of words, and the significance of things.
13. *Hypothetical* questions.
14. Questions calling for the appraisal of events and *actions*.

QUESTIONS UNSUITED FOR THE GENERAL PUBLIC

Of the fourteen categories of questions listed above at least seven of them suggest that the public's answers will have little value for policy makers in a direct, substantive sense. Answers to these queries may give indications, clues, hints, and other information of value, but not an answer which is better, or even as good, as some other source. These seven types of questions are:

1. Definition questions
2. Information questions
3. Prediction questions
4. Hypothetical questions
5. What to do questions
6. Questions regarding new policies, remedies, actions
7. Questions regarding the reasons for things

Of Definition

Definition questions indicate the degree to which the public comprehends the meaning of words, concepts, and phrases such as filibuster, Rule 22, jurisdictional strike, Common Market, Alliance for Progress, and so on. It goes without saying that the public is not the best source for correct answers to this type. Such questions are frequently used to screen the informed from the uninformed before further interrogation.

Of Information

Closely related to the above class of questions are information queries such as those regarding the extent to which Negro children can get as good an education as white children; how, according to the proposed law, the Medicare plan would be paid for and who would be covered by the plan; whether the President is anti-business; whether there is a Biblical basis for segregation; whether Negroes can live a happier life today in the North or in the South; whether religion is increasing or losing its influence on American life. Answers to such questions presuppose a considerable amount of factual knowledge, specific information regarding Negro education; the proposed Medicare law; what the President has said and done; etc. The public in general would hardly be the best source for valid answers to these questions asked in 1962.

Of Prediction

Polling organizations are fond of asking prediction questions such as the following posed by Gallup in 1962: Will President Kennedy go more to the right, more to the left, or keep to the middle of the road politically? Will the people of Cuba overthrow Castro and the Communists within the next two or three years? Will all Christians—Catholics and Protestants— ever unite? Will life for the people get better or worse? Will prices go up in the next six months? Will there be more people out of work? Will the average price of stocks be higher or lower in three months? Is peaceful settlement with the Reds possible? Is the standard of living going up?

There is little evidence to prove that the clairvoyant powers of the masses are greater than those of more select groups. There is no apparent law of statistical probability which states that the larger the number of guesses about the future the closer to the truth the average of such guesses becomes. It is of course true that the kind of future we anticipate often influences our behavior and, in a sense, affects the future. But the nature and degree of this relationship is most uncertain.

Of Hypothesis

For several reasons hypothetical questions call forth answers of little direct value to policy makers. The circumstances and issues hypothesized may never arise in exactly the form stated. If they should, public opinion may have changed regarding them. Furthermore as judges have discovered, it is very difficult to project oneself into the future, to anticipate all of the relevant factors needed in making a decision, and to render an opinion with that degree of seriousness that a live question produces. Nevertheless, Gallup has asked such questions as these:

(a) Suppose there were only two major parties in the United States, one for liberals and one for conservatives, which one would you be most likely to prefer?

(b) In the event that you should have another chance now as in 1933—to vote for or against a man like Hitler, how would you vote? (Asked in Germany)

(c) Do you think business conditions in this country would be better or worse today if a Republican President were in office?

Such questions usually precipitate the initial response, "it all depends." What do you mean by liberal and conservative parties? What would they stand for? Who would lead them? What about their relative numerical strength in the country at large, and in my own community? In practically all such cases, the inability to spell out in significant detail the nature of the contingency means that the answers will be of little value when such a contingency arises, since it will probably have little relationship to the questioner's or the public's image of the anticipated contingency.

Of Decision

Once in a while the public is asked what it thinks should be done to solve a problem or deal with a situation. It is possible but unlikely that the public's answers to such questions would have much intrinsic merit. As many sages have remarked, the masses are more capable of venting grievances than inventing remedies. Solutions to problems require an astute analytical capacity, an ability to identify and weigh variables and causes, a knowledge of alternative solutions, time and patience which the ordinary person does not have. Certainly the general American voter would have little of substantive value to give to the question—What should the United States do about Egypt's taking over the Suez Canal? This is not to say that on some questions which relate to the everyday experience of people such as keeping city streets and parks clean or simplifying income tax returns, popular suggestion might not be fruitful.

Of New Policy

A very large proportion of policy questions used by polling agencies call for the public's evaluation of proposed, and in many cases, new policies. For example, according to questions used by Gallup during 1962, the American people:

(a) Would ban cigarette sales to youths under 16   79%
(b) Like the idea of a Presidential Honors List   70%
(c) Back standard national tests for High School people 77%
(d) Favor a domestic Peace Corps to work in poor areas 62%
(e) Back laws requiring safety belts in all cars   54%
(f) Do not favor United States invasion of Castro's Cuba at present (October 14, 1962) 63%
(g) Say birth control data should be available to anyone 72%

(h)	Do not think work week in most industries should be cut from 40 to 35 hours	64%
(i)	Divide on merits of sending food to the Red Chinese	48-43%
(j)	Divide on readiness to accept "freeze" on wages and prices	40-46%
(k)	Split on proposals to raise air mail and first-class mail rates	1st 45-50% Air 48-44%
(l)	Split on banning prize fighting	47-37%
(m)	Back a "Freedom Academy" to train Cold War strategists	69%
(n)	Favor law stopping union "featherbedding"	55%
(o)	Favor reviving Civilian Conservation Corps concept	79%
(p)	Back medical care of aged through social security	55-34%
(q)	Back new type hospital for those not critically ill	58-31%
(r)	Support resumption of nuclear tests above ground	66%
(s)	Back official review of speeches given by top military leaders	59%
(t)	Oppose United States getting out of the United Nations	90%

Many students of public opinion believe that voters are far more capable of judging the results of existing policies than they are of passing on proposed policies. As the above questions suggest, it is not always easy to separate the new from the old. One's opinion of a new policy may be based primarily on existing or old policies. This would be the case with such proposals as banning cigarette sales to youths under 16, upping postal rates, banning boxing, cutting length of work week. In fact, proposals to ban existing practices or rules or to change or modify them—all involve to a considerable extent judging the results of such practices or rules. Few, if any, proposals are wholly unrelated to the past. Most of them give rise to such questions as, is there a need for change? If so, is this particular change the most desirable one? The capacity of the public to opine intelligently on such proposed policies will depend, therefore, on many factors: the extent to which the policies are related to existing or past policies familiar to the respondent, the extent to which they fall within the experience of the average voter, how simple or complicated the proposal is, how widely it has been discussed, and so forth. Most of the proposals submitted by Gallup to the voting public in 1962 were related to past policies which were familiar and not too complicated. There were a few, however, that were not apparently within the general competence of the public. When asked in 1962 their views regarding the Kennedy Administration's tariff proposals for meeting the challenge of the European Common Market, Gallup discovered that only 13 per cent understood the proposal. It would hardly be worthwhile to poll the remaining 87 per cent, in the expectation that their opinions would be intrinsically valuable. Polls have shown that the public is often unaware of important legislative proposals and that only a small number understood them. Even fewer have discussed, or studied them.

Reasons

Another type of question seeks what the public thinks are the reasons for things. For example, in June, 1962, of those who had heard of the recent stock market slump, 85 out of 100 were asked "What do you think is the *chief* reason for the decline in the stock market?" And shortly thereafter the public was asked who they thought was more to blame for higher prices—employees or employers. On questions of this kind it seems unlikely that the public rather than the expert knows the answer. Economists, financiers, students of employer-employee relations, and other experts may not agree, but they should be able to give more informed answers than the average citizen. This is not to say that these two polls may not be useful for reasons other than the validity of the answers.

QUESTIONS SUITED FOR THE GENERAL PUBLIC

Seven categories of questions have now been considered; answers to these would seem to have little direct, substantive value for policy makers, however useful they might be for other purposes. The remaining seven categories would, on the contrary seem to supply answers intrinsically valuable. These are:

1. Appraisal of persons
2. Appraisal of non-governmental institutions
3. Appraisal of events and actions
4. Appraisal of the results of government policy
5. Questions of fact regarding oneself
6. Standards of fairness, justice, rightness, morals, and ethics
7. Goals and ends—relative values.

Appraisal of Persons

If the American voter has any special competence in the matter of expressing opinions, this would seem to be in choosing and appraising public officials. Students of public opinion and political theory have frequently stated that the public is more competent to judge men than measures. Certainly this seems to be the assumption in democratic forms of government where participation in elections and the choice of public officials is extensive and frequent. In the United States, for example, there are approximately 550,000 elective offices, and constituencies—national, state and local—appraise their candidates almost unceasingly.

The competence of the public to appraise persons, such as candidates for public office, depends in part on their knowledge of the person, on the personal attributes that are to be evaluated, and on the credentials offered by the candidate, his party, professional association, or record. In the political arena important distinctions have been made between filling legislative positions, top executive policy-making offices, administrative, technical jobs, and judicial offices. The founding fathers in the United States were very reluctant to entrust to the voting masses the selection of federal officials, and they did not do so in the case of the President, Vice-President, and members of the Senate. The difficult if not impossible chance of voter acquaintance with nation-wide and even state-wide candidates, the non-existence of responsible party organizations, as well as the peculiar requisites for these federal positions, seemed to justify an indirect method of selection. Views regarding the ability of the average voter to appraise candidates for public office have changed somewhat since that time, and notwithstanding a flurry of interest in allowing the voter to recall, if not choose, judges in some state jurisdictions, and to choose a number of state administrative officers, the general sentiment today seems to be to confine public appraisals to legislative representatives and a few, top administrative officials. The theory of representative government is that legislators are agents and the people are principals. So who is better qualified to select his agent than the principals? Somewhat the same argument also applies in the case of the popular election of top executive or administrative officials, although differences of opinion exist regarding the number of offices which should be made directly responsible to the voter.

Two additional points may be made. Whatever may have been the lack of competence of the nation-wide electorate to choose national officers in 1787, the situation today is vastly different. Due to the activities of political parties, pressure groups, and various non-partisan groups, such as the League of Women Voters, voters are probably better informed about their candidates than ever before. Newspapers, magazines, television, and other mass media provide much information and insight. Also, higher educational levels have given the people more historical and civic background and orientation information for judging personalities than heretofore.

A second point may be made that the voter in choosing a candidate today is also passing upon the results of legislative and administrative policy and action. The voter's decision is seldom a pure, exclusive appraisal of a person or persons. It is a composite of choices, congruent, conflicting, competent and incompetent. On the basis of what was said earlier regarding the voter's competence to assess results, a voter may be more capable of judging the incumbent than the hopefuls.

A very large number of Gallup's polls during 1962 asked for appraisals of candidates for President, Vice-President, and Congress. Repeatedly, over that year, he held what he called his "open primary," to test the appeal of nine potential Republican nominees for President. Polls of President Kennedy's popularity were taken every month, tested by the question "Do you approve or disapprove of the way Kennedy is handling his job as President?" This question calls for an appraisal of the man primarily in terms of the results of his administration's activity as well as of current events. Consequently, it is not surprising to find his popularity changing from a high of 79 per cent in March to a low of 66 per cent in August after the steel crisis and market slump, then rising to 74 per cent in December after he sent troops to Mississippi and the Cuban crises.

Appraisal of Institutions

In addition to appraising men, the pollsters often ask the public to appraise institutions of various kinds such as the United Nations, the John Birch Society, the Presidential press conference, the Common Market, and especially political parties. In the case of political parties the American voter was asked such questions as: which of the major parties will do the better job of keeping the country prosperous? Which would be more likely to keep the United States out of World War III? Which can do a better job of handling what you consider the most important problem facing this country today? Another type of assessment is obtained by asking various groups, such as business and professional, white-collar, farmers, skilled workers, and unskilled workers, which party they think serves their interests best? Finally, the public is repeatedly asked, during a Congressional election year, such as 1962, which party they would *like* to see win. In that year the preference for Democrats fell from 61 per cent in March to 55.5 per cent by the time of the November election.

How shall one appraise these appraisals? Are American voters as a whole more competent than any segment to say:

> Which party serves the interests of workers, farmers, business and professional people best.

> Which party is most likely to keep the United States prosperous, out of war, and to deal most satisfactorily with the country's major problems.

> Which party they would like to see win.

These three types of questions are appraisals of parties, only in a very general and possibly an indirect way. The most general question, perhaps, is the third. A voter may want a particular party to win for a great many different reasons, such as a desire to get a job, to see a friend put in office, to prove that he can pick a winner, because he has been a member of the party for years, and for other reasons more or less related to an appraisal of the parties as such. In a sense, the question is a question of fact, and the answers merely indicate, in fact, which party the voters would like to see win. As such, of course, no one is more competent to say than the voters themselves. Have they, however, made a wise choice? About all that one can say is that there are no objective standards of appraisal, and it is difficult, if not impossible to find a smaller, more competent group better able to assess all the multifarious dimensions of wisdom, including knowledge, reason, justice, and expediency.

The question as to which party serves the interests of particular occupational groups best, when addressed only to that particular group, raises a question which has been raised through the centuries—do people know their own best interests? Also it poses the question whether the voter really knows what interests particular parties serve. If voters do not know their own best interests who does? Someone will say, the experts do. But the trouble with this is: (1) that often the experts differ and the particular public has to choose between or among them; (2) when the experts are substantially agreed, it will usually be found that the public readily accepts the opinion of the expert; (3) in the few cases where the public does not do this, it may well be that the expert has taken into account only part of the voter's interest, not the whole. To allow the voter to define his own interest also avoids the possibility that the expert's definition of the public's interest may, in fact, be a definition of his own, which may not coincide with that of the public. And so, for many reasons, not a few students of government have come to believe that in the long run it is safer, and also wiser, to allow voters to define what is in their own best interest, while guided but not coerced by the advice of experts.

When voters are asked which party is most likely to keep the United States prosperous, out of war, and so on, they are really being asked to predict or prophesy rather than evaluate, though there is an element of appraisal in the replies. They are saying that this or that party is better able to do something than another party. Although it is comparatively easy to discover weaknesses in the public's capacity to make these discernments, it is far from easy to designate who are the reliable experts in this complicated task of evaluation and prophecy.

All in all, the questions asked voters regarding parties do supply answers of substantive value to policy makers, especially those questions which articulate the interests of particular groups as they perceive those interests, as well as those which indicate their party preferences.

In addition to expressing their views regarding political parties, American voters in 1962 were asked to give their opinions on a number of other institutions such as the Presidential press conferences, the United Nations, and the Birch Society. With reference to the Presidential press conferences 91 per cent of the public said they had a favorable impression of the way

President Kennedy handled himself in them; 61 per cent did not favor changing the procedure to have questions submitted in advance and in writing; and 84 per cent thought the questions asked by reporters were "passing" or better. These appraisals of the press conferences would seem to have considerable substantive value. A large majority of the people were familiar with the conferences (it was estimated that 78 million had seen or heard one or more); no special information was needed; they were designed to reach the largest audience possible; and the public generally was the best judge as to whether they did so successfully.

The polls regarding the United Nations showed that 83 per cent of the people thought it very important to make the United Nations a success; 78 per cent thought it was doing a good or fair job trying to solve the problems it has to face; and 90 per cent were opposed to the United States giving up its United Nations membership. In this case the public was being queried about an institution whose successes and failures are, for the most part, quite well-known. It is difficult to think of a group better able to weigh the over-all values involved than all of those ultimately affected.

Since only 53 per cent of the American voters in February, 1962, had heard of the John Birch Society, they were the only ones polled and the results showed 43 per cent had an unfavorable opinion of it, as against 47 per cent who had no opinion. However interesting these results may be for other reasons, they would seem to have little real value as a judgment of the Society. Doubtless, only a few of those "aware" of the organization knew very much about its aims or activities; few were acquainted with it from direct, personal experience. The public's views could well be a product of the image created by a small number of exposures to a few dramatic incidents or biased propaganda.

Appraisal of Events and Actions

Thus far we have considered the public's competence to appraise persons, such as candidates for public office, and institutions, such as political parties and Presidential press conferences. What about the public's competence to appraise and give an opinion regarding events such as the President's decision in October, 1962, to blockade Cuba? In a nation-wide poll completed a few hours after the President's announcement of his decision, 84 per cent of those who had heard about it approved the move. Many who approved thought it should have been done sooner; only one in five feared it would lead to war with Russia; but 31 per cent thought it was too early to foresee the consequences. This one survey suggests a few of the factors which have to be considered in judging the public's competence to express an opinion regarding events: To what extent and for how long has the thought or anticipation of such an event been considered? In this case, the President's action had obviously been considered for some time, and many had hoped it would occur. Although no one, not even the experts, could foresee all the consequences, probably most of those aware of the blockade took into account the possibility of all-out war with Russia. Even at the risk of war, the overwhelming majority believed that steps should be taken to remove the Cuban threat to national security. This may be regarded, not as a judgment on the basic question—to blockade or not to blockade—but as a mere vote of confidence in the President and the policy makers. An important element in the wisdom of any public policy decision is the approval or disapproval of the voters. It is not clear in this instance to what extent the President followed or was influenced in his decision by public opinion.

Appraisal of the Results of Government Policy

One of the distinctions frequently made in discussions of the competence of the public to pass on questions of public policy is that between appraising new policies, and evaluating the results of past and existing policies: the distinction between venting grievances and inventing remedies. Many would insist that the primary function of mass opinion is to render a verdict from time to time on the policies and operations of government, audit them, balance them, and say whether it finds them good or bad. If the public is capable of doing anything it is capable, the argument goes, of saying whether it is satisfied, happy, and favorable toward what is being done. One would expect, however, that the average citizen would be better able to judge the results of policies and actions that affect him directly than those far removed from his own immediate concerns. Moreover, he may not be able to find out himself exactly what the results are. It may require more than general information and first-hand experience to tell whether food and drug laws are being administered effectively, whether government spending is wisely and efficiently handled, whether or not officials are honest. Another difficulty stems from the public's ignorance of alternatives. Although ignorance may be bliss—that is ignorance of other choices or possibilities—when the public is asked to give its opinion of the American system of broadcasting, the methods of handling city traffic with which it is familiar, or the services rendered by public utilities —the fact is that this ignorance of alternatives certainly does impair its judgment. By and large, however, only the public itself can say whether a given administration or policy makes it feel better, more secure, more optimistic, gives it better working conditions or a higher standard of living.

Although, in general, the public's ability to judge results exceeds its talent for recommending new policies, comparatively few strictly "result questions" were asked by the Gallup poll in 1962. These few surveys showed that 58 per cent of those familiar with the Kennedy-Steel dispute favored the President's actions to get the steel companies to change their plans about raising steel prices; 64 per cent approved of labor unions in general; 48 per cent considered the amount of their Federal income tax too high (43 per cent felt they were about right); 72 per cent opposed a cut in Federal income taxes if it would mean the government would go further in debt; 44 per cent believed the practice of the President in appointing judges from members of his own party should be changed (41 per cent said no); 40 per cent thought Russia was ahead in the "propaganda war" (33 per cent felt the United States was); 78 per cent approved the way Kennedy was handling his job as President; 67 per cent approved his handling of foreign policy, whereas 72 per cent supported his handling of domestic problems. Also, 71 per cent were not in favor of "reverse Freedom Rides"—the action of White Citizen Councils in supplying free transportation North for unemployed Negroes; 35 per cent thought the Kennedy administration was pushing racial integration at just about the right tempo (32 per cent too fast, 11 per cent not fast enough). After the trouble at Ole Miss the above figures changed to 31 per cent about right, 42 per cent too fast, 12 per cent not fast enough.

Taken together these items differed in many respects, a fact which would affect the competence of the appraisal. Some subjects were close to and within the everyday experience of the average voter, such as income taxes, labor unions, and the problem of racial integration. Others, such as the appointment of judges and the international propaganda war, were remote from the lives of ordinary people. One may seriously question whether the views of the public on the latter would have much intrinsic value for law makers.

The items also differed in their degrees of generality. To invite an estimate of labor unions in general, the over-all performance of President Kennedy, or the rate of progress in racial integration was something quite different from asking questions about a somewhat exceptional, brief tussle between President Kennedy and the steel companies, or even the Reverse Freedom Rides, and, of course, the amount of information and the amount of time available for discussion varied. Thus it seems that on questions regarding the results of policy or action the views of the public have much intrinsic value, especially if those actions or policies personally affect the public, are very familiar to them, and require a general rather than a specific response.

Of Personal Fact

Pollsters go to the public quite frequently for facts regarding personal behavior, states of mind and health, expectations, hopes and desires. These are facts which, in most cases, the public and only the public can give. Actually, the data obtained is not opinion data, but factual data. In a sense it is also "information"—but this word has been reserved, as explained earlier, for facts external to the respondent, "cross-word puzzle" facts, facts in the public domain as it were, such as facts of history, science, literature, and current events. As a result of these fact, not information, questions in 1962, it was found:

> 40 per cent of the United States adult population went to church in a typical week.

> 50 per cent of the voters in the 1962 election split their tickets, and this tendency or practice is increasing.

> In November 16 per cent of 17 million Americans were planning a winter vacation trip away from home.

> 12 per cent have seat belts in their cars, and 51 per cent of these use them most or all of the time.

> In the 1962 campaign both major parties had about the same number of volunteer precinct workers—2,200,000.

> In October 69 per cent of the voters had given little or no thought to the Congressional campaign.

> Nationally, 28 per cent of the people describe themselves as Republicans, 22 per cent Independents, and 50 per cent Democrats. Outside the South the figures are 30, 24, and 46 respectively.

> 44 per cent of the parents of school children reported that religious observances took place in their community schools; 29 per cent said they did not; and interestingly enough 27 per cent didn't know. Also, 69 per cent reported that grace was said before meals at their home. In this connection it was also found that 79 per cent of all adults approve religious observances in the public schools.

> Some 12 million adults took a vacation of six days or more last winter, and most of them headed for the sunny climate.

> Although admitting there may be safer ways to travel, Americans prefer the convenience and the flexibility of the family car when it comes to taking a long trip.

> More Republicans (37 per cent) than Democrats (26 per cent) had a particular reason for wanting to vote in the Congressional election.

> 20 per cent of adults (20,000,000 people) said they had had a "religious or mystic experience"—that is, a moment of sudden religious insight or awakening. People reported five different types of such experiences: (1) mystic, hard to describe, other-worldly, a feeling of union with a Divine Being; (2) the same but carrying with it the conviction of the forgiveness of sins and salvation; (3) answers to prayers—often of a miraculous nature; (4) a turning to God—or a reassurance of His power and love in moments of crisis; (5) visions, dreams, or voices.

This kind of factual data, however useful and interesting it may be, is the kind that only the general public can give. No other group can claim greater expertness.

Five types of opinion data which the public in general seems competent, or as competent as any other group, to supply have been considered: data concerned with appraisals of persons, especially candidates for public office, appraisals of some non-governmental institutions, appraisals of certain acts and events, evaluations of the results of some government policies, and data regarding the respondents own behavior, thoughts, hopes, intentions. In each case, qualifications and exceptions were necessary. No fully conclusive answers could be given. Only very general probabilities were possible.

Of Moral and Ethical Judgments

Two remaining types of opinion data need to be considered: moral and ethical judgments, and statements regarding the ends and goals of public policy. Do the voting masses, taken collectively, have a superior sense of what is right, ethical, moral, fair and just? It has been held by some—A. Lawrence Lowell, for example—that public opinion is peculiarly competent to pass judgment on great moral issues.[3] Professor Carl Friedrich in his *New Belief in the Common Man* emphasizes the strength of character and the essential soundness of judgment of common men taken collectively. He says:[4]

> On any matter involving common values it stands to reason that three people consulting with one another are less likely to make an error in judgment than one, no matter who they are. . . . And the larger the collective group, the less frequent become the instances in which one person is apt to be right as against the collective judgment of all.

Leon Duguit, Hugo Krabbe, and other students of jurisprudence have professed to find in the sense of justice of the masses the foundation and justification for positive law.[5] This problem has engendered philosophical debate throughout history. Also, the pollsters have been impressed with what seems to them to be the common sense, wisdom, and high standards of right and fairness of the general American voter. On the other hand, there are some who are far less sanguine, such as Walter Lippmann, who dwells on the public's lack of standards, moral discipline, and a true "public philosophy."

In 1962, two questions of this ethical and moral type were asked of nation-wide publics, one in the United States and one in England. The American public was asked: "As you may have heard or read, an Arizona woman recently had a *legal* abortion in Sweden after having taken the drug thalidomide, which has been linked to birth defects. Do you think this woman did the right thing or the wrong thing in having this abortion operation?" For the American public as a whole 52 per cent said she did the right thing, 32 per cent the wrong thing, and 16 per cent had no opinion. As might have been expected only 33 per cent of the Catholics agreed it was the right thing; whereas 56 per cent of the Protestants supported the woman's action. Men and women differed about the same, 54 to 30 per cent in favor among the men; 50 to 33 per cent among the women.

In England the British public was asked: "Do you feel Britain is treated as an equal partner by the United States in affairs that concern them both, or don't you think so?" Only 22 per cent thought Britain was treated as an equal partner; 60 per cent thought Britain was not.

Many who would claim that in the final analysis it is the people in general who must say what is politically right and in the public interest, would balk, however, at the assertion that the general public is qualified to determine what is morally right. For them the standards of right and wrong can only be found in their own consciences, in some higher law, natural or divine, or in some divinely inspired book or person, in science, reason, or elsewhere. For the individual, what is right and what is fair, will always be an individual matter. For the democratic state, however, it will be a collective matter, the opinion of the people. In the long run the two will tend to merge as public opinion and individual opinion interact.

Moral standards and norms of fairness and justice are generally the product of longtime cultural development. In fact, it may be argued that any question which has been answered the same way for a sufficiently long time assumes a moral character. The distinction between moral questions and other types of questions seems to be losing some of its force. There are few so-called moral questions which do not involve economic, social, and political aspects. And, such amoral attributes have moral implications also. Questions are moral questions because their answers have been decided and imbedded in the crust of custom. In a very real sense the masses are the custodians of this custom. They are more inclined than any select group to uphold the decisions of the past and to support the heavy hand of custom, which in the final analysis comprises the accepted standards of right and wrong. During periods of rapid social change, when new questions are arising and old questions are being re-examined, the masses often find many of their accepted standards undermined. Ideas regarding standards of justice and morals become confused. However, the masses are the custodians of what Lowell has called "settled convictions" to the extent these convictions exist. For that reason they are peculiarly competent to answer questions "involving apparent harmony or contradiction with settled convictions." [6]

Of the Goals of Public Policy

Although many, if not most, students of public opinion agree that voters in general are better able to define the ends of public policy than to determine the means for realizing those ends, no questions dealing with the broad ends or goals of public policy were asked by the Gallup poll in 1962. It is difficult, of course, to differentiate ends and means, and ends tend to become means to other ends on a higher level of generality and comprehensiveness. In a certain sense most of the new, proposed policies discussed earlier, such as the Presidential Honors List, prize fighting, reviving the CCC, and establishing a 'Freedom Academy' were ends in a restricted sense, but they were also means to other ends such as rewarding excellence, preventing boxers from getting killed or seriously injured, deterring juvenile delinquency, and strengthening the position of the United States in the Cold War. But all of these ends may be regarded as means for promoting the health and well-being of the people in the United States.

One can easily list a long array of goals, more or less broad in scope, which most people endorse, such as security, health, justice, morality, public education, peace, progress, and many, many others. It is when these general goals are turned into concrete, specific proposals that differences of opinion arise, differences that increase when the means for realizing these goals are considered. It is sometimes said that our political parties, at least the two major ones, differ mainly over the means for attaining broad public policy objectives, rather than over the objectives themselves. Nevertheless, there seems to be justification for the general public's claim that it, and it alone, is competent to say what the ends of public policy should be. This rests on the assumption that government should serve the interests of all, not those of a segment or faction. There is also the assumption that each person should, as a matter of justice, have a right to participate in the decision.

NOTES FOR CHAPTER 5

Epigraph. James Bryce, *The American Commonwealth*, Chapter 87, Vol. 2, p. 367.
1. Compare an interview of the editors of the *Ladies' Home Journal* with George Gallup as reported by Gretta Palmer in that Journal, July, 1947 entitled "How Wise are We, the People" with either Walter Lippmann's *The Phantom Public* or *The Public Philosophy*.
2. Perhaps the most discriminating discussion of this problem is still that of A. Lawrence Lowell, *Public Opinion and Popular Government* (Longmans, Green and Co., 1913), esp. pp. 13-20; 46-53. See also Hall, Arnold Bennett, *Popular Government* (New York & London: The Macmillan Co., 1921), esp. pp. 50-62.
3. Lowell, A. Lawrence, *op. cit.*, p. 46.
4. Friedrich, Carl, *The New Belief in the Common Man* (Boston: Little, Brown, & Co., 1942).
5. See Duguit, Leon, *Law in the Modern State*, translated fr. the French by Freda and Harold Laski (New York: B. W. Huebsch, 1919), and Krabbe,

Hugo, *The Modern Idea of the State,* translated by George H. Sabine and Walter J. Shepard (New York: D. Appleton and Co., 1922).

6. Lowell, A. Lawrence, *op. cit.,* p. 46.

SUPPLEMENTARY READING

CANTRIL, HADLEY (ed.), and STRUNK, MILDRED A. (compiler). *Public Opinion 1935-1946.* Princeton, N. J.: Princeton University Press, 1951.

CHRISTENSON, REO M., and MCWILLIAMS, ROBERT O. *Voice of the People: Readings in Public Opinion and Propaganda.* New York: McGraw-Hill Book Co., 1962. Chapter 14.

COTTRELL, LEONARD S., and EBERHART, SYLVIA. *American Opinion on World Affairs in the Atomic Age.* Princeton, N. J.: Princeton University Press, 1948.

DAVIS, MORRIS. "Community Attitudes Toward Fluoridation," *Public Opinion Quarterly,* Vol. 23 (Winter, 1959-60), pp. 474-82.

ELDRIDGE, SEBA. *Public Intelligence.* Lawrence, Kansas: University of Kansas Press, 1935.

ERNEST, MORRIS LEOPOLD, and LOTH, DAVID. *The People Knew Best: The Ballots vs. The Polls.* Washington, D. C.: Public Affairs Press, 1949.

FENTON, JOHN M. *In Your Opinion.* Boston: Little, Brown & Co., 1960.

GALLUP, GEORGE. "The Absorption Rate of Ideas," *Public Opinion Quarterly,* Vol. 19 (Fall, 1955), pp. 234-42.

LANE, ROBERT E. *Political Ideology: Why the Common Man Believes What He Does.* New York: Macmillan-Free Press, 1962.

NAFZIGER, RALPH O., ENGSTROM, W. C., and MACLEAN, JR., M. S. "The Mass Media and An Informed Public," *Public Opinion Quarterly,* Vol. 19 (Spring, 1951), pp. 105-14.

PERRY, RALPH BARTON. *The Citizen Decides.* Bloomington, Indiana: Indiana University Press, 1951.

ROPER, ELMO. "American Attitudes on World Organization," *Public Opinion Quarterly,* Vol. 17 (Winter, 1953-54), pp. 405-42.

SCOTT, W. A., and WITHEY, S. B. *The United States and the United Nations: The Public View, 1945-55.* Published for the Carnegie Endowment for International Peace. New York: Manhattan Publishing Company, 1958.

Social Science Research Council. *Public Reaction to the Atomic Bomb and World Affairs.* Ithaca, New York: Cornell University Press, 1947.

STOUFFER, SAMUEL ANDREW. *Communism, Conformity and Civil Liberties.* New York: Doubleday & Co., Inc., 1955.

WITHEY, STEPHEN B. "Public Opinion About Science and Scientists," *Public Opinion Quarterly,* Vol. 23 (Fall, 1959), pp. 382-88.

VI · Formation of
Public Opinion

The public being but a congeries of individuals, the forces which mold individual character are, in final analysis, those which make public opinion.

—PETER ODEGARD

T O F I N D O U T how public opinion is formed is to find out how individual, personal opinions are formed. The public is always a group, a collection of individuals, never an organic entity with an existence of its own. Public opinion is always a collection of the opinions of these individuals constituting the public. How then are personal opinions formed? The answer is quite simple, so long as it is stated in very broad, general terms. Opinions are what they are because personal attitudes are what they are, and these attitudes stem from the nature of the personality, in turn the evolving result of the dynamic interaction of the person and his environment. From birth until death this interacting process goes on, producing ever-changing personalities, attitudes, and opinions.

There are, therefore, three basic elements in the opinion-forming process: the person, his environment, and the interaction between the two. It seems quite futile to ask, however, which is the most important of the three in this process, or even to ask which is the more important, the person and his heredity, or his environment? Both, and all three, are indispensable: as necessary as both blades to a pair of scissors. The blades may differ in size, fixity, or toughness, but they are equally necessary to the cutting process. So also with the person and his attributes on the one hand, and the environment on the other.

The words "person," "environment," and "interaction" are all broad, general, comprehensive terms comprising a great many aspects, elements, or attributes. As in the sciences generally, so in the study of public opinion and human behavior, larger entities are broken down into smaller parts for study. The person is subjected to physiological, biological, even chemical analysis. His bodily structure, nervous system, glandular make-up, muscles, circulatory system are noted. Psychologists explore his mental processes. Thus the word "person" comes to life as almost unlimited attributes, factors, variables which interact with each other and with the external environment. Nearly all of the tangible, visible parts of the human body have been identified and labeled, and for the most part, their functions have been described. Although many secrets remain, the progress of the biological and physiological sciences in recent years has been rapid and impressive.

PERSONAL FACTORS

Not all of man's personal attributes are tangible and visible, however. Neither his subconscious fears, conscious ideals, mental processes, feelings, nor emotions can be touched or seen directly, but some of their manifestations can. Yet these states of mind and body undoubtedly do have pronounced effects on the attitudes and opinions of the person. The following frequently used psychological terms and concepts will suggest the tremendous number of purely psychological attributes, which may constitute factors in the opinion-forming process in the individual: stereotypes, perception, identification, motives, frustrations, conflicts, tensions, anxieties, guilt feelings, habits, complexes, fixations, frames of reference, dissonance, cross pressures, ego defense, rationalizations, values, trauma.

Both tangible and intangible attributes of the person have been used as factors to explain personality, attitude, and opinions. Hippocrates wrote of the four humors and their bodily correlates: melancholy (black bile), choleric (yellow bile), phlegmatic (phlegm), and sanguine (blood). Ernst Ketschmer differentiated the asthenic (long, lean), pyknic (fat), and athletic personality types, somewhat related to the later and more familiar classification (Sheldon) of ectomorph, endomorph, mesomorph. These broader types have been subclassified, almost to the point of absurdity. Although these attempts to relate personalities, attitudes, and opinions to physiological factors have not proved generally useful, physical appearance is often indicative of mood and attitude, if not of specific opinions. The influence of certain physiological and biological attributes such as the nervous system, glands, and sense organs on personality and attitudes cannot be questioned.

Students of opinion formation have never been wholly unmindful of the intangible, psychological aspects of person and personality, and they have sought to find in them the clues to why opinions are what they are. Whether these factors are true causes, in the same sense as physiological attributes, or whether they are intervening variables, or merely constructs of the imagination, will not be discussed here. In any case, many of these processes, mental states, and psychological factors illumine the human personality, if they do not fully explain it.

In his 1913 study, *Public Opinion and Popular Government,* A. Lawrence Lowell called attention to the importance of a person's interests, emotions, attention, and the "ascribing of weight" to arguments and evidence. Possibly no one person has made as important a contribution to the understanding of opinion formation as Sigmund Freud, whose discoveries in the realm of the subconscious revolutionized thinking about the determinants of opinion. Nearly every psychologist and social psychologist has had something to say about psychological determinants of behavior and opinion, but only the conclusions of a few will be cited here. Gordon Allport, in his classic explanation of attitude formation,[1] gave prominence to four psychological processes: (1) accretion and integration; (2) individuation and differentiation; (3) traumatic experience; and (4) imitation. Daniel Katz adopted a functional approach to the study of attitudes and concluded that attitudes are formed to meet four basic psychological needs: (1) utilitarian needs (adjustive function); (2) to handle internal conflicts (ego-defensive); (3) to maintain self-identity and enhance the self-image (value-expressive); or (4) to give understanding and meaning to the outside world (the knowledge function).[2] Herbert C. Kelman, not unlike Professor Katz, distinguished "three processes of social influence, each characterized by a distinct set of antecedent and a distinct set of consequent conditions." The first is *compliance,* "when an individual accepts influence from another person or from a group because he hopes to achieve a favorable reaction from the other," not because he believes in its content. The second is *identification,* "when an individual adopts behavior derived from another person or a group because this behavior is associated with a satisfying self-defining relationship to this person or group." The individual is primarily concerned with meeting the other's expectations for his own role performance, and he actually believes in the opinions and actions that he adopts. Finally, "*internalization* can be said to occur when an individual accepts influence because the induced behavior is congruent with his value system. It is the content of the induced behavior that is intrinsically rewarding here." [3]

Psychologists have shown no little imagination and ingenuity in finding psychological factors or determinants. Mention has already been made of some of these such as stereotypes, dissonances, perceptions, frustrations, complexes and so on. Morris Rosenberg studied the effect of low self-esteem on political participation;[4] William A. Scott studied the relationship of values concerning interpersonal relations to opinions regarding foreign policy.[5] Angus Campbell concluded that "for many people Democratic or Republican attitudes regarding foreign policy result from a conscious or unconscious adherence to a perceived party line, rather than from influences independent of party identification." [6] M. E. Rosenbaum and I. M. Zimmermann explored the effects of committing oneself publicly to a point of view on subsequent attempts by others to change that viewpoint.[7] G. D. Wiebe discovered that "inappropriate" values acquired during childhood were prime determinants of public reactions to the Army-McCarthy hearings.[8] Heinz Eulau, studying the relationship between social class and political behavior, found that identification with social class "is more likely to be effective in connection with attitudinal than with role or functional dimensions of political behavior." [9] And Elliot G. Mishler found, in a study of the relationship between personality and social behavior, that "a particularistic role orientation is positively related to the characteristics of the authoritarian personality." [10]

In these studies a few, a very few, of the many psychological determinants used to explain opinion formation were cited: self-esteem, values concerning interpersonal relations, adherence to a perceived party line, public commitment to a point of view, values acquired in childhood, identification with social class, and a particularistic role orientation. The person which emerges from all these studies is a being, not only of bones, nerves, blood, and muscle, but of innumerable psychological states and processes, of cross pressures, dissonances, purposes, predispositions, loyalties, moods, and drives.

Although these words and expressions usually label or describe something meaningful within the person they give the impression that it is real and easily identifiable, and this is not always the case. In fact, these so-called psychological determinants present difficulties. Their existence cannot be proved directly, but it must be imputed from some form of overt behavior, such as the expression of opinions. How otherwise can one conclude that cross pressures, stereotypes, or dissonances exist? Even the existence of attitudes themselves must be deduced from some form of overt behavior such as laughing, shrugging the shoulder, or stating an opinion. This is not true, of course, for visible, tangible, biological or physiological attributes, for a brain tumor, a stomach ulcer, or defective eyesight. Not only is it impossible to locate and identify these intangible psychological constructs, but it is difficult if not impossible to describe, measure, or weigh their influence, since there is usually no agreed upon definition or measure of them. At best these psychological attributes of the person are intervening variables, deliberately placed between the expressed opinion and other types of overt behavior and the tangible, identifiable, physiological forces or factors. They are not true causes or influences, but rather feedbacks from preceding effects. For example, an internal bodily change or an external stimulus causes a person to move, laugh, make some other kind of noise, or state an opinion. These effects or forms of behavior in turn affect the body, relieving tensions, producing pain or pleasure, modifying muscular and nervous systems, or storing impressions in the brain. Patterns of bodily response and behavior develop, and it is to these patterns, or more or less habitual types of response, that these psychological names, such as dissonances, stereotypes, predispositions, complexes, attitudes, apply. As references to patterned, more or less structural responses, they are useful terms, but they should not be considered causes of, or determinants of anything. In this sense an attitude is not a determinant of opinion, but a word descriptive of a frequent, habitual behavioral response. To say that a person votes for X because he has a favorable attitude toward X is really not explaining why he votes as he does, but it does state that he has expressed a whole array of opinions favorable to X. Stereotypes do not cause a person to label a bushy-haired individual a communist; they are merely said to exist when a person repeatedly treats people or things or ideas alike simply because they have one or a few features in common. Similarly, with a great many so-called psychological determinants; they are names for patterns of behavioral responses, or imputed, hypothetical causes of those patterns.

These behavioral responses, whether in the form of opinions or bodily movements, are not only grouped to form psychological complexes, motives, pre-dispositions and the like, but they are extended to constitute traits, a much more inclusive grouping. Traits are combined to form types —the introvert or extrovert, the outer- or inner-directed, the liberal or conservative, the authoritarian or non-authoritarian. The more inclusive the categories, the greater the tendency to obscure important personality differences and deviations. The attempt to type individual personalities tends to overstress human similarities, whereas the avoidance of classification may exaggerate individual differences and obscure uniformities.

ENVIRONMENTAL FACTORS

Attitudes and opinions emerge, not as the sole result of the operation of factors and determinants within or attributable to the person, but in consequence of the interaction between the person and his environment. The environment as a whole is so extensive and inclusive as to be almost incomprehensible. It is as close to the person as the air he breathes and as distant as the outer limit of the universe. It includes physical, biological, and sociological factors; economic, religious, and political institutions; topographical, climatic, and demographic items; ideas, customs, and myths. To list, even, these factors in their entirety, is an impossibility. Sociologists, and others, have tried to classify the more important aspects or features of the environment, and they have then gone on to subclassify them and select for special consideration a few of the items in the subclasses. The family and its influence on its members' opinions and attitudes have been studied, along with many other kinds of small, primary (face-to-face) groups. Such institutions as the church, the school, and media of communication have received much attention. Governments of all kinds have been studied to ascertain their influence in the opinion-forming process, national, international, state and local. The role played by secondary groups, economic, professional, ethnic, religious, and special purpose has received a great amount of scholarly attention. But interest has extended far beyond the environment of persons and human institutions to include investigations of the influence of things, processes, and physical factors of many kinds.

Not all lists of environmental factors, however, even try to be comprehensive or schematic. Rather, they appear to be highly selective and haphazard, emphasizing the particular interests of the author. Two illustrations will suffice. Professor F. E. Lumley, in his *Means of Social Control* listed and discussed the following without indicating precisely why these, rather than other aspects of the environment, were selected: rewards, praise, flattery, persuasion, advertising, slogans, propaganda, gossip, satire, laughter, calling names, commands, threats, and punishment.[11] Except for the first and last, they all are forms of communication. Why were these rather than other types of communication chosen?

Curtis D. MacDougall in *Understanding Public Opinion* also presents a potpourri of alleged opinion determinants, most of them environmental, including customs, ideologies, propaganda, business civilization, Protestant tradition, legends, censorship, fashions, heroes, language, arts, religion, education, and journalism.[12]

Environmental factors as well as personal attributes may be general or specific, large or small, remote or proximate, stable or changeable, and may differ in many other ways. Students of public opinion have shown inventiveness and imagination in discovering, listing, and classifying determinants of both a personal and an environmental nature. But there appear to be a few categories within the environment of special significance: first of all, the so-called basic institutions; the family, church, and school. Through the formative years of early childhood and youth these agencies are usually very important, although the role of peer and other primary groups, the influence of geography, climate, and other physical factors, and the impact of many other environmental items are not to be ignored. The influence of these basic institutions, because it comes as early as it does, usually persists for years, often for a lifetime.

In addition to these basic institutions, there are other important environmental influences which tend to become more important over the years: the media of communication, especially the mass media; the professional, occupational, special purpose, and other interest groups to which a person belongs; and the government with its control over so many phases of human life, its outpouring of information and propaganda, and its ability to create news and events. Although determinants of great importance, each of these, however, comprises innumerable parts, elements, and attributes of varying significance.

It may be of some interest to note a few of the specific environmental factors which have been studied recently. Benton Johnson studied the effects of ascetic Protestantism in the United States;[13] Donald Stokes and Warren Miller, the records of major parties in Congress;[14] Herbert Menzel and Elihu Katz, the role of face-to-face contacts;[15] I. L. Janis, A. A. Lumsdaine, and A. I. Gladstone the effect of an "optimistic" communication just prior to a disturbing event;[16] and Warren Breed and Thomas Ktsanes the influence of other people's views.[17] In recent years such environmental factors as the press, radio, TV, advertising, public relations, opinion leaders, reference groups, small groups, press conferences, information services, propaganda, all kinds of pressure groups, customs, fashions, and –isms have been explored to determine their effect on public opinion.

RECENT THEORIES: SOCIAL PSYCHOLOGY

For many years the study of the individual and the study of the social environment went on in more or less segregated compartments, psychology and sociology. That the two acted on and reacted to each other was appreciated, but it wasn't until the advent of social psychology that this interacting process was systematically investigated. This discipline straddles the other two and seeks to understand and explain the dynamic process of personality development. This process is for the most part invisible and intangible. One can see or touch the environmental factor in the formation of opinion—the press release, the TV program, or the family group—and one may observe the effect as revealed in behavior, opinions expressed, or the acceleration of the heart-beat. But the dynamics of their influence and the interacting process remain hidden. A great many words are used to describe this process such as communicating, suggesting, conditioning, persuading, experiencing, and learning. It is not always easy or feasible to draw a hard and fast line between person and interaction on the one hand, and environment and interaction on the other. They are all part of the same over-all dynamic process.

Much of what has been written about opinion formation is theory rather than verified or tested fact. Stated conclusions are often more in the nature of propositions or hypotheses to be proved than the results of careful, scientifically conducted experiments. These theories may take one of several forms such as: (a) a single-factor approach; (b) a multi-factor approach; (c) the use of a "pat formula"; (d) attempts to formulate "laws" of opinion formation; (e) attempts to determine the relative influence of opinion determinants by correlational analysis; and (f) the attempt to do the latter experimentally.

In the single-factor approach one factor or determinant, or group of factors, is given a predominant place in the opinion-forming process. At one time some stressed the importance of heredity, and others emphasized the influence of the environment. Many have been much more specific. Karl Marx stressed the importance of economic factors; Freud stressed frustrated sexual urges and the role of the sub-conscious; Berman, the role of glands; Child, the importance of physiological factors; Turner, the frontier in American history; and others have underscored race, instincts, geography, technology, and power among others. Many philosophers have constructed entire systems on the narrow base of one or a few personality or environmental factors. There is less of a tendency today toward a single-factor approach, but many students have their favorites: reference groups, elites, primary or small groups, opinion leaders, events, stereotypes, personality, perception, psychological dissonance.

The multi-factor approach, as the name suggests, focuses on several factors instead of one. In his memorable study of voting behavior in Erie County, Ohio, Paul Lazarsfeld concluded that voting behavior in that area could largely be accounted for by three factors: social-economic-status (SES), residence (urban-rural), and religion (Protestant-Catholic). Taken together these constituted his index of political predisposition (IPP) which he used as a base for determining the effects of the 1940 Presidential campaign.[18] E. Jackson Baur, in a study of changing public opinion during a controversy over methods of flood control and water conservation in Kansas, concluded that "public opinion is formed through subtle processes of changing kinds of knowledge, affectivity level, and relative salience of values and interests" rather than "as a logical confrontation and persuasion by rival proponents in public debate."[19] L. A. Froman, Jr., and J. K. Skipper, Jr., tried to find the reasons why so many voters tended to misperceive or fail to understand how a political party stands on particular issues. They identified four of them: type of issue, education, party identification, and strength of issue orientation.[20]

Erich Reigrotski and Nels Anderson, on the basis of a study of stereotypes of Frenchmen and Germans, concluded that national stereotypes were due primarily to lack of foreign contacts, national stereotypes held by other peoples, and low educational levels.[21] S. M. Lipset studied student opinion at the University of California during the loyalty oath controversy in 1951 to find that it was in large part a product of previous experience and attitudes. Deviations from these predispositions were due primarily to cross pressures. The study was made especially useful because of the number and variety of determinants and relationships surveyed and analyzed: influence of college class or status, political attitudes, religion, newspaper reading habits, socio-economic status, occupation of father, residence in or outside the University, how financed through school, future job aspirations, major subject or department, significant group affiliations, perception of Communist influence in the University, participation in the university community.[22]

Edward A. Suchman and others studied the attitudes of 4,585 male students in eleven universities regarding the Korean War and identified what appeared to be three basic dimensions of those attitudes: ideological conviction (belief that Korean War was fought for an ideal), partisan allegiance (views regarding international relations), and political knowledge (information about Korean War). The interrelationship among these variables proved to be extremely complex, however.[23]

In 1952, Herbert E. Krogman made a preliminary report on the Appeals of Communism Project, which was concerned with what makes an individual become a Communist. One group of relevant factors was related to the individual's personal situation just prior to joining: his emotional adjustment problems, especially in the case of intellectuals, political pressure, previous political interest, unemployment, as an answer to fascism, in anger over the Depression, a dull, materialistic life. The specific attractions of the Communist Party comprised a second group of factors: idealistic (fight against injustice, fascism, poverty), romantic (defy authority, participate in danger and excitement), practical (seek knowledge, understanding, trade union skills, jobs), escape (avoid loneliness, meaninglessness, competition), status (to become part of an heroic, powerful or Bohemian elite), admiration (for members), tradition. The third group of factors could be labeled psychological needs which membership in the party satisfied to some extent: unconscious needs such as release from feelings of hostility, unworthiness, weakness, apathy, confusion, and isolation, and conscious needs such as jobs, belonging, satisfaction of curiosity, and the carrying out of obligations to trade unions, ethnic minority groups, and mankind in general. The unconscious needs were salient for intellectuals.[24]

Ira N. Brophy, in studying anti-Negro prejudice among seamen, concluded that a seaman's attitude in this matter was primarily a function of the union he previously belonged to, the number of times he shipped with Negroes, the comradeship and sense of group solidarity aboard ship, undergoing traumatic experiences with Negroes under fire, even his job location aboard ship, rather than a function of the usually accepted determinants such as place of birth or residence, amount of education, or class consciousness.[25]

Hans H. Toch was interested in pinpointing the situations or factors responsible for producing critical changes in ideological beliefs.[26] He identified them as: (1) long periods of solitary confinement, (2) encountering strong invalidating evidence, (3) a failure of important expectations; (4) shock of evidence coming "close to home"; and (5) an emotionally upsetting, traumatic experience. In a study of attitudes toward participation in civil defense, William A. Scott also attempted to isolate three psychological factors which seemed to induce people to volunteer for civilian defense: motivation (amount of concern regarding dangers of war), information (knowledge of CD organization and activities), and evaluation (apparent need for strengthening CD). The dominant influence was found to be evaluation. Information is of major importance for only a few. Concern about war has a general independent effect on only previous consideration of volunteering. Other factors, such as age, sex, amount of free time, may also be important, but the three mentioned seem to be most significant.[27]

This review of a number of the more recent attempts to identify, describe, and determine the influence of various factors in the opinion-forming process leads to several observations.

Because of the variety in nature, scope, and concreteness of the factors designated in the several studies, comparisons, correlations, and generalizations regarding the role of particular factors are impossible. The variety of special public opinion situations studied is matched by the variety of opinion determinants disclosed. Not only are generalizations well-nigh impossible, but the findings of one study cannot be checked against those of another.

In any public opinion situation the number of factors that could be isolated are almost limitless, depending on the power of the microscopic and macroscopic lenses used to define them. The number of environmental, personal, and interaction variables seems endless. Some are concrete, very specific, and capable of quantification; others are abstract, vague, difficult to define. It may often be the case that those factors most easily concretized and quantified are the least significant. How may some order be brought out of this confusing maze of innumerable variables? One way is to differentiate remote and proximate factors. Some writers have suggested breaking down the twofold grouping into numerous subgroups, each subgroup representing a different degree of proximity or remoteness to the end product, the opinion. The name "funnel of causation" has been given to these pyramidal-shaped layers of factors. In this case, factors would be arranged along a time continuum, and interest would focus on that factor or factors which, to use a lawyer's phrase, had "the last clear chance" to prevent or cause a change of opinion.

Studies so far indicate that the relative influence of factors varies considerably from issue to issue. Some order might be brought to the situation by focusing more systematically on particular types of questions such as those concerned with civil rights, morals, taxation, or race relations, in order to ascertain, if possible, information regarding the significant factors and their relative influence for each type. The counterpart of this would be to take a particular factor, such as TV, a decision of the Supreme Court, or an event, such as the sending of an astronaut into space, and concentrate on its effect on public opinion.

If this free enterprise in the study of opinion formation has produced an almost indigestible supply of findings, it has also supplied a rich variety of insights, hypotheses, factors, to say nothing of research techniques and methodologies. These findings provide a colorful mosaic, but sometimes it is as devoid of meaning as some abstract paintings.

The single- and multi-factor approaches to the study of opinion formation are the most frequent, but now and then scholars will try to present a more sweeping panorama of the process of opinion formation without carefully assessing the role of specific factors taken singly or in combinations. Blithely ignoring the hazards of generalization, they view the process of public opinion formation on issues—usually very broad ones such as civil rights, social security, foreign aid, or prohibition—as a movement which usually, if not always, passes through several stages. This may be labeled the "pat-formula" approach. A few examples of these attempts to standardize the opinion-forming process may be given.

The late Professor Clyde King, in his preface to W. B. Graves' *Readings in Public Opinion,* published in 1928, described the process of public opinion formation in terms of four stages. "The first stage in public opinion," he writes, "is discontent in a matter believed to be capable of remedy by group action." Then, this discontent finds general expression and there emerges an awareness of a common need. This stage is followed by a third in which issues are crystallized following discussion and controversy in the press. Finally, the stage of judgment and decision is reached.

W. P. Davison, writing in 1958, attempted to delineate the public opinion process in greater detail.[28] The following steps or stages may be discerned in his discussion, though they were not set forth quite so succinctly. (a) Issues take root when communicated from one person to another; (b) discussion becomes generalized and an issue arises and takes shape; (c) the issue is taken over by a hospitable group; (d) party leaders take up the issue; (e) mass media and professional agents enter the arena; (f) ideas are simplified and generalized; (g) the issue is now brought to the attention of many; (h) public opinion, in the sense of the opinion of "a large collection of individuals who do not know each other personally, but who react to an issue with the expectation that certain categories of others will display similar attitudes on the same issue," may or may not arise; (i) more face-to-face discussions begin, and a kind of circular process of action and interaction starts through personal contacts, the influence of the opinions and behavior of other groups, prestige suggestions, role of stereotypes, and the influence of personal expectations. Finally, (j) the issue as such disappears because new goals are found, new issues arise, or the issue becomes embodied in law, custom, or social norms.

A still more recent attempt to chart the process of public opinion is that of E. Jackson Baur.[29] He specifies three major stages in the formation of public opinion, which he calls (1) the mass behavior stage, when opinions take form in dispersed primary groups; (2) the stage of public controversy when the newly formed opinions are transmitted to large, secondary groups; and finally, the institutionalized decision-making stage. He emphasizes that at each stage a small, primary group plays an important role. Actually, he is able to subdivide these three stages into seven steps which describe the process of public opinion formation more concretely.

(1) Many separate individuals become concerned about a social problem, assimilating ideas from many sources.

(2) Some organized group proposes a solution to the problem, and a public emerges.

(3) When an organized opposition appears, one may say that a public is fully formed.

(4) The opposing factions, after solving organizational problems and becoming fairly well unified, turn for support to the uncommitted.

(5) It is out of this discussion and controversy that public opinion emerges.

(6) Following the emergence of public opinion governmental institutions are invoked to take decisive action.

(7) Finally, responsible persons do take action and make authoritative decisions.

The pat-formula approach, in contrast to the single- or multiple-factor approach, emphasizes the dynamic nature of the process of opinion formation. It also provides a theoretical model on which actual studies of opinion formation can be tried for fit. Although, in most cases, the fit may be far from perfect, discrepancies can be noted and studied, and the model improved. If the theoretical model is not too "pat," or the "patness" accepted too uncritically, this approach can be very useful.

Another approach to the study of opinion formation has involved the so-called laws of public opinion. In a sense this is a "pat" approach also, and perhaps even more ambitious than the attempt to delineate stages in the formation process. Studying the fluctuation of public opinion in the United States in relation to events during World War II, Hadley Cantril reached a number of conclusions regarding the process of opinion formation which he undertook to generalize as psychological principles.[30] These principles are not, of course, laws in any scientific sense, since they fail to specify the conditions when they validly apply. However, they serve as interesting hypotheses or propositions against which to test empirical evidence. Five of the twenty "principles" are cited below for illustrative purposes:

(1) An opinion is formed when, and only when, you face a frustrating situation where a judgment is required on which you must base action that will help you carry out a purpose.
(2) An opinion is built up from past experience as a guide to purposive action.
(3) An opinion is based chiefly on unconscious cues which are mustered together and integrated when their relevance in forming a value judgment for purposive action is aroused by some situation.
(4) Knowledge and rational thought serve the function of bringing into the process of value judgment (opinion formation) more cues to be weighed.
(5) Knowledge must not be confused with understanding. Understanding, as distinguished from knowledge, means that knowledge has been put to some concrete test in purposive action.

In this list of "principles" Cantril seems to be saying that the starting point for any analysis of public opinion formation is acceptance of the premise that man is by nature purposeful, and it is only when purposes are frustrated that opinions are formed. Frustration starts the process and other factors guide it, such as past experience, unconscious cues, knowledge, rational thought, understanding, change of purpose, failure of opinions to work, tests of concrete opinions by self and others, sense of surety, former standards, new and emergent situations, expectancies, events, relative importance of purposes, and the purposes of others. This is an imaginative and insightful list of determinants. Difficulties arise, however, in assessing their relative influence or even stating the conditions when they exert their influence. The list of "principles" proves to be only another list of potential factors.

RESEARCH AND NATION-WIDE OPINION DATA

Many of the attempts to explain the opinion-forming process are little more than pure speculations, more or less shrewd according to the experience and insight of the observer. Likewise most of the assertions regarding the importance of opinion determinants have yet to be proved. In a few cases experiments have been undertaken to test hypotheses, but with publics so small as to make generalizations hazardous. The opinion data collected by nation-wide polling agencies, however, is exceptionally useful since it concerns mass publics, relates to a very large number of questions, and can be "broken down" for analytical study. Now this data does not answer directly the question how public opinion is formed, but it does throw light on the relative influence of certain factors or determinants in the process.

Using data collected by these nation-wide polling agencies it is possible to ascertain the distribution of opinion on questions within various age, sex, income, racial, religious, and residence groups. It is possible to find out, not only how the American people as a whole think about a given matter, but how men think, how those over fifty years of age, or those living in a particular state or region think. For the country as a whole, and for each of these subgroups, it is possible to determine the degree of agreement on a question, that is to say the difference between the percentage of those who say "yes" and those who say "no." For example, if all those in a given group, all men or all those living in New Jersey, think the same on a question we say that the degree of agreement is 100. If there is an equal split, that is 50 per cent say "yes" and 50 per cent say "no" there is a 0 degree of agreement. In other words we may indicate varying degrees of agreement by figures 0 to 100, the particular figure in each case obtained simply by subtracting affirmative from negative opinions or vice versa, depending on which is the larger.

Information concerning the varying degrees of agreement in various subgroupings provides clues to an understanding of the relative influence of the factors used as bases for these subgroups. For example, if analysis shows that there is an even distribution of opinion in all subgroups but one, and in that one everybody thinks alike, then the factor determining the subgroup is obviously very important in the opinion-forming process on that question. If age groups, income groups, sex groups, all groups in fact except one, political parties, show an index of agreement of almost 0, but for Republicans and Democrats the index of agreement is over 90, the predominance of party influence is clearly indicated. For practically every question asked by the nation-wide polls over the years it is possible to ascertain the index of agreement for numerous subgroups, and a comparison of these indices gives a general idea of the relative importance of the several factors involved.

Some years ago the American Institute of Public Opinion asked a question regarding the desirability of wives working outside the home, for example in industry. The results of the survey showed that for the country as a whole 78 per cent said "no," and 22 per cent said "yes." The index of agreement for the country as a whole was 56, indicating a fairly high degree of unanimity. The division of opinion by subgroups by per cent and indices of agreement for each are given in the table.

	YES	NO	INDEX OF AGREEMENT
National	22	78	56
Sections			
New England	23	77	54
Middle Atlantic	21	79	58
Eastern Central	19	81	62
Western Central	20	80	60
South	29	71	42
Rocky Mountain	21	79	58
Pacific	21	79	58
Sex			
Men	19	81	62
Women	25	75	50
Rural-Urban			
Urban	20	80	60
Farm	20	80	60
Small Town	20	80	60
Economic Status			
Wealthy	29	71	42
Average plus	29	71	42
Average	24	76	52
Poor plus	24	76	52
Poor	16	84	68
On relief	16	84	68
On old age assistance	16	84	68
Age			
Under 32	25	75	50
32 to 52	23	77	54
Over 52	16	84	68

It is evident from an inspection of the above opinion data that economic status and age are the more important determinants, since those in the lowest economic brackets and those over 52 years of age display the highest degree of agreement, an index of 68, which is considerably higher than the index of agreement for the country as a whole, 56. Interestingly enough the most pronounced differences of opinion are to be found in the southern section of the country and among the wealthy where the index of agreement is only 42.

The question may be asked as to how the results of a survey should be interpreted if all the breakdowns show substantially the same divisions of opinion, the same indices of agreement. In such a case one might properly infer perhaps that none of the factors was significant, or that they all were important but equal. The question calls attention to the fact that variations in degrees of agreement only indicate the relative influence of the factors listed. It is always quite possible that an important factor or even a significant number of factors have been left out of consideration altogether. In those cases where breakdowns do not produce any very substantial variations in indices of agreement, the student of public opinion is really presented with an invitation to try and find more significant factors, factors which produce atypical degrees of agreement.

Over the years the polling agencies have asked literally thousands of questions. By using the breakdown data in the manner indicated above it should be possible to arrive at some convincing as well as interesting conclusions regarding the role of certain factors in the opinion-forming process. Do breakdowns tend to show wide variations in the degrees of agreement, thereby pointing to the relatively greater influence of certain factors than others? Are there certain factors, such as economic status, which seem to be of greater importance than the others on practically every type of question? Is there a pattern of relative importance among the factors for all types of questions, or only for certain types? For what types of questions is the sectional factor important, the age, sex, economic, and other specific factors? Are the degrees of agreement within the breakdowns on some types of questions so uniform as to suggest that perhaps real account has not been taken of the determining factor? When such uniformity exists the student of public opinion will be eager to know if some other factor can be unearthed which displays a high index of agreement.

A Single Determinant Study

The possibilities of research along the lines mentioned is suggested by a little study which the author made to determine, if possible, the role of section, particularly the South, on the formation of opinion on national issues in the United States. About fifty questions on national issues asked by the American Institute of Public Opinion were used—questions for which sectional breakdowns were available, and questions dealing with a variety of issues and problems. The accompanying table lists the question topics and the indices of agreement for each question by geographical sections. The highest degrees of agreement for each question are in bold face.

The study, although incomplete and unsatisfactory in many respects, does call attention to some noteworthy facts. It shows that there are comparatively few issues on which sectional opinion is atypical, that is on which the degree of agreement is greatly out of line with all the other sections of the country. In only six instances was the degree of agreement in the South so atypical as to suggest a peculiarly southern slant: agricultural resettlement, fingerprinting, press treatment of labor, mercy deaths, medical care, and women as teachers. The study shows how varied are the degrees of agreement on different questions. It also indicates how difficult it would be to discover a general, common pattern of sectional influence. The influence of determinants varies markedly from question to question.

GEOGRAPHICAL SECTIONS AS OPINION DETERMINANTS
(Indices of agreement by geographical sections on selected issues)

ISSUE	NORTH-EAST	MIDDLE ATLANTIC	EAST CENTRAL	WEST CENTRAL	SOUTH	ROCKY MOUNTAIN	PACIFIC
Agriculture							
Resettlement	36	38	36	38	**48**	40	42
Americana							
Daylight Saving	**46**	44	6	8	4	10	26
Thanksgiving Date	50	30	42	54	54	**60**	34
Business							
Big vs. Small	10	**32**	10	18	10	0	8
Civil Liberties							
Academic Freedom	**18**	2	0	2	16	10	8
Fingerprinting	62	58	68	72	**82**	74	?
Voting by Reliefers	60	58	64	60	30	**70**	70
Communications							
Press treatment of labor	28	16	6	22	**38**	24	10
Education							
Value of College	62	52	66	**68**	52	30	66
Family							
Birth Control	42	40	44	40	36	48	**52**
Divorce	68	29	70	**76**	60	64	60
Sterilization	50	60	76	66	68	**84**	84
Government							
Constitution-amending							
process	14	10	16	**22**	4	14	4
Unicameral legislature	30	**32**	29	4	8	16	4
Civil Service	42	28	44	34	38	50	**52**
Federal Employee							
Unions	44	38	50	56	56	**58**	42
Sales Tax	**66**	**66**	56	42	64	64	60
Government and Business							
Chain Stores	34	**40**	**40**	**40**	**40**	30	22
Government Ownership							
Coal Mines	24	32	40	52	49	**54**	38
Munitions Industry	**54**	38	50	22	16	38	38
Electric Power	42	32	20	24	42	40	**60**
Railroads	12	28	30	**48**	37	36	40
Regulate Big Business	34	**44**	40	24	38	32	38
Regulate Insurance	**18**	2	14	14	14	0	**18**
Health							
Medical Care	14	6	10	22	**40**	8	24
Mercy Death	8	2	4	6	**38**	22	?
Isms							
Dictatorships	**36**	16	2	24	**36**	**36**	28
Labor							
Regulation of Wages	22	26	8	18	10	**28**	4
Morals							
Gambling	4	**32**	4	8	10	4	26
Prohibition	**52**	30	30	22	6	36	?
Women							
Wives working	54	58	**62**	60	42	58	58
Women as Teachers	14	0	6	20	**48**	6	?

On comparatively few issues does there appear a markedly high degree of agreement in any section, which would seem to indicate that the sectional factor was not a pronounced influence in a large majority of the cases on the questions asked.

A Multiple Determinant Study: The Stoddard Study

At the suggestion of the author, William G. Stoddard undertook a much more extensive study of opinion determinants than the one cited above.[31] Whereas the latter took into account only the sectional breakdowns and was limited to approximately 50 questions, Stoddard examined the results on 250 questions and used four breakdowns: sex, political affiliation, age, and economic status. His primary objective was to determine the relative influence of these four factors for different types of questions. To do this he followed a procedure similar to the one previously explained. He classified the 250 questions into eight broad, general categories and a number of subcategories. For each question the degree of agreement was ascertained within each of the subgroups of the four breakdowns, so that he was able to give the index of agreement on each issue for the following groups:

> Sex
> Men
> Women
>
> Political Affiliation
> Government
> Opposition
>
> Age
> 21-29
> 30-49
> over 50
>
> Economic Status
> High
> Middle
> Low

The 250 questions studied were those asked by the British Institute of Public Opinion during the years 1939-46. Mr. Stoddard was obliged to use this British data because he was unable to obtain breakdown results for a sufficient number of questions asked in the United States. Since he was not interested in specific answers to questions, nor in any special public, but only in the relative influence of certain determinants for different types of questions, British opinion data was quite as acceptable as any other. Perhaps the most serious limitation to the study was the small number of factors available for study: sex, political affiliation, age, and economic status. At best his conclusions could deal only with the relative influence of these four, and it is reasonable to suppose that on many issues other factors might have been of equal if not greater significance. However, a very high index of agreement for any of these four factors would be very indicative. It should be remembered that a uniformly low degree of agreement for all factors suggests that none of them are significant so far as the particular question is concerned. A uniformly high degree of agreement raises the question whether the factors are important or not. Where the high degree of agreement is uniform it is possible that some other factor or factors are primarily responsible for the result. Variations in degrees of agreement from factor to factor suggest, however, relative degrees of influence. (See the accompanying classification of questions used in the study.)

CLASSIFICATION OF 250 QUESTIONS ASKED BY THE
BRITISH INSTITUTE OF PUBLIC OPINION, 1939-46

1. Rationing
    a) Food
    b) Fuel
    c) Clothing
    d) Black Market
2. Political Leaders
    a) British
    b) Enemy (World War II)
3. Wages
    a) General regulation
    b) Specific question
4. Socialism and Social Welfare
    a) General Socialization of Industry
    b) Socialized Medicine
    c) Social Security
5. Domestic Issues
    a) Taxes
    b) Employment After the War
    c) Parliamentary Elections
    d) Military Preparedness in Peacetime
    e) Political Party Issues
    f) Communism
    g) Reconstruction and Private Industry
6. Domestic War Issues
    a) War Regulation and Restrictions
    b) War Effort
    c) Use of Man Power
       (1) Conscription
       (2) Armed Forces
       (3) Demobilization

7. Foreign War Issues
   a) War Aims
   b) Military Operations
      (1) Europe
      (2) Far East
   c) Allied Cooperation
   d) Collaboration with Pro-Axis Neutral or Former Pro-Axis Individual
8. Foreign Affairs
   a) The British Empire
      (1) India
      (2) Egypt
   b) Allied Cooperation After the War
      (1) General
      (2) United Nations
   c) Peace Conditions
   d) War Crimes Trials
   e) British Attitude Toward Various Foreign Countries
      (1) France
      (2) Russia
      (3) Poland
      (4) Spain
      (5) Enemy Countries
      (6) Ireland

As indicated previously, the study suffered from certain shortcomings and cannot be accepted as altogether conclusive. There may be some objections to the way in which the questions were classified for purposes of analysis. Possibly different groupings would have been more significant. On quite a large number of questions there was no data available for making the political affiliation breakdown; this was an important lack since this factor frequently appeared as the most important when data regarding it was at hand. Furthermore, in a number of the subcategories there were so few questions (only one or two) that valid conclusions regarding the category were impossible. This was the case with:

Rationing
    Fuel (1b)
    Clothing (1c)
    Black Market (1d)
Political Leaders
    Enemy (2b)
Foreign War Issues
    Military Operations
        Far East [7b(2)]
    Collaboration (7d)

Foreign Affairs
    The British Empire
        Egypt [8a(2)]
    War Crimes Trials

In the first place the study shows very clearly that the relative influence of such factors as economic status, political affiliation, age, and sex varies from question to question. It emphasizes the necessity of guarding against hasty generalizations regarding the opinion-forming process in general. The process is highly individualized, and until we know more than we do about the formation of opinion on specific questions, it will be hazardous to posit general conclusions. It would seem, however, that on questions of the type included in the 250 studied, the economic factor is the most important of the four in the majority of cases. However, this conclusion must be somewhat tentative since there are so relatively few questions, for which there are also breakdown data for the Political Affiliation factor. It is interesting to note in this connection how frequently a very high degree of agreement appears in the upper income bracket.

Next to the income factor comes the age factor. The questions with the highest degrees of agreement here had to do with Socialized Medicine (4b), Employment After the War (5b), and Reconstruction and Private Industry (5g). In only one category of questions did the sex factor appear to be relatively the most important—issues concerning Demobilization [6c(3)]. In only one group of questions was Political Affiliation the prime determinant, namely, British Leaders (2a), and even here the economic factor was quite as important. As mentioned earlier, on many questions, data on political affiliation were not available.

In the case of seven of the subcategories the divisions of opinion were so similar in all the breakdowns that it seemed reasonable to assume that the four factors were about equally significant; or one factor would be the most important on some questions, another factor on other questions. No conclusive answer can be given regarding the relative influence of the factors on questions dealing with Specific Wage Matters (3b), Parliamentary Elections (5c), Communism (5f), War Regulation and Restriction (6a), War Effort (6b), Armed Forces [6c(2)], General Allied Cooperation After the War [8b(1)].

The degrees of agreement for the country as a whole on all 250 questions asked is interesting. If anything from a 50-50 to a 60-40 split of opinion can be considered a decided difference of opinion then we find that on approximately one-third of the questions asked there was this "decided difference of opinion." If we take 75-25 and upwards as indication of a high degree of agreement, then we find this high degree of agreement on from one-fifth to one-fourth of the questions. Interestingly enough the question "Do you think Hitler, Himmler, and Goering should be pun-ished?" produced an index of agreement of 90 which indicated that only 5 per cent of the British people opposed such punishment in 1944 when the question was asked. The accompanying table indicates the distribution of the different degrees of agreement from the 250 questions.

INDICES OF AGREEMENT	NUMBER OF QUESTIONS
0-9	35
10-19	46
20-29	42
30-39	39
40-49	32
50-59	24
60-69	17
70-79	8
80-89	5
90-99	2
	250

This table may be used as reasonable assurance that the people of a country do not necessarily exhibit great unanimity of opinion. It is some-times said that democracy cannot function satisfactorily in an environment where there are fundamental differences of opinion, where the minority is not willing from conviction to acquiesce in the opinions of the majority. Without going into the question as to how many of the above 250 questions are fundamental, it is important to note that the questions selected by the British Institute of Public Opinion for submission to the people of England were not selected with a view to finding out what the questions were on which the British people were generally agreed. The picture one obtains from these 250 questions is probably not a fair picture of the extent of agreement at all. It is conceivable that the questions were selected because they were under discussion, because there were differences of opinion on them, and therefore because they were newsworthy. If that were the case, then the results would overemphasize the extent of disagreement on matters of general public policy. For the student of public opinion and public pol-icy the question arises of the effect upon public opinion of focusing atten-tion upon those issues which are the center of controversy. How is it going to be possible to give the people some idea of the bases of psychological unity which undoubtedly exist in every nation? Perhaps this is not the function of the polls, but it is as important to appreciate the arena of agree-ment as well as that of conflict.

An examination of the degree of agreement within the various categories and subcategories also shows a preponderance of questions on which there are relatively sharp divisions of opinion. There are no questions on which all men and all women, or all of those in separate income, political, and age categories think alike. That would be too much to expect. But there are surprisingly few questions on which there is even a marked tendency toward agreement. This fact would suggest that for a great many questions the four factors employed for setting up the sample are really not very significant as opinion determinants. This is perhaps one of the most important results or conclusions of Mr. Stoddard's study. In some cases the importance of the factor is clearly indicated. But in other cases what are the important factors? If there is a 50-50 division of opinion down the line through the various breakdowns then the student is presented with a real challenge. What factor or factors really do determine thinking on these questions?

As the nation-wide polls supply more and more breakdowns of their opinion data, it will be possible to answer much more completely than at present a great many questions concerning patterns of public opinion. On what types of questions, if any, do women tend to think alike? Some studies, as for example Dr. Lazarsfeld's surveys of Erie County, Ohio, would seem to indicate that on political questions, at least, women tend to follow the lead of their husbands or other male members of their families. Some students of the subject claim that the advent of woman suffrage increased the quantity of voters without changing to any marked extent the outcome of elections. Breakdowns of polling data should give more detailed and reliable answers to the question. Likewise with age, income, residence, and other factors it should now be possible to speak convincingly of the pattern of ideas of numerous groups. Of course it is important to distinguish causation and relationship in this connection. A close relationship between two factors does not necessarily mean that the relationship is a causal one.

It is not at all unlikely that further analyses will show that the organized groups to which a person belongs furnish the key to his opinions on many types of questions. On some questions the church to which a person belongs may be the proximate determinant; on others his trade union; on still others his fraternity, lodge, or political party. It would be interesting to find out what degree of agreement is obtained when opinion data is broken down by the media to which one adheres, such as the newspaper or newspapers the respondent reads, the radio and television stations he customarily attends to, the occupational or professional journal he reads. It is to be hoped that survey agencies will find the means for obtaining more data than is available at present for just such breakdowns. In view of the fact that such a large number of the breakdowns now employed do not yield high degrees of agreement, it is reasonable to suppose that for a great many questions the really important factors are missing. Only by trying out new factors and by incessant experimentation, will it be possible to enlarge the scope of our understanding of the question of what influences and forms public opinion.

As indicated above, one way to test hypotheses regarding the opinion-forming process is to classify opinion data by various factors and note the relative degrees of agreement obtained from the several breakdowns. This is about the only method available for ascertaining the influence of age, sex, race, and other factors which are incapable of human manipulation. It is obviously impossible to change the age of a person to measure the effects of the change upon his attitudes and opinions. The next best thing is to classify people by age groups and to note the difference of opinion, if any, from group to group.

There are, however, a number of potential factors or determinants that can be humanly manipulated, and are, therefore, susceptible to use in a controlled experiment. Advertisements, editorials, news, events, music, broadcasts, and various symbols and representations can be manufactured and controlled. Hence, attempts have been made to measure the specific influence of such factors on public opinion. Professor Gosnell essayed an early experiment of this kind to ascertain the effect of a non-partisan mail canvass to "get out the vote" in selected districts in Chicago.[32] His sample included voters living in twelve districts which were composed of populations typical—in economic and racial characteristics—of the city as a whole. The sample was then split in two in such a way that the two groups would not differ fundamentally in regard to age, income, race, and so on. One group was subjected to a barrage of non-partisan appeals through the mails. The other was not. Since the two groups were presumably similar in all other respects, except that one was subjected to the mail canvass, the difference in voting behavior of the two groups was presumed to be a measure of this mail appeal. This method measures the effects on public opinion of advertisements, speeches, and various means and devices used to mold public opinion. The success of the experiment depends upon the success attained in eliminating the influence of all factors except the one to be tested, upon the representative nature of the samples used, and upon the actual similarity between experimental and controlled groups. However, it is an expensive and cumbersome procedure at best, and especially when employed to study effects on mass opinion.

Multiple Factor Analysis

A recent device for determining the relative influence of factors in the opinion-forming process is the statistical technique of partial correlations, which has been simplified and called the method of multiple-factor analysis. By means of available statistical data it seeks the same result obtained by the controlled experiment method. It undertakes to hold constant, simply by neutralizing their effect statistically, important factors in the process of forming opinion, and to determine the effect of one of these factors. Professor Gosnell applied this technique to a study of the influence of the press on public opinion.[33] He stated his problem as follows: "There are many difficulties confronting any attempt to estimate the role of the press in the democratic process. Are the newspapers molders or followers of public opinion? How can the incidence of the policies of the press be separated from the many other complex variables which are woven together in a complicated pattern?"

Without attempting to explain the statistical techniques used, the procedure may be summarized as follows: Information on the circulation of four leading daily newspapers was obtained for 47 selected areas in the city of Chicago. For these areas the votes received by nine candidates at primary or general elections during a given period were obtained and expressed as percentages of the total vote cast. The attitude of the newspapers toward these candidates was determined by estimating the number of column inches in each devoted to editorial and cartoon endorsements of a given candidate. Eight other variables were then selected, each of which was assumed to have some relation to the election results. A master table expressing these 21 variables in percentage form was then prepared for the 47 areas. Product-moment coefficients of correlation were then calculated for all possible combinations of the 21 variables and presented in symmetrical form, providing what is commonly known as a correlation matrix. The question was: Did these intercorrelations show patterns of behavior which could be interpreted in the light of the newspaper recommendations?

Factorial methods assume that there are primary tendencies which are to be estimated in terms of the variables given. The aim of factor analysis is to ascertain how many general and independent factors must be postulated to account for a whole table of intercorrelations. It seeks to reduce a complicated set of relationships to a relatively small number of factors. In the problem at hand it was discovered that the 210 intercorrelations could be satisfactorily explained in terms of four general factors.

These illustrations of current activities in the field of public opinion research call attention to the complexity of the problem of analyzing the process of public opinion change. It is not enough to list and classify the numerous factors involved. We need to know more precisely what their specific and relative influence is.

NOTES FOR CHAPTER 6

Epigraph. Peter Odegard, *The American Public Mind,* p. 1.
1. Allport, Gordon W., "The Genesis of Attitudes," in *A Handbook of Social Psychology,* ed. Carl Murchison (Worcester, Mass.: Clark University Press, 1935), pp. 798-844.
2. Katz, Daniel, "The Functional Approach to the Study of Attitudes," *Public Opinion Quarterly,* Vol. 24, pp. 163-204.
3. *Public Opinion Quarterly,* Vol. 25, pp. 57-78.
4. *Ibid.,* 26:201-11.
5. *Ibid.,* 24:419-35.
6. *Ibid.,* 15:623.
7. *Ibid.,* 23:247-54.
8. *Ibid.,* 22:489-502.
9. *Ibid.,* 20:529.
10. *Ibid.,* 17:134.
11. Lumley, F. E., *Means of Social Control.* New York: The Century Co., 1925.
12. New York: The Macmillan Co., 1952.
13. *Public Opinion Quarterly,* Vol. 26, pp. 35-46.
14. *Ibid.,* 26:531-46.
15. *Ibid.,* 19:337-52.
16. *Ibid.,* 15:487-518.
17. *Ibid.,* 25:382-92.
18. Lazarsfeld, Paul F., Berelson, Bernard, and Hazel Gaudet, *The People's Choice: How the Voter Makes Up His Mind in a Presidential Campaign* (2nd ed.; New York: Columbia University Press, 1948).
19. *Public Opinion Quarterly,* Vol. 26, p. 226.
20. *Ibid.,* 26:265-72.
21. *Ibid.,* 23:515-28.
22. *Ibid.,* 17:20-46.
23. *Ibid.,* 17:171-84.
24. *Ibid.,* 16:331-54.
25. *Ibid.,* 9:456-66.
26. *Ibid.,* 19:53-67.
27. *Ibid.,* 17:375-85.
28. *Ibid.,* 22:91-106.
29. "Public Opinion and the Primary Group," *American Sociological Review,* Vol. 25 (April, 1960), pp. 208-19.
30. "Opinion Trends in World War II: Some Guides to Interpretation," *Public Opinion Quarterly,* Vol. 12 (Spring, 1948), pp. 30-44.
31. "Breakdown Factors of Public Opinion Polls," manuscript prepared by the author for graduate seminar in Public Opinion, Princeton University, Department of Politics, 1950.
32. Gosnell, H. F., *Getting Out the Vote: An Experiment in the Stimulation of Voting* (Chicago: University of Chicago Press, 1927).
33. Gosnell, H. F., and Margaret J. Schmidt, "Relation of the Press to Voting in Chicago," *Journalism Quarterly,* Vol. 13 (June, 1936), pp. 129-47.

SUPPLEMENTARY READING

ALBIG, WILLIAM, HARTLEY, E. L., FISHER, B. R., HYMAN, HERBERT, LEISERSON, AVERY, and ALPERT, HARRY. "Processes of Opinion Formation: A Symposium," *Public Opinion Quarterly*, Vol. 14 (Winter, 1950-51), pp. 667-86.

ALLPORT, G. W. "Attitudes," in *A Handbook of Social Psychology*. Edited by Carl Murchison. Worcester, Mass.: Clark University Press, 1935. (Chapter 17.)

BAUR, E. JACKSON. "Public Opinion and The Primary Group," *American Sociological Review*, Vol. 25 (April, 1960), pp. 208-19.

BERELSON, BERNARD (ed.). *The Behavioral Sciences Today*. New York: Basic Books, 1963.

BERELSON, BERNARD, and STEINER, GARY A. *Human Behavior: An Inventory of Scientific Findings*. New York: Harcourt, Brace, and World, 1964.

BOGARDUS, EMORY STEPHEN. *The Making of Public Opinion*. New York: Association Press, 1951.

BURDICK, EUGENE, and BRODBECK, A. J. *American Voting Behavior*. Chicago: The Free Press of Glencoe, Ill., 1959.

CAMPBELL, ANGUS, GURIN, G., and MILLER, W. E. *The Voter Decides*. Evanston, Illinois: Row, Peterson, 1954.

CAMPBELL, ANGUS, *et al. The American Voter*. New York: John Wiley and Sons, 1960.

CANTRIL, HADLEY. "Opinion Trends in World War II: Some Guides to Interpretation," *Public Opinion Quarterly*, Vol. 12 (Spring, 1948), pp. 30-44.

DEWEY, RICHARD, and HUMBER, W. J. *The Development of Human Behavior*. New York: The Macmillan Co., 1951.

EYSENCK, HANS JURGEN. *The Psychology of Politics*. New York: Frederick A. Praeger, 1955.

HALL, C. S., and LINDZEY, G. *Theories of Personality*. New York: John Wiley and Sons, 1957.

HOVLAND, C. J. *Communication and Persuasion*. New Haven: Yale University Press, 1953.

HYMAN, HERBERT. "Reflections on Reference Groups," *Public Opinion Quarterly*, Vol. 24 (Fall, 1960), pp. 383-96.

IRION, FREDERICK C. *Public Opinion and Propaganda*. New York: Thomas Y. Crowell, 1950.

JACOB, PHILIP E. *Changing Values in College: An Exploratory Study of the Impact of General Education in Social Sciences on the Values of American Students*. New Haven, Conn.: The Edward W. Hazen Foundation, 1957.

JANIS, IRVING L., and HOVLAND, C. I. *Personality and Persuasibility*. New Haven, Conn.: Yale University Press, 1959.

KATZ, DANIEL. "The Functional Approach to the Study of Attitudes," *Public Opinion Quarterly*, Vol. 24 (Summer, 1960), pp. 163-204.

KATZ, ELIHU, and LAZARSFELD, PAUL. *Personal Influence*. Chicago: The Free Press of Glencoe, Ill., 1955.

KATZ, DANIEL (ed.). "Attitude Change," *Public Opinion Quarterly*, Vol. 24 (Summer, 1960). Special issue devoted to the subject.

LAZARSFELD, PAUL F., BERELSON, BERNARD, and GAUDET, HAZEL. *The People's Choice: How the Voter Makes Up His Mind in a Presidential Campaign*. 2nd ed. New York: Columbia University Press, 1948.

LIPSET, S. M. *Political Man: The Social Basis of Politics.* Garden City, N.Y.: Doubleday & Co., 1960

MACDOUGALL, C. D. *Understanding Public Opinion.* New York: The Macmillan Co., 1952.

ROSENBERG, M. J., HOVLAND, C. I., MCGUIRE, W. J., ABELSON, R. P., BREHM, J. W. *Attitude Organization and Change: An Analysis of Consistency Among Attitude Components.* New Haven, Conn.: Yale University Press, 1960.

SMITH, M. BREWSTER, BRUNER, JEROME S., and WHITE, ROBERT W. *Opinions and Personality.* New York: John Wiley & Sons, 1956.

VII · Influence of Family, Church, and School

The major institutions forming public opinion are the family, churches, and schools. . . . So familiar are we with our forms of family organization, religion, and education that the very familiarity may have blinded us to their significance.

—FREDERICK C. IRION

OF THE ENVIRONMENTAL factors which contribute to the formation of public opinion the influence of family, church, and school is decided. The role of each of these basic institutions in the opinion-forming process is forever changing, and it is by no means clear what their relative influence is. It is useful to consider some of these changes and to speculate regarding their impact on personality, attitude and opinion.

THE FAMILY

Many writers have emphasized the importance of the family as a molder of attitudes and opinions. One writer says,[1] "Out of the vast amount of scientific data of recent years, two facts stand out in clear relief: One is that the foundations of human personality are laid in early childhood; the second, that the chief molder of personality thus becomes the family." He goes on to say, "It is in the unit of interacting personalities that the child learns to live, in which his personality first takes form, and in which this personality continues for a number of years to be confirmed and enriched." Another writer states,[2] "From birth to grave there is scarcely any great action of consequence that can be performed by a person, even in our free society, that is not guided and colored by family relations." And still another student writes:[3] "Fundamental attitudes toward love, mother, individualism, conformity, social status, competition, and goals, doubtless

138

find their origin in the family." There are innumerable studies of family influence which support these claims: studies of voting behavior which show the extent to which families vote as a unit, studies which show the close religious ties of families, and studies which show the role of the family in influencing educational and occupational choices of children, their motivations, habits, and attitudes.[4]

There are said to be approximately 60,000,000 families in the United States, varying greatly in numerical size, degree of interrelationship, activities, living and working conditions, and in many other respects. Starting with a minimum size of two (mother and child, husband and wife and so on) the number of family members living together in one household may increase to include many children, grandparents, aunts, uncles, and cousins. The tendency today is for the family living in a single household to become more compact and more closely related. The average family, according to the United States Census Bureau, has about five members. Although the influence of the family on its members is really the influence of each member on every other member, one usually thinks of family influence as the influence of parents on children.

Changes in the Modern American Family

Many changes are taking place in the American family; some certainly have an important effect on children's attitudes. The physical environment of the family has changed, and is changing with the increasing urbanization of American society as well as changes in the type of house, its location and number of rooms. Also significant have been the changes in home furnishings, the increased use of electrical equipment, better lighting and refrigeration, more reading materials, radio and TV, automobiles and other facilities for transportation. In an increasing number of homes laborious housework has given way to electrically aided pickups and cleanups, pre-processed meals as well as food—all of which has resulted in greater mobility for all members of the family.[5]

The functions of the average household have also changed, with a consequent effect on family attitudes. As an economic unit more of its members are engaged in gainful employment—not only the husband, but often the wife and some of the older children. The total family income has, on the average, increased noticeably in recent years. There has also been an increase in home ownership. The family as an educator and religious guide has lost some of its influence. A larger number of children are sent to pre-schools at earlier ages. The older members of the family, many of whom are gainfully employed, have less time to give younger members of the family. The schools not only take children at an earlier age, but they train and supervise them for longer periods during the day and for more days and even years. The expansion of extracurricular activities to social clubs, in sports, as well as in workshops and after hours in classrooms, has been considerable. It is probable that the parents play an even smaller role than formerly in religious education. The modernization and liberalization of church programs, the virtual abandonment of religious instruction in homes, all point to an increasing dependence on church schools for whatever religious teaching is received. It is difficult to estimate, in this connection, the educational, and possibly the religious effect of radio and TV, though some attention will be given to this in a later chapter.

The family has also been changing in other ways. People tend to marry earlier than they did fifty or more years ago and to have a moderate rather than a large number of children. The number of marriages that end in divorce is increasing, not only absolutely, but in proportion to the population.[6] This may be due to the fact that divorce has, in many cases, taken the place of desertion or informal separation. Divorcees remarry more frequently than before. Over two-thirds of the population over 14 years of age are married. By 1950 about two out of every three (661 out of 1000) marriages ended in divorce. The influence of divorce and a broken family is very great on the attitudes and opinions of children in such homes. Not infrequently it amounts to a traumatic and devastating experience.

Finally, some mention should be made of changes taking place in the composition of the family. In most sections of the country, the family is thought of as the immediate blood group, and does not include the broader, more inclusive kinship relationships. The child moves more closely and more frequently with a clique, a peer group, rather than his own clan. All members of the family, including the children, have greater freedom. Family decisions are more prompt and positive. There is a marked tendency for parents to compare the attainment of their children horizontally with those of other children of comparable age. This often leads to an emphasis by the child on conformity, to a tremendous drive for achievement, and to a basic feeling of insecurity. Many students of the family detect a growing gap between the parents and the children in ideas, occupations, outlooks, and standards.

Is the parental influence on children's attitudes and opinions increasing or decreasing? The answer is not clear. Some trends enhance their influence, although these trends are by no means universal and may not be predominant. Most families continue to be economically interdependent. Children, to the age of adulthood and even beyond, look to their parents for necessities, for schooling, and even for aid in getting started in business or in raising a family. As the costs for all these items increase, there is undoubtedly a growing interdependence in thought and attitudes as well as in dollars and cents.

In many homes the prestige of parents remains high, although it may well be that for the majority of homes, parental prestige is declining more rapidly than previously. Modern urban living, with its many diversions, almost unlimited transportation, and ample outside-the-home attractions, leaves little time for the family as a whole to be together and for parent-child relations to intensify. Nevertheless, to the extent that these relations are kept close and the amount of time spent together expanded, the influence of parents on children will increase. On the other hand, many factors definitely lessen the influence of parents: notably the multiplication of outside, diverting influences, such as recreational facilities, school activities, stronger emotional ties to peer groups, weakened parental authority, family mobility, family instability, and the employment of women, particularly mothers, outside the home.[7]

Parental Influence on Attitudes and Opinions

How does the family influence the attitudes and opinions of its members? It is in the family that the small child usually receives his first impressions, forms his early habits, develops early prejudices, likes and dislikes, desires, wishes, goals. Moreover, the parents and family have virtually a monopolistic control over the stimuli affecting the child, especially during the early years. It is during this period that the intimacy of family life intensifies the importance of imitation, repetition, and suggestion. Habits of eating, sleeping, playing develop early, and the experiences multiply and cast attitudinal forms. It is during these early days that the child discovers the nature of authority, at least the kind of authority which prevails in the household. It is in the home that experiences and influences have their emotional colorings, and some of them may be intensely traumatic. Although the family is not the teacher of years past, it still plays an important role in the development of skills, motivations, emotions, aspirations. It influences directly or indirectly the selection of childhood companions, the schools attended, and attitudes toward an infinite variety of subjects. It is in a real sense a giver of status, and a major agent for the transmission of culture, for the development of general and central attitudes as well as many specific opinions. It may not be altogether true that a person's way of life, his basic outlook and attitudes, become fixed during the first five years of life, but the shaping process has indeed gone far by that time.

In what areas is the influence of the family, especially of the parents, most pronounced? Many studies have shown that failures of the home and family life are the major cause of juvenile delinquency. In one of the most comprehensive studies of the causes of juvenile delinquency ever made Professor Sheldon Glueck and Dr. Eleanor T. Glueck of the Harvard Law School found that if the child's family life was adequate, the chances were only 3 in 100 that he would turn out to be a delinquent, whereas if his family situation was poor the chances were 98 out of 100. Lax, overstrict or erratic discipline, a mother's neglect, parental rejection, and a home which was "just a place to hang your hat" were among the important factors present among delinquent boys. They concluded that the kind of relationships that existed in a home between the boy and his parents had far more to do with his delinquency than whether he lived in a slum area, or grew up among conflicting cultures, or came from a large family, or from a family where there was much ill health, or whether he had a high or a low I.Q.[8] It is quite clear that family life has a profound influence on the character, morals, motivations, and ideals of children.

Family life also affects markedly the child's attitude toward religion. From 65 per cent to 85 per cent of the young people cling to their parents' religion. This religious solidarity of the family is matched by its political uniformity. Charles Merriam and others have found that similar percentages of young people follow the partisan affiliations of their parents. Other important areas of parental influence are: economic, since parents' example and admonition frequently guide, if they do not direct, the child's occupational choices; educational, because a child's educational career is largely directed by parents, or at least conditioned by them; and the personal habits which become fixed in early life. Attitudes toward men and women, toward marriage, toward the nature and requisites of success, toward authority, toward other races, all become well-established in the home. Writers have detailed the scope and nature of this influence in many ways. F. C. Irion finds that a number of basic traits are formed in the home: good nature and toughness, views regarding romantic love, the idealization of motherhood, conformity, the need always to keep going, egocentrism, the notion of social levels, prejudice and intolerance, the nature of success, the importance of fashion and of machinery.[9]

It is by no means easy, if at all possible, to isolate the family, or the parents, and to trace their influence and effect on the minds and attitudes of children. Besides the family there are the schools, the mass media, peer groups and many other salient variables. There is need for much more information than we now have on what parents tell children, what parents are told to tell children, and what the effects are. As guides to children's attitudes and opinions, parental behavior and environmental circumstances are important. In fact, these circumstances, and especially the behavior of the parents, are decisive and significant, and they may often deviate from or conflict with their spoken words.

How may one obtain this information? There are songs and lullabies, children's books, "readers," comics. There are training guides in which parents are taught what to say and do. What of trends in religious instruction, ethics, sex? What of the attitudes toward parents and other members of the family, toward work and play? To realize the nature and extent of parental influence, one must also note children's personal habits—eating, sleeping, cleanliness, their relations with others, their basic values.

THE CHURCH

Membership

The *Yearbook of American Churches for 1963* reports a total church membership in the United States of 116,109,929 distributed among 258 religious bodies. This is approximately 63.4 per cent of the estimated population of the country. Of this church membership 64,416,233 are Protestants and 42,876,665 Catholics. Close to five and one-half millions are Jews, and about two and three-quarter millions belong to the Eastern Orthodox Church. Slightly over ninety per cent of all Protestants are in twenty-two major "families" of which the following are the largest:

1. Baptist bodies	22,028,365
2. Methodist bodies	12,769,065
3. Lutheran bodies	8,549,906
4. Presbyterian bodies	4,320,686
5. Protestant Episcopal Church	3,344,523
6. Churches of Christ	2,185,127
7. United Church of Christ	2,015,770
8. Disciples of Christ	1,797,466
9. Latter Day Saints	1,751,445
	58,762,353

Reports from 227 church bodies showed a total Sunday or Sabbath School enrollment of 44,434,291 persons in 286,661 schools. Since 1900, the percentage of the population who are church members has risen almost steadily, from 36 to its present 63.4 per cent. Since 1926 the proportion of Protestant members has grown from 27 to 37 per cent, and for Catholics from 16 to 26 per cent.

Communication

There are many channels through which church leaders communicate with their members and with outsiders. In addition to formal worship services on Sundays and Sabbaths, members meet in large or small groups during the week. Most of the religious bodies hold conferences or conventions during the year. Practically all of them issue magazines and other types of printed material. Noteworthy among the religious periodicals of the country are the *Christian Century, Christian Herald, Christian Advocate, Presbyterian Life, America, Catholic Age, Catholic Action, Catholic World, Commonweal,* and the *Harvard Theological Review.* An increasing number of church leaders use radio and television to communicate with members and outsiders.[10]

Organizations

Closely associated with the church bodies themselves are many organizations and associations which supplement, assist, and cooperate with them. Among the more important are: the National Council of the Churches of Christ in the United States of America, established in 1950; the American Jewish Committee dating back to 1906; the National Catholic Welfare Conference originating in 1919; the American Council of Christian Churches (1950); the Education and Publication Board of the Northern Baptist Convention (1944); the National Conference of Christians and Jews (1928); B'nai B'rith (1843); the Young Men's and the Young Women's Christian Association (1844, 1855). These groups provide opinion leadership and guidance for their members in many areas, both inside and outside the church bodies themselves.

It is quite difficult to describe, much less sketch, the over-all impact of these many religious bodies on their members, to say little or nothing about the influence on those who are not members. In most cases, the church begins to exert its influence when the child is very young and continues to do so throughout life. In some cases, the church provides the individual with a substantial core of beliefs, attitudes, and opinions regarding God, Christ, the Bible, life after death, salvation, and many other tenets which guide, if they do not control, his views on other, non-religious matters. For others, church membership is nominal, and its influence on attitudes and opinions is incidental.

Doctrines and Beliefs

Practically all Protestant and Catholic religious bodies propagate beliefs in God, Christ, sin, salvation, life after death, the Bible, and the essentials of a Christian life.[11] Some lay greater emphasis on faith and beliefs; others, on works, behavior, and conduct. In some cases, the differences in belief are fundamental; in others, they relate to incidental, even trivial matters. The Roman Catholic Church stresses its alleged pre-eminence as the one true church, its organization, the infallibility of the Pope, the distinctions between clergy and laity, the importance of the seven sacraments, the divinity of Christ, the Virgin Mary, and other aspects such as the Trinity, indulgences, purgatory, and atonement. The Baptists emphasize the importance of baptism by total immersion, favor a closed communion for believers only, and are generally decentralized in their national organization. Methodists lay much stress on method and organization, have a system of probation for new converts, and often stress class meetings, exhorters, local preachers, itinerary, presiding elders, and bishops. Lutherans lay great emphasis on justification by faith alone and adhere to the

Apostles', Nicene, and Athanasian creeds, also the unaltered Augsburg Confession, the Schmalkald Articles, Luther's two catechisms, and the Formula of Concord. In policy they are fundamentally congregational, although they do confer some authority on their Synods.

Presbyterians are Calvinistic in doctrine and emphasize the right of all members to share indirectly in its government through elders, the recognition of only one order in the Christian ministry, the unity of the whole church as expressed in a graded system of church courts composed of ministers and elders. Episcopalians stress the supreme authority of the bishops rather than of the Pope, as stressed by the Roman Catholics.

The smaller churches in the United States differ in many respects. The Church of Jesus Christ of Latter Day Saints, commonly called the Mormon Church, accepts the infinite atonement of Christ and believes that all men may be saved through obedience to the principles and ordinances of the gospel of which the most important are faith in God, specifically in Jesus Christ as Redeemer and Saviour of the race, repentance for sin, baptism by immersion for the remission of sin, and the laying on of hands for the reception of the Holy Ghost. They believe in prophecy, continued revelation, visions, healing, tongues, and all the gifts and powers of the primitive church. Their early practice of plural marriage was banned in 1890.

Adventists preach that the second coming of Christ and the end of the world are near. Assemblies of God stress sanctification, premillennialism, and pacifism. Disciples of Christ, sometimes called "Christians," reject human creeds and sectarian names, hold the Bible alone to be the rule of faith and practice, celebrate the Lord's Supper every Sunday, and baptize by immersion only. The Church of God practices immersion and footwashing. Eastern Orthodox Churches have sacraments, venerate the saints, and revere icons. They reject the supremacy of the Pope and exclude the *filioque* from the creed. Quakers, or "Friends," call special attention to the importance of the "inner Light" and stress simplicity, peace, and friendship. Mennonites stand for Scriptural authority, non-resistance, plainness of dress, rejection of oaths, adult baptism, aloofness from the state, restriction of marriage to the clan, and footwashing. There are numerous other religious or quasi-religious bodies including the Pentecostal Assemblies, Reformed Bodies, Spiritualists, Unitarians, Jehovah's Witnesses, Evangelicals, and Nazarenes.

Principal Trends

What are the principal trends among church bodies in the United States today? Church membership increases steadily, though not quite as fast as does the total population. The Roman Catholics increase in numbers a little more rapidly than Protestants. Notwithstanding the appeals for church unity and the merging of a few denominations from time to time, the absolute number of churches continues to grow. Some religious bodies stress the social gospel more than others, and one may discern a somewhat general liberalization of religious beliefs. There remain, however, a great many smaller groups or sects with firm if deviant ideas. On the whole, the larger church bodies, feeling the impact of education, travel, and the mass media among other influences, lay less and less emphasis on doctrine and creed and more on community services and aid to individual members. Most of the church denominations have schools and seminaries for training their clergy, and an examination of their curricula and faculties will show increasing emphasis on broad, cultural subjects and on the practical, day-to-day tasks of the ministry rather than on pure theological training. There is, of course, a great difference in the training of the clergy from denomination to denomination and from sect to sect. In general one finds that the training is becoming more scholarly, more general, especially in the fields of the social sciences and humanities, and the whole approach is more open-minded and less dogmatic. According to the U. S. Office of Education there were 5,184 bachelor or first professional degrees in theology conferred in 1959-60, and 3,024 in religious education and the Bible.

Creeds and dogmas still have their places in the manuals of worship, and lip service still is paid to them but the severity and impact of their message has been lost for a majority of the younger generation. Efforts to modify the creeds and try to adapt them to the changing times have not been too successful. Worship services and meetings of all kinds continue with many changes. In the Protestant churches at least much stress is placed on the Sunday morning worship service, whereas evening services, either on Sunday or during the week, have been more or less abandoned by some of the larger denominations. More and more attention is being given to religious education, and many churches have tried to revise their Sunday school treatment of religious instruction to bring it into line with the forms, if not the substance, of secular education.[12] Boys and girls, men and women, are organized into a host of circles, clubs, institutes, and fellowships to serve social and educational, as well as religious needs. Around the core of church activities are many specialized study groups, classes, and meetings catering to the varied needs of members. Many churches are highly organized to take care of infants and very young children during worship services, to minister to the sick and needy, to make the lives of elderly people more meaningful, to cooperate with other churches and community undertakings. In fact, as the work of the church expands to meet the desires of various groups and interests, it loses its ideological focus and becomes a great congeries of decentralized and to some extent uncoordinated activities and routines.

AREAS OF CHURCH INFLUENCE

How may one estimate or appraise the influence of the church? This is difficult. With a total membership of nearly two-thirds of the population, with a professional clergy of hundreds of thousands devoting full time to their work, with innumerable worship services and meetings, with one day in seven set aside primarily for them, and with a great many closely affiliated organizations and associations, the churches would seem to be very influential. But any simple conclusion of this nature is ill-considered.

On a great many subjects there is probably considerable agreement among most of the Christian church members: belief in God and Jesus Christ, the inspired nature of the Bible, prayer, and the efficacy of faith. However, the farther one goes in this list of religious teachings, the greater the differences of opinion, the divergences and deviations. Among the various churches there are more or less important differences of opinion regarding baptism, the sacraments, faith-healing, predestination, and especially regarding church organization and authority. One will also discover disagreements regarding the infallibility of the Bible, the role of the Virgin Mary and the Saints, the nature of Sin, Hell, Purgatory, the Trinity, Atonement, Miracles, Transubstantiation, the second coming of Christ, the relative emphasis to be given to faith and works, the eternal life, and many, many others.

Religious, Moral and Ethical Beliefs

The importance of religious beliefs rests, not only on the specific beliefs themselves, but on their by-products, on their influence on so many different facets of daily thinking and behavior. Much emphasis is given to religious differences, and these are extremely important, but so also are the points of agreement—the almost universal belief in God, in a future life, and in the merits of a good life, in prayer, and in faith. These fundamental ideas, when held firmly, color and channel a great many other phases of life.

Closely related to the strictly religious influences of the church, are its moral, ethical and marital views. Most churches subscribe to some code of moral conduct. It may be closely related to the Mosaic stipulations of the Ten Commandments, or it may be far less or much more rigid. Most religions have a place for sin, which is often defined in terms of overt behavior as well as subjective deviance. Although the definition of sin changes and will continue to change, its fundamental content remains fairly stable. Whatever the church's views regarding dancing, card playing, gambling, and drinking, it will always make positive assertions regarding murder, theft, extreme selfishness and pride, intolerance, and many other undesirable or even infamous aspects of human conduct. Moreover, most religions have much to say regarding marriage and the relations between the sexes, and these prescriptions have had far-reaching influences on courtship, marriage, and family life.

Economic Attitudes

The influence of the churches in other areas grows more and more complex, even confused. In the field of economics, writers have argued that the Protestant churches have been ardent supporters of private property, free enterprise, and private capitalism, but there are many complicating factors. In the first place, there has always been a kind of correlation or coincidence between wealth and church affiliation. Frequently, studies have shown that the Protestant Episcopal and Presbyterian churches have a much larger proportion of wealthy members than do the Baptists, Methodists, or Pentecostals.[13] This finding does not indicate which is the cause, and which the effect. In any case this tendency toward economic and social stratification of the churches seems quite well-established. As a consequence church teachings regarding wealth, production, distribution, and consumption, regarding employer-employee relations, regarding profits, interest, capital, and wages will differ from church to church. In some there will be few, if any, specific references to these economic topics; in others, references will be made with more or less tact. The Bible and Christ's teachings provide considerable latitude for interpretation of these matters, with the result that nearly all points of view are represented in the teachings, from outright Christian communism to the most vivid exponents of free, capitalistic enterprise.

Political Attitudes

In politics, too, there is a tendency for the churches to follow their economic and social stratification, although there are certainly many other factors than religion determining political behavior. One of the principal political cleavages of the churches is that between the Roman Catholic and Protestant Churches in the United States. Whether due to ethnic backgrounds, or because of income and social status, there has been a very marked tendency for the Catholics of the eastern and north-central sections of the country to vote Democratic, particularly in the larger cities and metropolitan areas. Paul Lazarsfeld found in his Erie County, Ohio, studies that anywhere from 65 to 80 per cent of the Catholics in that area could be counted on to vote Democratic regularly.

One of the basic issues dividing Catholics and Protestants is that of separation of church and state. The Catholics, as a rule, oppose rigid separation and favor financial and other types of aid to their parochial schools by the states and the Federal government. In Latin America and other countries where Catholics predominate, additional ties between church and state are established which often place the schools in a close and dependent relationship to the church. The same may be true of ecclesiastical salaries, churches themselves, and many other related offices concerned with marriage, divorce, and death.

The Catholic Church in the United States has always played a role in state and local elections. Although many Catholics had won seats in the United States Senate and House of Representatives, as well as several governorships, not until 1960 did a Catholic capture the Presidency. This was the first time that a Roman Catholic had been elected to this office, although Al Smith, a Catholic and the Democratic nominee failed to win the office against the Protestant Herbert C. Hoover in 1928. The victory of John F. Kennedy in 1960 may indicate a marked decline in religious bias since 1928, but it does not signify the disappearance of church influence from politics. In fact, it may heighten political-religious controversies. In State and local politics where political candidates of different religious persuasions have vied with each other for years, such political-religious controversies continue to wax and wane.

Not only the Roman Catholic Church, but many of the larger Protestant denominations take emphatic stands on issues not closely related to religion. The Roman Catholic Church frequently issues manifestoes on educational matters other than governmental financial aid, on birth control, censorship, McCarthyism, relations between employer and employee, civil rights, and relations with foreign countries, especially those in which the Church is strong. The role of the Methodist Churches in the movement for national prohibition is well-known. Its national boards have always been very active in the areas of peace, civil rights, temperance, and industrial relations. This is also true of the Baptist and Presbyterian bodies. The social pronouncements of the General Assemblies of the Presbyterian Church deal with such topics as international relations, the United Nations, disarmament, economic policies, Arab-Israeli issues, refugee resettlement, immigration, freedom and civil liberties, racial and cultural relations, agriculture and rural life, industrial relations, alcohol, juvenile delinquency, gambling, narcotics and the field of education.

Although churches vary greatly in the amount of attention given to secular issues, and also, in the extent to which they manage and direct the thinking of their members, their influence at times can be considerable. One student, referring to Roman Catholic voting habits, says, "The Catholic Church's influence on the political attitudes of Catholics is pervasive and profound. Ranging from birth control, where the Church's influence was direct and most apparent, to the right to work, and civil rights for Negroes, where influence was subtle and derived from certain basic values of the Church, the Catholic Church in each case evidently had a greater impact than Protestant churches on the thinking and thus the political behavior of its members." [14]

Other Attitudes

There are other substantive areas in which churches may exercise much influence, aside from religion, economics, and politics. Attitudes toward science and the scientific method are still influenced by the teachings of some church bodies, and most devout churchgoers maintain some subtle, inescapable feeling of distrust for science. The Catholic Church, especially, vigorously opposes divorce, and in some countries this results in various kinds of subterfuges and devices for escaping the full effect of the bans on divorces. Attitudes toward the use of alcohol and gambling, toward war and Communism, toward faith and healing, toward labor, welfare, sex, and international relations—all may be profoundly affected by church membership.

From time to time Gallup and other nation-wide polling agencies probe the public mind regarding the church and religious questions. Belief in God is almost universal—at least nearly everyone says he believes in a God of some kind. The polls also indicate a general decline in religious bias, particularly during the last twenty-five or thirty years. The great majority of people in the United States, including many Catholics, affirm their belief in the separation of church and state. They also express a desire for greater church unity. They believe that religion is gaining rather than losing importance, but they feel that economic security is as important as religion, if not more so. The American people as a whole lament the secularization of Christmas and Easter, believe in God's incarnation in Christ, believe that true Christianity means belief in God which finds expression in moral obligations. Other opinions and attitudes touched on concern the attitudes of church members toward members of other churches, the extent to which pious people are hypocrites, the relationship between religion and morals, United States guarantees of religious freedom, and the attitudes of young people toward religion.

As stated earlier, it is not easy to isolate the influence of the church from other factors—ethnic, economic, occupational, and social. Reference has already been made to several attempts to do this. The Erie County, Ohio study found that on no economic or social level was the Democratic proportion among Catholics less than 71 per cent, and the more devout the Catholics the larger the Democratic percentage.[15] Studies of the Michigan Survey Research Center showed that Catholics voted two to one for Truman, whereas the Protestant vote was about even. John H. Fenton in his analysis of the Catholic vote found that "the Catholic Church does influence strongly the political behavior of its members." But Peter H. Odegard concluded that "Save on some particular issue at some particular time, in the context of some particular set of circumstances, there is no Catholic, Jewish, Protestant, Negro, etc., minority vote." [16]

HOW THE CHURCH INFLUENCES

Argument

One final aspect of the influence of religion on public opinion needs to be noted, and that is, how it influences. In the first place, it influences by the strategy of argument: by appealing to the authority of Pope, Bible, statements of church leaders, experience, and logic. Sermons, articles, and books seek, by means of the evidence available, by reference to authorities, and by logical reasoning to convince the member and non-member alike.

Persuasion

The church also uses the strategy of persuasion: by appealing to the emotions, to fears, hopes, faith, idealism, and anxieties. Some church bodies make far more extensive use of such appeals than others, Nazarenes and Pentecostals more than Unitarians and Quakers. All rely on such appeals to some extent and to the use of more or less elaborate rituals, processions, pageants, symbols, crucifixes, icons, candles, incense, robes, color, and other forms of religious observance. Curiously enough, some denominations and sects disdainful of emotional appeals through words and music, rely very heavily on rituals and signs.

Organization

A third important strategy by which religious bodies manage opinion is by organization. Here again, they differ greatly in their emphasis, from the Roman Catholic, Eastern Orthodox, Episcopalian, and Presbyterian bodies at one end of the scale, to the loosely organized Quakers, Baptists, Unitarians, and Pentecostals at the other. The Roman Catholic Church has been particularly successful in encompassing the life span of the member from birth to death, through schooling, social life, marriage, children, and occupation. Most churches seek as total an involvement as possible with their members, but few have been as successful as the Roman Catholic Church. Membership, attitudes, and opinions are further cemented by various kinds of stewardship programs, financial obligations and benefits, services of all kinds, membership rituals, and the fostering of social relations. The Roman Catholic, and members of other churches to some extent, begin to look to the Church for satisfactions at an early age, and throughout life build up a powerful hierarchy of relationships, dependencies, obligations, and benefits which are extremely difficult to sever.

Publicity

Finally, there is the strategy of publicity, which seeks to use to the best advantage possible, the pulpit, religious training, personal contacts, meetings, conventions, and conferences of various kinds, and the mass media. No group has been more skilled in the arts and sciences of public relations, propaganda, and publicity than religious organizations. Against formidable obstacles, the early church fathers and martyrs spread the Word; churches were established throughout the western world; and church membership grew. During the Renaissance in Northern Europe, the Protestant Reformation challenged the role of the Roman Catholic Church, until denominations and sects multiplied, and missionaries spread out to the far corners of the earth. Preaching, publications, personal contact, and organizations went hand in hand. In the training of church leaders, special emphasis was placed on opinion leadership. With the advent of modern communication media, many churches provide religious programs for radio and television. The great religious organizations of the earth continue to function as substantial molders of mass opinion in our times.

THE SCHOOL

In the United States in 1961 there were approximately 1,458 senior colleges and about 527 junior colleges. Ninety-four of these colleges had an endowment of $10,000,000 or more; the University of Texas had the largest amount (almost four hundred million dollars), followed by Harvard, Yale, Chicago, Columbia, California, Massachusetts Institute of Technology, Cornell, Stanford, and Northwestern. Enrolled in all higher educational institutions in 1961 were 3,891,000 students. In that same year there were over twenty-four million elementary school pupils, and nearly thirteen million secondary school students, or a total of 37,504,190 being taught by nearly one and one-half million teachers. During the preceding year, 1959-60, nearly 395,000 students received their bachelor or first professional degrees; almost 75,000 their master's degrees; and nearly 10,000 a doctoral (Ph.D., Ed.D., etc.) degree. During the last sixty years there has been a steady, in some cases a phenomenal, increase in school enrollments, average daily attendance, number of teachers, financial outlays. In 1900, the number of students enrolled was five-sevenths of the population five to seventeen years of age; today it is six-sevenths. During this period, the average daily attendance has tripled, as has the number of teachers, and the total expenditures for public schools has shown a phenomenal increase of almost 72 times its 1900 point.[17]

GROWTH TABLE OF PUBLIC EDUCATION IN THE
TWENTIETH CENTURY IN THE UNITED STATES[a]

	1900	1960
Population 5 to 17 years	21,404,322	43,927,801
Pupils enrolled	15,503,110	36,146,846
Average daily attendance	10,632,772	32,468,772
Teachers	423,062	1,369,800
Total expenditures	$214,964,618	$15,643,519,000

[a] *The World Almanac*, 1963, p. 542.

Changes in the Modern School System

CURRICULA. The foregoing discussion is sufficient to point up the scope of educational activity in the United States, but it fails to take into account the many changes that have taken place in the total educational picture: the changes in curricula, in teacher training, in methods of instruction, in equipment, and in problems of finance, relations with the government, segregation, and many others.[18] It is hazardous and probably misleading to attempt generalizations in these areas, but a few observations may be of use. The number of subjects taught has increased greatly at all levels. In fact, the variety and specialized nature of many courses have invoked complaints that more basic areas are being neglected or avoided altogether.[19] The curricula today reflect more than ever the schools' goal of satisfying the community's need for education and the training of the masses, not merely the training of a select few.

Teaching Aids

The manner of teaching has also changed with the availability of many new teaching aids which supplement the traditional text and blackboards. Various experiments in classroom teaching are in progress—experiments in group learning, the use of educational television programs and classes, field projects, various kinds of informal procedures, use of games, and many different kinds of texts, manuals, and visual equipment. More emphasis is placed on supervision, motivation, learning and individual guidance. Efforts are made as never before to develop the total capacities of the child, not merely his intellect.

Professional Standards

Over the last sixty years new and more rigid standards have been imposed by law for entrance into the teaching profession. Nearly all states have their own teachers' colleges, and the training of both classroom teachers and school administrators has expanded. Most states now require specialized educational training of their public school instructors, and private schools and institutions of higher learning, as a rule, require advanced degrees.

Growth of Secularization

In recent years, other trends have affected considerably the influence of the educational system on the minds of the American people. One of these has been the growth of secularization. The history of public and private education in the United States was, from the beginning, closely related to religious institutions. Many, if not most, of the private schools and colleges were established, and for many years, were guided by religious denominations. The constitutional guarantees of religious freedom encouraged this, and Roman Catholic, Baptist, Methodist, Presbyterian and other religious schools evolved. The development of public schools, financed by taxation, during the early nineteenth century, evolved a new type of non-church-related school system, which, nevertheless, was strongly influenced by private school and Protestant traditions. The two systems have continued to the present but in both the religious influence has given way to secularization. With the exception of purely theological seminaries and a few private schools and colleges, the direct influence of religious control has largely disappeared. In the public school, vestiges of religious instruction, such as the reading of the Bible or morning prayers, have now been banned. To a very large extent this has left most of the schools and colleges without a generally accepted philosophical point of view, without a goal, other than the obvious, but equally obscure, search for truth. This search has led to numerous diversities of opinion, and to a widespread feeling of intellectual confusion, hopelessness, and oftentimes futility. In place of goals, ends, and ideologies, there has come about an emphasis on methods of teaching, science, and innumerable types of business-fund-raising, globe-trotting, speech-making, and public-relations activities as the primary function of university and educational administrators.

Movement Toward Social Desegregation

Another major trend has been toward desegregation. With the upsetting of the "separate but equal" doctrine by the Supreme Court in 1954, the day of segregated schools in the United States was brought legally to a close, although, after a decade, there remains strong resistance to desegregation in a few southern states as well as in other Northern areas in the United States. The problem of school segregation, which is most critical in the social relations between whites and blacks, also affects interracial tensions in other areas where economic, ethnic, and social differences, to say nothing of religious and political differences, are tense. Minority groups have always faced an uphill fight to obtain equality before the law, and thereafter economic and social equality. Legal equality in

the schools of the country now exists, but the road to its complete fulfill-
ment and enforcement is rough and will be traversed slowly.

Financial Aid to Private Education

Another trend, which is also a problem, is that of federal, financial aid
to private schools. From 1787 to the present, the doctrine of separation of
church and state has been an essential part of the constitutional structure
of the United States. It derived in part from the social experience in
Colonial times with various types of theocracies and government-aided religious and private schools. It also derived from the firm conviction that
schools that were in any sense supported by the public should serve the
public, that is all the taxpayers, and not a particular group or interest.
With the exception of the Roman Catholic Church, no other religious or
private group has ever argued very emphatically for changes in this rule.[20]
Roman Catholics, however, especially in communities and states where
their numbers have been strong, have tried in one way or another to overcome this doctrine. Their case has been, since they educate a considerable
proportion of the young people in these areas, the state should help them
do it. What they neglect to say, however, is that the state did not ask
them to do this job. This rift between parochial and public schools in
some areas will probably become more bothersome as the proportion of
Catholics to non-Catholics becomes more nearly equal. The pressure for
federal or state assistance to private schools will continue and in the end
will mean either a complete victory for the public schools and the gradual
passing of parochial schools, or it will mean a victory for the latter on an
increasingly broad educational basis. If this happens, the government will
undoubtedly extend greatly its control and supervision over these private
schools.

Finally, there has been a noticeable increase in the amount of adult
education. Many universities and colleges are conducting extension classes,
mainly for adults, and individual communities have developed their own
adult programs. These latter supplement to a degree the educational work
of television and other media.

Teaching of Social Science

There have been changes in the teaching of most subjects, but those
in the social science field are of special importance because of their impact
on the thinking of students about political, social and economic affairs.
For some, the schools may merely reinforce home teachings and inculcate
the habitual beliefs of our society. For most, the schools give an important
introduction to questions of broad community and national import. Prior
to 1890, virtually the only social science course given in secondary schools
was history. The principal aim of the teaching was to inculcate morals, to

develop the religious aspects of life, to inspire patriotism, to provide for the profitable use of leisure, and to train the memory. In the 1890s, however, there were two careful investigations of history teaching, but at the secondary level the instruction continued to be rigid and lifeless, and there were actually few changes in objectives or theory even down to 1940. At the elementary level, however, the child-centered ideas of Friedrich Froebel and Johann Herbart led to John Dewey's experiments in Chicago and emphasis on progressive education during the early 1900s and by 1930 to a society-centered approach. In 1922 the principal organization of social studies teachers in the secondary schools, the National Council for the Social Studies, was established. In 1938 the Educational Policies Commission of the NEA issued its famous report on "The Purposes of Education in American Democracy," which has been reissued in revised forms from time to time.

Within the last twenty or twenty-five years many notable changes have taken place in the objectives, content, and methods of instruction in the social studies at the secondary level. These changes have by no means been uniform throughout the country, but they are characteristic of leading public and private schools. In general, no attempt is now made to inculcate morals, promote the religious life, or train the memory as such. The earlier aims of imparting knowledge, encouraging constructive participation in society as a moral, democratic citizen, and enriching personal living are all retained. Within this general framework many specific changes have been made. More emphasis is given to learning by doing as well as reading, to the use, not merely the acquisition of knowledge, to today's problems, to reasoned understanding, to positive motivations rather than formal discipline.

One student, Ernest G. Miller, in a study of *The Latest Objectives of Social Studies Teaching in American Public Secondary Schools* undertakes to summarize these objectives in terms of attitudes which teachers are seeking to develop.[21] He lists these attitudes as follows:

(1) An inquiring mind and critical judgment.
(2) Respect for human dignity, and an inclination toward cooperative endeavor in social life.
(3) Concern for social justice.
(4) A positive inclination to participate in social and political activity, with emphasis on the "public interest" (a sense of social responsibility).
(5) Tolerance toward differing and sincerely held beliefs and "different" persons and social groups.
(6) Respect for law and order.
(7) Devotion to democracy as a way of life and a form of government.
(8) A sense of "world" social responsibility.

Along with subject matter changes in social studies teaching have gone transformations in method. There have been attempts to "correlate" materials as in courses entitled "Problems in Democracy"; to "fuse and integrate"; and to underscore "core programs" geared to student interests and needs. As one writer puts it, the primary aim is to relate course materials to the social life and personal experience of the students by (1) emphasizing the position of the individual pupil; (2) considering learning as an active process; (3) awakening pupil interests; (4) looking at education as a continuous process of reorganizing and reconstructing experience. To this end texts have been improved in format with many illustrations, charts, color, different types. Radio, television, slides, and many other kinds of audio-visual material are used. The structure and furnishing of classrooms have been made more mobile and adapted to specific needs. Various and varied techniques are used for group discussions, projects, problem approach, units, field trips and surveys. Current events are stressed, and every possible use is made of community resources in personnel, history, artifacts, experience, and equipment.

EDUCATIONAL CHANGES WITH NEGATIVE INFLUENCE

Variety and Freedom

Many factors both enhance and lessen the influence of the schools on public opinion. Those which enhance have been previously mentioned: the increased enrollments, the time spent in school, the decreased influence of home and church, the improved texts, methods of instruction, and so on. But many aspects of the changing educational scene are not contributing to an increased molding of public opinion. A major factor is the emphasis on variety and freedom which produces mental conflicts and cross-pressures and undermines conviction. The more facts that are acquired and the more information that is obtained regarding systems of thought, opinions, and philosophies, the more difficult it becomes to believe any one of them. It almost seems that as the realm of finite knowledge expands, the arena of skepticism, cynicism, and disbelief expands also.

Specialization vs. General Education

Again, the multiplication of specialized courses, subjects, and study areas has tended to produce more and more specialists, but fewer and fewer over-all, well-proportioned minds. Learning and knowledge have become increasingly departmentalized, with more and more emphasis on minutiae or weak generalizations. Educators, each with his followers, drift farther and farther apart, and this physical splintering is accompanied by an intellectual separatism. This is perhaps the inevitable consequence of freedom and the democratic processes as applied to education.

Extracurricular Activity

The multiplication of extracurricular activities—sports, clubs, numerous forms of recreation, the automobile, television, books and magazines—has also softened and blunted considerably the impact of the schools on the minds of students. Probably there has never been a time in human history when young people were acquiring as much information as they are today, in so many fields—such as science, music, anthropology, literature, the social sciences. Yet, there has not been a concomitant growth in thought processes—in the ability to organize, analyze, digest, interpret, and to anticipate consequences. Human beings generally, and young people particularly, are becoming human encyclopedias of knowledge—information that is often uncoordinated, undigested, and with little immediate use. The mind becomes an ever more confused pot of vague, mixed ideas, and notions. Although it has never been expressed, and probably few would agree with all its tenets, there does seem to emerge from this hodge-podge of facts, ideas, opinions, and notions a kind of educational syntax. Starting with a great variety of goals, aims, purposes, from emphasis on imparting information to acquiring skills, mental training, and adaptation to life, considerable emphasis is placed on freedom of thought and on objective, scientific skepticism. Equality of opportunity, with something for everyone, seems to be implicit in this very eclectic philosophy. Although there are a few notable exceptions, the goal of the "well rounded" person is salient. Although the religious base of education in the United States has been gravely scarred, if not uprooted, a very definite kind of socially purposeful humanitarianism has taken its place. Included in this is a continuous emphasis on individualistic, laissez-faire competition. Finally, mention should be made of the characteristic concern with the individual and his success, most recently manifested by the widespread use of vocational guidance, both theoretical and practical.

It is not clear, by any means, what effect these and the many other educational changes are having on the students. Their intake of facts and information of all kinds is tremendous. By and large young people seem to enjoy their schools more than they did earlier and do not cringe from it as many once did. Without doubt an increasing number get a much broader perspective of the earth, the world, and their components than their parents did. They are surrounded on all sides by visual and auditory aids to an understanding and appreciation, not only of their own communities but of other countries and of the entire world. They enjoy much more freedom than their predecessors, not only to choose what they will study, and how they will do it, but freedom to choose from a greater variety of diverting and pleasurable, non-academic activities. Yet the secularization of the schools, the usual absence of a clearly expressed goal or philosophy, and this very freedom and diversity, all too frequently leave the student confused and perplexed, desiring guidance but not knowing where to obtain it, retreating and withdrawing rather reluctantly to the immediate, tangible, nearby jobs of the day. It is this philosophical vacuum which produces in some the "go-go" spirit; in others withdrawal, reticence, excessive inner-directedness; and in still others tensions of varying degrees of gravity. The amount of knowledge is just too prodigious for the masses of men and women; the need for a unifying formula, a generally understood and accepted philosophy is imperative.[22]

MAJOR INFLUENCES OF MODERN EDUCATION

Traditional or Progressive?

What can be said regarding the general impact of this colossal educational structure with its more than one and one-half million teachers? How can one depict the influence of a single public or private school on each year's class, or even the influence of a single teacher, to say nothing of the mass influence of the thousands of schools from elementary to university, of theological, dental, trade, law and medical schools? About all that one can do is to hazard a few general hypothetical observations. Most public schools tend to reflect rather than create family and community attitudes, especially on political and economic matters.[23] The teaching in most elementary and secondary schools is, if anything, more conservative, perhaps, than the educational material carried in the mass media. This is especially true in science, literature, history, and the social studies. The steps taken years ago in Tennessee to bar the teaching of biological evolution and the efforts to discredit the United Nations in some Los Angeles schools after World War II emphasize how extreme this conservatism can be at times. Although the guards against new ideas or facts have been dropped in some areas and controversial subjects are debated quite freely in most public school systems, the system as a whole is more rather than less conservative than the community in which it functions.

At the college and university level the situation is somewhat different, extending from one extreme to another, with the majority of institutions in the van of liberalism. For many reasons, most of the institutions of higher learning in the United States today pursue the search for truth and its teaching, unhampered by taboos of any non-professional kind. There are still areas, however, in parts of the country where tactless, outspoken advocacy of certain points of view on economic or social questions may be treated intolerantly, especially in a few smaller, more specialized colleges; nevertheless, the freedom of speech of the academic world at the higher levels is marked. Whatever curtailment of freedom exists today comes from within, more than from without, comes from the long, laborious, screening process through which candidates for the top teaching and research positions in the United States must pass.

Impact on Religious Beliefs

A second general observation regarding the influence of the educational system on public opinion relates to its impact on religious beliefs. There can be little doubt that the over-all secularization of the schools, at least the public schools, and a large number of private schools, plus the critical, scientific approach to many subjects, have countered many of the primitive religious ideas inculcated by many families and churches. Much religious instruction has not kept pace in substance and understanding with the rapid scholastic changes occurring in the educational world. An increasing number of students are not equipped to meet the challenges of the secular schools. Whatever religious experiences students bring to the public school systems are often undermined or eradicated. It would be incorrect to say that the schools destroy the religious faith of young men and women. It would be nearer the truth to assert that the religious indoctrination of young people succumbs all too readily to educational ideas because it has not kept abreast of general world-wide developments. For many reasons, quite unrelated to either religion or formal education, an increasing number of young people experience no religious vs. education cross pressures, but for those who still do the impact of the educational process often is devastating, and the recapture of personal balance is difficult, if not impossible.

Changes in Social Attitudes

Another important area in which the schools have some effect is in attitude formation of a social nature such as prejudice, bias, and intolerance. The desegregation process, the day-to-day contact with peers coming from many different races and ethnic groups, the play periods, cooperative assignments, the very nature of the instruction—all help to break down many family-based prejudices. This is perhaps more true in public than private schools.

The school, from the age of four or five on, engrosses so great a part of the child's life and affects that life at so many points that it is impossible to isolate it and measure its influence. How may one determine the effects of specific courses—English, French, history, science, economics—and scores of others? Some of these effects may be immediate; others come into focus only after the passage of years. Ideas regarding geography, history, biology, or English may develop slowly over the years while some of them may take effect suddenly and dramatically. In general, the basic views of men and women in positions of responsibility and authority are often those acquired by them twenty to thirty years previously. Many prominent businessmen, government officials, and those in the professions are today implementing policies, theorems, and ideas acquired during their school years.

Changes in Curricula

Some of the general curricula changes may be mentioned to suggest, since they cannot prove, what education is doing to the minds of young Americans. Mention has already been made of the diversification of courses. Language instruction continues with less emphasis on Latin and Greek, more on French, Spanish, German, Italian, Russian. The study of English has broadened with an increasing emphasis on literature, less on grammar and sentence structure. In recent years many changes have taken place in the teaching of mathematics and science. The growth of the natural sciences has been little short of phenomenal during the last few decades, in almost all fields—physics, chemistry, biology, astronomy, and so on. The interrelationships have become clearer and have been marked by many new hybrid fields such as biochemistry, and astrophysics. Historical and social science studies have expanded to the point where considerable work in economics, sociology, political science, and even psychology and anthropology is done at the secondary level. All of these developmens in what might be called the traditional disciplines have been accompanied by the introduction of a great many subjects, new to the general educational system. These include a whole array of applied, almost vocational, studies in engineering, business administration, sales and advertising, commercial as well as creative art, speech and drama, health and vocational guidance, sex and marriage, and many others. The battle between traditionalists and innovators goes on, but for the former it is mainly a rearguard action. The curriculum continues to expand, the core of it more diffused, and the minds of students more confused. It is becoming more and more difficult to tie this proliferating, amazing, polyglot of fact, datum, and findings together. Individuals retreat to specialists; and specialists retreat to atomists and beyond. No one seems to be able to discover the formula to define its meaning. Some cling somewhat dispiritedly to old, and simple traditions; some ignore the whole matter, or try to, seeking peace of mind in work, specialty, or in energy itself; a few continue to struggle for enlightenment. Education seems to be flooding the earth with new information, which the mind of man, even with the help of educators, cannot digest and organize into any general pattern of wisdom. Men seek meaning and understanding in what they can see, handle, and control in pictures, in workshops, and in machines. But man has somehow lost his sense of meaning of the ends and goals of life.

The only alternatives he knows are focusing on his specialty and the present, relying on the traditions and dreams of childhood, or forsaking formal religious security and becoming agnostic. The educational process has left man confused, so confused that he uses every psychological device possible to divorce himself from mind, and possibly wisdom.

NOTES FOR CHAPTER 7

Epigraph. Frederick C. Irion, *Public Opinion and Propaganda,* p. 225.
1. Bossard, James H. S. (ed.), "Toward Family Stability," *The Annals* of the American Academy of Political and Social Science, Vol. 272 (November, 1950).
2. *Idem.* See also Nimkoff, Meyer F., *Marriage and the Family* (Boston: Houghton Mifflin, 1947); Groves, E. R. and G. H., *The Contemporary American Family* (Rev. ed.; Philadelphia: J. B. Lippincott Co., 1947), Part II; and Kirkpatrick, Clifford, *The Family as Process and Institution* (New York: The Ronald Press Co., 1955). Also Winch, R. F., *The Modern Family* (New York: Henry Holt & Co., 1952).
3. Irion, F. C., *Public Opinion and Propaganda* (Thomas Y. Crowell Co., 1950), p. 227.
4. See Lazardsfeld, Paul, *et al., The Peoples' Choice, op. cit.;* Burgess, Ernest W., Locke, H. J., and Mary M. Thomas, *The Family—From Institution to Companionship* (3rd ed.; New York: American Book Company, 1963).
5. See Zelomek, A. W., *Changing America: At Work and Play* (New York: John Wiley & Sons, 1959).
6. Today, the United States has a greater proportion of its population married and living together than ever before, and a large percentage of divorced persons remarry. Talcott Parsons, *New York Times,* January 26, 1964, p. 80.
7. Dr. Neil J. Smelscr, Professor of Sociology at the University of California at Berkeley contends that the modern child is probably more exclusively reliant upon his parents as authority models than ever before and that the social challenge to the family is not so much the decline of parental authority as it is the lack of continuity between that and other types of authority. See *New York Times,* January 26, 1964, p. 80.
8. This study was described in the *New York Times* for October 22, 1950.
9. Irion, F. C., *op. cit.*
10. See Parker, E. C., *et al., The Radio-Television Audience and Religion* (New York: Harper & Row, 1955).
11. See Rosten, Leo, *The Religions of America* (New York: Simon and Schuster, 1963); Herberg, Will, *Protestant-Catholic-Jew: An Essay in American Religious Sociology* (Rev. ed., Anchor Books; Garden City, L.I., N.Y.: Doubleday & Co., 1960); Williams, J. Paul, *What Americans Believe and How They Worship* (New York: Harper & Row, 1952).
12. Smart, James D., *The Teaching Ministry of the Church: An Examination of the Basic Principles of Christian Education* (Philadelphia: Westminster Press, 1954).
13. See Niebuhr, H. Richard, *The Social Sources of Denominationalism* (Cleveland: Meridian Books, World Publishing Company, 1962).

14. Fenton, J. H., *The Catholic Vote* New Orleans, La.: Hauser Press, 1960, p. 56.
15. Lazarsfeld, Paul H., *et al., The People's Choice* (New York: Columbia University Press, 1948).
16. Odegard, Peter H. (ed.), *Religion and Politics* (Published for the Eagleton Institute of Politics by Oceana Publications, 1960).
17. The National Education Association in its annual survey, "Estimates of School Statistics, 1961-62," predicted that the total enrollment in 1962 would reach 38,600,000 and expenses would exceed $18,000,000,000 for public education through the twelfth grade. See Machlup, Fritz, *The Production and Distribution of Knowledge in the United States* (Princeton, N.J.: Princeton University Press, 1962), chap. IV.
18. See Brubacher, John S. and Willis Rudy, *Higher Education in Transition: An American History, 1636-1956* (New York: Harper and Brothers, 1958).
19. See Dreiman, David B., *How to Get Better Schools: A Tested Program* (New York: Harper & Row, 1963).
20. "A special commission of the 3.2 million member Lutheran Church in America has rejected the principle of 'absolute' separation of church and state in favor of a mutually beneficial relationship in which each institution contributes to the common good." *New York Times,* January 21, 1964.
21. This paper was prepared in 1955 to show "the kinds of social attitudes that teachers in the social studies are attempting to establish in the minds of their high school students." See also Cummings, Howard, "The Public Opinion the Schools Desire to Achieve," in the *Twenty-first Yearbook* (National Council for the Social Studies, 1950), pp. 1-10.
22. See Osgood, Charles G., "Education of Philosophers for Democratic Society," *Princeton Alumni Weekly,* January 27, 1956, pp. 11-15.
23. "In the largest sense the educational system is a great mechanism for conserving the values, the institutions, the practices of the political order, as it inculcates from the primary school even through college the memories, the unities, and the norms of the system." Key, V. O. Jr., *Public Opinion and American Democracy* (New York: Alfred A. Knopf, 1961), p. 343.

SUPPLEMENTARY READING

ANSHEN, RUTH. *The Family: Its Function and Destiny.* Revised ed. New York: Harper & Bros., 1959.
BESTER, ARTHUR. "Education and Its Proper Relationship to the Forces of American Society," *Daedalus* (Winter, 1959), pp. 75-90.
BRUBACHER, JOHN S., and RUDY, WILLIS. *Higher Education in Transition: An American History, 1636-1956.* New York: Harper & Bros., 1958.
BRUNER, JEROME S. *The Process of Education.* Cambridge, Mass.: Harvard University Press, 1960.
BURGESS, ERNEST W., and LOCKE, HARVEY J. *The Family—From Instability to Companionship.* 2nd ed. New York: American Book Co., 1953.
BUTTS, R. FREEMAN. *The American Tradition in Religion and Education.* New York: Henry Holt & Co., 1950.
BUTTS, R. FREEMAN. *A Cultural History of Western Education.* 2nd ed. New York: McGraw-Hill Book Co., 1955.
CALHOUN, A. W. *Social History of the American Family from Colonial Times to the Present.* New York: Barnes and Noble, Inc., 1945.

CHILDS, JOHN L. *American Pragmatism and Education.* Henry Holt & Co., 1956.

CHILDS, JOHN L. *Education and Morals.* New York: Appleton-Century-Crofts, 1950.

CLINCHY, EVANS. "The New Education: Survey of Developments in the U.S.A. That Have World-Wide Significance," *International Development Review,* Vol. 4, No. 9 (September, 1962), pp. 15ff.

CREMIN, LAWRENCE A. *The Transformation of The School.* New York: Alfred A. Knopf, 1961.

DEWEY, JOHN. *The School and Society.* Chicago: University of Chicago Press, 1900.

DEWEY, JOHN. *The Public and Its Problems.* New York: Henry Holt & Co., 1927.

DRAKE, WILLIAM E. *The American School in Transition.* New York: Prentice-Hall, Inc., 1955.

DWORKIN, M. S. *Dewey on Education.* New York: Columbia University Press, 1960.

EVERETT, JOHN R. *Religion in Human Experience.* New York: Henry Holt & Co., 1950.

GOOD, HARRY G. *A History of American Education.* New York: The Macmillan Co., 1956.

GREER, SCOTT. "Catholic Voters and the Democratic Party," *Public Opinion Quarterly,* Vol. 25 (Winter, 1961), pp. 611-25.

HARRIS, RAYMOND P. *American Education: Facts, Fancies, Folklore.* New York: Random House, 1961.

HERBERG, WILL. *Protestant-Catholic Jew.* Revised ed. New York: Doubleday & Co., Inc., 1960.

HYMAN, HERBERT, H. *Political Socialization.* Chicago: The Free Press of Glencoe, Ill., 1959.

IRION, F. C. *Public Opinion and Propaganda.* New York: Thomas Y. Crowell Co., 1950.

JACOBSON, PHILIP. "Religion and the State: A Year's Review. July 1, 1960—June 30, 1961." *American Jewish Yearbook.* Vol. 63, 1962.

JAMES, WALTER. *The Christian in Politics.* New York: Oxford University Press, 1962.

JOHNSTONE, JOHN W. C. *Volunteers for Learning: A Study of the Educational Pursuits of American Adults.* Published by National Opinion Research Center, University of Chicago (February, 1963).

KERR, CLARK. *The Uses of the University.* Cambridge, Mass.: Harvard University Press, 1963.

KNOWLES, MALCOLM S. *The Adult Education Movement in the United States.* New York: Henry Holt & Co., 1962.

LIEBERMAN, MYRON. *The Future of Public Education.* Chicago: University of Chicago Press, 1960.

MASON, R. E. *Educational Ideals in American Society.* Boston: Allyn and Bacon, 1960.

MCGRATH, JOHN L. (ed.). *Church and State in Our Land: Cases and Materials.* Milwaukee, Wis.: The Bruce Co., 1962.

MILLER, DANIEL R., and SWANSON, GUY E. *The Changing American Parent: A Study in the Detroit Area.* New York: John Wiley and Sons, 1957.

National Education Association, Research Division. *Estimates of School Statistics, 1962-63.* (The NEA, December, 1962).

NOBLE, STUART G. *A History of American Education.* 2nd ed. New York: Rinehart, 1954.

ODEGARD, P. H. (ed.). *Religion and Politics.* Published for the Eagleton Institute of Politics by Oceana Publications, 1960.

RIESMAN, DAVID. *Constraint and Variety in American Education.* New York: Doubleday & Co., 1958.

ROSTEN, LEO. *The Religions of America.* New York: Simon and Schuster, 1963.

RUSK, R. R. *The Doctrines of the Great Educators.* New York: St. Martins Press, 1954.

SMART, JAMES D. *The Teaching Ministry of the Church: An Examination of the Basic Principles of Christian Education.* Philadelphia: The Westminster Press, 1954.

STACE, W. T. *Religion and the Modern Mind.* Philadelphia: J. B. Lippincott Co., 1952.

"The Supreme Court, the First Amendment, and Religion in the Public Schools." *Columbia Law Review,* Vol. 63 (January, 1963), pp. 73-97.

SYMONDS, P. M. *The Dynamics of Parent-Child Relationships.* New York: Columbia University Press, 1949.

TROELTSCH, ERNEST. *The Social Teachings of the Christian Churches.* New York: The Macmillan Co., 1931.

VEBLEN, THORSTEIN. *The Higher Learning in America.* New York: Huebsch, 1918.

WELTER, RUSH. *Popular Education and Democratic Thought in America.* New York: Columbia University Press, 1962.

WESTOFF, C. F. *et al. Family Growth in Metropolitan America.* Princeton, N. J.: Princeton University Press, 1961.

YOUNG, KIMBALL. *Personality and Problems of Adjustment.* New York: F. S. Crofts & Co., 1952.

VIII · Role of the Press

The first requirement is that the media should be accurate. They should not lie.—COMMISSION ON FREEDOM OF THE PRESS, 1947

THE PRESS is an important factor in the formation of public opinion —some would say the most important, notwithstanding the influence of television. The word "press" is used with varying degrees of inclusiveness, sometimes referring only to the newspapers, sometimes to periodicals and general carriers of the printed word, or to all mass media, as was the case with the Commission on Freedom of the Press.[1] Here, the focus of attention will be confined to the American newspaper. After a very brief reference to the history of newspapers in the United States, three aspects of the subject will be considered in greater detail: major influences shaping the press, the influence of the press, and some of the important public opinion problems of the American newspaper today.

A BRIEF HISTORY

The history of the newspaper may be thought of as the history of the many elements and parts of which it is composed. The newspaper is both things and people, processes and effects, functions and accomplishments. To tell its story fully one would have to trace the evolution of printing and printing presses, of newsprint and ink, of engraving and stereotyping. The people who own newspapers, publish them, write, photograph, prepare copy, and report for them, distribute the papers and prepare the ads— all have their own stories to tell. Also, part might be told in terms of its changing content: news stories, editorials, advertisements, features, headlines, financial and sports pages, columnists and pictures. Processes, such as news gathering, news selection, and news presentation are also a part of the over-all history. Then there are the reader and circulation figures, pressure groups and laws affecting newspapers, trade unions, and associations

166

of editors and publishers. It is probably true to say that the complete history will never be written. The newspaper is, indeed, a many-sided institution, reaching to some extent and in some degree nearly all members of the American public.

It has been customary to divide the history of the American newspaper into several periods.[2] Such a chronological classification provides a useful frame for the unfolding picture. Period One may be called the early history of the newspaper; it covers developments in England and elsewhere before the establishment of the first paper in the United States in 1690. Before the advent of printing with movable type during the middle of the fifteenth century, news was transmitted by word of mouth, in letters, in song and story, poem and ballad, by proclamation, smoke signal, drum beat, poster, and pamphlet. Printing, of course, speeded up the process and increased the area of circulation. Printing was introduced into England from the Continent about 1476 by William Caxton, but it was not until 1622 that the first newspaper, the *Weekley Newes* appeared. Throughout this early period and down to the latter part of the seventeenth century the British government maintained a tight, monopolistic control over the press, and this control extended to the colonies. The first printing press in the American colonies was set up in Cambridge, Massachusetts in 1638. The first newspaper appeared in 1690, but it was suppressed after one issue. A second attempt was made in 1704 when the first issue of the *Boston News Letter* appeared; it continued for 72 years.[3]

Period Two, from 1690 to 1765 covered the Colonial era. By the end of this period there were 35 papers in the country and at least one in each colony. There were no dailies, and most of the papers were weeklies.

During Period Three, the Revolutionary period, from 1765 to 1783, many of the colonial papers took the lead in supporting the patriot cause. At the outset a few papers supported England, but in the course of the struggle they either ceased publication or went over to the side of the revolutionists. At the war's beginning there were thirty-seven papers in the country.

Period Four, from 1783 to 1830, is often referred to as the period of the party press. Most of the papers were extremely partisan, and were subsidized by party and private interests. In 1784 the first daily appeared, *The Pennsylvania Pocket and Daily Advertiser*. The papers took an active part in the fight for adoption of the new Federal Constitution, and the celebrated Federalist papers were first published in *The Independent Journal* established in New York City in 1783. The cleavage which developed between the Jeffersonians and the Hamiltonians was reflected in the partisan policies of the press. Both sides of the political battle recognized the importance of the press, and each of the leaders subsidized an organ of his own to present his case to the people.[4] As the momentum of the westbound population increased, the printing press and the newspaper kept pace. By 1810, the number of papers had increased to 363. Most of them, large, "blanket" papers, stressed business and political news and were too dull and expensive for the great majority of low income, poorly schooled working classes.

Period Five, beginning in 1830, brought unprecedented changes in newspaper publishing, notably the penny press. James Gordon Bennett and Benjamin Day, influenced to some extent perhaps by developments in England, successfully undertook to establish papers that would be profitable, that would not be compelled to accept subsidies from party and private interests, that could stand on their own feet. Thus the business formula of American journalism was employed: to increase circulation, to increase advertising, to increase profits. They increased circulation dramatically in their "penny" papers: by filling the pages with sensational news of crime, sex, and violence; by emphasizing human interest stories, and by printing the kind of material that would excite and hold the interest of the shipping clerk, dairy maid, bartender, and stevedore, and all others with no taste for the colorless menu of the staid old "blanket" newspaper. Prior to the "penny" papers the tendency had been to increase the size of the pages, and not their number.[5]

Although the introduction of the penny press was the most outstanding development of the period from 1830 to 1860, there were many other important changes, even though they were less spectacular. There were changes in the mechanics and technology of printing, in the speed and scope of news gathering, in the sale and distribution of papers, in news presentation, and in the number and circulation of papers.

Period Six has been labeled the period of editorial journalism. It began about 1860 and extended to the climactic election of 1896. The Civil War, in company with previous wars—the Revolution, the War of 1812, the Mexican War—greatly increased the demand for news. Every effort was made to satisfy this demand by sending more and better correspondents into the battle areas; by speeding up the process of news gathering by means of the fastest transportation and communication possible; and by increasing the number of editions, including a Sunday edition. After the Civil War, the industrial expansion in the North, improvements in communication, rapid economic growth of railroads, mass production, national advertising, combinations, trusts, and holding companies—all of these marks of economic growth and prosperity were accompanied by a comparable rate of growth and prosperity in newspaper publishing. But it was not the economic, but rather the editorial aspect of the papers that stood out. This was the era of such editorial giants as Henry J. Raymond, Joseph Medill Patterson, Horace Greeley, Edwin L. Godkin, Melville E. Stone, William R. Nelson, Henry W. Grady, and Henry Watterson.

Period Seven, from 1896 to World War I, saw the beginnings of the era of "yellow journalism," ushered in by the fiercest of all newspaper wars, that between Hearst and Pulitzer for capture of the New York market.[6] It witnessed a Cuban war, fully exploited, if not to some extent encouraged by power- and profit-seeking publishers. The structures of press associations were reorganized and the new Associated Press (AP) emerged, along with the United Press (UP) and later International News Service (INS).[7] Feature syndicates grew in numbers; the number and circulation of papers as well as newspaper chains expanded; many developments in printing improved newspaper quality and the speed of manufacture. Growth in national advertising greatly enhanced newspaper revenue, but paid advertising encountered increasing pressures from press agents, who sought to obtain free space and publicity. During this period schools of journalism appeared, and systematic efforts were made to train men and women for newspaper careers. The American Newspaper Publishers Association which had been formed in 1887 was followed by the American Society of Newspaper Editors in 1922, and the American Newspaper Guild in 1933.

The period between the two world wars, Period Eight, was one in which the preceding trends continued, although the number of daily papers in the United States reached a peak in 1917 and has since declined. The content of newspapers changed to include more news of foreign affairs, more pictures and maps, more features and departments, more attention to science and education. The size of Sunday editions grew to include weekly news digests, magazines, book review sections, special brochures on travel, art, and business; and women's sections, in addition to the standard comics, sports, and business sections. As radio extended its news reporting and coverage, the newspaper at first tried to ignore this competition, then fought it, but before the end of this period finally accepted it and adjusted to it more or less.[8] This competition between radio (and later television) and the newspapers for advertising revenue and news coverage continues, and it has affected the newspaper both in its content and its finances. The Great Depression and the New Deal that followed made Washington and the national government an unprecedented source of news, and the growing international tensions intensified still more the public's interest in public and foreign affairs.

The post-World War II period is the latest or modern period. This period has been marked by a further decline and finally a leveling off in the number of dailies, a slow but steady increase in total circulation, a decrease, almost to the vanishing point, of cities with more than one newspaper, a widening gap between the outstanding *New York Times* type of real *news*paper and the entertainment paper which specializes in feature material and sensational news. During this period the press has been frequently attacked for its alleged lack of responsibility, drawing much attention both inside and outside the profession. Indications are that national newspapers are coming into being, in the case of the *New York Times, Christian Science Monitor,* and *Wall Street Journal.* Several other papers also circulate widely beyond the boundaries of the cities where they are published. Many improvements have been made to speed up and extend the scope of news gathering. Likewise, the mechanics of typesetting and printing have been refined and made more efficient. Beset, however, by rising costs of printing, increased demands of employees, and resourceful competition from other media, especially radio and television, many papers find it hard to continue in the black. The strong seem to get stronger, the weak weaker. This trend may have fateful consequences in terms of news coverage, fairness, responsibility, and integrity.

Before considering the major influences shaping the newspaper press in the United States today, a bird's-eye view of their number and circulation figures may be instructive.[9] The total number of dailies reached its peak at 2,514 in 1917 and has decreased almost steadily to a figure of 1,761 in 1962. Of these, 1,458 were evening papers and 312 appeared in the morning. The number of foreign language dailies has dropped from 122 in 1948 to 76 in 1962. The number of Sunday papers has remained fairly stable, 558 in 1962. Weekly papers far outnumber the dailies, and all but about 350 of the total 9,000 appeared once a week in 1962. There are a few other papers, less than 100, which have bi-monthly, monthly, or semi-monthly schedules. Altogether, the newspaper press in the United States numbers more than 13,000 papers, with an aggregate daily circulation of approximately 60,000,000, and a Sunday circulation of close to 48,000,-000.

Commercially, newspaper publishing ranks high among the industries of the country in number of employees, in capital invested, and in value of product. More than $3,793,900,000 was spent on newspaper advertising in 1962, 31 per cent of the total 12 billion advertising dollars. The value and profits of individual newspaper properties are not generally known but certainly vary greatly. A few such properties have been sold in recent years for more than $20,000,000.[10]

INFLUENCES SHAPING THE PRESS

The newspaper in the United States is what it is today because of the influence and role of owners and publishers, of the staffs of the papers from editors and business managers to the typesetter, mechanic, reporter, and other staff workers, and of the newspaper reader. Technological invention and development have played their part too, as have the advertiser, the government, and pressure groups of all kinds.

Ownership

Newspapers are owned individually by families, collectively by corporations or partnerships, and in a few instances cooperatively by employees. They are also owned in groups or chains. In 1960, there were 109 groups of two or more general daily and Sunday newspapers under common ownership or control in two or more cities of the United States. The three largest groups were the Scripps-Howard (N.Y.C.) papers totaling 21 with over 3,000,000 circulation, the Lee, Mason (Davenport, Iowa) group with 18 papers and a circulation of 335,000, and the Hearst chain with 14 papers and a circulation of over 4,000,000. Other chains with 500,000 circulation or more were the Newhouse (L. I., N. Y.), Ridder (N.Y.C.), and Gannet (Rochester, N. Y.) groups. Altogether 560 papers with a circulation of 27,000,000 were owned in groups. However, the average number of papers per group was 5.1, below the peak of 5.6 in 1930. Mention should also be made of the Roy H. Thomson group with headquarters in Canada, perhaps the largest chain of newspapers in the world with 100 papers in England, Ireland, Nigeria, Canada, and the United States.

In his latest study of trends in newspaper ownership, Raymond B. Nixon found that in 1961 concentration of ownership in dailies was becoming more intensive and less extensive; that is, local monopolies, inter-city dailies, and small regional groups were on the increase, whereas the number of large national chains was decreasing.[11] He also reported that fears regarding local newspaper "monopolies" had largely subsided, and press ownership seemed to have stabilized at one publisher to a community except in cities of over a million population. In fact, only 13 cities have three or more dailies, and only six of these have more than two owners.

One of the most significant developments in newspaper ownership has been the emergence of media giants: communication empires controlling newspapers, radio, and television stations, and in some cases branching into book and magazine publishing, motion-picture production, and ownership of processing and manufacturing plants for needed raw materials. A number of the leading papers in the country have taken part in building up these cross-channel realms, notably the *New York Times, Philadelphia Inquirer* and *Bulletin, Baltimore Sun, Washington Post, Chicago Tribune, Los Angeles Times,* and *St. Louis Post-Dispatch.*[12]

The personality, talents, and aims of newspaper owners and proprietors have profound effects on the content of papers and on their role as leaders and reflectors of public opinion. William Randolph Hearst is a classic case, of course, but every owner is to some degree an example. These men affect editorial policy, news treatment and presentation, the reaches of circulation, and the financial success of the papers. They may be active or passive, remote or close to management, economically motivated or public spirited, revered or despised, but in any case they are powerful molders of newspaper form and character.

Technological Developments

Not only is the character of the newspaper influenced by who owns and controls the paper, but also by the tools, machines, and technologies available for its manufacture, for news gathering, news presentation, and news distribution. Improvements in transportation and communication from the days of sailing vessels and horseback riders to jet planes and tel-stars have speeded up the processes of news gathering and news distribution, while mechanical changes in printing and paper manufacture have accelerated the preparation of the paper and increased its size and quantity. The story of newspaper technology can be sketched very briefly.[13] From the advent of printing in Europe in the middle of the fifteenth century until the early nineteenth century all printing was done on hand presses. Then came the cylinder presses first used by the *Times* of London in 1814, and in the United States by the *New York Daily Advertiser* in 1825. Soon steam driven presses began to take the place of those operated by hand. About 1860 the invention of stereotyped plates for curved forms of type, cast in papier-mâché matrices, sped up and made more efficient the attachment of type to cylinder. The next major development was the use of linotype machines, first by the *New York Tribune* in 1886, then by the *Chicago Daily News*. Meanwhile, the use of electric power, improved cutting and folding devices, the rapid development of telephone and typewriter, improvements in engraving, use of color, better ink and paper all contributed to the mechanical and technological evolution of the modern newspaper. During the twentieth century there have been many refinements and improvements in existing machines and processes, and a few major changes, notably the invention of the teletypesetter (1928-31), which enables a typist in one place to set type in many other places almost simultaneously. Improvements in photography and the uses of color have brought greater emphasis and an increasing interest in pictorial journalism and in color work. Early in the nineteenth century newsprint made from woodpulp largely took the place of paper made from rags. Later the substitution of huge paper rolls for sheets made possible the high speed presses of today, capable of turning out 60,000 sixty-four page papers an hour, folded and ready for delivery. Probably no technological development is more illustrative of the benefits and also the problems of automation than the story of newspaper printing. The transmission of copy by type and electronic impulse from one master keyboard to presses near and far, where these impulses are automatically translated into papers, makes national and international newspapers possible, but it also threatens the jobs of many technicians and craftsmen.

It is difficult to overestimate the influence of newspaper technology on the character of the press. This influence has affected the size and quantity of papers, the content and its presentation, the speed and extent of newspaper coverage and distribution, its financing, the relations between newspaper proprietors and employees, and in many other overt and direct, hidden and subtle ways. The newspaper and its relationship to public opinion cannot be understood without some knowledge of this technological foundation and background.

Personnel

The most important factor determining the nature of the newspapers in the United States today is personnel—the men and women who publish, edit, administer, write, photograph, draw for, and otherwise produce the 13,000 newspapers in the country. They influence the product both as individuals and as members of organizations. It is impossible to measure this impact precisely or to explain it completely. Owners and publishers, who have been considered earlier, naturally have a degree of control unsurpassed by others; nevertheless, their influence in most cases tends to be general and not very closely related to the daily operations and content of a paper. Owners and publishers usually set the outside limits of policy within which others exercise discretion. There are, of course, many exceptions, and men like William Randolph Hearst, Adolph S. Ochs, E. W. Scripps, Robert R. McCormick, and Joseph Medill Patterson could be said to have made their papers in their own image. Today owners and publishers generally prefer to delegate much of their authority regarding content to subordinates.

The principal organization of publishers is the American Newspaper Publishers Association (ANPA), founded in 1887.[14] It has been primarily concerned with employee relations and government relations, as well as most of the business aspects of newspapers such as advertising, costs of newsprint, technological change. While it is primarily concerned with focusing the collective opinions of the publishers on government and institutions external to itself, the meetings of the ANPA, internal communications and contacts affect views and opinions of individual members.

The Editors

Next to publishers in their power to shape the newspaper are the editors. As newspapers have become more departmentalized and specialized, so also has the editorial function which includes managing editors, city editors, financial and sports editors, to mention only a few. Together they determine to a large extent what appears on the non-advertising pages of the paper as news, editorials, feature material, pictures. They may write editorials, but more important, they select, screen, evaluate, determine the priorities, place, and manner of presentation of the quantities of news items, features, editorials, comment, and other items that make up the paper. They, too, have their national organization, the American Society of Newspaper Editors (ASNE), formed in 1922, and several more specialized associations. The ASNE has been active in trying to promote the professional interests of editors, encourage high ethical standards, remove attacks on and obstacles to freedom of the press, and in general to preserve the essential character of the paper as news.

Closely related to this group are the columnists whose articles and comments are syndicated across the country and often contradict the views of a paper's own editors. These syndicated columns deal more or less seriously with public and community affairs, yet they constitute only a small part of the hundreds of syndicated items today, including comics, legal, health, marriage, and bridge advice, disquisitions on art and literature, poll findings, house furnishings, menus and so on. In many media and small papers such syndicated material may account for two-thirds or more of the non-advertising content of an issue of the paper.

The Reporters

The news function is, or perhaps should be, the primary function of the newspaper; at least, it may be considered the reason for its existence. The selection, editing, presentation, and distribution of news, important as they are to the news function, are all dependent on that of news gathering. Hence, the importance of the role of reporter and correspondent, the men and women in the field through whose eyes, or colored glasses, the world of reality enters the world of the newspaper, and eventually that of the reader. News gatherers have always been highly individualistic, competition among them has often been keen, and they are probably in a position to see life more realistically than any other group.

Trends in reporting which have a bearing on the influence of reporters on the newspaper are: (1) the rapid rise in the educational level of reporters. This means in many instances a college degree, often attendance at a school of journalism, and possibly special study or experience in public or international affairs, business, law, science, or some field which enables the reporter to approach his job with a broad cultural education and a specialized knowledge of a particular field. (2) There is also a greater appreciation by others of the importance of the reporter in establishing good relations between institutions and individuals on the one hand, and the public on the other. Although attempts to "use" reports for publicity and propaganda purposes are frequent, most news gatherers are aware of this. In any case, this appreciation of the importance of the reporter has often meant greater convenience and improved facilities open to him for doing his job, and sometimes easier access to news sources. (3) News coverage has expanded, not only world-wide, but to subjects philosophically complex and abstract, or scientifically specialized and detailed. International affairs covering the relations of 110 countries, plus the United Nations and other international bodies, make increasing demands upon the political, military, and economic resources of reporters. Likewise, science and technology, education and health, social welfare and industrial relations demand a broader, more analytical and insightful kind of reporting than do stories of crime, sex, and violence. (4) Finally, what is news has reached new dimensions, including subjects less concrete and obvious, more theoretical, subtle, and invisible. The public is less satisfied than formerly with news of surface symptoms. They want news of events below the surface, news of trends in underlying causes, of movements of hidden tendencies that will erupt on the surface later, knowledge now that will give meaning to future happenings and facilitate adjustment to them.

The Business Staff

Another important element in the working force of the newspaper is the business staff. On the average, anywhere from two-thirds to three-fourths of the revenue of a newspaper is derived from advertising. Newspaper sales account for most of the remaining revenue. The advertising and circulation managers can, through the policies they follow, do much to determine the paper's personality. Their skill, foresight, shrewdness, efficiency, and overall business acumen usually spells financial success or failure, though personnel groups already considered are quite as important. They have much to do with who advertises and who does not, with the quality and nature of advertising in the paper, and to some extent with the relations between the business and editorial sides of the paper. There can be little doubt that the two sides interact and influence each other. In the minds of some critics, financial pressures are frequently too great, and the non-advertising content is too often shaped by the demands of this pressure. Certainly the influence of both the business and editorial aspects are important in the development of a newspaper personality.

Besides the publishers, editors, reporters, and business managers, there are many other groups of skilled and unskilled workers in a newspaper enterprise. Many of them influence the paper directly as individuals and many through organizations, such as the American Newspaper Guild (ANG), founded in 1933, and trade unions such as the International Typographical Union and Newspaper and Mail Deliverers Unions. The unionization of printers and other skilled newspaper workers took place early in this century, but unions did not enter the editorial and higher level of commercial officers until the 1930's with the establishment of the Guild.

Labor unions have done much to improve wages, work hours, and the working conditions of newspaper employees, but the unions have contributed in no small way to the trends in increased costs, mergers and consolidations, local newspaper monopolies, automation, strikes, and all the many problems that face the newspaper world today.

EXTERNAL INFLUENCES AND THE PRESS: PRESSURE GROUPS

The American newspaper is not only the product of internal influences which shape and mold its character but of outside, environmental forces, particularly the pressures that come from innumerable private groups and institutions and from the government itself. Practically every group in society at one time or another affects the newspaper press, either through advertising, news publicity, or editorial comment. In fact, studies have shown that more than 50 per cent of the news content of an average paper will deal with group activities and to a large extent will be the deliberate, carefully prepared output of group publicity efforts. The amount of group-inspired publicity that comes into newspaper offices far exceeds that which is printed, but enough of it does appear in the newspaper columns, in one form or another, to give papers the appearance of a clearing house for pressure group publicity and propaganda. This is by no means cause for intemperate alarm. Much of what goes on in society is group initiated, and group activities are the source of a large proportion of worthy news. However, the multiplication of press agents and skilled publicity men, the staging of stunts and the manufacture of news, and the refined and skilled techniques of press relations have all combined to make it difficult for editors to separate real from fake news. There is also the problem of differentiating real news from free publicity. For years individual papers, as well as ANPA, have been vigorously striving to channel pure publicity into advertising rather than news columns.

The impact of pressure groups, publicity, and propaganda upon the newspaper press is many-sided and complicated. Consequently, the papers obtain much news they would or could not otherwise obtain, simply because they do not have sufficient staff to cover group activities adequately. In a sense, pressure groups are a real help to newspapers in supplying news, and valuable news at that. On the negative side, however, the publicity of pressure groups often distorts the real news picture, leads to the considerable use of pseudo, manufactured news, and results in a failure to give all important groups equitable access to the newspaper medium. Newspapers vary greatly in their attitudes toward particular groups, but the pro-business and pro-Republican bias of many papers is convincingly documented. Papers are by no means as pro-business and pro-Republican as in earlier days; the majority of papers try to keep this type of bias out of the news columns. Nevertheless, in defining news, gathering and selecting it, presenting and distributing it, few papers try conscientiously to give all groups—labor and business, party and profession, ethnic and religious—equal access to their printed pages. Of course, to say that this is pure bias may be to disregard different concepts of what is news, and what is important.

The Advertisers

To what extent are we able to confirm that the big advertisers influence and shape the newspaper and its contents? Since advertising revenue is such a large percentage of the total revenue of most papers, it would not be surprising to find a degree of the advertiser's influence on editorial and news content. The amount of influence in the case of a particular paper probably depends on whether the paper is dependent on a few or many advertisers, whether it enjoys a monopoly position in the market area it serves, whether the advertiser wants much, little or no publicity, whether or not the paper is in a strong financial position, and above all upon the editorial policy and courage of the paper and the willingness of advertisers to respect newspaper integrity and independence. Newspapers have been known, as favors to advertisers, to withhold information and to give free publicity on the editorial page or in news columns. Certainly private interests would not employ public relations and publicity staffs to obtain such favors, if they did not succeed to some extent. In the experience of many papers, the granting of one favor only leads to demands for more by one and all advertisers. It seems to have become obvious to most papers, however, that fair and equitable, nonpartisan treatment of all groups and all advertisers is good policy and good business. It is none the less true that newspapers, especially daily newspapers, as big businesses dependent on advertising, naturally have a point of view which is sympathetic to that of advertisers and businessmen. The pressure of these considerations, rather than the pressure of individual advertisers, is what really shapes and colors newspaper content. It is this attitude that helps explain newspaper opposition to laws regulating business in general and advertising in particular. Newspaper attitudes toward tax programs, welfare measures, labor unions, postal legislation are basically the consequence of the fact that newspapers are usually big businesses and depend on big advertising.

The Government

In some respects the American newspaper today owes its character and its form more to the influence of government than to any of the factors already mentioned, important as they are. The constitutional guarantees of freedom of the press as amplified and protected by law and judicial decision have done much to give American newspapers the freedom and independence they enjoy. Censorship in almost any form is abjured and abhorred, and probably no country has greater freedom to print than the United States. Even in wartime this press freedom is preserved to some extent in name if not in fact through "voluntary censorship," a kind of self-imposed censorship under the guidance of government officials. To be sure, newspaper proprietors are subject to libel laws and laws respecting false advertising, but aside from these restrictions their limits of discretion are extensive. In company with other businesses, they are conditioned in their business operations by laws regarding postal rates and practices, tax laws, labor laws, and many other statutes.

As government has become more and more the source of news—and it has to a remarkable extent in recent decades—it has affected profoundly the content of the newspaper. Government affairs, domestic and foreign, comprise an ever-increasing proportion of news space. The number of Washington correspondents increases, as do the correspondents in some state capitols. To meet the insatiable demand for government news, government agencies have enlarged information staffs and information output. They have, at times, gone beyond the mere release of information and propagandized to win public support. This latter effort arouses charges of "managed news," the conscious and deliberate furnishing or withholding, playing up or playing down, creating or concealing, juxtaposing or segregating of facts—in short, manipulating the news to create a desired effect.[15]

The Readers

In the final analysis, the influence of the newspaper reader is decisive. Unless readers in sufficient number buy and read newspapers, advertisers lose interest, and soon the paper folds. In a sense, the story of the newspaper in the United States is the account of an unending striving to attract new readers. Benjamin Day tapped the interests of the common man by crime and police court reports, Bennett by society news, church assemblies, Wall Street items, Hearst with items of concern to women and immigrants, Pulitzer with comics, Macfadden with "true stories." Throughout the nineteenth century primary emphasis seemed to be laid on searching for more new readers from lower and lower economic, educational, and cultural levels. With that area of circulation exploited, the search turned upwards, partly to find new readers, but perhaps to keep pace with the rising educational and cultural level of the population itself. This rising level of reader interest showed itself in more newspaper attention to literature, art, education, and science, and a more detailed and sophisticated treatment of politics, business activities, even of crime and personal tragedy.

The newspaper, in contrast to radio and television, for example, is able to cater more effectively to the interests of all readers and not merely to the majority. The newspaper is a package, a collection of items—news stories, features, editorials, and advertisements—designed to appeal to as wide a variety of reader interest as possible. It may pay to include items of interest to the minorities interested in coin-collecting or Chinese cooking, as well as news of public and international affairs or sports of interest to the majority. Unfortunately for the public, on radio and television the limitations of time and channels, with the salable standard unit of time 15-minute "chunks," mean that maximum revenue is usually obtained by presenting only those items with the widest possible appeal. Adding items with only specialized interest decreases rather than increases revenue.

The influence of readers is felt constantly, and newspaper proprietors are very sensitive to the revelations of reader surveys and to clues and crude indices of reader desires. Repeated surveys show the widespread interest in pictorial and graphic content, in a few outstanding news events, and in sports. In general, editorials and serious commentaries on the news rank low in the scale of interest, while the relative ranking of news regarding weather, deaths, business, amusements, science, and politics varies greatly from time to time and person to person. The newspaper reaches lower into the socio-economic scale than books and magazines but not as deeply as radio and television.

Readers, as a rule, do not take the initiative in bringing about changes in newspaper content, format, or practices, although letters to the editor or personal contact with members of the staff elicit suggestions. Changes are more likely to be made in response to suggestions by circulation, editorial, or other staff members, or by survey and promotional firms. Newspapers are in a better position than radio and television to test suggestions on a small scale. Not all newspapers sacrifice other important motives to maximize circulation. Other influential factors may include promoting causes, building a reputation for newspaper excellence, or serving the interests of a social, economic, intellectual, or ethnic class. Only a comprehensive review of the many reader surveys that have been made and the newspaper changes which resulted would pinpoint the influence of the reader on newspaper form and operations. The obvious concern of newspaper executives with readers and circulation is convincing evidence of this reader influence.

It should be emphasized, in concluding this survey of some of the major influences shaping the newspaper, that all of these factors—ownership, technology, personnel, pressure groups, advertisers, government, and reader —intermix and interact to produce the end result. It is virtually impossible to rank and measure them in the order of their importance, and little would be gained by trying to.

THE INFLUENCE OF THE PRESS

Much has been written about the influence of the newspaper press. Its power is reputed to mold public opinion, to shape public policy, to create and destroy governments, to make war and maintain peace, to preserve the status quo and to reconstruct society. Its alleged power to do all these things is extolled by many, questioned by some, and feared by others. Although it is extremely difficult to separate the influence of the newspaper from other influences with which it is intertwined and even more difficult to measure that influence precisely, its influence is widely accepted on other less scientific, but none the less convincing evidence. Logic strongly suggests that that something which governments have so frequently tried to suppress, control, or use, to which individuals and organized groups so zealously try to gain access, and which circulates so widely and is read so persistently must have considerable influence. Certainly advertisers, politicians, organized groups, promoters of all kinds, business and religious leaders would devote far less time and money than they do to relations with the press if they did not believe the newspaper was a powerful molder of opinion. Although a few attempts have been made to measure the precise influence of particular papers and groups of papers in particular situations and at certain times, convincing generalizations from the meager evidence available are almost non-existent.[16]

There are numerous factors that affect or condition the influence of newspapers, such as the nature of the object or target of influence, the number and character of the competing influences, the extent to which the object of the influence is exposed to the newspaper, the subject matter or direction of the influence, and the predispositions of those to be influenced. These are some of the variables in what may be called the influence situation. It may be easier for a paper to influence children than adults, women than men, long-term rather than short-time subscribers. Influence may be greater when other media support rather than oppose, when competing organizations in the public opinion arena are not very strong. It would seem plausible that influence would vary more or less with the amount and nature of direct exposure to the pages of the paper. Also, influence may be greater on generally approved subjects, than on controversial matters. Finally, the existing attitudes, traits, and predispositions of the reader will hinder or facilitate the projection of influence. Influence will also vary with the prestige of the paper or writer, and the information the reader already has about the subject. Well structured opinions, opinions held for a long time, and opinions based on known facts and personal experience are generally difficult to change. In this respect the influence of newspapers in matters of foreign policy or international relations or even national policy may be far greater than in matters of local concern which fall well within the everyday experience and knowledge of the average reader.

Consumer Buying

Probably the most important area of newspaper influence is consumer buying. Over three and three-quarter billion dollars (1962—$3,793,900,-000) are now spent yearly on newspaper advertising, 21.6 per cent of it on national advertising and 78.4 per cent on local advertising.[17] In spite of advertising competition from television and other media, newspaper revenue from advertising as well as the proportion of newspaper space given to advertisements continues to increase. The vote of confidence by advertisers in the selling power of newspaper advertisements is very impressive and convincingly demonstrates the power of the press in the market place.

Politics

The influence of the press in politics is not as clear as it is in advertising. By virtue of editorial policy there are many more Republican than Democratic papers, though the difference grows smaller and the proportion of independent papers grows. The political influence of a paper may reflect the content of its news columns as much as, if not more than, its editorial columns. This is a tribute to the laudable attempt to keep partisanship or editorializing out of the news columns. Papers today are far from perfect in this respect, but progress since the nineteenth and early twentieth century is noticeable. It is much easier to see the political direction of editorials than of news columns; moreover, the newspaper as a whole, with its variety of news stories and columnists, may be such a confusing and conflicting complex of influences that it is virtually impossible to determine the direction of its over-all influence, to say nothing of its strength.

Not only do different elements within a paper often negate each other's influence, but a newspaper's influence may often be lessened by the selective reading habits of a large number of people. Innumerable studies show that readers tend to read what they agree with, approve, or like.[18] Republicans read Republican and Democrats read Democratic output. To the extent this is true, much of what is overtly partisan only reaches the faithful. The rapid disappearance of competitive newspapers in a single town may mean that readers will be forced to cross party lines in their reading habits, where one paper only is available. It will also be likely that these monopoly papers, whether from self interest and advertising pressure, or from a greater sense of public responsibility, will move in the direction of non-partisanship or omni-partisanship. Their influence will be less partisan and directed toward individual men and measures, toward arguments directed to the merits of proposals and policies.

The influence of newspapers in elections is far from clear, perhaps because so few attempts have been made to determine precisely what that influence is. That politicians, candidates, and party organizations think papers are influential is shown by the efforts made to secure favorable publicity, both free and paid for. Nevertheless, the frequency with which victory goes to the side with little or no newspaper support, has led some to conclude that a law of inverse relationship exists. In city after city, candidates and parties have won in the face of 100 per cent newspaper opposition. The repeated victories of Franklin D. Roosevelt against overwhelming newspaper opposition seemed to prove the electoral impotence of newspapers. But who could say what would have happened if the press had not participated? What of the point that FDR victories only showed that front page news was more influential than editorials? Many factors are involved in the outcome of any election—the strength of party organization, issues, personalities, political traditions, economic conditions—and the role of the newspaper in many cases may be of only marginal importance although in close elections this marginal impact could be decisive.

Some have argued that the power of the press is more negative than positive. As T. S. Matthews puts it,[19] "The press has a negative power— to titillate, alarm, enrage, amuse, humiliate, annoy, even to drive a person out of his community or his job. But of the positive power to which it pretends, and of which the Press lords dream—to make war and break governments, to swing an election, to stop a war or start a revolution— there is no tangible evidence." This may be true, no one really knows.

There are undoubtedly many instances where the deliberate attempts of newspapers to influence elections, editorially and otherwise, have borne fruit. Their influence on public policy would also seem to be considerable since many policy makers look to their favorite papers for clues to the popular will. Papers usually take an active part in furthering or hindering the adoption of constitutional amendments and legislative referenda. Many newspaper crusades have exposed governmental corruption, initiated reforms, and brought about changes in government personnel, organization, procedures, and policies.[20] In spite of the increasing influence of television in politics, the newspaper still remains the primary source of information regarding candidates and office holders, legislation and policies, and what is going on in government. For breadth of treatment, for variety of viewpoints, for interpretation and background, it really has no equal.

Crime and Morals

A third important area in which the newspaper apparently exerts much influence is that of crime and morals. Papers vary greatly in the amount of space given crime, sex, and violence and in the way they treat such news.

At one extreme is the temperate and conservative policy of such papers as *The New York Times* and *The Christian Science Monitor,* and at the other, the lurid sensationalism of the popular press. Studies of newspaper sensationalism have plotted and diagrammed the column inches and pictorial space devoted to this kind of reportage, and the statistics regarding vice, crime, and violence are available. The problem is to determine the extent of the causal relationship, if any. There seems to be some plausible evidence that exposure to such material has affected the behavior of children and young people, and in some instances, may have touched off a certain amount of imitative actions by people more or less predisposed to abnormal behavior of this sort. The extent of this influence, however, is unknown. At least this much is clear, the time spent reading this kind of newspaper fare must be taken away from time that might be given to more nourishing diets. Whether or not this sensationalism is a specific cause of anti-social behavior, it surely leaves mental images and impressions which condition and color behavior, albeit subtly and indirectly.

There are doubtless many other areas where the influence of the newspaper is felt, but precise knowledge regarding them does not exist. What of the influence of the various sections of the paper on the minds and behavior of readers: the business section, sports section, women's pages, book reviews, art, and entertainment. It is often more difficult to extricate and identify the slow-moving, long-term, but in many cases the more important effects, than it is to perceive the speedier, more dramatic, but perhaps fleeting effects. The publication of a news item regarding the President's concern about the walking ability or lack of it of military personnel may start a walking craze throughout the United States. The influence of the newspaper in this case is apparent, though not the kind of influence which will probably have lasting and profound effects. What students of newspaper influence would really like to know, however, are answers to far more important questions. What influence, if any, are newspapers in the United States having on the public's views regarding good government, the administration of justice, the process of law-making, and public administration in the public interest? Are papers making it easier or more difficult for public officials to do their job well and for democracy to succeed? What are the over-all effects of newspaper publishing on tensions between nations, between employers and employees, between ethnic groups? Do they, in their over-all effect, promote war and strife, or reconciliation and understanding? What of their impact on character, on the public's conception of justice and morality, on their idealism and cynicism? These are, indeed, difficult questions to answer. Their asking reveals how little we really know about the influence of the press, and what the challenge is.

How Does the Press Influence Public Opinion?

Finally, a word regarding the various ways in which the newspaper exerts its influence. It does this by screening and selecting the items to be printed, by the way these items are presented, the emphasis and treatment accorded them, the headlines and pictures used, the typography and format employed, the position in the paper, and the skill employed in the writing and pictorial presentation. During World War II, the U. S. Office of War Information used these and many other devices for exploiting news for propaganda purposes. News was played up and played down, dramatized, repeated, juxtaposed, spelled out, underscored, all short of actual falsification, to enhance its influence in desired directions. Thus, today, various techniques are used to make papers interesting, readable, attractive, stand out, entertaining, informative, exciting, shocking, ad infinitum, to enhance their influence.

PROBLEMS AND CRITICISM

The newspaper in the United States, notwithstanding the progress it has made and its many accomplishments, has by no means solved all its problems or attained all its goals. From time to time these goals have been defined by individual papers in their Volume I, No. 1. They have also been set forth by groups of editors or publishers, by special commissions established to study the press, and by students of journalism. Noteworthy in this regard are the "Canons of Journalism" of the American Society of Newspaper Editors, formulated in 1923, and the requirements of press responsibility enumerated by the Commission on Freedom of the Press in 1947. The aims of editors and students of journalism do not always jibe, however, with those of newspaper owners, and when profits and ideals conflict, it is usually the ideals which suffer. Profits may be sacrificed up to a point and for a period of time, but ultimately a limit is reached. The basic question which every newspaper proprietor faces is how good a paper he can afford to publish. To those less idealistically inclined, this may be a misleading question, since for them the standard of goodness is profitableness itself.

News versus Entertainment

Although newspapers perform many functions, their news function—the gathering, selection, treatment, presentation, and distribution of news—is, or should be, paramount. As the "Canons of Journalism" state, "The primary function of newspapers is to communicate to the human race what its members do, feel, think." The Commission on Freedom of the Press would require the newspaper to give "full access to the day's intelligence" and "a truthful, comprehensive, and intelligent account of the day's events in a context which gives them meaning." The literature of and about journalism repeatedly emphasizes the primacy of the news function, though other, supplementary goals are mentioned, such as interpretation of news, criticism of government, guidance of public opinion, projecting "a representative picture of the constituent groups in the society . . . presentation and clarification of the goals and values of the society," and providing a "forum for the exchange of comment and criticism." [21] Actually, the newspaper functions as an entertainer, a means of escape, an adviser, educator, exhorter, and advertiser, to mention only a few of its secondary and tertiary uses.

A large percentage of the criticisms of newspapers deals with their alleged failure as purveyors of news. Critics say that the news function is all too frequently subordinated to the entertainment function, that too little care is taken to get and present accurate and truthful news, that too often news is slanted, distorted, fabricated, and biased to favor special interests, that important news is frequently omitted in favor of the shocking, dramatic, and sensational items, and that news is presented, many times, in such a way as to obscure its meaning and significance. Not all of these criticisms will apply to all newspapers at all times, but there is sufficient evidence to justify the claims to some extent.[22]

There are many replies which newspaper proprietors can and do make. Some, and the number is small, insist that running a newspaper imposes no greater responsibility on the publisher than running a grocery business does on a grocer. So long as he stays within the law, including the law of libel, it is no one's business what he prints and how unimportant, incomplete, biased, unrepresentative, sensational, and meaningless it is. Less irresponsible publishers would not go this far, but they would claim that freedom of the press means freedom to print what the owner wishes to print within the limits of good taste, accuracy, and personal integrity. The more responsible editors and publishers would agree that, in return for the very special privileges accorded newspapers by the government and constitution and because of their importance in the democratic process, they have special and very important responsibilities in relation to their readers and the government. Some of them would argue, however, that any improvements in their performance of the news function would be too costly and would not, in fact, be appreciated by their readers. In the final analysis, they say, we are giving the people what they want. There is no evidence, they argue, that readers want more complete, more accurate, or less sensationalized news than they are getting. It is for the readers themselves to determine their newspaper fare, not for government, some intellectual elite, or even newspaper owners themselves to decide what the readers should get because someone else says it is good for them.

Press Freedom and Press Responsibility

The problem of newspaper responsibility is indeed a difficult one. To what extent are newspaper proprietors responsible for complete coverage of the day's news, for truthfulness and meaningful interpretation of the news, for representing all groups, for clarifying the goals and values of society? To be more specific: Is a newspaper under an obligation, a special obligation to further democracy and the United States' form of capitalism rather than authoritarianism and communism or fascism? Does it have a responsibility to strengthen rather than weaken the carrying out of United States foreign policies, to mitigate, at least not to aggravate, international tensions, and tensions between racial groups or labor and capital? Must it always be on the side of tolerance, non-violence, compromise, ethics, morality? Does it, in other words, have higher obligations than the obligation to get the news and print it, regardless of consequences? [23]

To define the extent of newspaper responsibility is to define the limits of press freedom. Press freedom and press responsibility are the two sides of one coin. There are already specific limits to press freedom in laws of libel and laws regarding false advertising. Beyond this, however, it is presumed that press freedom itself, the free competition of information and opinions in the market place, coupled with the pressure of public opinion, will set whatever further limits are desirable. Why, then, doesn't press freedom produce more newspapers that promote the good rather than the bad by deleting news that inflames tensions and hatreds, by leaving out items that cater to the morbid, the pathological, and the prurient or by refusing to publish news that is trivial, bizarre, or merely gossipy?

One reason, of course, is that there is actually no real newspaper competition in ninety-five per cent of the cities and towns in the United States today. Readers may grumble about the quality of their papers, as they do for example on the West Coast and in many cities across the country, but there is little they can do. It is merely a question of taking what they get or leaving it. But the question arises, why in these areas do the low rather than the high quality papers survive, and why in the few places where newspaper competition still exists, do the more sensational and lurid papers circulate more widely than a quality paper such as the *New York Times*? The answer seems to be that as papers decrease in number in any community, those remaining tend more and more to cater to the interests, and, one could say, the needs of the majorities. They approach a mean average of performance which is somewhere between the worst and the best. This mean average is rising as anyone can see who attempts to compare the typical monopoly newspaper in one-newspaper towns today with the papers that have fallen by the wayside during the last fifty years.

The loss of some very fine papers has been compensated for by the disappearance of some that merited extinction.

Will the passing of newspaper competition mean a redefinition of press freedom and an acceptance of greater responsibility by newspaper proprietors? There is some reason for optimism. Monopoly newspapers are likely to be more profitable and therefore financially able to raise quality, if they desire to do so. This desire may well be encouraged by competition from other media, if not from a growing number of regional and national papers on the one hand, and numerous, enterprising, and aggressive suburban papers on the other. Moreover the influence of the advertiser in maximum circulation may, in the case of papers in contrast to television, mean greater variety in newspaper content and efforts to win more readers from the higher rather than the lower cultural and intellectual groups. The success of books and especially popular magazines has always indicated the emerging interests of the reading public. Newspapers still have opportunities for exploiting these interests.

Even though the "monopoly" newspaper continues to follow rather than lead public opinion and persists in "trying to give the public what it wants," this must inevitably lead to better papers. Although the statistics regarding the educational revolution that has taken place since 1900 are available for all to read, mass media proprietors have been slow to comprehend the full impact of longer schooling, greater breadth of curriculum, and more intensive specialization on the intellectual and entertainment tastes of the general public. The American reader is far more discriminating than before, far more knowledgeable, and far more articulate. Even in one-paper towns greater newspaper responsibility is destined to come, either through the sharp pricking of editorial consciences or the falling off of circulation and advertising revenue.

There is a strong disposition these days to say that everyone, that is each person, is entitled to his own opinion and to his own philosophy of values. This sort of philosophical, cultural, and ethical anarchism is quite as objectionable as political anarchism, which pits each against all and destroys the very freedom it purports to foster. Government, law, and sanctions are not ends in themselves, but means to an end—the maximum freedom of all. The necessity for rules, standards, and laws in the fields of values and morals is quite as imperative as it is in politics and other fields. No rules or laws can control thinking per se, but when values and goals become articulate and actualized in behavior they do become of concern to all.

How then can true press freedom be realized? It must be freedom under law, not press anarchy. But whose law? Shall it be divine law or man made? If man made, by whom, the few or the many, the elite or the mass? In the realm of government and politics, some have said the few, others the many, and the forms of government and rule making have varied from pure democracy to naked dictatorship. The people of the United States have tried to avoid the extremes and adopt the mean, and to combine the insights and expertise of the few with the earthy wisdom of the many.

The Question of Standards

Similarly in the newspaper field, in the interest of real press freedom, standards are necessary—not only legal, but moral and cultural. One man's values are not necessarily as good as any other man's. There is probably no better way for determining those standards and values than to adopt what may be called the "mixed," "mean," or republican approach somewhere between the extremes of a plebiscite and a dictatorial edict. A system could be devised, without doubt, for arriving at canons of modern journalism that would balance the masses' concept of what is good or bad, right or wrong, moral or immoral with the views of the "experts," in such matters. It should be remembered that the term "freedom of the press," although it meant in earlier days merely freedom from government control for owners and publishers and freedom from governmental censorship and licensing requirements, has grown to mean freedom from all restraints business as well as governmental that interfere with its proper functioning. It has come to refer to the freedom of readers to know, as well as the freedom of proprietors to speak.[24] Perhaps it also means today freedom of access to its pages, as well as freedom to read what is printed thereon; freedom to receive fair wages as employees, as well as reasonable profits as owners. If it is essential that public policy, domestic and foreign, have a popular base as well as a detailed structure elaborated by experts, the same is true of newspaper policy. The editor and publisher, as architects, can design and suggest, but the ultimate decision will rest with the clients, the reading public.

Some have argued that newspapers are public utilities and should be regulated as such, either by government commission, or by some agency of self-regulation, as the motion-picture, radio, and television industries have attempted. It is not argued, as in the case of some accepted utilities, such as the railroads, that newspapers are natural monopolies. Rather the argument stresses that the importance of the press in the democratic process is so great that the newspaper publishers and editors cannot be left to their own whims and devices. The importance of the press—keeping the public informed regarding matters pertinent to their role as sovereign decision makers—is attested to by the special constitutional guarantees of press freedom. What might be gained by such enforced responsibility would be more than lost, however, by reinforced lethargy, lack of enterprise, and a weakening of corporate fiber and moral character. Far more could be accomplished in raising standards through pressure from readers, educating students in school, college, and professional schools in understanding the role and potentiality of the newspaper in a democratic society, and by fostering positive, progressive leadership within the profession of journalism.

The problems of biased news, sensationalism, emphasis on violence, sex, and crime, inaccuracy, meaningless news—all of these problems could be partially solved if editors and publishers really wished and willed to solve them. Education, training, and reader pressure, not enforced reform, is the best answer.

ASSESSMENT AND EVALUATION

How may the role of the newspaper be assessed and evaluated? Many different criteria of appraisal could be employed according to the function selected—news function, editorial function, advertising, or entertainment. From the point of view of government and the citizen a basic question is, how well is the press performing its functions of enlightening the people and helping them to decide wisely the questions they need to decide? It is because of this responsibility for enlightening the public that the press is accorded special constitutional and other legal privileges.

The competence of the public depends on the information it has and on its capacity to use that information wisely. Newspapers supply their readers with more information than ever before—more in quantity and variety, but also more in quality. Whether it is sufficient for the tasks confronting the citizenry is a question of some difficulty. Many of our oft maligned papers carry more significant news and information today than the most informative papers did a century earlier. But mere information isn't enough, even though it is comprehensive, accurate, important, and meaningful. In order for the public to use this information intelligently it must be able to think logically about it, which means the ability to arrange and organize information, to perceive issues and problems, to see relationships and identify causes, to anticipate effects, to recognize logical fallacies, and to be aware of alternative remedies or solutions.

What the public does with the news, facts, and ideas the newspaper brings to it is something over which the paper has little control. It cannot teach its readers how to think straight, which means thinking logically. Nor can it control the reader's center of attention. Readers are selective, and however newspapers may try to direct the reader's attention and manage the reader's selectivity, the limit of their efforts is soon reached.

There are other ways in which newspapers fail, some are remediable, others not. The newspaper, by its very nature, stresses the present out of proportion to the past or future. There is a wide difference, a marked lack of agreement, regarding what is and what is not newsworthy and important. Also, as indicated previously, the profit motive may, and sometimes does, lead to prostitution of news function and excesses of bias and sensationalism. Possibly the greatest weakness of the newspaper as an organ of popular enlightenment is the fact that its influence comes late, after the full impact of family, church, and school. This is not to say that the newspaper does not influence young people indirectly through parents, preachers, and teachers, but the basic institutions are still the primary influences during the formative years.

NOTES FOR CHAPTER 8

Epigraph. Commission on Freedom of the Press, *A Free and Responsible Press* (1947) p. 21.
1. Commission on Freedom of the Press, *A Free and Responsible Press.* (Chicago: University of Chicago Press, 1947).
2. There are several standard histories of newspapers in the United States, notably those of Frank L. Mott, Edwin Emery, W. G. Bleyer, J. M. Lee, George Henry Payne.
3. On early newspapers in England and the United States see Frank, Joseph, *The Beginnings of the English Newspaper, 1620-1660* (Cambridge, Mass.: Harvard University Press, 1961); Shaeber, Matthias A., *Some Forerunners of the Newspapers in England, 1476-1622* (Philadelphia: University of Pennsylvania Press, 1929); Hudson, Frederic, *Journalism in the United States* (New York: Harper and Brothers, 1873).
4. See Mott, Frank L., *American Journalism: A History, 1690-1960* (3rd ed.; New York: The Macmillan Co., 1962), ch. 6. John Fenno established the *Gazette of the United States* in 1789 to support the Federalists, and Philip Frenau launched the *National Gazette* in 1791 on behalf of the Jeffersonian Republicans. The latter ceased publication in 1793; the former continued to 1818.
5. See Carlson, Oliver, *The Man Who Made News: James Gordon Bennett* (New York: Duell, Sloan and Pearce, 1942).
6. See Seitz, D. D., *Joseph Pulitzer: His Life and Letters* (New York: Simon and Schuster, 1924); Swanberg, W. A., *Citizen Hearst* (New York: Charles Scribner's Sons, 1961).
7. See Rosewater, Victor, *History of Cooperative Newsgathering in the United States* (New York: Appleton, 1930); International Press Institute, *The Flow of the News* (Zurich, Switzerland, 1953); Gramling, Oliver, *AP: The Story of the News* (New York: Farrar and Rinehart, 1940); Cooper, Kent, *Kent Cooper and the Associated Press: An Autobiography* (New York: Random House, 1959).
8. See "The Menace of Radio," *History of the American Newspaper Publishers' Association,* chap. 8, pp. 196-211 (Minneapolis: The University of Minnesota Press, 1950), ed. Edwin Emery. Also, Chester, Giraud, "The Press-Radio War: 1933-35," *Public Opinion Quarterly,* Vol. 13 (Summer, 1949), pp. 252-64.

9. For latest summary of statistics see *Directory of Newspapers and Periodicals* (Philadelphia: N. W. Ayer & Sons, Inc., 1963), p. xix.
10. *Statistical Abstract of the United States* (1963), pp. 787-91; 524-25.
11. See Nixon, Raymond B. and Jean Ward, "Trends in Newspaper Ownership and Inter-media Competition," *Journalism Quarterly*, Vol. 38 (Winter, 1961), pp. 3-14.
12. See *Broadcasting*, March 13, 1961, p. 44.
13. See Edelstein, Alex, "The Challenge of Communications in Century 21," *Journalism Quarterly* (Summer, 1963). Special supplement. Steinberg, S. H., *Five Hundred Years of Printing*. (New York: Criterion Books, 1959).
14. See Emery, Edwin (ed.), *History of the American Newspaper Publishers' Association, op. cit.*
15. A panel of newsmen, for example, told Congress on March 19, 1963, that U. S. Government officials had manipulated the news and lied during the Cuban crisis in October, 1962. The group represented publishers, editors, broadcasters, and included James R. Reston of the *New York Times,* Herbert Brucker of the *Hartford Courant,* Clark Mollenhoff of the *Des Moines Register* and *Tribune,* and Gene Robb of the *Albany Times-Union.* Arthur Sylvester, Assistant Secretary of Defense for Public Affairs, defending government policy, said that the government had "a right, if necessary, to lie to save itself when it's going up into a nuclear war." The panel insisted on known censorship rules, if needed, not "management of the news." *Washington Post,* March 20, 1963, p. A1.
16. See Klapper, Joseph T., "What We Know About the Effects of Mass Communication: The Brink of Hope," *Public Opinion Quarterly,* Vol. 21 (Winter, 1957-58), pp. 453-74; and Davison, W. Phillips, "On the Effects of Communication," *Public Opinion Quarterly,* Vol. 23 (Fall, 1959), pp. 343-60.
17. See *Information Please Almanac,* 1963, p. 597.
18. See Lazarsfeld, Paul F. *et al., The People's Choice, op. cit.,* and Berelson, Bernard *et al., Voting, op. cit.*
19. *The Sugar Pill* (New York: Simon and Schuster, 1959), p. 166.
20. Weinberg, Arthur and Lila, *The Muckrakers* (New York: Simon and Schuster, 1961); Regier, C. C., *The Era of the Muckrakers* (Chapel Hill: University of North Carolina Press, 1932).
21. See *A Free and Responsible Press, op. cit.*
22. The number of newspaper critics is legion. Dean Edward W. Barrett of Columbia University's Graduate School of Journalism states that only 18 of the 200 major newspapers in the United States are first-rate, and that 50 are definitely bad, operating as though they were shoestore chains, motivated solely by profits, biased, ignoring local corruption, unable to recognize and reward talent (*New York Times,* May 26, 1963). Among newspaper critics the following have been outspoken: Robert M. Hutchins (speech before ASNE, *New York Times,* April 22, 1955, p. 16); George Seldes (*Lords of the Press,* New York: Julian Messner, Inc., 1938), and other writings; Upton B. Sinclair (*The Brass Check,* Pasadena, Calif.: The Author, 1920); H. L. Ickes (*America's House of Lords,* New York: Harcourt, 1939); Silas Bent (*Ballyhoo: The Voice of the Press,* New York: Boni and Liveright, 1927), A. E. Rowse (*Slanted News,* Boston: Beacon Press, 1957); A. J. Liebling (*The Press,* New York: Ballantine Books, Inc., 1961); Carl Lindstrom (*The Fading American Newspaper,* New York: Doubleday & Co., Inc., 1960).

23. See Gerold, J. Edward, *The Social Responsibility of the Press* (Minneapolis: University of Minnesota Press, 1963); Wiggins, J. R., "The Power and Responsibility of the Press," *Journalism Quarterly,* Vol. 37 (Winter, 1960), pp. 29-34. The Commission on Freedom of the Press, *A Free and Responsible Press* (Chicago: University of Chicago Press, 1947); Schramm, Wilbur, *Responsibility in Mass Communication* (New York: Harper & Brothers, 1957).
24. Hudson, Edward G., *Freedom of Speech and Press in America* (Washington, D. C.: Public Affairs Press, 1963); Cross, Harold L., *The People's Right to Know* (New York: Columbia University Press, 1953).

SUPPLEMENTARY READING

BENT, SILAS. *Ballyhoo: The Voice of the Press.* New York: Boni and Liveright, 1927.

BIRD, G. L., and MERWIN, F. E. *The Press and Society.* New York: Prentice-Hall, Inc., 1951.

BLEYER, W. G. *Main Currents in the History of American Journalism.* Boston: Houghton Mifflin Co., 1927.

CATER, DOUGLASS, *The Fourth Branch of Government.* Boston: Houghton Mifflin Co., 1959.

CLARK, WESLEY CLARK (ed.). *Journalism Tomorrow.* Syracuse, N. Y.: Syracuse University Press, 1958.

COHEN, BERNARD C. *The Press and Foreign Policy.* Princeton, N. J.: Princeton University Press, 1963.

Commission on Freedom of the Press, *A Free and Responsible Press.* Chicago: University of Chicago Press, 1947.

COOPER, KENT. *The Right to Know.* New York: Farrar, Straus and Cudahy, 1956.

EMERY, EDWIN, and SMITH, H. L. *The Press and America.* New York: Prentice-Hall, Inc., 1954.

HOCKING, W. E. *Freedom of the Press: A Framework of Principle.* Chicago: University of Chicago Press, 1947.

KIMBALL, PENN. "People Without Papers," *Public Opinion Quarterly,* Vol. 23 (Fall, 1959), pp. 389-98.

KOBRE, SIDNEY. *Modern American Journalism.* Tallahassee: Florida State University, 1959.

LEE, ALFRED McCLUNG. *The Daily Newspaper in America.* New York: The Macmillan Co., 1937.

LEE, JAMES MELVIN. *History of American Journalism.* Boston: Houghton Mifflin, 1917.

LIEBLING, A. J. *The Press.* New York: Ballantine Books Inc., 1961.

LINDSTROM, CARL E. *The Fading American Newspaper.* Doubleday & Co., Inc., 1960.

LIPPMANN, WALTER. *Liberty and The News.* New York: Harcourt, Brace and Howe, 1920.

MACDOUGALL, C. D. *Interpretative Reporting.* New York: The Macmillan Co., 1963.

MATTHEWS, T. S. *The Sugar Pill.* New York: Simon and Schuster, 1959. First published in London by Gallancz.

MOTT, FRANK L. *American Journalism.* 3rd ed. The Macmillan Co., 1962.

PRICE, WARREN C. *The Literature of Journalism: An Annotated Bibliography.* Minneapolis: University of Minnesota Press, 1959.

ROSEWATER, VICTOR. *History of Cooperative News-gathering in the U. S.* New York: Appleton, 1930.

ROSTEN, LEO C. *The Washington Correspondents.* New York: Harcourt, Brace, & Co., 1937.

SALMON, LUCY MAYNARD. *The Newspaper and Authority.* New York: Oxford University Press, 1923.

SALMON, LUCY MAYNARD. *The Newspaper and the Historian.* New York: Oxford University Press, 1923.

SCHRAMM, WILBUR. "Twenty Years of Journalism Research," *Public Opinion Quarterly,* Vol. 21 (Spring, 1957), pp. 91-107.

SELDES, GEORGE. *Lords of the Press.* Messner, Inc., 1938.

SELDES, GEORGE. *Freedom of the Press.* Indianapolis, Ind.: Bobbs-Merrill, 1935.

SINCLAIR, UPTON B. *The Brass Check.* Pasadena, Calif.: The Author, 1920.

SVIRSKY, LEON. *Your Newspapers: Blueprint for a Better Press.* New York: The Macmillan Co., 1947.

WILHELM, JOHN. "The Reappearing Foreign Correspondent: A World Survey," *Journalism Quarterly,* Vol. 40 (Spring, 1963), pp. 147-68.

WILLIAMS, FRANCIS. *Dangerous Estate: The Anatomy of Newspapers.* London: Longmans, 1957.

WOLSELEY, ROLAND E. *The Journalists' Bookshelf.* 7th edition. Philadelphia: The Chilton Company, 1961.

IX · Motion Pictures, Radio, and Television

I invite you to sit down in front of your television set. . . . I can assure you that you will observe a vast wasteland.

—NEWTON N. MINOW

THERE IS considerable justification for considering motion pictures, radio, and television together. They exemplify somewhat more exactly than the newspaper the concept mass media, although the newspaper press is properly included in that connotation. These three media reach out more broadly and down more deeply into the population strata than the newspaper press. Their listening and viewing audiences comprise nearly everyone capable of viewing and listening, from the littlest of tots to the most senior of citizens. Partly because of this fact and also for technical reasons, in the case of radio and television, these media have not enjoyed that degree of freedom from government concern or supervision granted the printed media. Motion pictures have from time to time been subjected to censorship in some of the states, and radio and television have long been regulated by the Federal government. Although their history is much shorter than that of the newspaper and the printed word, their impact on American culture and public opinion speedily approaches, if it has not surpassed, the impact of the press. Finally, these three media are closely related both historically and technologically.

HISTORY AND DEVELOPMENT

The story of the development of these electronic media illustrates in a vivid manner the history of science itself, the step by step process by which science moves ahead modifying, improving, and combining the discoveries and inventions of the past to create the new. In a sense the history of the latest, enlarged, color television screen goes back at least to the appearance of the "magic lantern" during the middle of the seventeenth century, and if one really wants to pinpoint the ultimate beginning it would have to be the beginning of science.

The Movies

Whatever the date of its origin, by the middle of the nineteenth century the development of the motion picture was rapidly on its way.[1] The principle of the persistence of vision had been discovered (1824), the "wheel of life" had been combined with the magic lantern (1853), photography was fairly well developed by 1860, a series of photographs had been applied to the "wheel of life" (1880), and with the development of photographic film (also 1880) and Thomas A. Edison's motion-picture camera, the Kinescope, in 1894, the motion picture was ready for business. The first public film showing, a four minute fight film, occurred on May 21, 1895. From then until the "talking" motion picture in 1928, the growth of the medium was truly phenomenal. Technical improvements and refinements were made in photography, films, and projectors, feature-length pictures supplemented the shorter subjects, and the artistic and dramatic quality of pictures improved, the rising demand for bigger and better pictures produced thousands of new motion-picture theaters, new and more efficient systems of distribution, and the Hollywood image which is still vivid throughout the United States and the world. No one probably ever can precisely define what this word "Hollywood" really means and what its impact has been on the public opinion of our times. It means so many things to so many different people—to many, glamour, success, and wealth; to some, unreality, tawdriness, and greed; to others, ruthlessness, immorality, and debasement—yet, nearly everyone seems to sense that directly or indirectly, over longer or shorter periods, the thing that was and is Hollywood has left an indelible mark on the American mind and character.

The introduction of sound motion pictures in 1928 added a new and important dimension to the medium and made possible the adaptation of a literary and dramatic output of greater intellectual depth and subtlety, as well as a world of music and sound. The motion picture as a medium in its own right reached its peak as a business and an art form in the 1930's.

Radio

Meanwhile, another medium had entered the arena of public opinion, and it was developing a mass audience of its own, overlapping both newspaper and motion pictures and also competing with them: radio.[2] The development of the wireless radio was preceded by almost 100 years of technical development in related areas of communication: the development of the telegraph (1832-44), the laying of transoceanic cables (1850-68), and the inauguration of the telephone (1876). The age of wireless began in 1873 after methods for producing and for detecting electromagnetic waves had been invented by James Clerk Maxwell and Heinrich Hertz, respectively. By 1896, communication by wireless was a fact, and the British Marconi Company had been established. By 1906, the human voice, as well as dots and dashes, were being broadcast. Until World War I when the United States government took over all senders, technical progress was rapid. Immediately following the war, with government encouragement, the Radio Corporation of America was founded to pool patents and facilitate research and development.[3]

Radio broadcasting on a commercial basis did not begin until 1920 when the first commercially licensed station, KDKA in Pittsburgh, began its broadcasts with news of the Harding-Cox election returns in November. There followed rapid demand for station licenses and within a few years hundreds of stations were in operation without attempt by the government to regulate or police the air waves. The confusion grew intolerable until in 1927 the Radio Act was passed. Meanwhile the National Association of Broadcasters was established in 1922, the industry turned somewhat reluctantly to advertising for revenue in 1923, and the NBC and CBS networks were established in 1925 and 1926 respectively. From 1927 to 1935 the radio industry expanded greatly and less chaotically. Air waves transmission was regulated and policed technically with more care. Licenses were granted and renewed with a more emphatic concern for the public interest. Although the act expressly forbade government censorship, it also stipulated regulation in the "public convenience, interest, or necessity." When dealing with program content the Federal Radio Commission (FRC) and its successor the Federal Communications Commission (FCC) often found it impossible to obey both mandates simultaneously; hence, a "hands off" program policy generally prevailed.

The FCC Act of 1934 expanded the jurisdiction of the new commission to cover all electrical means of communication including telephones, telegraph, and all forms of wireless transmission and radio broadcasting. The Commission was enlarged and procedures were changed somewhat. The ban on censorship was retained, as well as the "public interest, convenience, or necessity" clause. Freedom of speech for political candidates using the radio was guaranteed, as well as their right to "equal" time, a provision that gave some difficulty and was modified in its application during the Presidential election campaign of 1960.

The history of broadcasting since 1935 in the United States has been a history of technological change, notably the advent of FM, UHF (Ultra-high-frequency), and color television. It has also been a story of problems: some technical, some economic, some arising out of the competition for control of the medium. Before considering these, a brief mention should be made of the development of television to which both radio and the motion picture contributed.[4]

Television

Although light had been converted into electrical impulses as far back as 1873 and images had been transmitted in parts by the use of whirling disks in 1883, it was not until 1923 that an electronic method of scanning was developed. Considerable technological progress was made in the 1930's, both in the United States and abroad, and by 1936 FCC rules took cognizance of the new medium. By 1939 there were 23 licensed television stations, and in 1941 the Commission assigned 18 channels for their use. Between July 1, 1941 and the end of World War II further development was halted and because of the numerous and perplexing problems of allocation, standards, channels, and color—to mention a few—a "freeze" was imposed from 1948 to 1952, to give the Commission time to study these problems and chart a future course. Extremely important decisions had to be made: commitments that would affect the industry and the public for years to come. During the "freeze" extensive hearings were held on UHF and color television. The latter was authorized in 1951. Also, a nation-wide allocation table was set up, channels were set aside for educational television, and the ban on station editorializing was lifted.

The decade 1952-62 has been replete with radio and television problems, many of which remain unsolved. Technical problems of allocation, coverage, channels, program ratings persist. Even more pressing and significant are the problems arising out of the public responsibility of the industry, such as those of program content, cross-channel ownership, pay television, the political use of radio and television, self-regulation, monopoly, role of the networks, and the relation of the FCC to the Congress, to the broadcasting industry, and to the public.[5] The radio and TV dials may not be linked to a "wasteland" and, to be sure, the industry may point with pride to many fine programs, but most observers outside the industry seem convinced that technical progress has gone much farther than progress in over-all programming. The paucity of really good drama, worthwhile public affairs programs, entertaining entertainment, interestingly live broadcasts, significant information and the plethora of obnoxious advertising, violence, sex, and stupid and degrading entertainment suggest that there is room for improvement. Token excellence is no more satisfactory than token integration. A few worthwhile programs here and there hardly pay off the industry's debt to the public for wasting its time and investment.

ECONOMICS AND OWNERSHIP

The coming of age of television has by no means meant the end of the influence of the motion picture and radio. The advent of television has changed considerably the structure and output of the motion picture. To some extent the highly centralized and integrated corporate giants have given way to a multiplication of specialized, independent producers. The number of full length, feature pictures has dropped drastically from a yearly output of more than 600 to less than 200. Also, the motion-picture audience has fallen precipitously, but production of pictures for television itself, plus income from old releases, has helped greatly to offset losses. Nevertheless, the industry is still trying to find and stabilize its new position as a supplier of program content for television and as an independent medium, distributing and exhibiting images as well as producing them.[6]

The impact of television on radio seemed at first to be as menacing as its impact on motion pictures. Radio advertising revenue dwindled rapidly. Code regulations regarding advertising excesses and program standards soon lost much of their force, and many of them were discarded altogether in the panicky effort to check the fall of program ratings. But once the initial scare was over, it became evident that radio still had its place as an informer and entertainer. Actually, the number of radios in homes, office buildings, shops, cars, and elsewhere where TV was not always feasible or preferable, continued to increase.[7] Television certainly broadened the dimensions of broadcasting, but there still remained a very important role for radio, especially in the transmission of news, music, and programs where the visual image added little if anything to the audience appeal. Radio too is gradually finding an important and profitable place in the over-all communications pattern.

As in the case of the newspaper, a number of important influences have combined and interacted to produce the electronic media of the motion picture, radio, and television. Among the more important of these conditioning pressures are the owners and proprietors, the employees, the advertisers and advertising agencies, the Federal government, and the listening and viewing public. Each of these major groups comprises many subgroups with varying degrees of significance. The owners and proprietors are sometimes individuals, families, or partnerships. More often they are corporations. Not infrequently one owner or corporation will control a number of radio and TV stations to the extent allowed by law, plus several newspapers, and a few motion-picture companies. Then he will extend this media empire to include magazine and book publishing and even related businesses furnishing raw materials, manufactured products, as well as merchandising, transportation, and banking services. Among the more important of these media giants are the Time, Cowles, Triangle, Meredith, Whitney-Corinthian, Newhouse, Scripps-Howard, Cox, and Washington Post combines, with a number of regional publishing-broadcasting empires.[8] The Time group, according to the magazine *Broadcasting* in its March 13, 1960, issue, owned radio and TV stations in Denver, Indianapolis, Minneapolis, and Grand Rapids in addition to the magazines *Life, Fortune, Sports Illustrated,* and *Architectural Forum.* The Cowles group included *Look* magazine, and broadcasting and TV stations in Des Moines, Huntington (W. Va.), Minneapolis, and Wichita. Triangle could boast of an empire with stations in Altoona and Lebanon (Pa.), New Haven, Fresno, and Philadelphia. On the publishing side this combine comprised the *Philadelphia Inquirer* plus the Annenberg publications including *TV Guide, Seventeen, Daily Racing Form* and others. The Meredith Group with *Better Homes and Gardens* and its stations in Syracuse, Kansas City, Phoenix, Omaha, and Tulsa; the Whitney properties with the *New York Herald-Tribune* and its stations in Tulsa, Houston, Indianapolis, Fort Wayne, Sacramento; and the *Washington Post* with its *Newsweek* and stations in Washington and Jacksonville—all follow substantially the same pattern.

When newspapers first began to feel the competitive pressure of radio in the late twenties and early thirties their first reaction was to ignore it, then to fight it, and finally to join it. It was not long before newspapers were acquiring radio properties, and later TV stations, at such a rapid rate that it became necessary for the FCC to check the trend by limiting the number of papers and stations under a single ownership. These cross-channel, multiple ownership giants are significant, not so much because of the number of publications and broadcasting outlets they control (although this is important), but because of the location and signal strength of the stations and the circulation of their publications.

By far the great majority of radio and television stations in the United States are separately and individually owned. As of June 30, 1962, there were approximately 3,700 standard AM stations on the air, about 1,000 FM stations, and some 550 television stations. Notwithstanding earlier predictions that FM would soon drive AM stations out of business, the latter have increased steadily in number since World War II to a point where the FCC has been compelled to impose a partial "freeze" and to adopt "birth control" measures.

Following an initial, rapid increase in the number of stations soon after commercial FM was authorized in 1931, FM has not actually attained the rate of growth expected. The superior quality of FM reception was not generally matched by superior quality of programming, since FM programs often merely duplicated AM programs. Moreover, the limited range of FM signals, plus fewer FM than AM receiving sets, tended to make the FM medium less attractive to advertisers, hence often unprofitable. However, FM has found many specialized uses, especially at the local and community levels, and with the use of hi-fi and stereophonic recordings, many FM stations are beginning to flourish. Of the 1,000 stations on the air in 1962, there were 201 non-commercial educational stations, 325 were authorized to engage in multiplexed, subsidiary services, and 122 were programming stereo.

The development of television, especially after the end of the "freeze" in 1952 has been little short of phenomenal. In less than a decade the number of stations has increased five-fold. Growth in number of stations, however, reached its peak rather quickly because of the restricted number of TV channels available in the VHF (very high frequency) band. Efforts to encourage use of the UHF (ultra high frequency) band were slow to bring results, since most receiving sets were not equipped to tune to UHF. Actually, only 104 stations using UHF were on the air in 1962. On April 30, 1964, the requirement went into effect that manufacturers henceforward produce all-channel receiving sets. This should mean that this obstacle will be removed.

Among the owners of radio and television stations the major and minor networks play an important role. The NBC and CBS networks were established in 1925 and 1926 respectively, to be followed in 1934 by the Mutual Broadcasting System, and in 1942 by ABC. In addition to a few stations which each network owns or controls outright, the networks have "affiliates" which buy their program material and carry their advertising. The contractual relationships between network and affiliate have sometimes given rise to charges of monopoly and have been objects of extensive investigations by the FCC.[9] Since a considerable proportion of individual station program material is supplied by networks, their influence on the medium is great. Of 550 commercial television stations, well over 500 are affiliated with one of the major networks.

The business of radio and television is generally profitable.[10] The total revenue of television networks and stations has increased steadily from $1,900,000 in 1947 to $1,318,300,000 in 1961. Income before Federal taxes amounted to $237,000,000 in 1961. During the fiscal year ending June 30, 1962, an AM station in New York City sold for $10.9 million, the highest price ever paid for an AM station. Also, during that period, $10.6 million was paid for one-half interest in a Pittsburgh TV station. The buying and selling of radio and television stations reached a peak in 1959 when close to 500 stations changed hands for a total sales volume of $123,000,000.[11] In 1961, the number of stations sold dropped to 319, but the total sales price rose to $128,000,000. Usually the value of the license itself far exceeds the value of equipment or capital outlay. It should also be noted that the public's investment in receiving sets is much greater than the investment of proprietors. Prior to December 31, 1944, the original cost of 53,800,000 receiving sets manufactured during the previous eight years was over two billion dollars, whereas the original cost of all tangible broadcast property to licensees of all stations and networks, as of December 31, 1944, was about 83 million dollars.[12] Trafficking in station licenses is a problem with which both Congress and the FCC have been concerned.

The changes which have taken place in the economics and ownership of radio and television have had their repercussions in the motion-picture industry. The dominance of the "majors" which existed for so many years has disappeared and given place to a growing number of smaller, specialized producers. The motion-picture decree of the courts, which divested the large producers of their far-flung interests in theater properties, introduced new problems of film distribution and exhibition which further weakened the dominating position of the majors. In the motion-picture industry the real impetus to change was television, which attracted more and more theater-goers away from the box office to the home screen, and at the same time developed an almost insatiable demand for old and new movies. The result has been that old and new producers are devoting more and more of their time to meeting this demand, the ties between motion-picture producers and TV proprietors are getting closer, and media combines encompass more segments of the motion-picture field. A few pioneering motion-picture families are still important owners of motion-picture companies, but bankers, real estate interests, and actors and actresses are prominent.

WHO CONTROLS PROGRAM CONTENT

Personnel

Owners and proprietors provide the financial resources, the capital, the wages and salaries, and to a greater or lesser extent the general policies and objectives of the motion picture, radio, and television firms. The officers and employees, however, are the ones who really give form and shape to the industry's output. Probably no industry has such a large proportion of employees in higher income groups as managers, artists, or technicians. Altogether the payrolls of the three media contain over 1,000,-000 members. The more important organizations of workers are listed in the accompanying table.

ORGANIZATION	FOUNDED	MEMBERS
1. Actors' Equity Association (AAA-AFL)	1913	12,000
2. American Federation of Musicians (AFL)	1896	256,000
3. American Federation of TV and Radio Artists (AAA-AFL-CIO)	1937	26,000
4. American Guild of Musical Artists (AAAA-AFL)	1936	3,000
5. American Guild of Variety Artists (AAAA-AFL-CIO)	1939	78,000
6. American Society of Composers, Authors and Publishers (ASCAP)	1914	8,133
7. Associated Actors and Artists of America (AAAA-AFL-CIO)	1919	60,000
8. Association of Radio-TV News Analysts	1942	
9. Authors League of America, Inc.		3,600
10. Catholic Actors Guild of America	1914	1,250
11. Catholic Writers Guild of America	1919	300
12. Directors Guild of America	1959	2,187
13. International Alliance of Theatrical Stage Employees and Moving-Picture Machine Operators of the U. S. and Canada (AFL-CIO) (IATSE)	1893	61,037
IATSE also includes locals of laboratory technicians, make-up artists and hair stylists, assistant directors and script clerks, costumers, film editors, screen cartoonists, set painters, studio art craftsmen, studio cinetechnicians, electrical technicians, studio grips, projectionists, publicists, sound effects, scenic artists, set designers and model makers, stage employees, story analysts, studio mechanics, wardrobe attendants.		
14. National Association of Broadcasters	1927	3,119
15. National Variety Artists	1916	650
16. Screen Actors Guild (AAA-AFL)	1933	15,000
17. Society of Motion Picture and TV Engineers	1916	5,200

The offerings of the motion-picture screen, the voices on radio, and the visual presentations of television are the products of these employees. A few outstanding artists, a relatively small number of managers and technicians attain widespread publicity, but most of them are relatively unknown. Their impact on these media is very great, yet little is known of them—their personalities, their motivations, their methods of selection, how they work, or what specific and individual contributions they make. Owners and proprietors may exert a kind of negative control over program content, checking and retarding progress, but, in the final analysis, only the talents of artists, technicians, and managers, the innovators and creators, can raise the quality and level of mass media offerings.

Internal Regulation: The Industrial Code

Owners and, to some extent, the top officials and employees of the electronic media have exercised an important though negative influence upon program content through self-regulating authorities set up to enforce codes and standards of good conduct. For several reasons these media have gone further in the direction of self-regulation than newspapers.[13] In the case of all three there is a large audience of children. Also, with respect to radio and TV the audience is essentially a home audience which includes practically all members of the family. Moreover, programs are likely to have sudden and widespread effects, and if undesirable could do much harm. The threat of government regulation has also been an ever-present reason for maintaining minimum standards of performance, a threat which does not exist in the case of newspapers. Early in the history of motion-pictures, boards of censorship were established in several states and the movement for Federal censorship became quite vociferous in the early 1920's following a series of Hollywood scandals that shocked the nation. The National Association of Motion Picture Producers and Distributors responded by adopting a motion-picture code which was to be enforced by the newly established Hays Office.[14] Without legal authority to enforce its demands, this office did succeed in improving motion-picture standards for a time or at least in preventing the further lowering of them. In the 1930's the industry experienced perhaps its worst public relations and most vehement attacks because of its immoral excesses. Led by the Catholic Legion of Decency and supported by other religious bodies, the public boycotted the movie theaters to such an extent that code provisions were revised and enforcement was made more stringent. Since that time the Hays Office and its successor, the Johnston Office, have seemed to have less and less difficulty with the problem of good public relations, partly because of the greater willingness of producers to follow the guidance of their associational conscience, but especially because of marked changes in the moral and cultural precepts of the public's conscience. Certainly it is far easier for the motion-picture industry to adjust its product to the broadminded, super-liberal (some would say open-ended) public conscience of today than it was in the twenties and thirties.

The radio industry through its National Association of Broadcasters promulgated its first code of ethics in 1929. A new code was adopted in 1935 following the passage of the FCC Act in 1934. A revised edition of this code was issued in 1939. Benefiting from the experience in both the motion picture and radio fields, the TV industry was better able to meet its need for self-regulation, when in March, 1952, its first code went into effect. In 1962, approximately 400 of 571 commercial TV stations on the air were code members, as well as all three networks, and some 22 Code Film Affiliates. In addition to the NAB code, each of the networks and most of the stations also have their own codes which may or may not be more stringent and comprehensive.[15]

The TV Code of 1952 has been revised a number of times, the latest and seventh revision taking place in 1962. The Code seeks to provide guidelines in fourteen areas, eight of which deal with programming and production, and six with advertising. The first group deals with the advancement of education and culture, responsibility toward children, community responsibility, general program standards, treatment of news and public events, controversial public issues, political telecasts, and religious programs. The second group concerns advertising, including general advertising standards, presentation of advertising, advertising of medical products, contests, premiums and offers, and time standards. As set forth in this document the responsibilities of the telecaster are extensive and include the obligation to augment the educational and cultural influences of schools and colleges, the home, church, foundations and museums, the need to develop children's programs that avoid undue emphasis on violence, sex, and morbid suspense and foster instead the moral, social, and ethical ideals commonly accepted in American life. Telecasters have a special responsibility to ascertain and serve the needs of the community where they operate.

One of the longest sections of the code deals with general program standards regarding some thirty-two matters, such as the use of profanity and obscenity, words derisive of race or creed, attacks on religions, treatment of marriage and divorce, law enforcement, crime, sex relations, drunkenness, gambling, quiz programs, contests, subliminal perception, and payola. In treating news and public events, the station's news schedule should be adequate, well-balanced, and in good taste. Commentary and analysis should be clearly identified as such. News interview programs should conform to accepted standards of ethical journalism, and any advance restrictions on questions and areas of discussion should be clearly indicated. Telecasters have a responsibility to seek out and develop programs dealing with controversial public issues and to see that they give fair representation to opposing sides. Political telecasts should always be clearly identified as such, and religious programs should be made available which place emphasis on broad religious truths and avoid controversial or partisan news "not directly or necessarily related to religion or morality."

The advertising standards set forth in the Code are equally laudable. The Code member should not accept advertising of doubtful integrity, truth, or legality, or advertising believed objectionable "to a substantial and responsible segment of the community." The sponsors of all sponsored programs must be identified. Certain types of advertising are not acceptable, such as the advertising of hard liquor, fortune-telling, certain personal and intimate products, organizations or publications giving odds or promoting betting or lotteries, and "bait-switch" advertising. Advertising messages should be in good taste, avoid disturbing or annoying material, and harmonize with the program in which it appears. Great care must be exercised to avoid the presentation of false, misleading, or deceptive advertising, and especially advertising seeking to exploit children. Dramatized advertising involving testimonials by physicians, dentists, or nurses must be presented by accredited members of such professions. "Advertising copy should contain no claims dealing unfairly with competitors," and "a sponsor's advertising messages should be confined within the framework of the sponsor's program structure." Stations should not accept advertising of medical products which makes exaggerated claims regarding cures, harmlessness, and safety. Contests must be conducted fairly and not constitute lotteries. Offers of premiums should be carefully checked before advertised. Finally, the code sets certain time standards for advertising: not over four minutes of commercial material in any thirty-minute period of prime time, and not more than six out of thirty-minutes during non-prime time. Furthermore, there are specifications regarding advertising during station breaks, the integration of advertising and program material, exceptions for shopping guides, market information, and other special service programs, casual advertising, and advertising on stationary backdrops or properties.

The provisions of this Code have been described in some detail since they suggest the sort of programming problems facing the industry and show how the telecasters, through their national association, are trying to bring their influence to bear on the content of programs. Other forces are at work, however, and program content, even of Code members, to say nothing of non-Code members, may fall far short of these standards. The NAB through its Code Authority, Review Board, and TV Board of Directors, can give or withhold its seals of approval, but it has no legal or other powers to enforce compliance, except the power of persuasion and the support of public opinion. Complaints regarding programs to the FCC in 1962 reached an all time high of 12,000 letters, over one-third of them objecting to programs stressing crime and violence.[16]

Advertisers and Advertising Agencies

Advertisers and advertising agencies constitute a third major influence, in addition to owners and employees, who act individually and through their own voluntary associations to make the mass electronic media, especially radio and TV what it is today. In contrast to the motion-picture industry, which derives practically all of its revenue from ticket sales, and newspapers which obtain twenty-five to thirty-five per cent of their revenue from non-advertising sources, radio and television are almost entirely dependent on advertising for revenue. In 1962, out of a $12,258,900,000 total bill for advertising in the United States, newspapers accounted for $3,793,900,000, radio for $709,000,000, and TV for $1,744,800,000.[17] In contrast to newspapers, radio and TV not only carry a much larger proportion of national advertising, but also a comparatively small number of advertisers account for a very large proportion of station and network revenue. This fact, plus the role played by advertiser and advertising in program-making, has given the advertisers an extensive (some would say an excessive) influence, over program content. Whereas the newspaper sells advertising space and the advertiser uses all of it for advertising, the radio and TV advertiser uses only a fraction, two to three minutes out of fifteen, of the time he buys for advertising. Although he may not use the remaining time for strictly commercial purposes, he does try to control its use as a sponsor to attract the widest possible audience for the advertising message. Although the broadcasting station has full, legal responsibility for its programming, it cannot ignore and sometimes is unable to resist the program desires of sponsors. The tendency has been, under these circumstances, for stations and even networks to let advertisers or advertising agencies take the initiative in devising and preparing programs. The role of the station or network has tended to be passive or negative, and limited mainly to policing the programs to avoid violations of the law, FCC rules, and code provisions. Practice, however, is by no means uniform, and some stations take an active part, co-operating with clients in their selection of desirable programs. Many critics have claimed that radio and television stations have abnegated their responsibility as licensees by leaving so much responsibility for determining content to advertisers and advertising agencies. It is certain that the interests of the advertiser is the major determinant of the program content of sponsored broadcasts. The suggestion that radio and TV time sales follow the pattern of newspaper space sales or the "magazine" format and restrict sponsored time solely to purely advertising time, would give stations more programming responsibilities, but the advertising interest would still be primary and program content would probably be affected very little. Who pays the piper usually calls the tune, whether it is the advertiser, as in the United States, the set-owner through license fees, as in some countries, or the taxpayer through government subsidies in others.

Government Regulation: The Federal Communications Commission

Although newspapers and motion pictures are influenced by government in many ways, radio and TV come under almost continuous and direct pressure from government agencies, not only the FCC, but also the Federal Trade Commission, the Food and Drug Administration, the President, the Interstate and Foreign Commerce committees of House and Senate, special investigating committees of Congress, the Courts, and the Department of Justice. Three periods of federal regulation may be differentiated: the period before 1927 when the U. S. Department of Commerce had the responsibility for granting radio licenses and assigning frequencies, the period from 1927 to 1934 during which the Federal Radio Commission performed these duties and others prescribed by the Radio Act of 1927, and the period from 1934 to the present under the Federal Communications Act.[18] On the technical side the FCC has many responsibilities, such as classifying radio services and types of stations, assigning frequencies, setting engineering and operational requirements as well as eligibility qualifications, granting, renewing, and refusing to renew station licenses, and planning for effective use of the radio spectrum. In carrying out these technical responsibilities the FCC has developed a large and complex body of rules supplementing and interpreting the general principles of the FCC Act itself. The many broad and complicated technical problems which have confronted Congress and the FCC over the years have given rise to studies and investigations of one sort or another, such as those concerned with clear channels, ultra-high-frequencies, color television, satellite stations, all-channel sets, and subscription television. The decisions of the government affect decisively the coverage and the quality of technical performance. The FCC and other government agencies concerned with radio and TV have also followed, investigated, and regulated certain economic aspects of the media, such as monopolistic tendencies, network regulations, "trafficking in licenses"; and multiple and cross-channel ownership.

Not less important has been the influence of the government on program content. Almost from its beginning the FCC has been concerned with program standards, a concern which reached a peak in 1946 with the adoption of the "Blue Book." [19] This report indicated that the Commission would henceforth take a hard look at a station's programming when considering applications for licenses or their renewal; specifically, it would take a searching look at program structure to see if it was "balanced," if it carried enough local live talent programs, dealt with important public issues, and avoided advertising excesses. The industry responded with a hard look too and reacted negatively and vehemently. Very few, if any, stations failed thereafter to keep their licenses simply because of their programs, and the Blue Book really amounted to little more than a slap on the wrist.

As of February 1, 1964, there have been fifteen chairmen of the FCC. Except for James L. Fly and Wayne Coy, those serving during periods of crisis or suspended activity, chairmen served on the average for terms of less than two years. The chairmen varied greatly in their views of the responsibility of the FCC regarding programming. In the years following the episode of the Blue Book, the FCC seemed to follow a more or less passive, "hands off" policy, until the Kennedy victory in 1960, followed by the appointment of Newton Minow as chairman. His famous "wasteland" speech recalled the public interest concern of the Blue Book days.[20] Once again the industry rolled with the blow and came back fighting, and soon Minow seemed to indicate that he had had enough.

The influence of government on radio and TV programming is affected by a number of important factors: the personnel of the FCC, especially the chairman; the views of Congress, especially those of the members of the Senate and House interstate commerce committees, the attitude of the President, and the pressures from the radio and TV industry. The pressures from the industry are formidable, especially from the NAB, the networks, and from the media giants and combines. On occasion, when the need is great, large reserves from other media, the world of advertising and business itself can be wheeled into action. This pressure takes many forms and has influenced the selection of FCC, Federal Trade Commission and Food and Drug Administration personnel as well as interstate commerce committee personnel in Congress. These special interests have been adept in the strategy of argument, and in granting and promising favors. There are countervailing forces comprising groups of viewers and listeners, parent and teachers' organizations, women's organizations, educators, and even certain elements of the industry. These forces are so weak and sporadic that they seldom tip the balance in their favor. There are individual legislators who, from time to time, seek to speak out for the public interest, but as the Blue Book and Minow episodes revealed, the public interest as represented by these scattered and often weak voices, is an uncertain and ineffective reed for the would-be program reformers to lean on.

In many respects affecting programming, the FCC Act and supplementary rules are similar to the NAB Code, although the Code goes beyond the Act and rules, since the latter are minimal and legally binding. The Act definitely bans government censorship, but it also insists that stations operate in the public interest, convenience, and necessity. The industry argues that expressed government concern about programs, to say nothing about interference however slight, is censorship. The FCC, however, in its effort to balance public and private interests claims that it has the authority to lay down general program standards and refuse licenses to stations which do not live up to them. It differentiates between enforcing general standards and censoring individual programs.[21] Of course, stations, in company with media generally, are subject to laws against libel and slander, broadcasting lottery information, false advertising, and obscenity. Furthermore, in its Sections 315 and 317 the Act places certain restrictions on the political use of radio and television facilities by candidates for public office and requires stations to disclose any direct or indirect payments for use of broadcast facilities. Sections 508 and 509 deal with payola and contests of "intellectual knowledge, intellectual skill, or chance."

Although the FCC has virtually never refused to renew a station license solely because of objections to its programs, it has expressed disapproval of much of the advertising as well as content of programs banned by the NAB Code, such as advertisements for liquor and birth control preparations, racial and religious attacks, and programs prescribing medical treatments, giving horse-racing information or telling fortunes. On the other hand, the FCC has expressed approval of educational and religious programs and since 1949, has permitted station editorializing.[22]

In summary, therefore, it is clear that the threat of FCC refusal to renew station licenses is a stimulus to good behavior by radio and television stations, especially in the area of technical performance and to some extent economic performance as well. The influence of government on programs has probably been effective in a negative, minimal sense, but efforts to raise program standards by requiring "balance" or more emphasis on certain types of programs or de-emphasis on others has usually encountered almost decisive resistance.

The Listening and Viewing Public

Not yet considered is a factor or influence on programming which to some is the determining one and to others, purely passive or impotent—the listening and viewing public. Since attendance at motion pictures has declined so markedly during the last ten or fifteen years, and because its function is mainly entertainment, little attention will be given to the influence of the motion-picture audience on that medium. The motion-picture industry tries desperately to keep abreast of public tastes and wishes and to anticipate them as much as possible. In co-operation with public opinion survey firms, industry executives use a variety of survey techniques to probe states and trends in public attitudes toward pictures. One conspicuous result of this probing has been the discovery that the motion-picture audience is predominantly a teen-age and young adult public. The consequence has been an upsurge, over the years, of pictures catering to the interests of this public.

It is unlikely that radio and television will ever meet fully the needs of the motion-picture theater-goer: the need to "go out" for a change, the desire to see the very latest features, foreign as well as domestic, in color and on a screen that no TV set can match for size and quality, and the enjoyment that comes from the absence of commercials. Moreover, the motion-picture theater will always have an appeal for those wishing to get away from the living room with a companion, a group of friends, or alone to do something special, something different, or just to escape routine. Neither color TV nor pay TV will ever meet completely the variety of needs the motion-picture theater, walk-in or drive-in, satisfies.

Today, very few homes are without either a radio or television set, and many of them have several of each. Car radios, portable radios and TV receivers, transistors, to say nothing of TV and radio sets in office, school, store, club, and church have brought the American people within earshot and eyesight of the mass media day and night, at work or play. And they do look and listen. Radios may be left on for hours at a time, merely to provide a soothing background of soft music to make work or study more palatable and to mute annoying distractions. In the home the TV screen is being watched three to four hours daily, on the average, and in many cases much longer. The radio and TV researchers have made repeated studies of radio and TV audiences and their viewing and listening habits.

VIEWER STUDIES: RADIO AND TELEVISION

A study of the TV audience by Nielsen, reported in February, 1962, showed that 90 per cent or 46,900,000 United States homes had a TV set, that the peak viewing hours were from 8 to 10 P.M. and that during November and December, 1961, approximately 63 per cent of American homes were tuned in. It also showed that the size of the audience was increasing, especially in the high middle income category, that most of the viewing was done at night, that young families made up the daytime audience to a large extent, especially for AM radio, and were the highest users, and that program tastes tended to vary from season to season in almost a cyclical fashion.[23]

A study of the radio audience for WMCA by the Psychological Corporation, also reported in February, 1962, revealed that radio was definitely retaining a place for itself.[24] Specifically, it was found that:

(1) The listener spends more time with radio than generally supposed.
(2) He is surprisingly loyal to the station of his first choice (56 per cent of WMCA's core audience was loyal five to ten years).
(3) Interest in and dependence on news is substantial (25 per cent had not seen a paper the day before).
(4) Reliance on radio for diversion and entertainment is substantial (25 per cent had not watched TV and 64 per cent had not seen a magazine the previous day).
(5) One-third of the viewers complained about commercials but only 2 per cent switched stations because of them.
(6) In general, it would seem, that the mood of the listener or viewer de-

termines the station and type of program selected, and no single station can satisfy all moods.

From time to time Nielsen and other rating services report on the total or average audience for specific programs. The highest percentage of homes reached by all or any part of a TV program, except those viewing from 1 to 5 minutes, went as high as 48.2 per cent for a Rose Bowl game and 40.6 per cent for a National Football League world champion football game.

Of particular interest are children's listening and viewing habits. Children begin watching television at a very early age, and the amount of viewing increases until they reach twelve or thirteen years of age when it tapers off and becomes more selective. Interest in programs especially designed for children is soon supplemented and then supplanted by interest in adult pictures.

In addition to studies of viewing and listening habits of radio and TV audiences, numerous surveys have been made of the attitudes and opinions of these audiences regarding the industry and the programs it supplies. Many of these surveys are said by the industry to support its view that the public is getting what it wants, that criticism is mild and emanates from a few, and that the great majority is tolerably well satisfied. Following FCC Chairman Minow's wasteland attack on TV and radio programming, *Broadcasting* ran a story headline "TV's image shines untarnished," and went on to say, "Its programming is not considered 'a vast wasteland' by most people. As a 'moral problem' it gets low billing. As a source of news it still takes second place to newspapers (by a narrowing margin), but for reliability of news reporting it commands greater respect than newspapers do. It's the medium more people would keep, if they could keep only one." [25] An audience study of seven stations in New York City and four stations in Philadelphia reporting in February, 1962, however, indicated considerable dissatisfaction with the kind and amount of cultural programming. Almost the same pattern of dissatisfaction prevailed in both cities. In New York, of the 43 per cent that were dissatisfied, 56 per cent wanted more educational programs, 57 per cent more drama, 42 per cent more symphonic music, 31 per cent more opera, 29 per cent more international affairs, 21 per cent more national affairs, 17 per cent more news.[26] Not everyone would agree with Patrick M. McGrady's Fund for the Republic report on TV criticism which stated, "By and large, television criticism is the fitful labor of tired writers of monumental good will, a degree of talent, and a jaded perspective." [27]

The Steiner Report

Early in 1963, after three years of field work, tabulation, and analysis, the Bureau of Applied Social Research of Columbia University completed what is undoubtedly the most exhaustive study of TV viewer attitudes ever made. The study was financed by a $135,000 grant by CBS, and the field work was done by National Opinion Research Center of the University of Chicago and Elmo Roper Associates. The sample used consisted of a nation-wide cross-section of 2,427 adult viewers from 537 small areas, plus an additional group of 300 viewers in New York City. The interviewing was done in the spring of 1960.[28]

The study differentiates the "average American" viewer from the "average non-average" viewer; the latter being better educated, from a higher socio-economic group and inclined to be more critical of television. Both depend on TV for relaxation and entertainment, have their favorite programs, and seem to have a vague wish that programs could be more informative and educational, in an entertaining way. The "average viewer" finds TV well worth what it costs, a net advantage for children, programs good, even excellent at times, is aware of no "unbalance," rarely watches public affairs shows other than news and weather. He also thinks there is too much violence on TV and that parents should not be expected to do the screening for children. He wishes broadcasters would do something about the boring, repetitious, and irritating commercials. His real worry, however, is not television violence, nor commercials, but a feeling of guilt at the amount of time he "wastes" watching TV during his leisure hours.

The "average non-average" viewer is similar to the "average" viewer in many ways, but there are important differences. He is more critical of TV and more aware of its "costs" to him. He tends to select more information programs and is quicker to praise favorite programs, but he is less satisfied with television in general. He calls for more information programs, but he seldom has any specific suggestions to make. He seems to be genuinely concerned about the social and cultural implications of so much television and its use for "escape" by the masses, and he argues that the country needs more informative and educational TV, not for him, but for the good of others. "The big difference between the two groups," the study says, "is not so much in how they use it (TV), but in how they feel about it." Watching TV may be beneficial or wasteful, depending on what the viewer would otherwise be doing. For those who would otherwise be reading, doing something creative, serving the community, and so on, it may be a waste of time. For those, and they may be a majority, who would otherwise be loafing, gambling, or beating their wives, it probably represents a social gain. The study judges viewing largely in terms of the worth or worthlessness of what it displaces.

Both "average" and "non-average" viewers are critical of TV commercials and would prefer to have them shorter, fewer, less interruptive, less aggressive and distasteful, and more informative and entertaining. However, the study did not reveal any widespread desire to replace a commercial with a non-commercial system. The principal objections to commercials were their *content* (boring, dull, repetitive, misleading, dishonest, stupid, insulting to intelligence, bad taste, overdone) and their timing (interruptions in program, too many, too frequent, too long). The degree of objectionability may vary with the type of adjacent or interrupted programs, as well as with the content of the commercial and its timing. On the positive side, it was found that what people like about commercials is their entertainment and information value. However, from the advertiser's point of view, the excellence of a commercial is not its popularity but its selling power. Since there may be little relation between the two, it may be a long time before the industry itself will, of its own accord, remove or modify unpopular commercials with demonstrated selling power.

What is a "public service" program? When is a program schedule properly "balanced"? The author of the report, Dr. Gary A. Steiner, discusses these questions and argues that those who evaluate TV performance should consider entertainment as "a legitimate and perhaps not significant 'public service.' " In fact, he believes, that no distinction from the point of public service need be made between good entertainment and news, information, religious, and discussion programs. Entertainment shows, he claims, do many of the things the public service shows are supposed to do, and they do them better. This may be true in the case of a few entertainment and "public service" programs, but as a generalization it seems misleading.

With reference to the problem of "balancing" program schedules Dr. Steiner asks a few difficult questions. How should the proper proportion of time for different types of programs in the over-all schedule be determined? Should equal time be assigned to each type? Should the popularity, as determined by audience ratings, determine the distribution of time? Dr. Steiner seems to prefer the 'market place' ('cultural democracy') in preference to the Platonic approach which lays stress on providing programs "which are good for people."

The problem of "balance" will be considered later, but certainly there are alternative solutions to the two mentioned—equal time for each program type and apportionment based on popularity ratings. One would be to ascertain and identify the principal minority as well as majority interests and desires in the matter of programming and to assign frequencies and station power so that several minority desires, as well as the majority interest, can be satisfied simultaneously, or within a two or three hour time period. In view of the very limited amount of prime viewing time, it is most unfortunate that so many stations present the same type of programs at the same time. With greater co-operation among stations and networks serving a given area, it would be possible to avoid the same kind of programs at the same time. The difficulty is, however, that each station and each network wants to reach the maximum audience most of the time, seldom the minority. If station A, with a comedy program, attracts 55 per cent of the potential audience, other stations, instead of trying to present a program to attract the remaining 45 per cent, will tend to put on the same kind of program at the same time. It would seem that the public is best served when all the people can get the programs, or types of programs they want, when they want them.

But how can this be done in a way that is fair to all stations, in a way that will not give some the opportunity to serve the large audience and others the small? With as many AM, FM, VHF, and UHF stations as now exist it should be possible to do this in a financially equitable manner. As a first step, each radio corporation owning or operating channels on the four frequencies mentioned might be required to present a different type of program on each frequency at a given time, and within a given prime time period, say from 6 to 10 P.M., to offer a certain number of other types of programs. Each corporation would have to meet the needs of both majorities and minorities and would perhaps have to present less profitable as well as more profitable programs. Competition would then be between corporations, not solely on the most popular programs, but on total program appeal. Possibly, in the interest of public service programming, individual stations would be discouraged, if not discontinued, unless they belong to a corporation capable of providing at least four major types of programs simultaneously.

Other Surveys

A few other findings revealed over the years may be cited. Only a very small proportion of the audience (16 per cent in 1945; 9 per cent in 1948) have ever felt that the radio and television should be run by the government, as in the case of Britain's BBC.[29] The majority of listeners favor regulation of advertising by the industry itself, rather than by the government, though it is not clear what they want if self-regulation fails. Apparently, the great majority (78 per cent) prefer to have the programming financed by advertising rather than by license fees as in some countries. The attitudes of viewers and listeners vary all the way from vehement criticism, "willingness to put up with it," or "don't mind," to expressions of favorableness. The prevailing attitude seems to be resignation, dislike coupled with a feeling of futility. After all, what can be done about it? What alternatives are there? It is interesting to recall that during the early days of radio, when an effort was made to finance broadcasting by the sale of receiving sets, Sarnoff and other industry leaders seemed to think that sponsoring broadcasts by advertisers would be contrary to the public interest. This attitude did not last, and financing by advertising has long been the accepted method.

It is hard to think of an aspect of radio or TV broadcasting that has not been the object of survey questioning. On keeping the profits of stations from being too high, the audiences are about equally divided. On the fairness of station programs, only a small percentage (13 per cent) consider them biased, a much smaller number than those who criticize newspapers in this regard. Over half of the audience (52 per cent) seem to be interested in both entertainment and serious programs. Of the remaining 48 per cent, only 20 per cent listen primarily to serious programs. When asked, it turned out that only about one-third of the audience ever made a special effort to find new programs. With the ready availability of radio and TV guides in newspapers and magazines and the highlighting of special programs, there is undoubtedly more program selectivity than formerly, but there is also a persistent tendency to take what comes on one's favorite station.

Recently, Elmo Roper and Associates reported the comparative results of two surveys of "the public's attitudes toward television and other media" conducted in December, 1959, and November, 1961. Both surveys revealed that attitudes favorable to television heavily outweighed unfavorable attitudes. The specific findings of these studies are summarized in the following table.[30]

PUBLIC ATTITUDES TOWARD TELEVISION

(1) Television continues to be the major rival to newspapers as a news source.

(2) The public continues to be far less concerned about possible negative aspects of television than about other public issues.

    A larger per cent considers the problems listed below more serious moral problems than the bad effects of TV on children (42), rigged quiz shows on TV (41), disc jockeys taking money from record companies (34).

	1961	1959
Testing atomic bombs	86	65
Juvenile delinquency	80	89
Dishonest labor leaders	73	88
Government officials taking bribes	69	81
Disarmament	69	66
School segregation	64	71
Police beating and graft	60	74
False advertising	48	67
Sports fixing	46	45

(3) The majority continues to feel that schools, newspapers, and TV are doing a good job—not so local government.

(4) TV is considered the most believable source of news, newspapers the least.

(5) Given the choice of one medium to keep, the public continues to select TV by a large margin.

How should the over-all performance of TV be evaluated? Assuming it does rival the newspaper as a news source, does that prove that it is doing an excellent news job? The performance of the great majority of newspapers, as dispensers of news, is subject to ever-increasing criticism. Isn't the important question whether TV is doing the best news job it can do? How valid a standard are newspapers in general? There are obviously more important moral and social problems than rigging quiz shows, payola, and bad children's programs, but does this prove that TV is doing a good job, to say nothing of the best job possible? To imply that children's programs, quiz show rigging, and payola are the principal shortcomings of television is to overlook advertising excesses, insufficient local, live programs, public affairs programs, and really good entertainment. The basic moral question is, to what extent is the over-all TV performance helping to raise or lower the moral and cultural standards of the American people. One begs the real issue by limiting the "negative aspects" of TV to the three shortcomings mentioned.

The survey showed that a majority, 57-59 per cent, believed that TV was doing a good job. This may be a passing grade for some TV proprietors, but the fact that 41-43 per cent rated the performance only fair or less will be disconcerting to others. The trouble with that type of question is that there is no absolute standard of goodness or excellence given, nor is there a comparative basis for evaluation.

Finding that TV is considered the most believable and newspapers least believable, as a source of news needs to be carefully considered. By and large both media use the same news services, TV coverage is much more restricted than that of newspapers, and reports of major items covered by both media seldom conflict. Naturally, the larger the number of news items covered and the greater the detail, the more the chance for error. Whether the news performance of TV should be judged solely on the basis of believability without regard to the depth and extent of coverage is questionable. The attitude of the public in this matter may be because television stations do little or no editorializing and try to avoid the discussion of controversial issues as much as possible. The over-all effect of one, five, or fifteen minute capsule news reports, virtually no editorials, balanced, and limited discussion of controversial questions is, to be sure, an impression of objectivity, fairness, and credibility. To equate this with the highest excellence, however, may be placing too high a premium on doing very little, but doing it impartially and objectively.

Finally, if they had to choose between TV and newspapers, radio, or magazines more people would choose TV. What does this choice prove? Only a relatively small minority would be greatly affected by the loss of magazines, and radio has little or nothing to offer that TV cannot give, if it chooses to do so. The real choice is between newspapers and TV. It is true that 42 per cent preferred TV, but 58 per cent did not! At face value, these results seem to show that more people prefer viewing to reading (most studies show that reading declines markedly down the socio-economic scale), that more people prefer a larger proportion of entertainment to serious, informative programs or material, and that if they are forced to choose between entertainment and serious matter, they prefer to sacrifice some of the latter, rather than the former. These conclusions or findings are not surprising, in view of what is known of public tastes in general. To say that 51 per cent of the public probably prefers what it is getting on TV over what it receives from newspapers is really saying little about the relative excellence of the two media, or the absolute excellence of TV. It merely says TV is more popular with the masses than newspapers.

In addition to information regarding the personal traits and viewing and listening habits of TV and radio audiences, as well as their attitudes toward the media, a continuous stream of reports regarding audience program preferences pours forth. Rating services, using various indices and techniques, purport to give reasonably accurate figures of audience sizes, as well as public opinions and attitudes regarding any program, commercial or non-commercial, on the air. The influence of the public on TV and radio programming is forcefully indicated by the almost slavish regard given these ratings by sponsors, advertising agencies, and stations themselves. Often, solely on the basis of these ratings programs are accepted, retained, or discarded. As recently as 1962-63, serious questions have been raised regarding the accuracy of some of these rating procedures, and both the industry itself and Congress are investigating the matter. There is also the question of the extent to which radio and TV programs should cater to the wishes of the majority and to what extent those of the minority. This omni-present, ubiquitous problem of majority vs. minority, mass vs. elite, layman vs. expert, and public interest vs. private interests crops up here as it does in public opinion studies. It really isn't enough to say the two must be balanced. The crux of the problem is, where to strike the balance and what weights to use where.

THE AREAS OF INFLUENCE

The electronic mass media—motion pictures, radio, and TV—are not merely targets or objects of influence, they are agents or channels of influence. It is difficult, however, to determine with much precision what that influence is.[31] As with newspapers, it is almost impossible to isolate these media, separate them from other influences, and measure their effects individually or together. There is often a tendency to minimize or exaggerate their influence. To counter charges that motion pictures, radio, or TV are having a bad influence on children, spokesmen for these media sometimes plausibly argue that the alleged bad effect was primarily due to the child's predispositions, not to the medium. The programs were neither good nor bad in themselves, and they would not have been followed by reprehensible behavior of the child had he not been inclined in that direction.) The medium, or its content, could only be a contributing factor, not a primary one. Of course, it is true that any effect is the consequence of many interrelated and interacting forces, whether the effect is a change of attitude or a modification of behavior. At the most, the argument runs, the mass media are only minor, contributing influences, and the main reason for undesirable attitudes and forms of behavior must be sought elsewhere. Some go even further and differentiate the medium itself from its content and use, claiming that the medium is merely a common carrier, an inanimate link between communicator and respondent, that it has no influence, contributory or otherwise.

If media owners, in the face of public criticism, try to minimize the extent of their influence, they, along with social reformers, may also exaggerate the amount of influence when selling time to advertisers or searching for someone to blame for juvenile delinquency. It must be granted that there is very little accurate information about the precise influence of mass media on the attitudes and behavior of the American people generally, either in the short run or over longer time periods. There have been attempts to set up controlled experiments, designed to show what happens when a public, usually for a relatively short period of time is exposed to a particular medium of communication. An effort is made to neutralize the influence of all other factors than the particular one being studied. Usually these studies are limited in value because of the very special nature of the factor or influence being measured, the public whose responses are being affected, and the dated, special nature of the experiment as a whole. In the case of motion pictures a very elaborate series of controlled experiments of this general nature, the Payne Fund studies, were conducted in the early 1930s.[32] The purpose was to find out what motion pictures did to children. Numerous controlled experiments have since been conducted in the classroom by psychologists and students of public opinion and are more useful in suggesting new hypotheses than in testing or proving old ones. Probably more time and effort have been devoted to experimental tests of the effectiveness of advertising than to any other kind. Market researchers have shown much ingenuity in devising techniques for assessing the public impact of specific advertisements, radio, and television programs.

Much of the literature concerned with the effects or influence of the mass media is theoretical, the product of more or less imaginative insight based on a number of the special studies mentioned above, on rather general comparisons between media developments and political, social, economic, and public opinion changes, or simply on a thoughtful review of personal experiences with the media and their apparent effects.

William A. Belson has classified the theories regarding the effects of TV into four groups:[33] (1) those regarding the effect on social and group relations, including theories about family life, visiting, and general sociability; (2) those dealing with the effect on mental states and associated behavior including theories about interests, passivity, initiative, imagination, and creativeness; (3) the effect on general knowledge and matters related to education, including theories about the broadening of outlook, and (4) the effect on mores. Often the theories contradict one another; for example, Belson found that in England, where he served as Senior Psychologist in the Audience Research Department of the British Broadcasting Corporation,

> On the one hand television was said to be re-establishing the family unit, to be reducing irritability, and to be broadening the cultural horizons of the nation. On the other hand it was said to have reduced attendance at the cinema, at sporting events, at the pub; to have eroded club and trade union activity; to be killing the interests, the imagination, and the initiative of the public, to be turning England into a nation of sops. In short it has been regarded as an evil eye and as a thing of unlimited promise.

Since the theories of mass media effects are so numerous, only some of the general areas of influence will be considered.

Consumer Buying

A prominent student of the mass media once claimed that the only specific effect of radio broadcasting had been on the buying habits of the public. Certainly advertisers believe that advertising sells goods and services and justifies the total expenditure of over $12 billion dollars a year for advertising, much of which goes to the mass media. Not infrequently, advertising brings spectacular increases in the sales of particular products. The leading network advertisers are manufacturers of toiletries, food, drugs, smoking supplies, soaps, autos, house equipment. Each of seven companies spends over $5 million dollars a year on TV network ads alone— Proctor and Gamble, $12,000,000; American Home Products $9,000,000; Bristol-Myers $8,000,000; General Motors $7,000,000; R. J. Reynolds $6,000,000; Lever Brothers and Colgate $5,000,000.[34] Yet many questions remain unanswered. Does mass media advertising promote wise buying? Does it divert attention from the most useful to the less useful or even harmful? Does it create waste or ambitions and desires that are socially desirable? All too little is known about the less obvious, long term, and probably profound effects of the incessant din of radio and TV commercials.

Robert W. Sarnoff has argued that television "plays a role of decisive importance in stimulating economic growth and in reinforcing the strength of our democratic process." He says further, "in a free economy, production expansion depends primarily on using consumer demand; and in the mature American economy, rising demand requires, in addition to population growth, the continuous stimulation of consumer desires." Again, "The primary stimulant is advertising, and among all forms of advertising, television has unique capabilities that power the American economy." Also, he states, "Is the stimulation of private spending incompatible with meeting our public responsibilities? History argues otherwise, for as our consumption has increased, so has our allocation for essential services."[35]

Social Change

It is also alleged that the mass media are essentially a conservative force, at least in the realm of economics and politics. This is due, so the argument goes, to the emphasis, especially by radio and TV, on catering to the mass public, to the fear of more government control should media programs stir up controversy, to the fact that these media merely amplify, repeat, and diffuse existing tastes, standards, and interests, and to the fact that audiences are prone to view and listen to the views they already approve. These arguments seem convincing so far as they go, but they fail to take into account the impact of entertainment programs, which constitute so large a part of the program schedules, upon attitudes toward relations with others, morals and ethics, what is accepted behavior, and many other dimensions of life.

From some points of view, however, it has been argued that the mass media accelerate social change. Whatever impetus to change there is, is almost instantaneously communicated over wide areas, often producing simultaneous responses. The action of an enemy power, the discovery of a new drug, the debate of Presidential candidates, communicated to a nation-wide audience may produce a sudden and widespread reaction, with far-reaching effects.

Political Effects

Radio started its career broadcasting election returns, and like TV its impact on politics has undoubtedly been extensive. Observers claim these media have greatly enhanced public interest in election campaigns and are to a large extent responsible for the increasing proportion of eligible voters who go to the polls. Because of their nation-wide and rather uniform effect on their audience, they make the swing of the political pendulum more violent and extreme than would otherwise be the case. The likelihood of election landslides one way or the other has become greater.[36]

Certainly the advent of radio and television has brought great increases in campaign expenses. They have focused attention and awakened interest in national and international affairs to a degree never before attained, though some claim this has resulted in an increasing neglect of state and especially local affairs. Some ascribe considerable importance to the fact that radio and TV may relieve a political candidate or an officeholder from dependence on the coverage afforded him in a conservative, Republican-dominated press. Never before have government officials been able to project themselves, their viewpoints, and their activities so effectively and directly to the people. Hardly a day passes that the viewing or listening public doesn't find prominent national figures appearing on radio or TV. Are these mass media determining more and more the type of person running for office? Are they diverting public attention from issues to personalities? Are they making it easy for the slick solution to win public support, rather than the sound one?

Effect on Children

No area of mass media influence has received more study than the influence of radio and television on children, and several rather comprehensive surveys and analyses of this have been made.[37] These studies suggest that, from the long range point of view, TV viewing by children (1) may increase their excitement threshold to the point where they become addicted to that level and are seldom satisfied with activities less exciting; (2) may build habits of violence and aggression as well as reduce drives in that direction, especially if the need for aggression is aroused at some future time; (3) may make it more difficult for children to discipline themselves to delay their satisfactions at times; (4) by providing the child with too many avenues of "escape" from social pressures, mass media may retard the development of social responsibility; (5) may increase the child's tendency to obtain power satisfactions through particular kinds of power figures in later life; and (6) may interfere with the practice of real-life skills.

It has also been found that TV viewing may bring families closer together, but viewing does not bring greater interaction within the family and may reduce the amount of time the family spends together, exclusive of TV viewing. Also, viewing means less time spent with classmates, reduces amount of reading, play, and conversation, reduces amount of helping around the house, practicing on musical instruments, and engaging in creative activities.

The two to four hours a day that children spend before the TV screen, naturally has to be taken from some other activity—playing, studying, working, eating, sleeping, or something else. In many cases it is undoubtedly a substitute for less rather than more desirable occupations. To that extent it is a gain. In general, parents do not seem to find it harmful. In fact, they consider it enjoyable, instructive, and a remarkable pacifier and useful baby sitter. It may well be that its most important effect will be educational. Never before have younger children been brought face-to-face in a vivid, interesting fashion with so much information about people, their characters, problems, methods of getting what they want, their ambitions, and so on, with so much information about places, the physical environment, geography, science, even politics, economics, and sociology. The TV child is a sophisticated child, a child who has an unusually large and varied vocabulary, who has learned much, not only from the programs for children, but from those for adults as well. Whether his physical development and his moral progress are able to keep pace with his informational prowess is a crucial question. Unless his physical and moral development are as rapid as his informational, his premature introduction to adult themes and problems, to abnormal conduct and questionable behavior, to conflict, violence and adult misdoings, may retard, dwarf, or even prevent the development of a well-structured personality. Most studies of the impact of radio and TV on children have covered relatively short periods of time and a limited number of children. Only studies extending over several years at least can reveal the deeper, more fundamental effects.

Cultural Tastes

What effects, if any, do radio and television have on the public's musical, artistic, esthetic, dramatic, or literary tastes? According to a 1962 survey the ten most popular TV shows at that time were "Wagon Train," "Gunsmoke," Perry Mason, the Rose Bowl Game, "Bonanza," Garry Moore, Dr. Kildare, NFL World Champion Football, Tournament of Roses, and the Sugar Bowl Game.[38] This list emphasizes quite clearly that television is primarily an entertainment medium, and of the entertainment fare offered, the great majority prefer such items as outstanding sports events, westerns and mysteries, variety and comedy, and spectacles. The test of mass entertainment is how well and how many it entertains. Other types of entertainment have been offered from time to time, with greater or less informative and intellectual content, but the fact that the type of shows popular today are similar to those popular a decade ago would suggest very little change, if any, in the entertainment level.

Close to seventy-five per cent of radio time throughout the United

States is devoted to music, most of it popular, with now and then classical renditions. There are grounds for thinking that radio and TV, to some extent, have widely diffused knowledge regarding music of all types, and raised the level of musical tastes of a great many people. It seems to have done very little to raise the level of taste much above a modest level of interest in some of the more familiar classics, but it has brought these, formerly the property of the few, to the many. Put in another way, there is little for the expert, but much for the unlearned. The taste of the masses, the taste of the average listener, has been raised somewhat, and this is a social gain. This may be true in other fields such as architecture, home furnishings, dress, and manners as the man in the street is made aware, vividly and repeatedly, of what people do and how they live in different social strata, under varying economic circumstances.

Studies frequently show that radio and TV reduced the amount of time spent on reading. Whether this has meant a lowering of literary tastes depends on what, actually, was the type of reading sacrificed, and for what. There is evidence that the amount of serious reading, the reading of non-fiction, has increased, especially biography, history, and the social sciences. Also, it is known that those who are avid users of one mass medium tend to use others avidly as well. Interest in a subject, such as sports, science, or travel frequently means a multi-media attempt to satisfy that interest.

Entertainment

Entertainment seems to be a necessary part of life. It takes one's mind away from pressing problems for a time, relieves tensions, builds up morale, and may have many other salutary physical and psychological effects. It may well be that of all the effects of radio and television this is the most important. It relaxes the housewife as she struggles with children and housework; it relaxes the husband after the jolts and frustrations of the working day; it relaxes children and brings for a time at least a pause in their displays of restless energy. Perhaps its greatest contribution is that it provides an ever-ready pacifier for a people with ever-mounting tensions. To speak critically, or condescendingly, of its "escape" function may be to disparage what is really essential.

Education

The educational impact of the mass media is obviously considerable, whether the word "education" is defined in a narrow way to refer to what goes on in classrooms or is extended to include whatever serves to enlarge the mental capacities of man, whether through knowledge or the ability to use that knowledge. Whatever the purpose of education: whether it is to help people to adapt better to their environment, to teach them how to think straight and act wisely, to disseminate information and "truth," or to develop skills, the mass media have a role in it. The quantity of information projected by radio and TV is extensive, not only in their news and public affairs programs, but in entertainment programs as well. Information abounds regarding places and people, ways of doing things, issues and problems, reasons why courses of action are, or should be taken. Much of this information was obtainable before, but it wasn't pursued. Where the mass media fail, however, is that they are poorly equipped to instruct and train people how to use this knowledge, how to think straight, to see relationships, detect logical fallacies, anticipate effects, perceive alternatives, organize evidence, or devise remedies.

Some have argued that the mass media, mainly because of the rapidity with which information is presented, and the impossibility of interruption, questioning, or discussion, tend to frustrate thinking, and in a sense to dull the intellect. It is true that there is little time for reflection, appraisal, interpretation, analysis, or testing, as the programs roll relentlessly on. Perhaps this means that more attention should be given to a division of labor between the mass media and the classroom, taking advantage of the usefulness of the former for imparting information and of the latter for developing logical skills of application. As of the middle of 1962 there were 64 educational TV stations on the air (44 VHF and 20 UHF) and 309 channels reserved for their use.[39] New impetus has been given, not only by recent all-channel set requirements which will encourage greater use of UHF, but also by new legislation which will make $32 million of federal funds available in matching grants to the states for Educational TV. The increasing use of TV, as well as radio for educational use in the schools, plus the greater number of educational stations for general broadcasting signify an ever-rising educational effect in the broad, as well as the narrow sense, and especially on the informational level.

PROBLEMS OF PROGRAMMING

No attempt will be made in this chapter to consider all of the multifarious problems facing the electronic mass media. There are technical problems relating to radio and TV coverage, allocations, assignment and use of clear channels, color television, and quality of signals. There are economic problems stemming from the buying and selling of stations and their licenses, the tendency toward concentration of ownership, monopoly, and cross media combinations, dependence on advertising revenue, and such problems as payola, ratings, network relations with affiliates, and subscription television, as well as community antenna television. The major problems today, however, are really non-technical and non-economic from the general public's viewpoint, however critical they may be for individual station owners. The major problem, from the public's standpoint is that of programming and, in a broader sense, social responsibility. How shall this social responsibility be defined? Shall it be in terms of what the majority of viewers seem to want as programs, in terms of an ill-defined concept of "balanced programming"; in terms of what Congress and the FCC say it should be; or shall the definition of socially responsible programming be left to the market place, in the hope that free enterprise and competition will more or less automatically produce what is best?

There have been manifold criticisms of radio and TV programs and program schedules, focused on advertising excesses, emphasis on violence and sex, undesirable children's programs, too few informational, educational, and public affairs programs, too little in the way of local, live, community oriented programs, avoidance of controversial issues, dull, stupid, and low grade entertainment, lack of variety, balance, and programs of interest to special groups and interests. Needless to say, it is easier to criticize than to provide workable remedies.

What, after all, are the primary functions of radio and TV: to sell goods and services, to entertain, to inform, enlighten, educate? Who is to say? At present these media do all such things, and the great majority of the viewers and the public probably agree they should. Disagreement arises over the amount of time devoted to each function. The proprietors want to use the maximum time for selling, the majority of listeners want amusement, and the intellectuals and educators stress information and enlightenment. In the final analysis it is the FCC, under authorization of Congress, that must decide what distribution and weight shall be given to these several functions to further the "public interest, convenience, or necessity." It is clear that the station proprietors are not owners of the frequencies and channels they use, but lessees, licensees, and it is for the government, through the FCC and Congress, to define the terms of the licenses or leases. Air waves and frequencies are resources, national assets, which are limited and hence very valuable. Stations which command a sale price in the tens of millions are able to do so, not because of the value of the station's equipment and physical properties, but because of the value of an intangible right to use frequencies and channels, rights which are donated, given free of charge, to station owners. As the profits of station owners have soared and the "traffic in licenses" has grown, the question has been seriously raised whether the government should not charge fees for station licenses and set limits to what is a fair return on investment.[40] Whether or not this would be advisable is certainly open to question, but the right of the government to grant or withhold licenses on the basis of the "public interest" is clear. This means in part public interest in programming.

Now the FCC Act expressly forbids censorship by FCC. If by censorship is meant any interference with a station's right to do as it pleases then the assignment of channels, the restrictions on power, the very terms of the licenses themselves constitute censorship. On the other hand, if censorship is to be restricted in meaning solely to official blue-penciling of scripts it is probably much too narrowly conceptualized. Proprietors of radio and TV have frequently argued that they should be accorded the same degree of freedom constitutionally guaranteed the press. This claim would seem to be justified up to a point. Certainly station owners should be free to editorialize, to criticize the government, to express their opinions on public issues freely, so long as they do not violate laws regarding libel and slander, obscenity, and so on. In fact, the codes of most stations, the networks, and the industry as a whole go far beyond the officially pre-scribed legal requirements. The technical factors which restrict the num-ber of channels available, especially for TV, the family nature of the audience with a large number of child listeners, as well as the possibility of sudden, simultaneous response on a nation-wide basis, place these media in a somewhat different position, in relation to the general public, from that of the newspaper press.

Probably no agency or group is better able to "balance," or prescribe the weights to be given to different types of programs than the FCC. If leaving this decision to owners and proprietors exclusively is not desirable, neither is leaving it to the viewers, if by that is meant to 51 per cent of the viewers or to popularity program ratings. Although majority rule has always been an essential element of democratic institutions, emphasis has also been placed on minority rights. In a sense, this problem of balancing majority and minority rights is at the center of the programming problem of radio and TV. To some extent all stations, networks, and the industry as a whole are aware of this, and efforts are made to meet some minority interests and desires—educational, special interest, and the like. Some channels, and even stations, have been dedicated to educational use. UHF affords the possibility of a much wider spectrum for the specialized pro-gram. Nevertheless, in spite of the tremendous growth in number of AM stations during the last ten years and the increase in FM and TV outlets, the average listener or viewer is usually confronted with very few choices in types of programs at prime broadcasting hours. It should be possible to satisfy, not merely the majority, but many minorities as well, during these favorite hours with a much wider variety of program types, perhaps by grouping stations under a single ownership, by encouraging a larger number of networks with a limited number of affiliates, or through some other method of co-ordination and division of labor. The aim should be to have several types of program available to all listeners simultaneously, at least during the evening hours, and as often as possible throughout the day. This may mean that some of the more profitable stations will have to share their profitable time with a few of the stations serving special publics, that government, foundations, schools and colleges will have to fill some gaps, possibly with more stations of their own. The "wasteland," if wasteland there is, arises not only because of the audience's waste of time, but because of the economic and social waste of channels and frequencies duplicating each other throughout the day and night.

The problem of program quality, however, is not only a problem of duplication and lack of real choices, it is also a problem of creativity. The argument of program makers is that they are as eager to present new, exciting, high quality, live, informative programs as anyone, but where can they find enough of them to fill sixteen, twenty, or twenty-four hours a day of broadcasting time? Without tray after tray of taped soap operas, shelves of hi-fi recordings, and cans of old movies, how could they fill the long days and nights with sight and sound? In a very real sense the limited supply of talented musicians, artists, lecturers, creators simply does not meet the insatiable demand of sixty million families, and a potential audience well over 100,000,000. Mass consumption presupposes mass production, but mass production necessitates standardization, uniformity, exchangeable parts, minute division of labor, controls, and very little initiative once the production process is started. The result is duplication, maximum repetition, not maximum satisfaction. The need for a larger number of good programs of all types is great. Every effort should be made to provide the creative, productive talent necessary. The industry and the government can do much financially, and otherwise, to nurture creative talent; but more is needed. There must be a place for the output of such talent on the receiving sets of the country. Accomplishing this means a more co-ordinated, efficient, nation-wide pattern of TV and radio programming with more choices for the individual viewer at any given time and with less duplication.[41]

POLITICAL USE OF TELEVISION

A second major problem, not altogether unrelated to that of programming is the political use of radio and especially TV. There is the "equal time" problem and the problem of televising congressional proceedings and hearings. Stations are not required by law to give or sell time to candidates for public office. If they do, however, they are obligated to sell or give equal time to all other candidates running for the same office. Rules and practices have defined more specifically the meaning of "equal time" and of "candidate" as used in the law. A problem for the broadcasters arises, however, because of the number of candidates for some offices, and the fact that many of them have almost no popular support, no chance of winning the election, and sometimes are merely eccentrics, or ambitious publicity seekers. Rather than provide time for all candidates, many stations and networks have simply refused to give time to any. As a consequence, voters are deprived of the opportunity of seeing and hearing candidates. Yielding to public and industrial pressures, Congress in 1960 made an exception to the law in the Presidential election of that year, which made the Nixon-Kennedy debates possible without forcing the broadcasters to provide equal debating time for all Presidential and Vice-Presidential candidates. But this was an exception, and the equal time rule as set forth in Section 315 of the FCC Act still applies.[42]

Many broadcasters argue that the equal time rule should be dispensed with entirely, leaving to the stations and the networks the full responsibility for according political candidates an equitable if not an equal amount of time. They point to the fact that without the equal time provision they would still be obligated to a fair, balanced, and equitable presentation of controversial issues. As a matter of fact, there were few, if any, who criticized the exception made in 1960 or the use made of it by the broadcasters. The real difficulty would arise, however, if the equal time rule were abandoned in Congressional contests and in elections at the state and local levels. In these cases there are often several candidates for a particular office, and the distinction between the major and minor candidates is not so clear. Furthermore, previous experience would suggest that not all stations could be counted on to show the wisdom, and display the unbiased neutrality that major networks might exhibit in projecting candidates for President and Vice-President.

The argument for abolishing or modifying the equal time rule at the state and local level does not seem convincing. It would be virtually impossible to find a legitimate basis for treating official nominees for public office other than on an equal basis. Certainly a format or formula could be devised for affording all candidates equal time. Not every citizen could, under existing laws, qualify as a candidate entitled to a place on the ballot, and if a few publicity-seekers did qualify, the cost of giving them equal time could very well be charged to democracy's "cost of doing business." There is an important difference between the amount of listening time the public needs to judge a candidate's personality and learn his stand on public issues, and the amount of time a candidate would like to have to sell his candidacy. At the state and local levels the broadcasters might do what the League of Women Voters does at their candidates' meeting, and let all candidates state their views and answer questions. Stations might donate the amount of time necessary to broadcast or telecast such a meeting and give each candidate an additional 15 or 20 minutes during the campaign period.

Possibly, in the case of state-wide offices, such as governorships, or lieutenant governorships, a distinction might be made between major and minor candidates, prescribing equal treatment for each in their respective category. The criteria to use in differentiating major and minor candidates could vary from state to state. One criterion might be the number of votes he or his party received for that office in the previous election. Another might be demonstrated organizational (party and non-party) support. Still another, the ability to obtain a sufficient number of signatures to a petition in the state as a whole, and/or in a specified number of counties in the state. Doubtless there are other criteria. Since all candidates would have some public exposure, and the amounts in the major and in the minor categories would not differ greatly, marginal candidates would not be too adversely affected regardless of the category to which they would be assigned.

At the national level, for Presidential and Vice-Presidential candidates, the problem seems easier to solve on a major and minor basis. In the vast majority of Presidential elections there have been only two major parties, plus a number of very small parties. In a few instances, 1912 and 1924, for example, sizable third parties developed. With this experience in mind the category "major parties or candidates" might be defined to mean the two leading parties as measured by the votes for President and Vice-President in the preceding Presidential election. All other parties would be designated minor, unless in the opinion of the FCC, one or more of the minor parties had such large and widespread support that it would probably obtain electoral votes. In this case such a party or parties would be given equal time with the major parties. All parties and candidates would receive some radio and television time, and this would be equal within each of the two categories, major or minor.

Television and Congressional Hearings

Another problem of the political use of radio and television, is the televising of Congressional sessions and hearings, and the introduction of TV cameras into the court room. Following, or soon after, the sensational McCarthy hearings in 1954, Speaker Rayburn imposed his famous ban on the televising of Congressional hearings and sessions, a ban which has continued down to the present.[43] Many reasons for the ban have been given: (a) that the presence of TV cameras and equipment makes many potential witnesses at hearings reluctant to appear, or if they do appear, makes them much more fearful of projecting an unfavorable image of themselves, especially, if they are not photogenic; (b) those who conduct the hearings may be more concerned with the impression they make on the viewing audience than with the specific purposes of the hearings; (c) appearances before a nation-wide audience may have consequences, good or bad, which would be incalculable and tremendous, possibly catastrophic for the participants; (d) unless TV covered all hearings, or the hearings it did cover completely and did not merely portray the dramatic, it might give a distorted picture of the purpose, nature, and results of the hearings; (e) finally, it is argued that the presence of cameras, lights, wires, and other paraphernalia would impede and disrupt proceedings.

On the other hand the telecasters claim that the public, all the people, not only the few hundred present in the committee room, has a right to see what goes on at these hearings, that representatives of the press and other media are already allowed to attend and report their impressions, that with proper planning and staging of the hearings confusion and annoyances can be avoided, and that the performance of TV representatives at national party political conventions indicates that they can do their job to the general satisfaction of all.

The problem is a difficult and very complex one. In the first place, it seems clear that a large proportion of Congressional hearings and sessions are devoted to matters of a routine, technical, or mundane nature and would be of little interest to the public at large. The televising of such hearings and sessions would of necessity have to be highly selective. If one accepts as a criterion of selection, newsworthiness, then the question of definition becomes important. Shall it be the news definition of the *New York Times,* the *Christian Science Monitor,* the *Daily News,* or the *Police Gazette*? There will hardly be room for cameras representing many different points of view. Possibly this could be solved by granting admission to representatives of the three networks only. The principal problem will be two-fold, not to do injustice to the participants, especially the witnesses, and to give an unbiased and meaningful picture of the hearings as a whole, and their purposes. Probably neither of these goals can be attained by presenting the hearings live. However well the average legislator may be able to take care of himself before the cameras, as a consequence of much experience, the number of witnesses that can do so in an unrehearsed, unbriefed, and unmade-up situation, would be very few. It seems only fair, therefore, that participants be allowed to edit or delete the TV recordings, and this would necessitate the use of tape. Furthermore, the projection of such hearings should be in a context that would give them meaning. Either some member of the Committee staff could add this with introductory, explanatory, or summary statements from time to time, or this could be done by a special commentator for the network. What should be avoided at all costs is the selection of a few dramatic episodes out of context which distort the true meaning of what is going on and spread, across the TV screens of the country, images of public spirited citizens which may do them an injustice. Until then the Rayburn ban should not be lifted.

Television and the Court Room

The problem of televised court proceedings involves some of the same considerations mentioned in regard to Congressional hearings. The American Bar Association has repeatedly voted against putting such proceedings on the TV screen,[44] and the case for such a ban is convincing. In the first place, in most cases, civil as well as criminal, the private interests of plaintiff and defendant are paramount, not those of the public. The public's curiosity and desire for excitement and sensations, rather than any need for information or enlightenment, would be the primary motives for viewing the proceedings. Furthermore, the need for protecting the defendant and witnesses from the hazards of candid camera TV are greater even than in the case of witnesses at Congressional hearings. Most of the latter are voluntary witnesses; many of the former are reluctant and involuntary. Again, in criminal trials and others where a jury is used, the televising of proceedings may bring the public generally into the trial, in a manner that would seriously interfere with the jury doing its job effectively. Television could not give, even if a sizable number of viewers would watch the TV screen persistently enough, a complete view of the proceedings. In this case, a little knowledge—it could be no more than that—by the viewing public would probably be a very bad thing and fail to serve the ends of justice.

NOTES FOR CHAPTER 9

Epigraph. Newton M. Minow, reported in the *New York Times,* May 10, 1961, p. 79.
1. On the history of motion pictures see, Ramsaye, Terry, *A Million and One Nights: A History of the Motion Picture* (New York: Simon and Schuster, 1926), 2 vols. Also Bardèche, M., and R. Brasillach, *The History of Motion Pictures* (New York: W. W. Norton, 1938).
2. See White, Llewelyn, *The American Radio* (Chicago: University of Chicago Press, 1947), and Chester, Giraud, and G. R. Garrison, *Television and Radio* (New York: Appleton-Century-Crofts, 1956).
3. See *30 Years of Pioneering and Progress in Radio and Television* (Department of Information, Radio Corporation of America, 1949).
4. Bogart, Leo, *The Age of Television* (New York: Frederick Ungar Publishing Co., 1956).
5. See Elliott, William Y. (ed.), *Television's Impact on American Culture* (East Lansing: Michigan State University Press); weekly issues of *Broadcasting* magazine; the annual reports of the FCC.
6. Vernon Scott, in *"The Films: Then and Now,"* The Philadelphia Bulletin, February 18 and 20, 1963 notes the following trends:
   People watch TV instead of going to movies;
   many studios have disappeared;
   fewer pictures are produced;
   independent producers are used more frequently;
   many producers depend increasingly on the TV outlet;
   gross income has remained about the same for ten years $1.45 billion;
   costs so great that only one picture in five is profitable;

Hollywood reached its peak in 1936 with 621 full length pictures; only 143 produced in 1962;

good movies reap fortunes;

80 per cent of prime TV time is on film;

studios are selling films only a couple of years old;

about 40 per cent of TV time is devoted to old movies;

there has been a marked rise in number of independents;

networks are losing control to stars, agencies, and sponsors moving in to claim time.

7. FCC, *28th Annual Report* (1962), pp. 74-76.
8. See *Broadcasting,* March 13, 1961, p. 44. Representatives Emanuel Celler, opening the House anti-trust committee hearings March 13, 1963, cited three newspaper chains with 45 papers, 25 magazines, 10 AM, 7 FM, and 12 TV stations, 2 press associations, several photo services, syndicates, and feature services. These chains were Scripps-Howard, Hearst, and New-house. See *Broadcasting,* March 18, 1963, p. 62. "After deducting joint and multiple ownership, there are 4,993 separate and independent entities engaged in disseminating news—1,211 papers, 2,957 AM, 485 FM, 340 TV." *Idem.*
9. See Robinson, Thomas Porter, *Radio Networks and the Federal Government,* (New York: Columbia University Press, 1943), Chap. 6.
10. See FCC, *28th Annual Report* (1962), pp. 78-83.
11. *Broadcasting,* February 19, 1962.
12. See Irion, Frederick C., *Public Opinion and Propaganda* (New York: Thomas Y. Crowell, 1950), p. 118.
13. See Head, Sydney W., *Broadcasting in America* (Boston: Houghton, Mif-flin Co., 1956), esp. chap. 25. See also Inglis, Ruth, *Freedom of the Movies* (Chicago: University of Chicago Press, 1947).
14. See Moley, Raymond, *The Hays Office* (Indianapolis: Bobbs-Merrill, 1945). The Hays Office became the Johnston Office in 1945, and the organization of motion-picture producers, the Motion Picture Association of America (MPAA).
15. See Emery, Walter B., *Broadcasting and Government, op. cit.*
16. "Over 12,000 complaint letters were received during the year (1961-1962), which was a substantial increase over 1961. About 35 per cent were about programming, mostly objections to excessive crime and violence." FCC, *28th Annual Report,* 1962, p. 3.
17. *Information Please Almanac* (1963), p. 597.
18. In addition to Emery, Walter B., *op. cit.,* see *Broadcasting and Government Regulation in a Free Society* (Santa Barbara, California: The Center for the Study of Democratic Institutions, 1959).
19. The official title of the "Blue Book" is: *Public Service Responsibility of Broadcast Licensees* (Federal Communications Commission, March 7, 1946).
20. An account of and excerpts from the "wasteland" speech, *New York Times,* May 10, 1961, pp. 1ff.
21. In February, 1964, the Congress expressly refused to allow the FCC to prescribe rules restricting TV commercials.
22. See Emery, W. B., *op. cit.,* chap. 19, and discussion of a broadcast editorial bill sponsored by Representative John E. Moss, *New York Times,* July 16 and 17, 1963.
23. As reported in *Broadcasting,* February 19, 1962, p. 34.

24. *Ibid.,* February 5, 1962, p. 46.
25. *Ibid.,* February 12, 1962, p. 29.
26. *Ibid.,* February 26, 1962.
27. *Ibid.,* February 2, 1959.
28. Steiner, Gary A., *The People Look at Television* (New York: Alfred A. Knopf, 1963).
29. From a National Opinion Research Center survey as reported in *Broadcasting,* March 8, 1948.
30. See "A Comparison of Public Attitudes Toward Television: December, 1959, and November, 1961," A Memorandum to the Television Information Office from Elmo Roper and Associates, January 25, 1962.
31. See Klapper, Joseph T., *The Effects of Mass Communications* (Chicago, Ill.: The Free Press of Glencoe, Ill., 1958).
32. See Dale, Edgar, *The Content of Motion Pictures and Children's Attendance at Motion Pictures,* One Vol. (New York: Macmillan, 1935). Also Kimball Young's review of ten of the Payne Fund Studies, *American Journal of Sociology,* Vol. 41 (September, 1935), pp. 249-55.
33. Belson, William A., "Measuring the Effects of Television: A Description of Method," *Public Opinion Quarterly,* Vol. 22 (Spring, 1958), pp. 11-18.
34. *Broadcasting,* March 18, 1963, p. 30.
35. Sarnoff, Robert W., "Television's Role in the American Democracy," An Address before the Chicago World Trade Conference, Chicago, Illinois, March 5, 1963. Published by the National Broadcasting Company.
36. Campbell, Angus, "Surge and Decline: A Study of Electoral Change," *Public Opinion Quarterly,* Vol. 29 (Fall, 1960), pp. 397-418.
37. See Schramm, Wilbur L., Lyle, Jack, and E. B. Parker, *Television in the Lives of Our Children* (Stanford, Calif.: Stanford University Press, 1961). See also Maccoby, Eleanor, "TV: Its Impact on School Children," *Public Opinion Quarterly,* Vol. 15 (Fall, 1951), pp. 421-44; and vol 18 (Fall, 1954), pp. 239-44.
38. *Broadcasting,* February 5, 1962.
39. See Powell, John Walker, *Channels of Learning: The Story of Educational Television* (Washington, D. C.: Public Affairs Press, 1962); Institute for Communications Research, Stanford University, *Educational Television—The Next Ten Years* (1962). On May 1, 1962, Congress passed a law authorizing the Secretary of Health, Education, and Welfare "to make $32 million in matching grants to the States for the construction of non-commercial educational TV stations." FCC, *28th Annual Report* (1962), p. 63.
40. See *Broadcasting,* March 18, 1963, p. 100; February 19, 1962.
41. See "Program for FCC," *Consumer Reports,* February, 1960, pp. 93ff.; Elliott, W. Y. (ed.), *Television's Impact on American Culture* (East Lansing: Michigan State University Press, 1956); Emery, Walter B., *op. cit.,* chap. 24, pp. 303-14.
42. FCC, *28th Annual Report* (1962), pp. 48-51.
43. See *Broadcasting,* March 11, 1963, p. 80, and January 14, 1963, p. 64.
44. *Ibid.,* February 19, 1962, p. 53.

SUPPLEMENTARY READING

A. General

BERELSON, BERNARD. "The State of Communication Research," *Public Opinion Quarterly,* Vol. 23 (Spring, 1959), pp. 1-17.

BURTON, PAULA. *British Broadcasting in Transition.* Minneapolis: University of Minnesota Press, 1961.

COLE, BARRY G. and KLOSE, AL PAUL (compilers). "A Selected Bibliography on the History of Broadcasting," *Journal of Broadcasting,* Vol. 8 (Summer, 1963), pp. 247-68.

DAVISON, W. PHILLIPS. "On the Effects of Communication," *Public Opinion Quarterly,* Vol. 23 (Fall, 1959), pp. 343-61.

EMERY, WALTER BYRON. *Broadcasting and Government: Responsibilities and Regulations.* Lansing: Michigan State University Press, 1961.

KLAPPER, JOSEPH T. *The Effects of Mass Communications.* Chicago: The Free Press of Glencoe, Ill., 1958.

KRAUS, SIDNEY (ed.). *The Great Debates: Background, Perspectives, Effects.* Bloomington: Indiana University Press, 1962.

MACHLUP, FRITZ. *Production and Distribution of Knowledge in the United States.* Princeton, N. J.: Princeton University Press, 1962.

PARKER, EVERETT C., BARRY, D. W., and SMYTHE, D. *The Television-Radio Audience and Religion.* Harper & Bros., 1955.

PYE, LUCIAN W. (ed.). *Communications and Political Development.* Princeton, N. J.: Princeton University Press, 1963.

SCHRAMM, WILBUR. *Responsibility in Mass Communication.* New York: Harper & Bros., 1957.

SIEPMANN, CHARLES A. *Radio, Television, and Society.* New York: Oxford University Press, 1950.

SMEAD, ELMER E. *Freedom of Speech by Radio and Television.* Public Affairs Press, 1959.

B. Motion Pictures

BARDÈCHE, M., and BRASILLACH, R. *The History of Motion Pictures.* New York: W. W. Norton & Co., Inc., and the Museum of Modern Art, 1938.

BERTRAND, DANIEL, et al. *The Motion Pictures Industry: A Pattern of Control.* U. S. Temporary National Economic Committee, Monograph No. 43. Washington, D. C.: Government Printing Office, 1941.

CHARTERS, W. W. *Motion Pictures and Youth.* New York: The Macmillan Co., 1933.

INGLIS, RUTH A. *Freedom of the Movies.* Chicago: University of Chicago Press, 1947.

JONES, DOROTHY B. "Quantitive Analysis of Motion Picture Content," *Public Opinion Quarterly,* Vol. 6 (Fall, 1942), pp. 411-28.

KRACAUER, SIEGFRIED. *Theory of Film.* New York: Oxford University Press, 1960.

MOLEY, RAYMOND. *The Hays Office.* Indianapolis: Bobbs-Merrill, 1945.

PETERSON, RUTH C., and THURSTONE, L. L. *Motion Pictures and the Social Attitudes of Children.* New York: The Macmillan Co., 1933.

RAMSAYE, TERRY. *A Million and One Nights: A History of the Motion Picture.* New York: Simon and Schuster, 1926, 2 vols.

ROSTEN, LEO C. *Hollywood.* Harcourt, Brace, & Co., 1941.

ROTHA, PAUL. *The Documentary Film.* New York: W. W. Norton & Co., 1939.

SEABURY, W. M. *The Public and the Motion Picture Industry.* New York: The Macmillan Co., 1926.

WOLFENSTEIN, MARTHA, and LEITES, NATHAN. *Movies: A Psychological Study.* Chicago: The Free Press of Glencoe, Ill., 1950.

C. Radio

Federal Council of Churches. *Broadcasting and the Public.* New York: The Abingdon Press, 1938.

Fund for the Republic, Center for the Study of Democratic Institutions. *Broadcasting and Government Regulation in a Free Society.* Santa Barbara, California, 1959.

HERRING, J. M. "Broadcasting and the Public Interest," *Harvard Business Review,* Vol. 18 (Spring, 1944), pp. 344-56.

KERWIN, J. G. *The Control of Radio.* Chicago: University of Chicago Press, 1934.

ROSE, C. B. JR. *National Policy for Radio Broadcasting.* New York: Harper & Bros., 1940.

SIEPMANN, CHARLES A. *Radio's Second Chance.* Boston: Little, Brown & Co., 1946.

WHITE, LLEWELLYN. *The American Radio.* Chicago: University of Chicago Press, 1947.

D. Television

Anon. "Regulation of TV," *Harvard Law Review.* Vol. 72 (January, 1959), pp. 445-93.

Anon. "TV-the Light that Failed," *Fortune,* Vol. 58 (December, 1958), pp. 78-81.

BELSON, WILLIAM A. "The Effects of Television on the Reading and the Buying of Newspapers and Magazines," *Public Opinion Quarterly,* Vol. 25 (Fall, 1961), pp. 366-80.

BLUEM, A. WILLIAM, et al. *TV in the Public Interest.* Hastings House, Pubs., Inc., 1961.

BOGART, LEO. *The Age of Television.* New York: Frederick Ungar Publishing Co., 1956.

ELLIOTT, WILLIAM Y. *Television's Impact on American Culture.* Lansing: Michigan State University Press, 1956.

GLICK, IRA O. and LEVY, SIDNEY, JR. *Living with Television.* Chicago: Aldine Publishing Co., 1962.

HIMMELWEIT, HILDE T. *Television and the Child.* New York: Oxford University Press, 1960.

LAZARSFELD, PAUL F. "Why Is So Little Known About the Effects of TV and What Can Be Done About It?" *Public Opinion Quarterly,* Vol. 19 (Fall, 1955), pp. 245-51.

MACCOBY, ELEANOR E. "Television: Its Impact on School Children," *Public Opinion Quarterly,* Vol. 15 (Fall, 1951), pp. 421-44. Also *Public Opinion Quarterly,* Vol. 18 (Fall, 1954), pp. 239-44.

MEHLING, HAROLD. *The Great Time-Killer.* Cleveland: World Publishing Company, 1962.

PACKARD, VANCE. "New Kinds of TV: Where Do We Go From Here," *Atlantic Monthly,* Vol. 212 (October, 1963), pp. 68-74.

SCHRAMM, WILBUR. *The Impact of Educational Television.* Urbana, Ill.: University of Illinois Press, 1960.

SCHRAMM, WILBUR L., LYLE, JACK, and PARKER, E. B. *Television in the Lives of Our Children.* Stanford, Calif.: Stanford University Press, 1961.

Stanford University, Institute for Communications Research. *Educational Tele-

vision: The Next Ten Years. A report and summary of major studies on the problems and potential of educational television conducted under the auspices of the U. S. Office of Education. Stanford, 1962.

STEINER, GARY A. *The People Look at TV.* New York: Alfred A. Knopf, 1963.

TIENAMAN, JOSEPH. *Television and the Political Image: A Study of the Impact of Television on the 1959 General Election.* London: Methuen, 1961.

THOMSON, C. A. H. *Television and Presidential Politics.* Washington, D. C.: The Brookings Institution, 1956.

WEINBERG, MEYER. *TV in America: The Morality of Hard Cash.* Ballantine Books, Inc., 1962.

WIEBE, G. D. "Responses to the Televised Kefauver Hearings: Some Social Psychological Implications," *Public Opinion Quarterly,* Vol. 16 (Summer, 1952), pp. 179-200.

X · Pressure Groups

There is no public opinion that is not activity reflecting or representing the activity of a group or of a set of groups.

—ARTHUR F. BENTLEY

G ROUPS PLAY an important role in the formation of public opinion. Special consideration has already been given to the family as a relatively small, primary group, to religious groups, and to the schools. Later the role of government will be discussed. In addition to these groups, however, there are literally tens of thousands of groups of varying size and importance which may be labelled pressure groups, primarily because of the influence or pressure they exert on public opinion and public policy. These groups vary greatly in size, financial resources, objectives, organization, leadership, and influence. Some exert pressure very infrequently; others, almost continuously. Of primary importance are the large, powerful groups that do so much to mold and shape mass opinion and public policy.[1]

HISTORY AND DEVELOPMENT

Pressure groups are by no means new. They have existed throughout history, and today they may be found in all countries no matter how primitive and undeveloped some of them may be.[2] During the Colonial period in the United States there were religious and political groups, business associations and agricultural societies, chambers of commerce and organizations of labor. Noteworthy among the early pressure groups in the colonies were the Sons of Liberty and the Society of the Cincinnati. Following the framing of the federal constitution and the establishment of the new government, new groups appeared including peace societies, anti-slavery societies, and other reform movements. In 1789, one of the first temperance societies was organized in Litchfield, Connecticut, and in 1826, the American Temperance Society was formed. By 1830, there were more than one hundred anti-slavery groups in the United States, and in 1833, they federated to form the American Anti-Slavery Society. This organization was an unusually effective pressure group, and it exhibited most of the talents and strategies of the pressure groups of today, handicapped of course by lack of today's mass media. The industrial and railroad expansion of the mid-nineteenth century also produced powerful pressure groups. Many of the national organizations which are in existence today originated at this time: the American Medical Association (1847), the American Educational Association (1807), the United States Brewers' Association (1862), and the National Grange and the Grand Army of the Republic (1866).

The late nineteenth century witnessed rapid industrial growth, the westward movement, the emergence of trusts and monopolies, and nation-wide struggles over tariffs, currency, land policies, and government regulation of railroads and business. It also saw the growing influence of pressure groups and the beginning of efforts by the state governments to regulate the agents, the lobbyists, in the state capitals. The American Federation of Labor was founded in 1881-86; the National Association of Manufacturers in 1895, the Anti-Saloon League in 1893. The New York insurance investigation in 1905 was the first of several dramatic investigations of lobbying by the federal government as well as by the states. The most comprehensive undertakings by the federal government took place in 1913, 1927, 1935, and 1950.[3] In 1902, the Farmers Union was established, supplementing the National Grange, which had been in existence since the end of the Civil War. The creation of the American Farm Bureau Federation in 1920 completed the roster of the big three pressure groups in agriculture.[4] Although the American Federation of Labor remained the largest and most influential trade union, at least until the formation of the Congress of Industrial Organizations in 1936, there were other nation-wide labor organizations of importance among railroad workers, federal employees, and coal miners.[5] In the business arena the number of trade associations grew rapidly during the first three decades of the twentieth century, and in 1931, the Chamber of Commerce of the United States was formed to give state and local chambers, as well as many trade associations, a more unified and stronger voice in the determination of public policy. During the 1920's the Federal Trade Commission published its famous report on the efforts of associations and agencies of electric and gas utilities to influence public opinion in the United States,[6] and in the 1930's the attempts of the National Industrial Recovery Administration (NIRA) to recognize and institutionalize certain pressure groups as legal agents of particular trades and sectors of business, stimulated the growth and number of economic pressure groups.[7] Following the end of World War II, Congress passed the Legislative Reorganization Act which included a section dealing with lobbying groups, requiring them to register with the Senate and House, and to file certain information, including amounts spent to influence legislation directly or indirectly.[8] As indicated above, the last of the extensive congressional probes into lobbying activities took place in 1950. Since then the relations between Congress and the many groups that seek to influence it have been tolerably satisfactory, although, on occasion, some group, or array of groups will attract special attention.

For more than twenty years the *Congressional Quarterly* has been following very closely the work of Congress and the role of pressure groups in relation to it.[9] Its weekly publications and special reports, together with its yearly summaries, are a rich mine of information regarding the number of such groups active in Washington, how much they spend, their objectives, methods, and accomplishments. Much of its information is obtained from the reports of the groups themselves, submitted to the government under the law of 1946. Since the law went into effect the number of individuals, firms, and organizations registering each year has varied from a low of 204 in 1952 to a high of 731 in 1947. From 1954 to 1962 the number has been close to 400. The variations are due, not only to variations in the activities of groups, but to changing interpretations of the law. Some organizations, such as the National Association of Manufacturers (NAM), the American Bar Association (ABA), the Americans for Democratic Action (ADA), and the American Public Power Association (APPA), for example, no longer register because they do not believe they are engaged in activities covered by the law. From 1946 to 1962, there were 3,798 individuals, 231 public relations and law firms, and 557 organizations, or a total of 4,586 different lobbyists who had registered under the law. Of the 367 who registered in 1962, there were 239 who had never done so before. Since only 557 different organizations have filed since 1946 and since the number on file for any given year is much less than that figure (312 in 1961), it might be concluded that the most active and important pressure groups focusing their attention on the federal government during a single year would not be much over 300. However, this does not take into account the hundreds, even thousands of groups seeking to influence public policy and public opinion at the local, state, and even international levels. Nor does it consider the many groups that may be represented by these top 300, or those that seek to exert pressure very infrequently. Of the 312 groups which filed in 1961, 171 were classified as business groups, 52 as citizens groups, 40 in the labor-employee category, 22 farm organizations, 17 professional, and 10 associations of veterans or military people.[10]

Pressure groups in general do not report the expenditures of very large sums to influence legislation, that is large relative to the stakes involved, or the amounts spent by some business firms to advertise tobacco, cosmetics, and other commodities. The total expenditures reported for all the lobbyists registered went from $5,000,000 in 1947 to $10,000,000 in 1950 and back to about $4,000,000 in 1960 and 1961. The top spenders vary considerably from year to year, depending to a considerable extent on the prominence of issues and how crucial they seem. In 1961, the five top spenders in the order of their expenditures were the American Medical Association, the AFL-CIO, the American Farm Bureau Federation (AFBF), the American Legion, and the United States Savings and Loan League. In 1959, however, the top spenders were the International Brotherhood of Teamsters, the Temporary Committee on Taxes of the Mutual Life Insurance Companies, AFL-CIO, National Committee on the Income Tax, and the National Education Association (NEA). And so it goes from year to year, with some associations spending over $200,000 one year and perhaps less than $50,000 the next. Note that there are many groups that rank high as spenders nearly every year, even though they are not always near the top.

INTEREST PRESSURE GROUPS

A convenient and useful distinction may be made between interest pressure groups, and idea groups. Many, if not most, of the really powerful groups in the country are in the first category and include business, labor, agricultural, religious, professional, and ethnic groups. In the case of business there are the two summit organizations, the Chamber of Commerce of the United States and the National Association of Manufacturers, literally thousands of trade associations, and finally, the larger corporations which frequently exert much pressure directly, as well as through associations, on the public affairs of the country. The trade associations may be conveniently subdivided into five groups: (1) those whose members extract or deal with basic raw materials and power such as the American Mining Congress, American Petroleum Institute, American Gas Association, National Coal Association, American Iron and Steel Institute, and the American Public Power Association; (2) those concerned with manufacturing and processing such as the American Cotton Manufacturers Institute, the National Lumber Manufacturers Association, Automobile Manufacturers Association, and the National Association of Frozen Food Packers; (3) those involved with communication and transportation, the Association of American Railroads, the National Association of Broadcasters, and the American Trucking Associations; (4) associations in the areas of merchandising and advertising, for example, the American Association of Advertising Agencies, the American Retail Federation, and the National Retail Dry Goods Association; finally, (5) associations of firms concerned with banking and insurance, such as the American Banker's Association, the Life Insurance Association of America, and the United States Savings and Loan League. At each step of the business process from raw materials, through manufacturing, to transportation, selling, and financing, American business is well represented by pertinent pressure groups.

Reference has already been made to corporations as pressure groups because of their frequent efforts to influence government policies as well as public opinion. This is true of many of America's largest companies— American Telephone and Telegraph, General Motors, du Pont, Standard Oil of New Jersey, General Electric, United States Steel, and many others. Sometimes these individual corporations prefer to act through the associations to which they belong; at other times they bring their pressure to bear directly on government and public opinion.

The principal interest groups in the labor field have been mentioned— the AFL-CIO, the Railway Brotherhoods, Federation of Federal Employees, International Brotherhood of Teamsters, and the United Mine Workers. Aside from producer's groups and cooperatives, the top organizations in agriculture are the AFBF, the National Grange, and the Farmer's Union, each representing a slightly different constituency and section of the country. Interest groups also comprise the nation-wide professional organizations of doctors, lawyers, teachers, engineers, nurses and many others. There are over 300 religious denominations in the United States, and some of them attempt at times to influence public policy and public affairs. In addition to their separate organizations, however, there are three important, over-all agencies for representing Protestants, Catholics, and Jews; namely the National Council of Churches, the National Catholic Welfare Conference, and the American Jewish Committee. Each of these summit bodies undertakes to serve as the voice of its adherents, particularly on public problems and policies of special interest to its members. Mention should also be made of ethnic, racial, and nationalistic interest groups. Included, also, among interest groups are many government agencies, national as well as state and local.

IDEA GROUPS

Interest groups, as distinct from idea groups, have as their primary basis for organization some broad interest such as business activity, occupation, profession, religion, race, sex, or age. This general interest brings the members of the organization together and many different policies, positions, activities, or pressures serve that general interest. Idea groups, however, focus their attention on one or more ideas such as prohibition, crippled children, tariffs, constitutional government, and innumerable others. The yearly editions of the *World Almanac* usually have a section devoted to associations in the United States. In 1963, more than 1,000 were listed, and a large proportion of these were idea groups. Although the differences between idea and interest groups are fairly clear, some groups are difficult to classify. The National Association for the Advancement of Colored People, the Republican Party, the National Audubon Society, and the Isaak Walton League of America have each rather specific ideas to promote, yet one could validly speak of a race, a political, a bird, or a fishing interest. In spite of these difficulties at times, the distinction seems useful.

Some years ago a study was made of the general fields of interest of national associations in the United States. Approximately 4,000 associations were found, distributed as follows:[11]

Manufacturers'	800
Distribution (wholesale and retail)	300
Transportation, finance, insurance	400
Other business associations	300
Professional and semi-professional	500
Labor	200
Women's	100
Veterans and military	60
Commodity exchange	60
Farmers'	55
Negroes'	50
Public officials'	50
Fraternal	25
Sport and recreation	100
Other	1,000
Grand total	4,000

WHY PRESSURE GROUPS?

Enough has been written to suggest, at least, the scope of the pressure group problem in the United States. Other countries will reveal much the same situation, although there will be differences in the number, objectives, resources, organization, and relative influence of the groups from country to country. How may one account for the rise of pressure groups, and their proliferation, in the United States? What public services, if any, do they perform? Have there been any recent and important changes in their methods of exerting pressure? What seem to be the more salient and significant trends in pressure group activity today?

Many reasons may be given for the emergence and multiplication of pressure groups. The advantages of organization for the attainment of goals is quite obvious. As technology progresses, the population increases in number, and new problems, desires, and needs arise; new organizations are formed to meet the situation, and to further these desires and needs. As new groups appear, however, they may threaten, or appear to endanger others, and groups tend to beget groups. In an environment of ever-increasing specialization, the specialists are continuously facing the prospect of infringements, burdens, costs, and in some cases even extinction. Competition from other groups is one threat, but there is also the fear of adverse government action, or the desire to enlist government aid. Thus government itself has been a powerful, generative factor in the growth of pressure groups.

There are other conditions which have facilitated the "pressure group explosion," such as the rigidity of the constitutional structure of the United States with its doctrine of separation of powers, periodic elections, and difficult processes of amendment; the difficulty of making citizen ideas and wishes known to government without organizational links; and the inability of political parties, at times, to push for specific policies and legislation. Moreover, government has become increasingly important in the daily life of its citizens, making them more and more dependent upon it, not only for safety, but for security and welfare. Government powers, at least the exercise of them, have grown, the costs of government have rocketed upward, problems have become more intricate, technical, and complex, government regulations have mounted, and the average citizen feels an increasing need for specialized groups to represent him, speak for him, and further his needs and goals. As problems of government grow in number and complexity, representative bodies turn more and more to the executive branch, and to unofficial specialists for information and guidance. Because of this, and because of the frequently clashing interests within Congressional bodies, they become less and less able to meet satisfactorily the demands placed on them. With their failures, citizens turn more and more to groups and to the executive office of the President for leadership. The relative weakness of legislative bodies, their divisiveness and lack of leadership and party discipline tend to encourage pressure groups to use individual legislators whenever possible. The intricacies of the legislative process, House and Senate rules, committee systems, all enhance and facilitate the tactics of pressure groups. In other words, pressure groups have emerged and spread in the United States for a great many different reasons: to promote, defend, threaten, inform, educate, destroy, and so on. The array of assisting factors is equally numerous and varied.

Pressure groups have been the objects of much criticism, and the alleged evils will be examined presently. Remember, however, that most of these groups arise because of real needs, and that they usually perform useful services for their members, for other groups, for the government, and for society at large. They inform and educate their members regarding public affairs and matters of special concern to them. They represent their members before government agencies in public hearings and elsewhere. They serve to help bridge the gap between the citizens and their government and vice versa. In many instances they furnish legislators and other public officials with needed and valuable advice. They serve as checks on and critics of the government, and, with political parties, help to bring important social, economic, and political issues to the general public, albeit one-sided and biased in many cases. They are one of the most effective channels through which the individual citizen can bring his wishes and problems to the attention of public authorities. They protect citizens against injustices and alleged encroachments by government, and through them the right of petition is jealously guarded, and frequently made effective. Pressure groups also serve as training schools for political leaders, and even more effectively than political parties at times, they succeed in enforcing political responsibility. Not the least of their services is the fact that they frequently raise the level of self-interest among their members. It is still self-interest, but one that has been leavened by the meetings, conferences, conventions, publications, leaders, and contacts of a large organization, with national rather than parochial concerns.

Many of these pressure groups are interested in many different legislative policies and measures, and they are able to give legislators expert advice and guidance. Often they draft legislative bills and perform tasks which harassed public officials would find no time to perform. It is difficult to see how public officials could perform as well as they do without the researching and assistance these groups supply. To a minor extent, some of the groups assist in law enforcement and public administration. To enumerate these many services and contributions is not to say that all groups do these things, nor does it mean that pressure groups as a whole are exemplary. There are deficiencies, shortcomings—possibly evils—in the functioning of pressure groups in the United States today. Before these drawbacks are considered, some attention may be given to the methods and strategies of pressure groups for gaining their objectives.[12]

METHODS AND STRATEGIES

Pressure groups, in company with all individuals and institutions, have their publics, which usually include at least their own members, prospective and potential members, other groups, the government with all its branches, levels, subdivisions, and agencies, political parties, and community, national, even international publics. With each public the pressure group will use one or more of the four strategies of organization, argument, persuasion, and publicity. By multiplying offices, involving members in the organization, cementing their allegiance, monopolizing their time as completely as possible, the organization strategy is used to bind members together into a close and cohesive unit. Churches, trade unions, military units, and Communist and Fascist parties have been especially adept in this practice. The ties that bind members to these groups are usually very strong and capably fastened.

Nearly all groups use the strategy of argument to appeal to the minds, the intellects, the reasoning capabilities of their audiences. Most of the groups publish annual and special reports, pamphlets, periodicals, books, films, and pictures to argue their cases. Science, the Courts, the Bible, and numerous other authorities are appealed to. The arguments may vary greatly in the cogency of their logic, the weight of the evidence, and in the profundity of their appeal. Some religious and political groups rely heavily on the authority of some bible, divine or secular. More and greater reliance today is placed on empirical evidence, on scientific experiments, on univacs and elaborately programmed computers. Briefs go to law courts, committee hearings, and to opinion leaders. Carefully reasoned reports are prepared as well as pamphlets and articles. Speeches are delivered, press conferences engineered, also fireside chats, press releases, and panel discussions. In the final analysis, the propagation of group ideas is basically the dissemination of evidence and arguments for them; for certain important targets only, it is the cold, logical argument which counts.

But the strategy of argument is also accompanied by the strategy of persuasion, and it is often difficult to separate the two, although the latter is primarily concerned with emotions, motivations, and will. All kinds of techniques may be employed to arouse hate, love, fear, hope, despair, or any other emotion that will transform mere intellectual conviction and acceptance into votes, attendance, purchases, and loans. The prestige of the group's cause may be enhanced by the names of prominent business, religious, or professional leaders. Narrow, selfish, material objectives may be clothed in broadly based, humanitarian terms geared to the public interest. The baser motives may be appealed to, powerful, affirmative symbols will be appropriated, objectives will be dramatized, and every device for giving thought the driving force of will, will be harnessed. It may be stated that group leaders everywhere are quick to appropriate and apply whatever psychological, sociological, or other findings about human nature will serve their purposes. They are perhaps not quite as quick to do this as advertisers and public relations counselors, but neither do they tarry far behind.

Finally, all groups use the strategy of publicity to call attention to their appeals. This device is concerned with the most effective use of communication media, not only of mass media, but of personal contact, small groups, local papers, bill boards, radio and television stations. Today, there are not only general, but very specific specialists in publicity and communication, men and women capable of using and advising on the use of the various kinds of media.

Methods used by pressure groups to exert pressure may be good or bad according to the standards of evaluation. From the viewpoint of the pressure group, the only question is, does the method get results. Does it change opinions and attitudes in the desired direction? Does it win votes, produce sales, promote attendance? From the public's point of view, however, the more important question or questions may be does it enlighten or deceive? Does it help the public to make wise or foolish decisions? Many groups are almost exclusively interested in realizing their own private goals, and often they use whatever tricks, deceptions, falsifications seem to contribute to that end. Group aims are sometimes cleverly presented as in the public interest, or as aims of the whole public. Events are manufactured to attract attention, divert attention, enhance prestige and credibility, falsify trends. Individuals and institutions of prestige, whether educational, medical, research, or scientific, are used to give authority and glamour to the pressure group and its causes. False fronts are used to conceal origins, aims, methods, responsibilities, and everywhere there may exist indirection, subterfuge, chicanery, secrecy—anything but clear, candid, truthful exposition of facts and opinions. As instruments of mass communication have greatly widened the distance between the communicator and the receiver of the communication, and the speed of communication and the size of audiences have greatly increased, the possibilities for evil doing have multiplied. The voice of a single broadcaster may reach hundreds of millions of listeners. These listeners are ill-equipped to judge the accuracy, the motives, the character, the supporters, or the true objectives of the speaker. Real, self-appraisal by the listener is virtually impossible. The rectifying influence of competition is feeble.

The methods employed by pressure groups are the same as they have always been. Changes, such as they are, have come mainly because of new media of communication and improvements in the old which have created large, world-wide publics and almost instantaneous delivery and reception of messages. Publics have become better educated, more articulate, they have broader and higher expectations, and they have a much wider array of ideas and opinions. They live longer, have a higher standard of living, crowd into cities and urban communities, move farther and more often by car, plane, boat, and train, and think and talk of space flights, computers, dancing the twist, forty million dollar movies, and seventeen foot pole vaults. They have bulky, wordy, dull newspapers, sexy, prurient, cheesecake books and magazines, comics and science fiction, to say nothing of pre-breakfast educational TV, midnight movies, daytime news and commercials, and once a week symphonies. Change there has been, but the basic strategies of pressure groups remain—organization, argument, persuasion, publicity.

PRINCIPAL TRENDS

What are the principal trends today in pressure group activity? New groups are forever entering the pressure group arena, such as organizations of the aged, of scientists, and new idea groups. Other groups are dropping out. The balance of power among the groups is constantly shifting. The relative influence of business, farm, and labor groups is ever-changing. Certainly, over the last thirty years, the fortunes of labor and the farmer have risen, but business has maintained a strong position, and the over-all balance today seems more satisfactory than ever. Pressure groups have always tried to win public support as well as to lobby support in Congress and governmental agencies. Where the relative emphasis will be placed depends on the group, its objectives and resources, as well as surrounding circumstances. The American Red Cross or the American Cancer Society will of necessity focus their pressure on public opinion, whereas those primarily concerned with legislation or public administrative action will turn to government. There is an increasing emphasis on public opinion, both as an end in itself and as a means for bringing pressure on public officials.

The increase in number, tempo, and intensity of pressure group activity seems to have leveled off, following the explosive decades immediately preceding World War II. There is some evidence of an increase in the number of ad hoc groups to deal with special issues and problems. Government agencies, as well as state and local governments are becoming increasingly active as pressure groups. Teachers and public officials, for example, are taking their own interests into their own hands more and more.

Pressure groups have always sought alliances with other groups, and this practice continues. The 1936 split between the AF of L and the CIO was partially healed by the reunion in 1955, but tensions continue, and several large and important unions remain independent of this super AFL-CIO organization, notably the Teamsters, United Mine Workers, Railroad Brotherhoods, and various organizations of federal employees, telephone, electrical, mine, and laundry workers, longshoremen and lithographers. Most groups profess to be non-partisan, but this does not mean that they are non-political. Labor, and to some extent farm groups, screen candidates for public office very carefully, try to enlist member support for friends, and to defeat enemies of the group. Business groups, too, are generally neutral and non-partisan, but, in spite of exhortations from leaders, are even less susceptible to political or candidate guidance than labor or agriculture. Studies of the Presidential election of 1960 indicate the importance of the religious factor and the greater degree of political preference among Catholics and Jews than among Protestants. This agreement, however, while greater among the two minority religious groups, has never come close to unanimity, even in 1960.

Trends in pressure group methods show many refinements, but few basic changes, except that most groups try to take full advantage of improvements in the communication media, especially television. In so far as finances permit, all groups continue to use the press, radio, television, all kinds of publications, telephone, telegraph, the mails, speeches, pictures, conventions, personal contacts, stickers, billboards, and other communication agencies to persuade, convince, organize, and publicize. Media, organization, fund raising, and pictorial specialists of all kinds abound, and this fact emphasizes more and more the need for propaganda and promotion teamwork. As pressure group campaign budgets increase, larger sums are spent, not only for media and functional specialists, but for top-flight engineers in over-all public relations management.

Brief mention will be made of several other trends that persist and grow. The advent of public opinion polls seems to make mass opinion a more effective check on the tendency of some groups to exaggerate their numerical size and representative character. By highlighting the wishes of the general public, the polls make it a little more difficult for special interests to confuse public and private interests. The trend toward official recognition and institutionalizing of pressure groups probably reached its peak in the United States during the nineteen-twenties and early thirties. The Department of Commerce of the United States greatly expanded the idea of trade conferences and the use of representative economic councils. Other government agencies also used the economic advisory council to transmit policies as well as to collect opinions and views. This trend, as previously indicated, reached a climax with the passage of the National Industrial Recovery Act with its comprehensive plan for giving pressure groups not only official recognition but duties and responsibilities as well. Declared unconstitutional by the United States Supreme Court, this experiment failed, and there is no prospect at the moment that it will be revived. Advisory councils continue to be widely used; government officials frequently recognize the existence of pressure groups in hearings, conferences, and publications, but no attempt is being made to re-institute the idea of a corporative state in even a very mild form.

Students of pressure group politics have frequently called attention to the advantages pressure groups have over government in the competition for public support and power.[13] In some cases they have a more ready access to media of communication, better paid personnel, greater continuity of purpose, staying power, secrecy, and invisibility. Moreover, private pressure groups are much freer from public accountability than government agencies, can choose the specific targets for their pressure, of which there are many, and in the case of some business groups, they have controls over technology and applied science, which the government does not have. The advantages are by no means all on the side of the private group, however, for the groups are usually competing with each other, thereby nullifying to a considerable extent their advantages vis-a-vis the government. If the government is divided in its councils, private groups are even more so, and when the government does speak, it speaks with overwhelming, physical and legal force. Moreover, the government speaks on a higher level of public interest than any group can.

Of course, the government of the United States never has, and probably never will become a monolithic, neutral, bureaucratic group, above and outside the pressure group arena. It is both a part of the arena, and in some respects the arena itself. Within its branches, departments, and agencies the pressure group struggle goes on quite as vigorously as it does outside in the market place and before the bar of public opinion—in the Office of the President, governor, and mayor, in the halls of Congress, and in most of the departments, agencies, and committees. When pressures are overwhelming in one direction, government action may be speedy. If closely divided there may be long delays and possibly no action. The case of civil rights is illustrative. The walls of injustice are falling, but only as the preponderance of pressures cause them to fall. In a very real sense the government of the day, in the United States or elsewhere, is a government representing a particular complex of interests, that is, a complex, complex of interests, for the distribution of interests among groups is far from being systematic, clear, or even non-contradictory. The government can never be extricated from this maze of pressures, it can only rely on law and established procedures to resolve the conflicts.

Are pressure groups more powerful than the government, or becoming so? This is probably an absurd question or at least a misguided way of putting the question. The real question always is what groups, what pressure group complexes, are for the time being dominant? How shall one describe the balance of power at the moment? Here we discover both the reality and the complexity of the pressure group problem. There is actually no one balance but hundreds of balances on all kinds of bills, laws, decrees, actions. The United States is ruled, not by a majority, but my majorities. There is never merely one balance, but a maze of balances. We may try to simplify the explanation by citing election statistics, and party strength in Congress and in the state legislatures of the country, or we may list bills enacted into law and those defeated. None of these indices, however, will remove the darkness that shadows the intricate, confusing, crisscrossing pattern of the balances of group pressures.

CRITICISM

Notwithstanding the many services performed by pressure groups they have been severely criticized. In the first place it is often charged that such groups put self-interest above the public interest. As one writer stated: ". . . not only individuals but powerful groups have been operating on what might be called the Me First Principle. Their eyes have not been seeing America as a whole. When they have had to choose between behaving like Americans or behaving like, say, coal miners or steel men, they have behaved like coal miners or steel men." [14] Such critics are not silenced by the reply that the sum total of group selfishnesses is really the public interest.

A second criticism which is expressed often is that pressure groups use reprehensible methods. They lie, deceive, bribe, create false fronts, employ sophisticated, psychological tricks, inflate their size, degree of agreement, and motives. They flood the offices of legislators and administrators with fake, or phony telegrams; they strive to engender fear, suspicion, and hate; and they may even resort to violence.

A third charge is made that many groups are not democratically organized. The rank and file of members are said to have little to do with the selection of officials and leaders, and even less perhaps with the making of group policies. Too many groups, so the argument goes, are dominated by some cliques who have little if any concern for the desires and interests of the membership as a whole. Conventions are often rigged, so it is claimed, and few if any opportunities are given for all members to participate and express their opinions. Closely related to this contention is a fourth allegation, that pressure groups frequently claim to speak for and to represent more people than they actually do. Membership lists may be padded, and officials may indulge in all kinds of unauthorized statements and claims.

Other indictments of pressure groups assert that they promote factionalism and disunity in the community and throughout the nation and that their pressure on public officials, including threats as well as enticements and blandishments, make it difficult for public officials to do their jobs honestly and effectively and thereby tend to weaken governmental authority and responsibility. Also, charges are made that instead of informing and enlightening public opinion, these groups only confuse, befuddle, and exploit it, thus making it more difficult for government to function in orderly, effective, and democratic ways.

In many cases pressure groups are criticized, indirectly and covertly, if not directly and openly, for the policies and views they advocate, in spite of the constitutional guarantees of free press, speech, and opinion. For such critics there are good and bad pressure groups, the latter being those whose aims and programs are distasteful. People are certain to differ about what is good and bad. This is the basic premise of democracy. It is the function of pressure groups to present different values and preferences that the voters and legislators may decide.

If one examines carefully the several particulars of the indictment of pressure groups, there emerges a rather general, fundamental, if unexpressed criticism, which is that some groups exert more influence than they should. In reality, this is the basic issue. Do some groups because of their size, distribution of membership, financial resources, leadership, cohesion, and methods exert more influence than they should? Does the NAM, the AFL-CIO, the AMA, the American Legion, or the NAACP exercise more influence than it should? But what influence *should* a group exert, and what influence *does* it exercise? Because of, or possibly in disregard of, the difficulties of measuring pressure group influence and deciding on a formula for determining what influence a group should have, democracy simply allows groups to compete for influence under certain conditions. The theory is that by so doing groups will simply have the influence they are entitled to, *provided,* and this is most important, *provided* they compete in an arena where certain rules of the game are enforced. Through law and the establishment of regulatory commissions, notably the Federal Trade Commission (FTC), Securities Exchange Commission (SEC), and Federal Communications Commission (FCC), certain "rules of the game," certain conditions of pressure group competition, have been prescribed. The purpose of these rules is to assure that the success of pressure groups will depend, not merely on the size of membership, the amount of money they have to spend, or even the naked, political force at their disposal, but rather on the excellence of their programs and the real merits of the arguments and evidence used to support them. Many will claim, however, that these rules and their enforcement are far from adequate. Nevertheless, the democratic method is generally preferred to the authoritarian procedure of deliberately assigning to each group the measure of influence it should have and holding or trying to hold it to that influence.

PROPOSALS AND REMEDIES

Regulation

Various remedies and solutions have been proposed to deal with the pressure group problem. The most prevalent, perhaps, has been regulation. Laws regarding bribery, libel, slander, and the illegal use of the mails have existed for a long time.[15] The states began passing lobbying laws toward the end of the nineteenth century, requiring lobbyists to register and file expenses. State laws differ in details: California declared lobbying a felony; Colorado regulates specifically the right of access to the floor of the legislature; Connecticut forbids improper entertainment of legislators; Mississippi outlaws logrolling; and many states regulate or forbid contingent fees. Alabama was apparently the first to outlaw corrupt solicitation in 1874. Massachusetts was the first to go into the matter thoroughly in 1890, and soon thereafter Wisconsin went beyond reliance on measures to insure adequate publicity to lobbying practices to define permissible activities.

The disclosures of the New York insurance investigation in 1905 did much to speed the passage of state legislation.

Congress did not regulate lobbying until 1946, when regulatory provisions were included in the Congressional Reorganization Act. The provisions applied to "any person who solicits, collects, or receives money to be used principally to influence Federal legislation." Lobbyists were required to register with the Clerk of the House and Secretary of the Senate, and file financial statements and other information regarding their employers and the lobbying work they did. Penalties were provided for violations of the provisions. The federal legislation and also the state lobbying laws have been severely criticized for many reasons: their vagueness and lack of a clear definition of who should register as a lobbyist; the unsatisfactory nature of the information forms to be filled out; and above all the lack of a proper agency to summarize and publicize the information, and to enforce properly the regulatory provisions. The ineffectiveness of state and federal lobbying regulations to date have led a number of students of the problem, especially academic scholars, to recommend more emphasis on pitiless publicity of lobbying activities rather than regulation and penalties. Legislators and public officials, however, seem to feel that regulatory laws are necessary, but that they should be improved by closing loopholes and curbing abuses. A California Joint Interim Committee, for example, after conducting a general investigation of lobbying activities recommended that:[16]

(1) Lobbying legislation should be confined to professional lobbyists, that is, to representatives who work for compensation.

(2) Responsible legislative representatives should not be hampered or discredited.

(3) Professional advocates should be required to register, disclose employer, nature of his activities, the qualifications of the person to be a professional lobbyist, his experience, education, etc., and financial arrangements with his employer.

(4) An enforcement agency is needed, with power to investigate and to set up specific standards of conduct. It might be a joint legislative board.

(5) The lobbyist would be required to make monthly reports regarding his legislative activities only. Excessive expenditures would be investigated.

Strengthening Governmental Institutions

A second approach to the pressure group problem comprises measures to strengthen our governmental institutions. The evils of pressure group activity arise, so it is claimed, because of the weaknesses and short-comings of our governmental system. Legislative lobbying, so it is said, would have few pernicious effects if all legislators were strong, courageous statesmen of the highest ability and character; if legislative procedures were efficient, open, and gave all groups a fair opportunity to present their views; and if legislatures were capably organized and equipped to do a responsible job. The influence which groups exert on public policy depends, not only on the pressure the groups themselves can and do exert, but also on the countervailing ability of public officials to ward off undue pressure in seeking to conserve the public interest.

No attempt will be made to review all the types of suggestions made to improve the functioning, not only of the legislative branch, but also of the administrative and judicial branches. In 1946 and the years following, Congress underwent an extensive reorganization to promote efficiency and greater effectiveness, and further improvements have been made from time to time in parliamentary procedures, committee organization, hearings, and bill drafting.[17] The administrative branch has also been subjected to much pruning and trimming. Salaries have been increased; recruiting and promotion policies strengthened; the merit system extended—in short, there seems to be an upgrading of personnel policies, which should mean that government jobs would attract high caliber men and women. Not unrelated to this task of strengthening government and its personnel against the aggressive and sometimes rapacious designs of self-seeking groups are efforts to improve electoral procedures, raise the quality of legislative and administrative leadership, and to solve knotty problems like seniority, filibustering, conflicts of interest, ethical standards of civil service employees, and party discipline. Competent, efficient, streamlined legislative and administrative bodies can be a formidable bulwark against undue group pressures. However, it is not sufficient merely to block undesirable pressures. It is quite as imperative to encourage the use of the many services which pressure groups can legitimately perform.

Will the strengthening of political parties also help to curb pressure group excesses? It is quite likely that strong and disciplined parties are less likely than weak parties to be preyed upon by pressure groups. They are, in a sense, pressure groups themselves, with at least one very important difference—the responsibility for nominating candidates for public office. It should be remembered that there are minor as well as major parties and that minor parties, regardless of the firmness of their organization and the strength of their leaders, may be unable to withstand group pressures. Strong major parties may be able to use pressure group services without being dominated by them, unless their strong leadership echelons are not well grounded in the rank and file of membership. Otherwise, they may succumb to group pressures, or be swallowed up by them entirely. In their relations with political parties, pressure groups may try to play one against the other, bore from within, try to capture one or the other, form their own parties, or simply remain neutral.[18] The strength of the political party in itself is no guarantee, however, that parties can remain immune from the influence of groups.

Institutionalization of Relations

In addition to the regulatory and strengthening-of-government approaches to the pressure group problem, there is the institutional approach. This approach stresses the positive rather than the negative, and utilizes groups rather than just restraining them. It assumes that groups are here to stay, that in spite of some abuses they perform many useful functions, hence, an effort is made to tie them into government. One method was occupational representation, whereby occupational groups rather than geographical areas were made the basis for representation in legislative bodies. Following the First World War several European states experimented with various types of economic councils designed to represent the principal groupings of the country according to a formula that would give each group its proper weight in the councils of the nation. These councils were designed to supplement, and in a few cases to supplant even, the traditional legislative assemblies. The German National Economic Council was the most outstanding example of such a body.[19] Proposals for minority and proportional representation constitute attempts to institutionalize pressure groups, since they too seek to give groups their proper share in government.

Institutionalization of pressure groups reached its fullest expression in the Fascist Corporative State and to a certain degree in Germany under National Socialism. In Italy, under Mussolini, all interests, non-economic as well as economic, were separately represented in an hierarchy of associations, federations, and confederations culminating in a corporative parliament taking the place of the geographically based assembly. In Germany, the Nazis also attempted to give formal recognition to group interests through estates, but the plan was not fully completed.

In the United States the National Industrial Recovery Act (NIRA) of the early New Deal days was a major attempt to institutionalize pressure group relationships with the government. Groups had always, to some extent, been represented at Congressional hearings, or investigative boards and commissions, and in government advisory councils. But the NIRA undertook to incorporate economic groups more completely into the governmental process, and to give them certain administrative and even legislative responsibilities. By attempting to legalize and formalize government–pressure group relations, it was hoped that the concept of self-government in industry would be vitalized. Although the Blue Eagle experiment suffered an early constitutional death, it did stimulate the formation of pressure groups, called attention to their potentialities as servants of the state, and underlined some of the problems of the institutional approach. Some believe that the sudden dropping of the whole idea was far from being a judicious, discriminating action. It may well be that there are more uses for the institutional approach than the detractors of the New Deal perceived.

Highlighting the Public Interest

There remain for consideration three more approaches to the problem of pressure groups which may be explained briefly. The first endeavors to counter pressure group emphasis on self-interest by highlighting the public interest. It tries to improve methods of identifying and informing the public regarding what the public interest is. It encourages the creation of expert boards and commissions to survey social, economic, and political trends, to look into the future and plan alternative courses of action, to anticipate problems, to find remedies. In other words, it seeks to mobilize intelligence and wisdom that they may survey the human terrain, as well as the non-human, so that the highest conception possible of what the public interest is, can be found. An effort is also made to encourage the creation of organizations for important interests which are not adequately represented in the pressure group arena. It is hoped that by so doing the resultant of group pressures will be policies and programs on an even higher level of the public interest. The public opinion polls by showing the opinions and desires of the masses may also help expose to public view, interests, which, if not the true public interest in all cases, are more nearly so than narrowly-based, group interests.

Equalization of Group Resources

Some students of the pressure group situation believe that much that is objectionable would disappear if only pressure group resources, especially financial resources, were more equitably distributed. At this point the pressure group problem is seen to be inextricably involved with the gigantic problem of the distribution of wealth. In a very real sense, the pressure group struggle is a war to win subsidies, tariffs, tax reductions, pensions, depreciation allowances, social security payments, and numerous other kinds of financial emoluments and advantages. Although most students of the problem would probably agree that financial and material resources should be distributed more equitably among pressure groups, vigorous, even violent differences of opinion exist as to what is equitable. The haves advocate what is, and the have-nots what is not, and in between are those with all kinds of formulas and standards for making things equitable. Should the material resources of a group be commensurate with its numerical size, with its intelligence, brains, culture, with its ideals? These are questions difficult, if not impossible, to answer. Thus, democracy, despairing on agreement as to what formula or standard to apply, relies on competition to find the answer—a competition which uses "rules of the game" to help insure that merit, rather than money alone, will give the answer.

Five approaches to the pressure group problem have been explained: regulation, strengthening the government, institutionalizing group-government relations, highlighting the public interest, and equalizing group resources. There are those who argue, however, that none of these are adequate. They insist that the roots of the problem penetrate much deeper than these proposed solutions suggest, and they propose sweeping social and economic reforms along socialistic or communistic lines. They claim that the main evils of the pressure group system derive from the capitalistic, free enterprise, profit system. Only when the state itself is the primary producer and distributor of wealth, only when people serve the state and do not strive for profits, and only when pressure groups, instead of bringing pressure on public officials and public opinion, serve as agencies for helping the state to carry out its aims and purposes, only then will the pressure group problem be solved. This is not the place to explore the role of pressure groups under Communist or Fascistic regimes. A strong, totalitarian regime can utilize, can destroy, or can grant whatever degrees of freedom it wishes to pressure groups. A democratic regime is committed to the greatest degree of freedom under law, that is under established conditions or "rules of the game." These rules will be framed to insure that pressure group competition will be competition, not to see who can spend the most, who can deceive, trick, and befuddle the most, or who has the greatest physical strength measured by membership. The aim of the rules will be the removal of the influence, of such extraneous factors and the prescription of standards that will make the struggle a competition for excellence, enlightenment, intellectual merit, and victory for the best rather than the worst interests.

There is probably no single or best approach to the solution of the pressure group problem, or problems. Without abandoning the democratic goal of freedom, regulatory rules can be improved and strengthened, more consideration can be given to institutionalizing groups, to giving them a more useful place in the governmental process, and greater efforts can be given to place the public interest over against the various private interests through top level research and planning programs, and by dramatically highlighting these findings. It will also be very important to strengthen government in all its branches, but not that a stronger and more efficient government may destroy, or even curb pressure group freedom, except insofar as that freedom is abused. Perhaps what is really needed is not just a stronger, more stubborn, less sensitive government, but a government of men with moral character and the wisdom to parry, foil, or utilize group pressures in the public interest.

Undoubtedly, extremes of wealth and material resources tend to undermine the democratic objectives of balanced pressure group competition. Government action will be necessary to bring about and maintain some degree of balance, of equitable distribution of material resources among pressure groups. A sound system of taxation and public finance is essential, though agreement on what is sound is difficult, if not impossible. The balance can never be perfect, but the government can try to see that no significant group lacks the resources to make its needs, desires, and hopes known and that no significant group is barred from the pressure group arena. Furthermore, it can reduce extremes of wealth and material resources, especially when they are used to defeat the public purposes of the pressure group competition. When material pressure group resources are used to crush opposition rather than convince it, to purchase acceptance rather than win it with argument and persuasion, the whole structure of democratic government is threatened.

NOTES FOR CHAPTER 10

Epigraph. Arthur F. Bentley, *The Process of Government* (1908), p. 223.

1. The literature on pressure groups is copious, comprising publications of the groups themselves, reports of Congressional hearings, studies of particular groups, comparative surveys and analyses, studies of group pressures on selected policies, processes, or institutions. Weekly issues of the Congressional Quarterly, summarized annually in the Congressional Almanac, are very valuable sources for current information regarding group activities in the United States. A few of the recent studies are: Ziegler, Harmon, *Interest Groups in American Society* (New York: Prentice-Hall, 1964); Milbrath, Lester, *The Washington Lobbyists* (Chicago: Rand McNally, 1963); Wilson, H. H., *Pressure Group: The Campaign for Commercial TV in England* (New Brunswick, N. J.: Rutgers University Press, 1961); Potter, Allen, *Organized Groups in British National Politics* (London: Faber & Faber, 1961); Eckstein, Harry, *Pressure Group Politics: The Case of the British Medical Association* (Stanford, Calif.: Stanford University Press, 1960).

2. See Ehrmann, Henry W. (ed.), *Interest Groups on Four Continents* (Pittsburgh: University of Pittsburgh Press, 1958); Sklar, R. L., *Nigerian Political Parties: Power in an Emergent African Nation* (Princeton, N. J.: Princeton University Press, 1963).

3. See Tompkins, D. C., *Congressional Investigation of Lobbying* (Berkeley: University of California Bureau of Public Administration, 1956).

4. See Kile, O. M., *The Farm Bureau Federation Through Three Decades* (Baltimore, Md.: The Waverly Press, 1948).

5. V. O. Key, Jr., *Politics, Parties, and Pressure Groups* (4th ed., New York: Thomas Y. Crowell Co., 1960) provides an excellent survey of the leading pressure groups in the United States and their activities.

6. U. S. Federal Trade Commission, *Efforts by Associations and Agencies of*

Electrical and Gas Utilities to Influence Public Opinion, Senate Document 92, Part 71 A, 70th Cong., 1st Sess., 1934.
7. See Lyon, L. S. *et al., The National Recovery Administration: An Analysis and Appraisal* (Washington, D. C.: The Brookings Institution, 1935).
8. See Zeller, Belle, "The Federal Regulation of Lobbying Act," *American Political Science Review,* Vol. 42 (April, 1948), pp. 239-71.
9. Offices of the *Congressional Quarterly* are located at 1156 Nineteenth Street, N. W., Washington, D. C.
10. *Congressional Quarterly Almanac,* Vol. 18 (1962), p. 934.
11. McCamy, James L., *American Government* (New York: Harper & Brothers, 1957), p. 488.
12. See Herring, E. P., *Group Representation Before Congress* (Baltimore: Johns Hopkins University Press, 1929); Childs, Harwood L., *Labor and Capital in National Politics* (Columbus: The Ohio State University Press, 1930); Truman, David, *The Governmental Process* (New York: Alfred A. Knopf, 1951).
13. Blaisdell, Donald C., *American Democracy Under Pressure* (New York: The Ronald Press, 1957).
14. Chase, Stuart, *Democracy Under Pressure* (New York: The Twentieth Century Fund, 1945), pp. 4 and 43.
15. Logan, E. B., "Lobbying," Supplement to Vol. 144 of the *Annals* of the American Academy of Political and Social Science (July, 1929).
16. California Legislative Assembly, Interim Committee on Governmental Efficency and Economy, *Federal and State Laws on Lobbying* (Sacramento, 1950).
17. See Burns, James, *Congress on Trial* (New York: Harper & Row, 1949); Young, Roland, *The American Congress* (New York: Harper & Row, 1958); Galloway, George B., *History of the House of Representatives* (New York: Thomas Y. Crowell Co., 1961); Wahlke, J. C., Eulau, Heinz, Buchanan, William, and Leroy Ferguson, *The Legislative System* (New York: John Wiley and Sons, 1962).
18. See Calkins, Fay, *The C.I.O. and the Democratic Party* (Chicago: University of Chicago Press, 1952).
19. Lindner, E., *Review of the Economic Councils in the Different Countries of the World* (Geneva: League of Nations, Economic Relations Section, II B9, 1932).

SUPPLEMENTARY READING

BENTLEY, ARTHUR F. *The Process of Government.* Chicago: University of Chicago Press, 1908.
BLAISDELL, DONALD C. *American Democracy Under Pressure.* New York: The Ronald Press Company, 1957.
BLAW, PETER M., and SCOTT, W. RICHARD. *Formal Organizations.* San Francisco: Chandler Publishing Company, 1962.
CHASE, STUART. *Democracy Under Pressure.* New York: The Twentieth Century Fund, 1945.
CHILDS, HARWOOD L. *Labor and Capital in National Politics.* Columbus, Ohio: Ohio State University Press, 1930.
CHILDS, HARWOOD L. (ed.). "Pressure Groups and Propaganda," *Annals* of American Academy of Political and Social Science (May, 1935).

CHILDS, HARWOOD L. "Pressure Groups and Propaganda," *The American Political Scene.* Edited by E. B. Logan. Harper & Bros., 1936.

Congressional Quarterly Almanac.

Congressional Quarterly Weekly Report.

ECKSTEIN, HARRY. *Pressure Group Politics: The Case of the British Medical Association.* Stanford, Calif.: Stanford University Press, 1960.

EHRMANN, HENRY W. (ed.). *Interest Groups on Four Continents.* Pittsburgh: University of Pittsburgh Press, 1958.

GARCEAU, OLIVER. *The Political Life of The American Medical Association.* Cambridge Mass.: Harvard University Press, 1941.

GRUENING, ERNEST. *The Public Pays: A Study of Power Propaganda.* New York: The Vanguard Press, 1931.

HERRING, E. P. *Group Representation Before Congress.* Baltimore, Md.: Johns Hopkins University Press, 1929.

LATHAM, EARL. *The Group Basis of Politics.* Ithaca, N. Y.: Cornell University Press, 1952.

LOGAN, E. B. "Lobbying," Supplement to Vol. 144 of *The Annals* of the American Academy of Political and Social Science. (July, 1929).

ODEGARD, PETER H. *Pressure Politics: The Story of the Anti-Saloon League.* New York: Columbia University Press, 1928.

POTTER, ALLEN M. *Organized Groups in British National Politics.* London: Faber & Faber, 1961.

RUTHERFORD, M. LOUISE. *The Influence of the American Bar Association on Public Opinion and Legislation.* Philadelphia, Pa.: The Foundation Press, 1937.

ST. JAMES, WARREN D. *The NAACP.* New York: Exposition Press, 1958.

SCHATTSCHNEIDER, E. E. *Politics, Pressure, and the Tariff.* Englewood Cliffs, N. J.: Prentice Hall, Inc., 1935.

STEWART, J. D. *British Pressure Groups: Their Role in Relation to the House of Commons.* New York: Clarendon Press, 1958.

Texas Legislative Council. *Lobby Regulation.* Austin, Texas: The Council, 1956.

THOMPKINS, DOROTHY LOUISE CULVER. *Congressional Investigation of Lobbying: Selected Bibliography.* Berkeley, Calif.: Bureau of Public Administration, University of California, 1956.

TRUMAN, DAVID B. *The Governmental Process: Political Interests and Public Opinion.* New York: Alfred A. Knopf, 1951.

U. S. Congress, House, Select Committee on Lobby Investigation. *Hearings,* 63rd Congress, 1st Sess., 4 vols. 1913.

U. S. Congress, Senate, Committee on Judiciary. *Hearing on Maintenance of a Lobby to Influence Legislation.* 63rd Congress, 1st Sess., 1913.

U. S. Congress, House, Select Committee on Lobbying Activities. House Resolution 298—*Buchanan Committee Hearings,* 81st Congress, 2nd Sess., 1950.

U. S. Federal Trade Commission, *Efforts by Associations and Agencies of Electric and Gas Utilities to Influence Public Opinion.* 70th Congress, 1st Sess., Senate Document 92, Part 71 A, 1934.

WAHLKE, JOHN C., EULAU, HEINZ, BUCHANAN, WILLIAM, and FERGUSON, LEROY C. *The Legislative System.* New York: John Wiley & Sons, 1962.

WILSON, HARPER HUBERT. *Pressure Groups: The Campaign for Commercial Television in England.* New Brunswick, N. J.: Rutgers University Press, 1961.

ZEIGLER, HARMON. *Interest Groups in American Society*. Englewood Cliffs, N. J.: Prentice-Hall, Inc., 1964.
ZELLER, BELLE. *Pressure Politics in New York*. New York: Prentice-Hall, Inc., 1937.
ZELLER, BELLE. "The Federal Regulation of Lobbying Act," *American Political Science Review*, Vol. 42 (April, 1948), pp. 259-71.

XI · Advertising and Public Relations

You can tell the ideals of a nation by its advertisements.
—NORMAN DOUGLAS

THE DELIBERATE effort to influence public opinion takes many forms—propaganda, preaching, teaching, salesmanship, press agentry, advertising. Advertising is closely associated with the selling of goods and services and refers to notices and announcements used to that end. It, too, has many forms and styles such as classified ads, department store advertising, legal notices, television commercials, exhibits, good will and institutional ads. It is well to keep these different types in mind since their relations to and impacts on public opinion differ.[1]

In its broadest sense advertising is as old as communication itself; it is much older in fact than newspapers, criers of the Middle Ages, or the public notices of classical times. But it is advertising, especially in the United States today, which is of primary interest in this chapter. The annual advertising bill in the United States today is well over twelve billion dollars, and a large proportion of these outlays are used to try and sell drugstore merchandise, such as drugs, toiletries, soap, tobacco, as well as automobiles, and some foods.[2] Practically every large business firm has its advertising department, which may or may not employ an advertising agency to place its ads in appropriate media. Procter and Gamble was the largest spender in 1962 with an advertising budget over twelve million, followed by American Home Products, Bristol-Myers, General Motors, R. J. Reynolds, and Lever Brothers, each with advertising expenditures during the year over five million.[3] There are hundreds of advertising agencies in the United States, several of whom have many large clients and do millions of dollars of business each year. Advertisers and advertis-

262 PUBLIC OPINION: NATURE, FORMATION, AND ROLE

ing agencies have their professional and trade associations, notably the American Association of Advertising Agencies (AAAA), the Association of National Advertisers (ANA), and the Advertising Federation of America (AFA).

The rapid growth of industry after the Civil War forced manufacturers to find larger markets, and this led to national advertising on a large scale. During the last two decades of the nineteenth century nation-wide magazines, slogans and brand names multiplied, and by the 1920's advertising had reached a stage of stable economic maturity with clubs, conferences, trade journals, and the other earmarks of an established profession. Crusades were launched to win the confidence of business and the public, businessmen to some extent relied upon advertising as a substitute for competition, and many new unfamiliar products were advertised. Many advertisers considered themselves pioneers and economic reformers, creating new wants, stimulating consumption, promoting good will for business, and introducing new methods of persuasion.[4]

The competition of advertisers for the consumer's dollar has often led to advertising excesses and abuses. Patent medicine advertising during the latter part of the nineteenth century was notorious for its false claims, distortions, and naked lies. After a bitter war, reformers finally secured the passage of the Food and Drug Act by Congress in 1906, a truth-in-labeling statute of limited application, and the Federal Trade Commission (FTC) Act of 1914.[5] The threat of more regulatory legislation, perhaps, more than these acts themselves, brought some improvement. But these acts were not self-enforcing, and without adequate funds and staff, widespread abuses continued. Although the Federal Trade Commission is primarily responsible for regulation at the national level, other agencies, notably the Federal Communications Commission, the Post Office Department, the Federal Alcohol Tax Unit of the Treasury Department, the Securities and Exchange Commission, and the Food and Drug Administration, share this responsibility to some extent. In 1911, *Printer's Ink* started a movement for a model state statute prohibiting false advertising. Most of the states now have laws against false advertising, although enforcement of them has not been altogether effective.

Prior to 1938, and the passage of the Wheeler-Lea amendment to the FTC Act of 1914, the power of the Commission to regulate advertising was limited to unfair trade practices, not to advertising merely unfair or injurious to the consumer. The Wheeler-Lea Act, however, enabled the Commission to protect the consumer as well as the competitor and extended its powers to regulate false advertising of food, drugs, cosmetics, and medical devices. Its regulatory activities are preventive, rather than punitive. It investigates, issues complaints, conducts hearings, and issues cease-and-desist orders which may be appealed to the courts. The Commission sponsors many trade practice conferences to establish rules of conduct for the industry, including acceptable advertising procedures. Over 160 industries have established such rules.

For several years the FTC has been reporting periodically on its advertising activities in its publication *Advertising Alert*. The issue for April 24, 1963, for example, summarized actions taken regarding "spurious television demonstrations" of shaving cream, misrepresenting correspondence courses, misrepresenting savings available to purchasers of "railroad furniture salvage," deceptive means to sell real estate, and "misleading and coercive tactics to sell dance instruction courses." During 1962, the Commission acted to prevent false advertising of vitamins, sleeping bags, drugs, leather products, bathroom scales, textiles, freezers, toys, paints, furniture, watches, wrapping paper, TV sets, sporting goods, chemicals, electric appliances, and scores of other products. The Commission, also, requests all commercial radio and television broadcasting stations to submit scripts of their commercials: the networks for one week each month, individual radio and TV stations less frequently. A staff of four monitors reads about 50,000 scripts a month, some of them several pages long. The monitors segregate suspicious items and route them to attorneys for further examination and action, if called for. Printed advertising is also monitored systematically. A cross section sampling of newspapers is examined daily, and a somewhat similar approach is followed in the case of magazines.[6]

Many leaders in advertising and industry are fully aware of excesses and abuses, but they advocate self-regulation by industry in preference to government regulation. Newspaper and magazine publishers, and later radio and television proprietors, in some cases tried to check, if not eliminate, false advertising in their own media. Locally, and eventually on the national level, better business bureaus attacked the problem. Pressures from influential writers, governmental officials, and academic students had an effect. Stuart Chase's *Other People's Money* was one of a number of influential books, that highlighted the nature and scope of the problem. Also, consumer organizations were established to test products and inform their members of the comparative merits and shortcomings of products and merchandise. Bureaus were established to audit the circulation claims of papers and magazines, and rating services undertook to measure the appeals of radio and TV programs. Anyone who compares the advertisements of today—in newspaper or magazine, television or radio, in subway car or on billboard—with those of fifty or sixty years ago, will realize that much progress has been made in truthfulness, attractiveness, and style. Still the urge to overstate, to put the best foot forward—in short, to sell—is omnipresent, and abuses persist.[7]

THE EFFECTS OF ADVERTISING

What is, or what are the effects of advertising on public opinion? Generalizations are difficult and very hazardous. There are many different kinds of advertisements and various publics. Numerous studies have been made of the pull, appeal, or persuasiveness of particular ads and of individual campaigns, but there is very little empirical evidence to support broad generalizations on the merits of advertising as a whole. Nevertheless, a few statements may be made, more as tentative suppositions and hypotheses than definitive, proven conclusions.

Thought and Behavior

First, it seems clear that advertisements have various effects on the thinking of people: some good, some bad, some contradictory, others promoting harmonious behavior. Advertisements inform and misinform, enlighten and confuse, induce and obstruct purchases, please and annoy, elevate and debase, and even cause candidates to win or lose. In fact, advertisements may be a determinant for almost any type of behavior, and a given ad may, under certain circumstances, produce quite different effects, depending on who sees or reads it.

Consumer Habits

Secondly, advertisements have certainly had a profound influence on the buying habits of the American people. They help manufacturers and distributors introduce new products. They help to increase the sale of particular products, thereby often decreasing the unit costs of those products. They may even increase the demand for products as a whole, improve the quality and range of merchandise available, and play a part in increasing the real national income. What effect do ads have on distribution costs, concentration of supply, price competition, and fluctuations of the business cycle? Generalizations are hazardous.[8]

Since advertisers have spent so much to promote sales of drugs, cosmetics, tobacco, automobiles, and soap, it is reasonable to assume that these expenditures have had much to do with the sales of these items. Critics of advertising claim that the large sums spent to extol the virtues of one soap over another, one car over another, or one kind of cigarette over another are largely wasted from the social point of view. This is doubtless true in part because the differences between some soaps, some cars, and some cigarettes are largely psychological, at best. But for most competing products there are differences, often significant differences, which need to be explained, and can be by advertisement, if intelligent choices are to be made. In the purely economic sense competition is often wasteful, unless the excessive costs are counter-balanced by the gains in market stimulation, enterprise, and the creative improvements which come when markets are not assured.[9]

Has advertising tended to channel purchases from the more socially useful, to the less socially desirable? Has it encouraged people to buy cigarettes and liquor instead of good food and education, frills and fads instead of lasting goods and services? Although governments and other institutions place controls and limitations on individual spending through tax and social security laws and the individual himself may restrict his day to day spending by mortgages, installment buying, and other types of loans, the average person in the United States still exercises considerable freedom in the way he spends his income. He can buy peanuts or popcorn, yachts or country estates, depending on his income. Each individual is presumed to know his own best interests. That he doesn't always do this is suspected by many, but his freedom is revered, even though it may be exercised unwisely. Numerous curbs have been placed on the advertising of particular products—liquor, drugs, medical devices and contraceptives, lotteries—in the public interest, both by government and the industry. It may be expected, however, that further pressures within and without industry will direct advertising toward the socially useful rather than the harmful products. Researches into the relation between smoking and cancer have raised again the spectre of private versus public interest.[10] One of the largest advertising agencies dropped the *Reader's Digest* account because of a conflict of interest with a much more lucrative tobacco account.[11] Another agency, however, felt compelled to drop tobacco accounts as a consequence of its researches. In November, 1962, LeRoy Collins, as President of the National Association of Broadcasters, took a courageous and vigorous stand against cigarette advertising and urged that cigarette commercials be brought within the purview of the National Association of Broadcasters (NAB) code of good practices.[12]

Communication of Information

Mention has been made of the varying relations between advertisements and publics and of some of the economic effects of advertisements. In the third place, mention should also be made of the informative and educational impact they have. Reference is made primarily to classified ads, much department store advertising, notices in specialized magazines and trade publications, book and mail order catalogs. Advertising is by no means limited to blatant, noisy, repetitive TV commercials, or to full-page, colorful, imaginative but empty magazine or billboard ads. A sizable proportion is truly informative, guiding the would-be purchaser to the object or service desired because of the information given. It is quite possible that women and many men read department store notices in their local papers quite as intently and regularly as the non-advertising content. The copy in many magazines and catalogs also attracts much serious attention.

Promotion: Non-commercial

(In the fourth place, mention should be made of certain types of advertising that play a special role such as church advertising, political commercials, professional ads, and government notices. Doctors, lawyers, and clergymen, as well as a few other professional people, usually refrain from direct, obvious appeals, and they lean backward to avoid ostentation or flamboyancy.[13] Nevertheless, there are many subtle, covert ways in which they can advertise and sell themselves. Church publicity is primarily local, but it is quite extensive, regular, and informative. Political advertising, as distinct from political press agentry and publicity, is irregular, and limited largely to election campaigns. Many types of media are employed, particularly television. In many political campaigns today from one-half to three-fourths of the advertising budget may go to radio and TV. From time to time government agencies, national, state, and local use advertisements for military recruiting purposes, to sell bonds, to publicize legal notices of various kinds, to dispose of surplus stocks of goods, and for many, diverse purposes.)

Values

Finally, what may be said of the long range effects of advertising on the values of the American people, their ideals, hopes, aspirations? Has advertising made them more materialistic, more interested in things than people, more concerned with material, financial, and social success than virtue, nobility, character? Have the national advertisements, with their labels and slogans, tended to standardize the buying habits of the American people and to induce an ever-increasing amount of cultural conformity? It is virtually impossible to say with the data at hand. Advertisements constitute only one of numerous factors in the opinion-forming process, and it is not easy, and perhaps impossible, to isolate this factor for study. Meanwhile, progress seems to lie in the direction of curtailing as speedily as possible the obvious falsities, unnecessary annoyances, repetitiveness, and competitive wastes, at the same time expanding the educative and informative aspects. The educational level of the American people has risen by a large margin in recent decades; knowledge, understanding, tastes, and expectations have likewise risen. The opportunities of the advertiser to inform and educate, to introduce and explain, to notify and attract are truly great. It would be regrettable, indeed, if the billions of dollars spent for radio and television time, as well as for print and display, were not used to inform and enlighten, rather than to trick and falsify. The advertisers who first fully appreciate the masses' desire for information and try to satisfy them, not with color, jingles, noise, repetitive slogans, and gimmicks, but with information, real news, and good entertainment will be serving their private needs and also the public interest.)

PUBLIC RELATIONS DEFINED

"Public relations" means different things to different people. For some it is merely a new name for publicity, propaganda, and promotional activities. For others it connotes relations between an organization or individual and their publics, relations which are always two-way and which may be good or bad. Today most people use the expression to mean more than merely publicity or propaganda, and they think of a broad spectrum of relationships between organizations and their public or publics.[14]

In the most inclusive sense, public relations are simply the relations of a person, group, or organization with their publics. In the case of a business firm, the term would refer to its relations with employees, customers, stockholders, suppliers, government, the general public, and other groups, which are important to it.[15] The salient publics of business firms may be different from firm to firm, and quite different from those of government agencies, political and religious organizations, artists, actors, or teachers. Whoever or whatever the person or institution, their public relations may be good or bad, good with some publics, bad with others. The basic problem of public relations involves doing whatever is necessary to create and maintain good relations and to avoid or remove bad relations. If bad relations are due to ignorance or misunderstanding by the public concerned, an educational or informational campaign is indicated. If bad relations are due to company or institutional policies, these policies may have to be modified. Sometimes, bad relations arise out of real conflicts of interest, and compromise, negotiation, and some form of adjudication are necessary. Bad relations between countries, businesses, races, individuals, and groups are caused by these and many other circumstances, and the remedies called for are as varied as the causes. In some cases publicity, information, advertising, and other types of propaganda are necessary. At other times, quiet, behind-the-scenes negotiation may be preferable. In still others, there may be the problem of modifying personal behavior or organizational policy, or of referring the matter to some outside agency for mediation, reconciliation, or adjudication.

Before going further it must be emphasized that many of those concerned with public relations problems, especially public relations firms and their clients, take a narrower view of the whole problem than this. All too often they act as though the job was to remove ill will and bad relations without removing the real causes of the bad relations, especially if the causes are bad policies rather than misunderstanding. For such practitioners, the emphasis will be one-way, and that way will be to propagandize in order to persuade the public to accept, to believe, and to act as the propagandist wishes. Such a person or organization is little interested in the views or interests of the other fellow. He is basically concerned with getting his way, usually at all costs, and he is interested in good relations to the extent that they assist that end.

In contrast to the individual, firm, or institution which is unwilling to modify behavior and policy to improve public relations are those who are all too willing to follow public opinion and to change their corporate policies or individual view to promote harmony and good relations. From the "public be damned" policy of the late nineteenth century many have moved to the extreme, "the public is always right." There are undoubtedly limits to the extent one should go in trying to maintain good public relations, limits that must be set by one's convictions and values. This is an ethical problem which cannot be easily solved.

Many books and articles have been written on the so-called strategies and techniques of public relations, but few stress both sides of the situation, the person or organization and their responsibilities on the one hand and the public's on the other. Instead, these studies dwell on the means and tools available for modifying the opinions and attitudes of publics, press relations, publicity, techniques of propaganda, uses of mass media, and psychological strategies. Very little emphasis is placed on the necessity for studying the over-all public relations situation, probing for the basic causes of bad relations and then seeking to find the appropriate solutions. Propaganda, publicity, and advertising may well have an important place in the solution, but, again, they may have little to do with it. Only careful analysis and study can give the needed answer.

THE PUBLIC RELATIONS SITUATION

The basic principles of public relations can be easily and quickly stated. Their successful application, however, is often complicated, tedious, and frustrating. The first step is to make a careful survey of the opinions and attitudes of relevant and significant publics in order to identify the extent and nature of bad relations. Such surveys may be as elaborate and detailed as time and money will allow. The second step is to analyze these survey findings to determine the principal causes or reasons for the bad relations. Finally, in the light of these findings, suitable procedures and remedies must be devised to remove these causes.

In dealing with problems of bad public relations it is desirable to keep in mind what the over-all public relations situation is: what attributes of the client, whether individual, business firm, or government agency, are possible causes of bad relations; what aspects of the public or publics may be the causes; and similarly, what features of the communication processes may cause difficulties. The public relations situation is always composed of three elements: client (individual, agency, institution), public or publics, and communication processes. Each of these can be further broken down into features or aspects, which, if they malfunction may cause bad relations. The accompanying chart attempts to detail the over-all public relations situation.

PUBLIC RELATIONS SITUATION
(Partial Breakdown)

A. The Agency or Institution
  1. Policies
     (a) Nature of aims and objectives
     (b) Methods followed in adopting them
     (c) Degree to which groups affected participated
     (d) Effects of their formulation
  2. Personnel
     (a) Methods of recruitment and selection
     (b) Qualifications and competence
     (c) Honesty and integrity
     (d) Tact and courtesy
     (e) Morale of personnel
     (f) Extent and nature of training
     (g) Conditions of employment—wages, hours, security, promotion, etc.
     (h) Leadership
  3. Procedures
     (a) Simple or complicated (excessive forms, red tape)
     (b) Fair or unjust (adequate notice, equal treatment)
     (c) Efficient or inefficient (buck passing, mistakes)
     (d) Convenient or inconvenient (appointments, facilities)
     (e) Responsiveness (handling of complaints)
     (f) Responsibility (definition of functions, lines of authority)
     (g) Fast or slow
  4. Organization
     (a) Proper differentiation of jobs and functions
     (b) Clear lines of authority and responsibility
     (c) Clear job descriptions
     (d) Properly balanced responsibility and work load among organizational units
     (e) Good lines of communication
     (f) Responsibility commensurate with authority
  5. Physical Equipment and Appearance
     (a) Attractive arrangement and design in keeping with current modes and tastes

   (b) Functional adequacy

   (c) Cleanliness

   (d) Adequate equipment: information centers, washrooms, waiting rooms, lighting, heating, cooling, safety, guides and signs, parking, lifting machines, furniture, etc.

  6. History and Tradition

   (a) Reputation of institution

   (b) Previous actions and outstanding events

   (c) Previous leaders and notable personalities

   (d) Tradition reminders—ceremonies, symbols, ritual, songs, poetry, pictures

B. The Public

  1. Attitudes and opinions

   (a) Content and focus of the opinions

   (b) Degrees of agreement

   (c) Degrees of favorableness or unfavorableness

   (d) Intensity

   (e) Quality

   (f) Stability

   (g) Formation

   (h) Distribution

  2. Knowledge

   (a) Content

   (b) Source and reliability

   (c) Comprehensiveness

   (d) Distribution

   (e) Understanding and interpretation

  3. Interests

   (a) Degree to which clearly defined

   (b) Degree to which they may conflict with the interests of the institution or agency

   (c) Degree to which they are fixed or flexible

  4. Experience—especially with institution or agency

   (a) As users or clients of agency

   (b) As subjects of agency rules and regulations

   (c) As persons affected directly or indirectly by the work of the agency

   (d) As visitors to the agency or institution

  5. Participation

   (a) Attendance at meetings

   (b) Attendance at hearings

   (c) Membership on agency committees

C. Communication Processes

  1. Media of communication and contact

   (a) Press, publications, releases, conferences, etc.

   (b) Radio, TV, and other forms of electrical transmission

  (c) Advertising, films, art, exhibits, etc.
  (d) Owners and proprietors
 2. Content of communication
  (a) Clarity
  (b) Credibility and convincingness
  (c) Accuracy
  (d) Attention provoking
  (e) Persuasiveness
 3. Conditions of reception
  (a) Public or private
  (b) Alone or with large or small groups
  (c) Competing stimuli
  (d) Physical surroundings
  (e) Audience preparation or conditioning
 4. Communication agents and agencies
  (a) Experience
  (b) Reputation
  (c) Qualification of personnel
  (d) Coverage
 5. Techniques of communication
  (a) Variety
  (b) Adaptability to audience
  (c) Record of effectiveness
  (d) Imagination
 6. Time, place, manner of communication
 7. Censorship and control
  (a) Basis for
  (b) By whom
  (c) How
 8. Selection, presentation, distribution
 9. Flow of communication—aids and obstacles
 10. Audience
  (a) Composition
  (b) Reading, viewing, listening habits
 11. Effects
  (a) Direct and indirect
  (b) Specific and general
  (c) Durability

No attempt will be made to explain and discuss this table in detail, but a few points may be emphasized. To ascertain the causes of bad relations, if any, after a survey of publics is made, one may begin with the agency or institution itself, its policies, personnel, procedures, organization, physical equipment and appearance, history, and traditions. Under each of the main subdivisions, several aspects are listed which may have caused bad relations. Such questions as these may be pertinent: Do the aims and objectives of the client cause antagonisms? Are the client's employees honest, tactful, well-trained? Are institutional procedures complicated, unfair, inefficient? Is the organization of the firm adequate and well designed, its equipment attractive? Has anything in the history and traditions of the organization been responsible for unfavorable images in the public's mind? These are only a few of the many questions which are suggested by the breakdown of the public relations situation and by the public opinion surveys. Remedies may differ for different aspects. Changes in policies, personnel, or procedures may be necessary, more information and publicity may be requisite, or, perhaps, real differences of opinion and values may require negotiation and compromise.

An analysis of the public's side of the situation would follow a somewhat similar course: a careful study of its attitudes and opinions, how they were formed, the basic determinants, the knowledge on which they were based, the interests of the public, and numerous other sociological, psychological, and economic attributes of the public. Such questions as the following might arise: Does the public really know the facts? What contacts has the public had with the institution, and are they typical and representative? To what extent do the agencies' interests really conflict with those of the public or publics?

Finally, the basic causes of bad relations may be found in the communication processes, in the lack of clarity, credibility, accuracy, persuasiveness, and pertinence of media content. Possibly the conditions of reception for messages may lessen their acceptance and effectiveness. To what extent do those engaged in the communication processes between client and publics have the necessary qualifications and experience? What about the appropriateness and adequacy of the techniques of communication?

It must be repeated that few, if any, public relations firms or departments follow completely the steps outlined above. In fact, the majority probably focus attention primarily, if not exclusively, on their publics, seeking in one way or another to mold and manage the opinions of these publics in a pre-determined direction. It is well to keep this model of the over-all public relations situation in mind, as the perspectives of publicity men, even the outlooks of those who call themselves public relations executives, rise. The task of creating and maintaining good public relations is a continuous one. It is usually much easier to prevent bad relations from arising, or to forestall their spread, than to try and apply remedies after bad relations are rampant. This fact necessitates close and continuous watch over policies, publics, and communication processes. It is often difficult to alter policies and objectives once they have been adopted, hence the need for considering all foreseeable public relations problems before rather than after important policy decisions are made.

THE RISE OF THE PUBLIC RELATIONS COUNSEL

The history of public relations is so closely and inextricably related to that of publicity, press agentry, advertising, and propaganda that it is difficult, at times, to separate them. The difficulty is greatly aggravated by the varieties of definitions in practice. Advertising has a clearer concept, by referring to paid notices and announcements. Press agentry, on the other hand, is usually thought of as the effort to obtain free publicity particularly in the press. Many of the early public relations people, such as Ivy Lee and Edward L. Bernays, began as press agents and later saw the broader implications of public relations.

The rise of the professional public relations counsel was due in large part to the failure of business leadership to solve its public relations problems. Various branches of business had always been more or less aware of the importance of their relations with the voting public and more or less successful in their dealings with it. The degree of success depended to a large extent upon the qualities of business leadership present. In many fields of human relations, such as politics, religion, teaching, and law, few persons attained leadership and power without possessing or acquiring some public relations sense—not only an understanding of the importance of the voting public, and the many publics of which it is composed, but also competence in dealing with them. Business leadership, on the contrary, on many occasions and in many areas of economic activity, notoriously failed in this respect.[16]

Many reasons may be given for the failure of American business to obtain adequate public relations leadership. For example, many positions of leadership in business are inherited, rather than earned, by men and women who may be quite incapable of dealing with public relations, to say nothing of the technical, production, and marketing operations of the business. Then again, positions of leadership often fall into the hands of those who have gained pre-eminence because of their contributions to the selling, technical, or scientific side of business, and not because they possess an aptitude or understanding of public relations.

Also, the financial structure of many businesses often influences the character of business leadership. Such positions often go to the highest bidder, because of his ability to purchase and control stock. Often real control over business policies rests with absentee groups—bankers, holding companies, or trustees. The divorce of ownership and control places the real determination of policies in the hands of salaried employees lacking the true qualities of leadership.

It would be a mistake to assume that all businesses need the services of outside public relations counsel. In many instances such leadership is already present. The Bell Telephone System was especially fortunate, for example, in having as its president during its early years a man of the type of Theodore Vail. Mr. Norton E. Long in a careful study entitled "Public Relations Policies of the Bell System" states:[17]

> He (Theodore N. Vail) has claim to be ranked as one of the first leaders of American industry to appreciate the problems of public relations in a far-sighted manner and to seek a basis for their long time adjustment.

At a time when the Bell System was following a "take it or leave it" attitude toward the public, ruthlessly stamping out competition, and being subjected to an increasing amount of violent opposition, Mr. Vail assumed the leadership. With foresight he effected a revolutionary change in corporate policy and laid the foundations for the eminently successful public relations practices that have been followed since that time. Instead of crushing competitors he followed a policy of "taking them into camp" and using them as allies in the battle for public favor. In response to the public demands for more efficient and adequate service, he launched an operating program designed to follow public tastes and desires. Instead of stubbornly opposing all forms of public regulation, he accepted the fact that monopoly required some degree of social control, and he came out boldly for regulation by state commissions, thereby warding off more drastic regulation by federal agencies, and more uncertain, political control by state legislatures. He inaugurated the policy of using all the working personnel as instruments for creating public good will, of training them to be ambassadors of good will, both on and off company time. He undertook to humanize the leadership and to dramatize the contributions of the telephone industry to the social well-being of the country. In short, he was not only a business executive but a real leader, adept in bringing corporate policies and practices into tune with public opinion.

In striking contrast to the effective business leadership of Vail, we have the picture of John D. Rockefeller, a shrewd, two-fisted, fighting, efficient business executive who rose to power by the sheer force of a bold, relentless, driving personality. Quick to sense values and to take advantage of competitors, master in his own corporate household, he was a tiger in business warfare but totally inept in meeting the public relations problems of his empire. It was his lack of public relations sense that helped give birth to the professional public relations counsel, the advisor who supplies talents which business executives sometimes lack.[18]

When John D. Rockefeller's miners struck at the collieries of the Colorado Fuel and Iron Company in 1912 and the public gasped with horror at the news that armed agents of the company had fired at and killed scores of miners and members of their families, Ivy Lee had just returned from a two-year stay in Europe as manager of a Wall Street banking firm. Born in Cedartown, Georgia, son of a Methodist preacher, he had spent the years following his graduation from Princeton, in 1898, reporting for the *New York Journal,* the *New York World,* and the *New York Times.* In 1903, however, he gave up reporting to serve with the press bureau of the Democratic National Committee and soon thereafter became director of publicity for the Pennsylvania Railroad, a position which he held until he went to Europe in 1910.

During his years of service with the Pennsylvania Railroad, Lee had made some notable changes in the relations between that corporation and the press—changes that undoubtedly came to the attention, not only of the chief executives of the railroad, but of Rockefeller himself, who had a considerable financial stake in the road. Lee introduced an entirely new news policy. Instead of trying to get as much favorable publicity into the papers as possible, by devious, indirect, anonymous methods, he wrote directly to newspaper editors and told them that he proposed to supply them from time to time with news with accuracy guaranteed regarding the Pennsylvania Railroad, over the signature of responsible executives of the corporation. If in the opinion of the editors such statements were of news value, then he hoped they would be published; otherwise he would be glad to have them thrown in the waste basket. In other words he substituted for the aggressive techniques of the traditional press agent, a technique of press relations based on mutual confidence between business and newspaper. Instead of trying merely to promote the interest of his employer, he undertook to serve both corporation executive and newspaper editor. He asked for no favors. Unless the material he submitted measured up to the newspapers' standards of good reporting he expected no publicity.

This man Rockefeller brought in to assist him in reconstructing his corporate relations with the public—relations which had never been good but had become critical following the revelations of mining conditions in Colorado. Lee did not become an executive of the Standard Oil Company, nor of any other Rockefeller corporation. He set up his own office and served Rockefeller as an advisor. In the course of time his clients included the Pennsylvania Railroad, United States Steel, and a large number of important corporations as well as non-business institutions, and foreign governments. As a rule he was allowed a responsible part in the determination of corporate and institutional policy; he was able then to integrate public relations policies on all fronts, and anticipate and avoid public relations difficulties before they arose. Most of his clients had their own publicity departments, which he encouraged to follow what he considered the basic principles of sound press relations. He recognized the importance of group leaders in the formation of public opinion and through personal contact and correspondence systematically built up a wide acquaintance with outstanding leaders in all fields of human activity. His correspondence was extensive; he followed very closely the writings, speeches, and activities of all who might influence opinion on subjects or institutions in which he was interested. At one time he numbered among his clients the Bolshevik government of Russia, and in connection with his campaign to secure American recognition of Russia following the First World War, he built up a library of books, pamphlets, and clippings of extraordinary completeness. This material was deposited with the Princeton University Library following his death. Ivy Lee was one of the first, outstanding, professional public relations counsels.

World War I marked a new stage in the evolution of the public relations counsel. In the propaganda campaign launched by the Creel Committee on Public Information a number of men, journalists, press agents, and advertisers, suddenly perceived, not only the importance of mass opinion, but also the possibilities of molding and managing it. Among these were Carl Byoir, John Price Jones, and Edward L. Bernays. Bernays perceived the significance of the part played by group leaders in forming opinion, the variety of channels that might be used to influence opinion, the mass appeal of dramatized events and manufactured events, and the importance of translating private ends into terms which expressed the public interest. In short, he came to realize the many dimensions of propaganda of which press agentry and publicity played only a small part.[19]

Edward L. Bernays, born in Vienna in 1891, moved as a boy to New York. Following the completion of his public school education, he attended the New York State Agricultural College affiliated with Cornell. Bernays, however, was not destined to become a farmer. In 1913 he became the editor of the *Dietetic and Hygienic Gazette* and assistant editor of the *Medical Review of Reviews*—periodicals on the Bernarr Macfadden model dedicated to the enlightenment of the public on health and sexual matters. Shortly thereafter he helped to publicize Brieux's *Damaged Goods* for Richard Bennett.

Following a trip to Europe he wrote publicity for Klein and Erlanger productions, managed the tour of the Russian Ballet in 1915, and in 1917 was publicity manager for Caruso. Then came the war. During it he served on George Creel's Committee on Public Information; of this experience Bernays has written: "It was the war which opened the eyes of the intelligent few in all departments of life to the possibilities of regimenting the public mind."

After the war he was employed by the War Department to see that employers lived up to their pledge to return jobs to soldiers relinquished when they went to France. Then he went into business for himself to "serve the public interest."

Bernays' contributions to the rise of the public relations counsel have been marked. In the first place he has tried through his speaking and writing to give the vocation a rationale, a philosophy, and a professional status. He was first and foremost propaganda's own propagandist. Propaganda as a concept was in disrepute. Bernays undertook to translate his own self-interest as a propagandist into terms expressing a public interest. His argument was that co-operation is necessary for a smooth functioning society, that it was impossible for the average citizen to form intelligent opinions on complex issues, and that the conscious and intelligent manipulation of the organized habits and opinions of the masses is an important element in democratic society. "It might be better," he writes, "to have, instead of propaganda and special pleading, committees of wise men who would choose our rulers, dictate our conduct, private and public, and decide upon the best types of clothes for us to wear . . . But we have chosen the opposite method, that of open competition."

With the First World War fresh in the memory of the public, it was not difficult for Bernays to convince himself and others of the power of propaganda. His second major contribution was to show the dimensions and possibilities of the field. Public relations was defined in terms of propaganda: "The important thing for the statesman of our age," he said, "is not so much to know how to please the public, but to know how to sway the public." And so he proceeded to demonstrate how this could be done.

When the business depression of 1929 struck the country, business leadership suffered a severe loss of prestige—a loss that was further increased by the political situation and the avalanche of criticism that was directed at business from all quarters. This turn of affairs offered golden opportunities for the professional public relations counsel. At the time there were few individuals or firms in a position to assume this responsibility. Bernays and Lee were about the only exponents of this new occupation, but the demand did not long outrun the supply. Press agents and publicity men changed the nomenclature of their letterheads; many of the larger advertising firms created public relations bureaus; merchandisers and salesmen entered the field; fund raising organizations that had prospered gloriously during the boom days of the twenties reorganized their setups along public relations lines. Many corporations created vice-presidents-in-charge-of-public relations; trade associations began to call some of their activities public relations work.[20] A new profession was born, but it lacked many of the attributes of a profession: qualifications were not clearly defined, there was no accepted code of ethics, and no systematic scheme of professional training.

Various attempts were made to put the work on a professional, recognized basis.[21] Bernays was extremely active in this. He organized a Council on Public Relations, composed of various specialists in the field as well as academic students of the subject. There was considerable bewilderment among the members, uncertainty as to what it was all about. The desire to be "in the know" was counteracted by a suspicion that the Council itself was only a propaganda device for enhancing the prestige of the sponsors. Other attempts were made to organize the profession and define the scope of the field, and exercise a restraining hand on its abuses. One such organization which has enjoyed a longer life than most is the National Association of Accredited Publicity Counselors. It is far from being national in scope and is composed largely of a few men in the New York area.[22]

A few attempts were made to start a public relations magazine. A young man named Pryor made three such attempts, yearly for three years, but owing to financial difficulties he never got any farther than Vol. I, No. 1, each time. Meanwhile, the number of public relations counselors increased in other cities. After the election of 1936, many business leaders began to rank public relations as "Industry's Number One Problem"— notably Paul Garrett of General Motors, Colby Chester, then President of the National Association of Manufacturers and of General Foods, Edward Stettinius of United States Steel, Arthur W. Page of the American Telegraph and Telephone, and many others. Trade associations usually placed the subject of public relations high on their convention programs. During 1938-39, the McGraw-Hill Public Relations Forums were inaugurated; they were sponsored by a publishing house whose scores of trade journals brought it in contact with many branches of business.[23] During this period Princeton University established *The Public Opinion Quarterly* (1937), and most of the larger firms in the country established or expanded their public relations activities. Even before the United States entered World War II, public relations as a one-sided single-purpose activity engaged in promoting a positive image of the client before his public had reached a state of poised maturity in the business life of the country. Public relations had also invaded the educational field, religious organizations, social welfare work, political parties, and many other professional and special service organizations.

PUBLIC RELATIONS SINCE WORLD WAR II

No attempt will be made here to spell out in detail the history of public relations since World War II. Only a few of the major trends and problems may be noted. In the first place, public relations, in a limited, vague sense, has gained increasing acceptance as an important phase of business activity. Most of the large corporations have their public relation departments, and most of the smaller ones make use of public relations specialists.[24] Educational institutions, medical and other professional groups, political parties, government agencies, and all kinds of groups pay homage to the term. Local, regional, and national associations of public relations practitioners have been formed. Courses and departments of public relations have been added to the curricula of colleges and universities, and at one, Boston University, advanced degrees are now offered by its School of Public Relations and Communications. In 1946, according to Professor A. M. Lee, thirty of fifty-nine major educational institutions offered forty-seven courses under public relations titles, a large proportion of them in journalism schools. Ten years later a much more detailed survey was made by a committee of the Public Relations Society of America, showing that of the 653 institutions replying, 163 provided public relations training in some degree.[25] Fourteen of these institutions offered a public relations major. In 1956, the Council on Public Relations Education was created as a subunit of the Association for Education in Journalism.[26] Opinion leaders, and business leaders especially, are more conscious than ever of the importance of their public relations. Business executives are recapturing some of that confidence in their own ability to lead opinion which many had lost during the 1930's.

Improved Methods

In the second place, one may discern many improvements in the methods used to create and improve public relations. The methods employed by gas and electric utilities in the 1920's to high-pressure the press and to influence social science instruction in the public schools are generally avoided. There are exceptions, however, as the struggles between truckers and railroads during the 1950's showed.[27] In the dispute between U. S. Steel and President Kennedy regarding steel prices in 1962, that perceptive public relations sense one would expect of the management of one of the largest corporations in the country was lacking. Nevertheless, the methods used to win public support are generally more empathic, more restrained, more geared to revering rather than damning public opinion. Many of the larger corporations—notably du Pont, Standard Oil of New Jersey, International Harvester, General Electric—have well organized public relations departments, manned by college trained experts in consumer relations, journalism, and public opinion.

Corporations vary greatly in their public relations organization, its inclusiveness and comprehensiveness, its relation to policy-making, the size of its budget relative to the corporation budget itself. Some firms place the public relations department close to the president, with a vice-president in charge; some include within it employee relations, advertising, marketing research, stockholder, government, as well as public and customer relations. Corporations also differ in the extent to which they use independent public relations firms. The variety of structures and relationships within the company, and between the company and outside specialists, defy easy summation. The sort of public relations organization and functioning which is most expedient for a particular company depends on many factors such as the size of the company, budget, nature of products and services, customers, and not least the history, traditions, and top personnel of the firm. There is probably no one, single set-up that is necessarily best under all circumstances.[28]

Reappraisement

Thirdly, even though "public relations" as a term is as familiar as air, it still lacks a precise, generally accepted definition.[29] Many public relations personnel think of themselves primarily as promoters, rather than as specialists in reconciliation and creators of better understanding. Their major task seems to be to win public approval at any cost, not to bring corporate policy and activities into tune with public opinion, and vice versa. Quite recently, one of the senior, outstanding experts in public relations announced the forthcoming publication of a public relations counseling letter which would cover a long series of topics, nearly all of which were concerned with the public and winning its support, not with the other side of the public relations' situation, the corporation itself and its policies.[30] The counseling letter would deal with industrial relations, controversies and disputes, fund raising, public relations for banks, brokers, and investment counselors, unfavorable publicity, corporate images, timing of campaigns, launching a new product or service. These are assuredly the main topics which engage the attention of most public relations counselors. The problem of the future will be to make public relations activities more of a two-way street, not merely one-way propaganda.

The Ethical Problem

Finally, attention may be given to one of the basic problems affecting public relations work—the ethical problem. The efforts on the part of business and other groups, the voting public and the various groups of which it is composed, have not always met with the public response desired. The efforts by associations and agencies of electric and gas utilities to influence public opinion during the twenties, although successful for a time in terms of the amount of publicity received, finally ended in catastrophe. Many of those engaged in publicity and public relations activities are suspect, and legislative investigations occur frequently. The words, "public relations," "propaganda," and "publicity" often carry with them an invidious, socially reprehensible connotation. Why?

One of the reasons for this state of public apprehension is that public relations activities as they are conducted today lack the controlling influence of an acceptable code of ethics. Now codes of ethics, in and of themselves, do not mean a great deal unless they coincide with practice.

Various public relations firms and associations have published such codes, for example the Public Relations Society of America. It adopted its first code of ethics in 1954 and revised it in 1959 to tighten its procedures for hearing and dispensing of complaints. The Society, however, through its Board of Directors, can only censure, suspend, expel, or exonerate those charged with violating the code. Numerous public relations counselors have, in their published writings, undertaken to set forth their philosophies of sound public relations practice. Still, public suspicion persists, partly because the statements of policy are individualized and not generally accepted, partly because they are regarded as pious nonsense and not actual guides to practice. Public relations practice has been guilty of three major abuses: It has corroded communication channels with cynicism. It has cluttered them with pseudo events and phony phrases that confuse public issues that need clarification. It pollutes "the opinion stream with the debris of diversion and distortion." [31]

There are other aspects of public relations practice which are criticized. It is charged that those engaged in this work are insincere, that they materialistically sell their services and talents to the highest bidder regardless of the cause he is promoting, that they do not seek to enlighten the public mind with the facts of a given public situation but seek to promote the interests of their employer even to the extent of whitewashing conduct they know is socially reprehensible. Furthermore, there is a widespread belief that those engaged in this work will use their expert knowledge of mass psychology to arouse emotions, distort, fabricate even, whenever the circumstances seem to make it expedient. Even those who realize how profitable the services of an expert in public relations may be, are often dubious concerning the social merit of the activity.

Raising Professional Standards

Two problems are involved in the task of raising the standards of public relations practice: the first is to formulate a code of ethics generally acceptable to public relations executives, their clients, and the public; the second is to provide the machinery for enforcing it. The latter is without question the more difficult. This whole problem cannot be solved satisfactorily without the fullest understanding and co-operation of those who use the services of public relations experts. The standards which prevail will ultimately be determined by the client—in the case of business, by management. Regardless of the ideals of the public relations counselor, in practice he cannot rise much above the level of the person who employs him. He can advise, cajole, and remonstrate, but in the final analysis he will have to abide by the decision of the management or forgo his role altogether. If public relations counselors would take a united stand in this matter, they could undoubtedly exert tremendous influence, but without the fullest co-operation of business leaders their efforts to raise standards will be difficult indeed. The business executive who insists that his advisor win public support and approval for his firm without showing the least disposition to modify the corporate conduct which lies at the basis of public ill will, not only jeopardizes good public relations, but makes it extremely difficult for his public relations counselor to follow sound ethical practice.

But the difficulty goes deeper. It actually stems from a competitive—an unregulated, non-socially controlled—economic system which forces individual business men to adopt unethical practices which they would really prefer not to employ. A few chiselers, as practice has so frequently shown, if not controlled can undermine completely the morale and standards of an industry. How to curb these minority practices and make it possible for the leaders of an industry to maintain standards is a crucial question. Thus, the public relations counselor and the business executive find themselves enmeshed in the complexities of a system out of which it is increasingly difficult to create and maintain a workable code of standards.

Various methods have been employed to meet this situation—government regulation, self-government in industry, public education in one form or another. It is a curious fact, but none the less true, that the laws on our statute books, the regulatory agencies that have been established, and the far-flung machinery of courts, enforcement agencies, and social control are made necessary by the conduct and activities of minorities rather than majorities. The great majority of citizens who are decent, law abiding, well-intentioned, and high principled have to pay, in various forms of restriction, for the misdeeds and shortcomings of a comparatively small number of their fellow countrymen. The Securities Exchange Commission, the National Labor Relations Board, the Federal Trade Commission, to say nothing of our courts, police agencies, as well as the high taxes, and high insurance rates which result from existing circumstances are the product of a system which enables a small but unsocial group to set the pace. So it is in the field of public relations, publicity, and propaganda. The great majority of high minded men and women engaged in public relations work have to endure the public disfavor and odium generated by a relatively small, irresponsible group.

Propaganda, as the advocacy of ideas and doctrines, has a legitimate and desirable part to play in our democratic system. In the final analysis public opinion, the opinions of the masses, is the court of last resort, whether it be in the fields of business, government, or morals. The problem is to make that public opinion as enlightened as possible. How can this be done? There are those who have said and say today that the masses are incapable of arriving at enlightened opinions without an elite, a body of philosopher guardians, a college of cardinals, or a dictator to tell them what to think. Others do not subscribe to this philosophy. The masses, however, can never afford to place all their confidence in any small group or succession of leaders, no matter how humanly wise and socially motivated the group or leaders seem to be. Not only would the masses surrender the right to form their own opinions, but in so doing they would forfeit their right to judge the capacity of any such elite to lead them. The stunting of their own capacities to think and evaluate is the inevitable consequence of this particular solution to the problem of public enlightenment.

Perhaps the best way to produce an enlightened public is to provide for the widest possible advocacy and dissemination of ideas. A multiplicity rather than a monopoly of propaganda is to be preferred. Even if this process of enlightenment is slower at times than the other and if the masses prove inexpert at times in making their decisions, there is always the assurance that the human personality is developing rather than being stunted by authority, that the source of public policy is located at the base of power, and that mistakes, if and when made, can be remedied. The social justification for a competitive arena of propaganda—in the final analysis it must have a social justification—must be found in the contribution it makes to public enlightenment. The test of the soundness of any public relations policy as it involves advocacy, special pleading, publicity, and propaganda is whether it contributes to public understanding. It is not for a business leader, a public relations counsel, or for a group of business leaders and counselors to say what the public interest is or is not. It is for the voting public to say. The function of the public relations counsel is to present the facts, to give reasons, to present a point of view as clearly, logically, and understandably as possible.

REPREHENSIBLE PUBLIC RELATIONS TECHNIQUES

It is worthwhile at this point to undertake a summary statement of public relations techniques which are socially indefensible in the light of the public relations philosophy stated above.

(1) Deliberate falsification, distortion, colorization.

It is out of the question to expect that advocates of causes, special pleaders, and propagandists will be able to present all the facts relating to a special situation, problem, or issue. Some selectivity is inevitable, but the public has a right to insist that individuals and groups who appear before the bar of public opinion do their best to get all the facts so far as they can, and to use all the care possible to see to it that the facts so presented are accurate. Experts should be consulted; an opportunity for critics and opponents to check statements should be allowed. Errors are unavoidable, but if propagandists would simply refrain from deliberate manipulation of information there would be remarkable progress.

(2) Failure to reveal the identity of the cause, the promoter, and the source of the information.

Ivy Lee was definitely of the opinion that the greatest evil in public relations practice was the failure to disclose the true identity of the propagandist. There is certainly nothing reprehensible about special pleading or propaganda per se. It has a definite function to perform. Why should public relations counselors seek to hide the identity of their clients? In many cases, there are no valid reasons for doing so. In other cases, the reasons will not bear inspection. That the attitude of the profession is becoming enlightened on this point received gratifying confirmation sometime ago when full page advertisements in 2,600 papers over the country announced with candor the relation between Carl Byoir and Associates and the Great Atlantic and Pacific Tea Company in their joint efforts to promote the interests of the chain stores and defeat the Patman Bill. Identifying the sponsors of the campaign and a clear and frank statement of the purposes was an aid to public understanding and in no way injured but aided the cause.

Nevertheless this failure to identify the propagandist prevails all too generally throughout the propaganda arena. In spite of the fact that a large per cent of the news content of daily papers stems from interested sources, it is difficult if not impossible for readers to identify the source. The use of by-lines in the case of special correspondents, and the easy identification of columnists are both aids to public understanding which are widely used by newspapers today. This practice of identifying the source of news might well be extended to "free publicity" items generally.

SUMMARY

What can validly be said about the over-all influence of public relations specialists on public opinion? Have they altered the direction of public thinking? Have they modified public behavior? Have they reduced controversies and tensions between groups and individuals? Have they promoted justice between such groups and facilitated democratic processes of government? Answers based on hard facts are difficult. Only hypotheses, suppositions, guesses, actually, can be offered. In a broad sense public relations experts have helped to direct public thinking toward products and services and the goals of all kinds of enterprises, but they have probably had very little to say regarding the goals themselves. In varying degrees they may influence policy decisions, but they are seldom the basic determinators. Many public relations specialists lament this, and they insist that they should have a prominent role in policy making—some do, but the number is relatively small.

To somewhat the same extent public relations people have influenced and modified behavior, encouraged customers to buy this product or that service, urged patrons to attend meetings and exhibitions, recruited students for schools and colleges. Yet, in company with advertisers, publicists, and propagandists their influence is one among many variables and one that cannot be measured and weighed easily.

Probably the most important influence of public relations, as distinct from that of advertising and publicity, is its impact on the relations between groups and individuals. Public relations counselors are, in a sense, the peace makers of modern civilization, or they would be if they really devoted themselves to their two-way task of reconciliation. In so far as they have been successful in bringing merchant and customer, employer and employee, government and citizen closer together; in so far as they have brought competitors and antagonists to see the other's point of view; and in so far as they have brought about better understanding on the part of publics, and, at the same time consideration, empathy, willingness to adjust, compromise, and change on the part of their clients—they have undoubtedly poured oil on the hot bearings of this machinery we call civilization. However, it must be repeated that this reconciliation approach is all too often supplanted by the purely propaganda approach, the approach of the one-sided advocate.

Propaganda and public relations flourish in an open society, in a liberal democracy. The livelier the competition of ideas, the better. The greater the variety of public relations counselors, the keener the competition for the public mind. If the competition is to see who can present the most logical arguments and the arguments best supported by evidence, the quality of public opinion and its decisions rises. If not, and purely demagogic, emotional, tricky, and misleading appeals and activities abound, the contrary will be the case. There is unfortunately no outstanding evidence that public relations, in itself, has done very much to raise the intellectual level of argument and advocacy, and therewith public opinion and its decisions.

NOTES FOR CHAPTER 11

Epigraph. Norman Douglas, *South Wind.* Chapter 7.
1. On the history and practice of advertising see, Frey, Albert W., *Advertising* (3rd ed.; New York: The Ronald Press, 1961); The Editors of Fortune Magazine, *The Amazing Advertising Business.* Simon and Schuster, 1957; Ogilvy, David, *Confessions of an Advertising Man* (New York: Atheneum Publishers, 1963); Presbrey, Frank S., *The History and Development of Advertising* (Garden City, New York: Doubleday-Doran, 1929); Lederer, W. J., *A Nation of Sheep* (New York: W. W. Norton & Co., 1961);

Sandage, C. H. (ed.), *The Promise of Advertising* (Homewood, Ill.: Richard D. Irwin, 1961); Selden, Joseph J., *The Golden Fleece: Selling the Good Life to Americans* (New York: Macmillan, 1963); Pease, Otis A., *The Responsibilities of American Advertising: Private Control and Public Influence, 1920-1940* (New Haven, Conn.: Yale University Press, 1958).

2. See Machlup, Fritz, *The Production and Distribution of Knowledge in the United States* (Princeton, N. J.: Princeton University Press, 1962), pp. 266, 269.
3. See *Broadcasting,* March 18, 1963, p. 30. Also, *ibid.,* February 25, 1963, p. 70.
4. See Pease, Otis A., *op. cit.*
5. See Welch, Henry, and Felix Marti-Ibañez (eds.), *The Impact of the Food and Drug Administration on Our Society* New York: MD Publications, 1956.
6. See Federal Trade Commission, *Advertising Alert,* February 12, 1962, p. 1.
7. At a recent meeting of the National Retail Dry Goods Association, Eldridge Peterson, editor of *Printer's Ink,* warned that criticism of advertising was not coming from "crackpots" or "Commies," as it had in the past, but from very responsible people. The main causes of complaint, he said, were half truths, exaggerations, bad taste, and repetitiveness. He went on to say, "It is extremely hard to legislate against half-truths, exaggerated claims based on very minute differentiation between competitive products, phony research claims, vulgarity, etc." *New York Times,* June 28, 1952, p. 23.
8. See Borden, Neil Hopper, *The Economic Effects of Advertising* (Chicago: Richard D. Irwin, Inc., 1947).
9. One enthusiastic writer asserts: "Consumer advertising is the first rough effort of a society becoming prosperous to teach itself the use of the relatively great wealth of new resources, new techniques, and a reorganized production method. . . . Advertising, whether for good or ill, is the greatest force at work against the traditional economy of an age-long poverty as well as that of our own pioneer period; it is almost the only force at work against puritanism in consumption. . . . The waste is not in advertising but in the competitive system." "Advertising," *Encyclopedia of the Social Sciences,* Vol. I, pp. 474-75.
10. The *New York Times,* Sunday, January 12, 1964, pp. 64-65, printed the summary and conclusions of the Federal advisory committee's report "Smoking and Health," issued by the U. S. Public Health Service.
11. See story by Carl Spielvogel in the *New York Times* stating that Batten, Barton, Durstine, and Osborn, Inc., resigned the advertising account of the *Reader's Digest* after twenty-eight years because of a conflict of interest with the American Tobacco Company whose account it also handled. B.B.D.O. denied, however, that this action resulted from pressure by the American Tobacco Company, manufacturers of Lucky Strike, Pall Mall, Herbert Tareyton, and Hit Parade cigarettes. The company spends about $22,000,000 yearly on media advertising.
12. Jack Gould in the *New York Times* for November 28, 1962 stated, that "The future of LeRoy Collins as president of the National Association of Broadcasters is the subject of rising controversy following his outspoken disapproval of tobacco advertising designed to encourage young people to smoke cigarettes." Mr. Collins gave the admonition in a speech on November 19, 1962, in Portland, Oregon. It hit the broadcasting industry with

unusual force since, according to *Television Magazine,* the gross revenue derived by TV in 1961 from cigarette concerns amounted to $104,254,325, and that obtained by radio $30,000,000. Mr. Collins cited statistics to show that 20 per cent of boys had started smoking in the ninth grade; and that 30 per cent of all girls smoke before they graduate from high school.

13. In recent months, however, the advertising extremes of some funeral directors have evoked strident ridicule from such writers as Jessica Mitford.

14. The literature on public relations is voluminous and somewhat repetitive. Only a few distinctive books will be cited.

> BERNAYS, E. L., *Public Relations* (Norman: University of Oklahoma Press, 1952).
>
> CUTLIP, SCOTT M., and ALLEN H. CENTER, *Effective Public Relations* (Englewood Cliffs, N. J.: Prentice-Hall, Inc., 1958).
>
> GRISWOLD, GLENN and DENNY, *Your Public Relations* (New York: Funk and Wagnalls, 1948).
>
> HARLOW, REX F. and MARVIN M. BLACK, *Practical Public Relations* (New York: Harper & Brothers, 1947).
>
> JONES, J. P. and D. M. CHURCH, *At the Bar of Public Opinion* (Inter-River Press, 1939).
>
> KELLEY, STANLEY, *Professional Public Relations and Political Power* (Baltimore: Johns Hopkins Press, 1956).
>
> LESLY, PHILIP, *Public Relations Handbook* (New York: Prentice-Hall, Inc., 1950).
>
> PIMLOTT, J. A. R., *Public Relations and American Democracy* (Princeton, N. J.: Princeton University Press, 1957).
>
> RUBIN, BERNARD, *Public Relations and the Empire State* (New Brunswick, N. J.: Rutgers University Press, 1958).
>
> WEDDING, NUGENT, *Public Relations in Business* (Urbana: University of Illinois, 1950).

15. For amplification of this point see Childs, Harwood L., *An Introduction to Public Opinion* (New York: John Wiley and Sons, 1940).

16. See, for example, Long, Norton E., "Public Relations Policies of the Bell System," *Public Opinion Quarterly,* Vol. 1 (October, 1937), pp. 5-22, and Gras, N. S. B., "Shifts in Public Relations," *Bulletin of the Business Historical Society,* Vol. XIX (October, 1945).

17. Long, *loc. cit.*

18. See obituary of Ivy Lee in the *New York Times,* November 10, 1934.

19. See Pringle, Henry F., "Mass Psychologist," *American Mercury,* Vol. 19 (February, 1930), pp. 155-62, and Flynn, John T., "Edward L. Bernays: The Science of Ballyhoo," *Atlantic Monthly,* Vol. 149 (May, 1932), pp. 562-71.

20. See Griswold, Glenn, "The McGraw-Hill Public Relation Forums," *Public Opinion Quarterly,* Vol. 3 (October, 1939), pp. 704-09.

21. See Decker, Francis K., "The Path Toward Professionalism: PRSA's Code and How it Operates," *Public Relations Journal,* Vol. 19 (April, 1963), pp. 7-10. The Public Relations Society of America adopted its first code in 1954, and this article discusses the code adopted in April, 1960, and describes in detail the procedures for hearing and disposing of complaints.

22. There are now several organizations of public relations people notably the Public Relations Society of America, 375 Park Avenue, New York City; the American Public Relations Association, 1010 Vermont Avenue, N. W.,

Washington, D. C.; and the American College Public Relations Association, 1785 Massachusetts Avenue, Washington, D. C.

23. See Griswold, Glenn, *op. cit.*

24. See Bristol, Lee Hastings, *Developing the Corporate Image* (New York: Scribners, 1960); Eells, Richard, "The Corporate Image in Public Relations," *California Management Review*, Vol. 1 (Summer, 1959), pp. 15-23. Hill, John W., *Corporate Public Relations: Arm of Modern Management* (New York: Harper & Brothers, 1958); Henderer, Frederic Rhodes, *A Comparative Study of P. R. Practices in Six Industrial Corporations* (Pittsburgh: University of Pittsburgh Press, 1956).

25. See Lee, Alfred McClung, "Trends in Public Relations Training," *Public Opinion Quarterly*, Vol. 11 (Spring, 1947), pp. 83-91, and Cutlip, Scott M., "History of Public Relations Education in the United States," *Journalism Quarterly*, Vol. 38 (Summer, 1961), pp. 363-70.

26. See Lewis, David L., "The Basis for that Common Body of Knowledge," *Public Relations Journal*, Vol. 19 (February, 1963), pp. 18-21.

27. See discussion of the case of Noere Motor Freight, Inc. *et al.,* versus Eastern Railroad Presidents Conference under title "Supreme Court Exonerates P. R. as Agent for Lobbying-Railroads and Byoir Win Case," *Editor and Publisher* (February 25, 1961), p. 11. See further *U. S. Law Week*, Vol. 29, No. 32 (February 21, 1961) and 155 F Supp. 768; 166 F Supp. 163.

28. The "typical" PR executive is 43 years old, has been in his present position for seven years, has a staff of nine. Eighty-two per cent of PR executives are college graduates, and all but 34 per cent started their careers in journalism, publicity, public relations, advertising, radio, TV, or teaching Journalism, English or Speech. See Barbour, R. L. *Who's Who in Public Relations* (Meriden, N. H.: PR Publishing Co., 1959), pp. XXVIII.

29. For a useful collection of definitions of public relations, see Barbour, R. L., *op. cit.*

30. "A Preview of the Bernays Public Relations' Counseling Letter." No date.

31. Cutlip, S. M., "A Re-examination of Public Relations Platitudes," *Public Relations Journal*, Vol. 19 (January, 1963), pp. 13-16.

SUPPLEMENTARY READING

BERNAYS, E. L. *Public Relations*. Norman, Oklahoma: University of Oklahoma Press, 1952.

BERNAYS, E. L. *Crystallizing Public Opinion*. New York: Boni and Liveright, 1923.

BERNAYS, E. L. *Propaganda*. New York: Horace Liveright, 1928.

BORDEN, NEIL HOPPER. *The Economic Effects of Advertising*. Homewood, Ill.: Richard D. Irwin, 1947.

BRISTOL, LEE HASTINGS. *Developing the Corporate Image*. Charles Scribner's Sons, 1960.

BURNETT, VERNE EDWIN. "Solving Public Relations Problems," *Forbes* (New York: 1952).

CANFIELD, BERTRAND R. *Public Relations: Principles, Cases, and Problems*. 3rd ed. Homewood, Ill.: Richard D. Irwin, 1960.

CARLSON, ROBERT O. "The Use of Public Relations Research by Large Corporations," *Public Opinion Quarterly*, Vol. 21 (Fall, 1957), pp. 341-49.

CUTLIP, SCOTT M., and CENTER, ALLEN H. *Effective Public Relations.* New York: Prentice-Hall, Inc., 1958.

Fortune. "The Amazing Advertising Business." Simon and Schuster, 1957.

FREY, ALBERT W. *Advertising.* 3rd ed. New York: The Ronald Press, 1961.

HARLOW, REX F. *Social Science in Public Relations.* Harper & Bros., 1957.

HARRIS, RALPH. *Advertising in Action.* London: Institute of Economic Affairs, 1962.

KELLEY, STANLEY. *Professional Public Relations and Political Power.* Baltimore: Johns Hopkins Press, 1956.

KENNER, H. J. *The Fight for Truth in Advertising.* New York: Round Table Press, 1956.

KOLBE, RICHARD LEE. "Public Relations and American Administration." Unpublished Ph. D. Thesis, Politics Department Princeton University, 1962.

LEDERER, WILLIAM J. *A Nation of Sheep.* New York: W. W. Norton & Co., Inc., 1961.

LESLY, PHILIP. *Public Relations Handbook.* 2nd ed. Englewood Cliffs, N. J.: Prentice-Hall, Inc., 1962.

MAYER, MARTIN. *Madison Avenue, U.S.A.* New York: Harper & Bros., 1958.

OGILVY, DAVID. *Confessions of an Advertising Man.* New York: Atheneum Publishers, 1963.

PACKARD, VANCE. *The Hidden Persuaders.* New York: David McKay Co., Inc., 1957.

PEASE, OTIS A. *The Responsibilities of American Advertising: Private Control and Public Influence, 1920-1940.* New Haven, Conn.: Yale University Press, 1958.

PIMLOTT, JOHN A. R. *Public Relations and American Democracy.* Princeton, N. J.: Princeton University Press, 1951.

PRESBREY, FRANK SPENCER. *The History and Development of Advertising.* Garden City, New York: Doubleday-Doran, 1929.

ROSS, IRWIN. *The Image Merchants.* Garden City, New York: Doubleday & Co., Inc., 1958.

RUBIN, BERNARD. *Public Relations as a Function of Modern Government: A Case Study of New York State Administration, 1943-1954.* 1 reel, University Microfilms, Ann Arbor, Mich.: Doctoral Dissertation Series, 1954.

RUBIN, BERNARD. *Public Relations and the Empire State: A Case Study of New York State Administration, 1943-1954.* New Brunswick, N. J.: Rutgers University Press, 1958.

SANDAGE, C. H. (ed.). *The Promise of Advertising.* Homewood, Ill.: Richard D. Irwin, Inc., 1961.

SCOTT, JAMES DACON. *Advertising Principles and Problems.* New York: Prentice-Hall, Inc., 1953.

SELDIN, JOSEPH J. *The Golden Fleece: Selling the Good Life to Americans.* New York: The Macmillan Co., 1963.

TOSDAL, HARRY R. *Selling in Our Economy.* Homewood, Ill.: Richard D. Irwin, Inc., 1957.

TURNER, ERNEST SACKVILLE. *The Shocking History of Advertising.* London: Michael Joseph, 1953.

TYLER, POYNTY (ed.). *Advertising in America.* New York: H. W. Wilson, 1959.

WALKER, S. H., and SKLAR, PAUL. *Business Finds Its Voice.* New York: Harper & Bros., 1938.

WEDDING, C. NUGENT. *Public Relations in Business.* Urbana: University of Illinois Press, 1950.

WOOD, JAMES PLAYSTED. *The Story of Advertising.* New York: The Ronald Press Co., 1958.

XII · Government and the Formation of Public Opinion

The supporters of government information are between the devil and the deep sea. If the information is poorly contrived, we do not want it. If it is well contrived, it arouses the jealousy of Congress and the press.
—ZECHARIAH CHAFEE

THE RELATIONSHIP between government and public opinion is a two-way relationship. Public opinion influences government and government influences public opinion. This relationship exists at all levels of government—national, state, and local. The relationship is not only two-way; it may also be reciprocal and cyclical; moreover, the relationship may be close and direct, or remote and mediated. It varies greatly from time to time, place to place, and with changes in surrounding circumstances and conditions.

Public opinion influences government directly through elections, referenda, and public opinion polls. Indirectly, in a manner which may be less representative and true, it brings its influence to bear through pressure groups, public hearings, personal contacts, letters, demonstrations, and especially through the press and mass media. There are also many other clues to the nature of public opinion, which may be less obvious and indicative, but which a government official, sensitive to public opinion trends, often finds important, such as changes in consumer buying habits, attendance or non-attendance at meetings, compliance or non-compliance with laws and regulations, and other forms of behavior revealing favorable or unfavorable attitudes toward government policies, personnel, and activities.

No attempt will be made at this point to discuss the influence of public opinion on government, either directly or indirectly. It may be noted in passing that, notwithstanding the accumulation of much data regarding

291

voting behavior in elections and referenda, mounting quantities of opinion survey data, and many specialized studies of pressure groups, the mass media, and other links between citizens and government, few of the many hypotheses and speculations on the influences of public opinion on government found concrete, empirical verification. Specifically, even though public opinion is expressed regarding a specific public policy, it is seldom known which officials or agencies were aware of this state of public opinion, and what, if anything, was done about this awareness.

HOW GOVERNMENT INFLUENCES PUBLIC OPINION

Government influences public opinion in many ways, but mainly by its actions and by its words. The statements, acts, and even the behavior of the President have a profound and far-flung influence on public opinion. Through press conferences, radio and TV appearances, messages to Congress, speeches and addresses of many kinds he reaches the mass public directly; through interviews, conferences, correspondence, dinners, and telephone calls he influences opinion leaders and other links between himself and the larger public. In a somewhat similar manner, Cabinet members and other high officials have an impact on public opinion, but it is not quite so extensive. It is also true that congressmen, as well as the Supreme Court justices, via hearings, speeches, judicial proceedings and opinions, legislation, and court decisions influence public opinion to a great extent. Some of this influence may be unconscious or unintended, but much of it is deliberate and quite intentional. Government influences public opinion positively and negatively, by giving and by withholding information. The growth in government information and publicity activities has been marked. Many top officials and practically all branches, departments, and agencies of the federal government employ or use specialists in press relations, ghost writing, public relations, legislative relations, in the use of mass media, and in government reporting to assist in molding and informing public opinion.

On the negative side, various policies and procedures are followed to influence opinion by withholding information. Throughout the government, classification systems serve to conceal with varying degrees of tightness a large amount of information. Many types of documents and information have been officially cut off from the public's gaze by Congressional statute. Many departments and agencies have instituted control systems to prevent unwanted disclosures. It is sometimes said that zealous publicity and public relations staffs, by flooding the channels of disclosure, often succeed in obstructing if not blocking them. It is very difficult to draw a precise line where, in the public interest, concealment should end and disclosure should begin. In a democratic, free society the presumption always favors disclosure. The burden of proof always rests on those who would conceal to justify their position.[1]

Democracies are by no means the only governments concerned with public opinion. Nor are democracies to be differentiated from dictatorships on the ground that as democracies, they primarily reflect rather than mold public opinion. The fact is that all governments seek to guide and manage public opinion to some extent. In recent years, this emphasis by the United States government on opinion leadership, government propaganda, and information has increased—some feel to an alarming extent.[2] There are many reasons for this.

GOVERNMENT CONCERN WITH PUBLIC OPINION

One is the public's increased need for information and guidance due to the increased number, as well as the technical and complex nature, of public and national problems. Secondly, as the role of government has changed from a police to a welfare state the nature of government activities has changed, calling for a wider, and more understanding support on the part of the people. This is true in many areas, especially where compliance is necessary, but sanctions are difficult to impose when non-compliance is widespread, as in the areas of civil rights, civil defense, labor relations, agricultural stabilization, and tax payments.

Also, over the course of the last three decades and especially since World War II, the United States has assumed an ever-increasing number of international responsibilities vis-à-vis European countries, its friends in other parts of the world, undeveloped countries, the United Nations, the Americas. As leader of the non-Communist world, the United States finds it imperative to do all that it can to win public support for its policies both at home and abroad.

In the fourth place, as the Executive branch of the government has taken greater initiative in legislative matters, in formulating new policies, drafting legislation, and seeking Congressional approval, it has often turned directly to the people for support. Recent examples would be President Kennedy's tax program of 1963, the Medicare legislation, federal aid to Schools, foreign aid, and civil rights. Turning to the people for support often encounters spirited and formidable opposition and competition from unofficial, organized, as well as individual, would-be leaders of opinion. To get its case before the people effectively, the government now finds itself compelled to resort to financial outlays, techniques, opinion specialists, and information campaigns.[3]

Finally, to appreciate why there has been this increasing emphasis on public opinion leadership and management, one should also take into account the changing role of public opinion itself and the technical developments within the mass media which greatly facilitate the job of opinion leadership. As the public becomes better educated, more aware of public affairs, and more immediately and directly affected by public policies relating to war and peace, to his job, his wages, his whole life and standard of living, the public becomes more interested in such policies and more articulate about them. Then over-simple, evasive, and dubious answers will not suffice. Then the public will demand more information from the government—information that explains, gives meaningful answers to problems, points up issues, spells out reasons why, indicates alternatives and implications.

Never before have government officials had the tools and streamlined facilities and equipment for molding public opinion for good or evil that they have today, and they have access to them to an extent that nongovernment individuals and groups do not. Speeches of the President and many of his top advisers have free and relatively easy access to the air waves day and night because it is news and because it is, for the media and the officials, public service. It is regrettable that the approach of the official to the use of these instruments is more often than not that of the publicist rather than the educator.

FEDERAL AGENCIES IN PUBLIC INFORMATION AND EDUCATION

From the beginning, officials of the federal government of the United States have been sensitive to public opinion trends, and they have made efforts to influence them. In the early days of the Republic the newspaper press was an organ to be solicited. Until the middle of the nineteenth century, the press was vigorously partisan, and government reporting in the press usually followed this prejudiced pattern.[4] Thomas Jefferson was keenly conscious of the influence of the press, and many papers followed the leadership of his party's *National Gazette,* founded and edited by Philip Freneau. Andrew Jackson was equally aware; his "Kitchen Cabinet" included at least three prominent newspaper editors.[5] No very detailed studies have been made of the public opinion activities of government officials during the first half of the nineteenth century. There were doubtless few, if any, specialists in publicity or press relations on the government payroll, and Cabinet members and other top officials were largely their own leaders of opinion, exercising their opinion leadership through speeches, reports to Congress and the public, through correspondence with opinion leaders, and now and then through an article in a magazine or newspaper. Some government reports, such as Hamilton's "Report on Manufactures," circulated rather widely, and by the 1830's Congressional debates were being reported quite fully in the *Niles' Register* and other journals.[6]

Gradually, federal departments and agencies became more and more aware of the need for educational and information activities. Not infrequently they were expressly instructed to acquire and diffuse information. This was true of the Department of Agriculture, established in 1862, of the U. S. Office of Education dating from 1867, the Public Health Service beginning in 1893, the Departments of Commerce and Labor, and others.[7] Not only were many of the newer agencies expressly called upon to assume these public opinion responsibilities, but they found it expedient in order to sell themselves and their job to the public. In contrast to the Departments of State, War, Navy, Treasury, Justice, and Post Office, these newer agencies like Agriculture, Commerce, and Labor primarily served a sector of the public, and it required special efforts to maintain, to say nothing of enhancing, their positions.

By the turn of the century some of the Departments and Bureaus had expanded their publicity activities considerably. Apparently, the success of the Press Chief of the Post Office Department in getting space in the newspapers was arousing some jealous concern in other departments and unfavorable attention in Congress.[8] At about the same time (1909), the U. S. Forestry Service was forbidden to supply articles to newspapers and magazines. Various people inside and outside of Congress called for a curb on publicity activities by Executive agencies, the Senate deleted funds for an advertising agent for the Marine Corps, and finally in 1913, Congress expressly barred the employment of publicity experts by government agencies unless they were specifically authorized by Congress.[9] Although this law remains on the statute books, such experts manage to find their way into government payrolls under other titles.

During World War I, the United States government embarked on a gigantic effort to win public opinion support for the war effort at home and abroad.[10] Although the problem of maintaining morale and winning support was present during previous conflicts in which the United States had been involved, the First World War dwarfed all others in comparison. Although the war's end brought a quick dismantling of the Creel Committee and its propaganda machine, the experience left its mark on government relationships with public opinion. It brought to the minds of many the power and potentialities of propaganda as an instrument of public administration at home and a tool of diplomacy abroad. Although this lesson was not taken to heart by government officials in the United States until the coming of the New Deal, it was not forgotten by the Nazis and Fascists abroad when they came to power nor by the swarms of experts in publicity and public relations who invaded the market place at home. The spokesmen of business and other special interests were quick to take full advantage of the new techniques of opinion management learned during the war. They hastened to exploit the new findings of psychology which revealed the weaknesses of human beings, their irrationality, suggestibility, and subconscious motivations, and they speedily began to use the new media of mass communication, radio and motion picture. The publicity and information activities of government agencies reverted, by and large, to their pre-war status.

The coming of the New Deal, following the Great Depression, brought a renewed emphasis in Washington on public opinion management by government agencies. The action programs to revive the economy and start the country on the road to recovery required strenuous selling campaigns. As new government agencies multiplied, publicity staffs expanded, and the rising flood of press releases and propaganda aroused apprehension, especially in anti-administration circles. The most spectacular of the propaganda campaigns of the "alphabet" agencies was the NRA or Blue Eagle campaign engineered by General Hugh Johnson, its director.[11] In scope, intensity, and method it was reminiscent of the Creel Committee and the propaganda of World War I. Older departments and agencies, as well as the newer ones, crusaded for the short and the long run goals of the Roosevelt administration as well as for the means to attain them. A study of 50 government departments and offices in 1936 revealed in cold statistical terms the rapid upsurge in the number of full-time and part-time publicity people employed by these agencies, the outpouring of press releases, pamphlets, and other printed materials, and the variety of tools, techniques, and media used. Many agencies, especially the newer ones, made use of motion pictures, documentaries, radio broadcasts, exhibits, and public opinion surveys for the first time.

Meanwhile, developments overseas grew steadily more menacing. The rise of Fascism, and especially the coming to power of Hitler, followed by increasing tensions in Europe, finally touched nerves of concern in the United States as evidence came to light of Nazi inroads in Latin America. In 1937, a Division of Cultural Relations was established in the Department of State to bring the Americas closer together, not only culturally, but also politically, to check further Nazi infiltration. This marked the beginning of a succession of United States agencies created to deal with public opinion and propaganda problems arising before and during World War II, which continued during the Cold War which followed. This story is told elsewhere,[12] but suffice it to say here that in contrast to World War I, the major emphasis in World War II was on public opinion problems abroad, rather than at home. The Domestic Branch of the Office of War Information dwindled in importance as the war continued, whereas the Overseas Branch grew in stature and responsibility by leaps and bounds.

Following the war the public opinion problems of international and foreign policy of the United States government remained paramount, almost crucial. To handle them the United States Information Agency was created and it continues to the present.[13] Domestically, however, the departments and agencies continued to handle their public opinion problems individually, with such guidance and direction as the President and his assistants might give. Since World War II, there has been no phenomenal expansion of staff to handle public opinion problems on the home front. There has, however, been some expansion, and some refinements in method. Departments and agencies seem to have a greater awareness of their public relations problems as distinct from purely publicity and information problems.

From time to time surveys have been made of the information and publicity staffs of federal government agencies, and the amounts spent on their work. Precision in these matters is difficult because some of the personnel of these staffs are part-time workers, because definitions of the publicity function will differ, and accounting procedures for allocating funds to this function are often debatable. Certain conclusions, however, seem convincing. The Department of Defense and its principal components, the Army, Navy, and Air Force, together, have a far larger publicity and information staff than all the other federal agencies combined.[14]

INFORMATION PERSONNEL: ARMY, NAVY, AIR FORCE

	OFFICERS	ENLISTED MEN	CIVILIANS
Department of Defense	100		
Army	600	2,150	250 ± 50
Navy	212	500	
Air Force	650	1,400	230
	1,562	4,050	480 ± 50
	(Grand Total: 6,092 ± 50)		

The following civilian departments and agencies usually have the largest publicity budgets and staffs:

INFORMATION PERSONNEL: SELECTED CIVILIAN
DEPARTMENTS AND AGENCIES AS OF 1952

1. Agriculture	
Department	120
Principal Bureaus	269
2. Department of State (domestic)	198
3. Commerce	
Department	12
Principal Bureaus	68
4. Interior	
Department	9
Principal Bureaus	66

5. Federal Civil Defense Agency	52
6. Veterans Administration	41
7. Treasury	36
8. Atomic Energy Commission	36
9. Labor	29
10. United States Information Agency (domestic)	23
11. Housing and Home Finance	21
12. Post Office	15
13. Justice	13
14. Tennessee Valley Administration	12
Grand Total	1,020

RECENT TRENDS

What have been the outstanding trends in the public opinion activities of national government agencies in recent years? Possibly the most significant has been a greater sensitivity to public opinion developments, a greater appreciation of the need for creating and maintaining good relations with the major publics whom the agency contacts, and the need for listening to, as well as merely reciting to, the publics. This greater awareness of public opinion and its importance pervades the governmental hierarchy from the President down. It is reflected in the use of press conferences, the attention given to public opinion surveys and other indices of public opinion, in improvements in government reporting, in efforts to explain more fully the content of public policies and the reasons for them, in higher quality government reports, in the more frequent use of representative advisory commissions, and in the use of better trained personnel, such as public opinion analysts, public relations experts, radio and TV technicians, authors, and scholarly researchers.

Secondly, there seems to have been a somewhat greater appreciation of the over-all scope of the information and public relations function of a governmental agency. On the information side, the job is finding out what information the public wants and needs, and making this information available. Often in the scramble to get news stories for reporters, the real information the public needs is lost sight of. The information function no longer emphasizes solely its publicity feature but its educational obligation as well. This is more true of the Departments of Agriculture and Interior and some of their bureaus than it is of other government units.[15] The Defense Department, as well as Justice and Treasury, have yet to perceive the broad outlines and perspectives of their true informative functions.

There is also a clearer understanding of the true nature of the public relations function: the objectives and the means available for creating and maintaining good relations with contact publics of the agency. This involves a clear identification of these publics, a careful study of them, particularly their attitudes and opinions, an analysis of the causes for bad relations where they do exist, and finally, a sincere effort to remove those causes where it is in the public interest to do so. Many departments and agencies maintain close liaison with relevant publics, particularly organized publics, through conferences, advisory and consulting committees, and meetings of all kinds.

In the third place, although there has been a leveling off in growth of agency public opinion staffs since the war (in most civilian agencies the changes have been small), there have been refinements in method, some improvement in quality of output, and the use of a greater variety of media. The evidence of far-sighted public relations and public opinion planning is spotty and virtually nonexistent in some agencies.

It is significant to mention at this time a trend which is primarily outside the realm of government, but which affects the relationships of government and public opinion markedly: the considerable increase and improvement in private and unofficial reporting of public affairs. Certain newspapers, notably the *New York Times,* the *Washington Post,* the *Christian Science Monitor,* the *Wall Street Journal,* the *St. Louis Post Dispatch,* and a few others have provided more and better coverage. Weekly news magazines, private news services, publications of organized groups, to say nothing of television, radio, popular magazines, and trade publications, all carry an increasing amount of news of public affairs.

PUBLICITY OBJECTIVES OF GOVERNMENT AGENCIES

The developing and changing relationships between government and public opinion have left a number of old problems, modified them to some extent perhaps, and created new ones. One important problem persists: the objectives, goals, and aims of the government toward public opinion problems. In his study of federal publicity, published in 1939, James L. McCamy found that the 50 departments and agencies he surveyed had one or more of the following publicity or public opinion objectives:[16] (1) to capture public attention; (2) to influence legislation; (3) to answer attacks; (4) to distribute publicity among or for the clients of an agency; (5) to report, without particular aims, routine news of government; and (6) to attempt infrequently to avoid publicity. This catalogue of aims is still valid, in all probability, but it suggests quite clearly the absence of over-all planning and the lack of a positive, public relations approach to the information and publicity problems of a government agency. The ultimate public opinion goals of an agency are to be found first of all within a public relations context, and secondarily, in terms of information and education needs. The public relations goal is always to promote and maintain good relations with the important publics of the agency, so far as this can be done without jeopardizing the public interest. This may involve more and better information, but the information problem is usually much broader than this. It requires that the agency carefully determine the informational needs of the several pertinent publics, find out to what extent those needs are being met, and plan the program necessary to meet those needs.

Of the six aims actually pursued by government agencies, according to McCamy, only two seem to have much to do with meeting actual information needs of the public, i.e., distributing publicity and reporting routine government news. The remaining aims are essentially unrelated to these needs or contrary to them, such as capturing public attention, influencing legislation, answering attacks, avoiding publicity. Very few, if any, government departments or agencies seem to grasp fully the dimensions of their public relations and information job. The general public, and specialized publics as well, are woefully ignorant of governmental departments and agencies, of what they are trying to do, how they are doing it, what it is costing, how successful they are, what problems are encountered, what critical decisions are faced, the alternative answers, general trends in the areas served by the agencies, the centers of power and responsibility within the agencies, pressures on it from outside, and many, many more aspects. Now and then, here and there, some of this information comes to light in dramatic news stories, in the revelations of probing columnists, and the findings of Congressional committees. For the most part, however, the job —of keeping the public fully informed regarding what it should know to decide intelligently how good and efficient its government is—is not being done. A few illustrations will underscore this point and the size of the problems.

The Defense Department is responsible for spending over half of the national budget, yet the procedures followed in spending these huge sums, in letting contracts, in stockpiling, and in weapon selection are largely hidden, even from congressmen, to say nothing of the general public. How can the public, even Congress, possibly appraise intelligently the work of this Department under these circumstances? The Department of State is similarly lacking in a positive information program, and the public remains largely ignorant of what our policies and commitments are in many areas of the world, what the critical issues and problems are, where the centers of responsible decision making are, and so on. Only recently has Congress undertaken to find out what pressures are being brought on the American public, as well as on the Department of State and other government agencies, by foreign lobbyists and pressure groups.[17]

A few other evidences of informational needs are: (1) ignorance of certain results of the present tax policies of the federal government, i.e., revenue by income groups, compliance by income groups, the administration's new tax program; (2) the policy of the government regarding nuclear weapons; (3) business practices inimical to the welfare of the consumer, such as false advertising, misbranding of products, false weights and measures; (4) the facts behind labor relations, i.e., extent of collusion between unions and management; (5) economic effects of strikes on the parties and the communities concerned; (6) the actual role of government; (7) the facts behind the FCC, i.e., outside pressures, internal decision making, obstacles to public interest broadcasting; (8) the facts behind the AEC, FTC, SEC, and regulatory commissions. With the possible exception of the Department of Agriculture and certain divisions of the Interior and Labor Departments, information programs seem to be formulated, not in terms of what the public wants and needs to know, but what the agencies want them to know. If a more positive approach is to be achieved, it will probably have to come by Congressional mandate. However much departmental heads may want such an approach (it is by no means certain that many do) the ability to carry it out will depend in large part on Congressional appropriations. Congress can make or break an effective information and public relations program by control of its purse strings.

CENSORSHIP AND SECRECY

A second public opinion problem of government agencies is that of censorship and secrecy. As indicated before, in discussing trends, this is a problem of long standing. It appears to be primarily a problem of balance: the need for weighing the public interest in government secrecy over against its concern and desire for disclosure. The general principle seems to be that the balance should be tipped in favor of disclosure and open government, except when the need for withholding information is proven. In certain matters the need for secrecy is generally accepted, as in the case of information of value to the enemy in war time, some military and diplomatic records, FBI material, crop records and tax information, and also some types of business intelligence submitted to regulatory agencies relating to financial records, trade secrets, and technical processes.[18]

Congress itself has really been responsible for much administrative secrecy, although at times it argues vehemently against practices of administrative agencies which impede its work, as for example in the area of defense policy. In setting up government departments and bureaus Congress often authorizes or prescribes information and educational functions. The press has generally been very critical of government secrecy, especially when it is thought that such secrecy is unnecessary, or being used to hide inefficiency, incompetence, or corruption.[19] Another group quite critical of government secrecy are the scientists who have been increasingly active in public policy making since World War II. They argue that such secrecy stifles technological progress, especially when imposed on scientific information, and that it is really unnecessary and futile.[20]

This problem of censorship and secrecy is a continuing one. While there are many areas of widespread agreement, there will always be marginal ones where it is difficult to decide whether to hide or disclose. Since there seems to be a natural tendency in large and small scale bureaucracies, to conceal rather than reveal, to classify more readily than to declassify, it may be that the public has more to fear from secrecy than from overzealous pressure from Congress and the press in the other direction. The problem remains, and the burden of proof will continue to rest on those who wish to withhold information. The question remains who shall decide when argument and negotiation between press or Congress on the one side and department or agency on the other fails? Should Congress itself be the arbiter, and if so how could it enforce its decisions? Should the matter be decided by the courts? Should there be an independent, intermediate authority, and if so, what should be its composition and powers? [21]

GOVERNMENT PROPAGANDA

Closely related to the two problems just considered is the problem of government propaganda. Specifically, this is the problem of deciding where the line should be drawn in the public interest between desirable and undesirable propaganda activities by a government department or agency. During the New Deal period in the 1930's executive agencies of the government were subjected to much criticism for allegedly exceeding the limits of sound propaganda policy. Since then individual departments have been censured for propaganda excesses, notably the military in its efforts to promote Universal Military Training after World War II.[22]

In this connection the word "propaganda" is used in a rather narrow, specific sense to mean the spreading and dissemination of ideas and programs by the extensive use of suggestion and persuasive appeals to emotions. Within wide limits there is seldom much criticism of departmental distribution of specific facts and information, provided there is a demonstrable need for such, and waste is avoided. The problem really arises when an agency goes beyond this to use high-powered, persuasive techniques to win public support for a policy it favors. This the military agencies seemed to do on behalf of Universal Military Training. When that happens, few if any non-governmental institutions or groups, because of fewer resources, can compete on an equitable basis. A distinction can be made between official propaganda for policies and programs *after* they become law, when propaganda of a persuasive kind may be justified as a proper instrument to obtain widespread compliance and enforcement, and propaganda used *before* Congress has acted, while Congress and the public are trying to decide among several alternative policies. To allow government propaganda to enter the market place in large supply may obstruct the making of enlightened decisions by either the public or Congress.[23]

Even though the distinction is used between a policy on and not on the statute books, for in principle official propaganda for the latter is forbidden, a number of knotty problems arise in trying to apply the principle. Does this mean that top officials of a department or agency may not go beyond answering the requests of Congress for information and may only disseminate bare facts to the public? Does it mean that they are denied the right to try and win public or Congressional support for a program they believe in by using as persuasive techniques as possible? What limits should be placed upon their use of the resources of the department, in terms of money, time, and personnel, for propaganda purposes? Moreover, if the use of propaganda for a policy is contrary to the public interest before it becomes law, why will not the same dangers exist to some degree if a department is allowed to go all out for the policy once it has been made a law? Might not government propaganda, in such a case, be used to overpower efforts to change a law which may be backed by fewer propaganda resources? Of course there will always be the difficulty of differentiating in practice between so-called mere facts on the one hand and information and propaganda on the other.

ADMINISTRATION

A few more salient problems may be touched on rather sketchily. Problems have to do with the internal organization and administration of the public opinion function within the agency.[24] To what extent should the organization and control of public relations, publicity, and information be centralized, and to what extent should they be left in the hands of functional or regional divisions? How can the optimum amount of co-operation and co-ordination be obtained? What should be the relation between public opinion activities, and the over-all departmental making of policy? Should the top level of public opinion administration mesh directly with top policy-makers in the department, or at a lower level? And there will always be problems of personnel and finance. How can the proper number of well-trained and qualified public opinion administrators and specialists be obtained? This, and related problems of recruitment, promotion, transfer, removal, and similar personnel problems are not too unlike other problems throughout government service, though the newness of the public opinion function makes some of these issues difficult.

The problem of finance is difficult, and to some extent the same in its relation to public opinion operations as it is to other governmental responsibilities. To get adequate funds it is necessary to persuade Congress and the public of the need for implementing a more broadly based, positive public opinion program than is usually envisaged by Congressional lawmakers. This is often difficult, not only because of the inability or unwillingness of Congress to think in these positive terms regarding government information and publicity, but because of certain apprehensions. Congressmen often fear that resources appropriated for departmental public opinion operations may be used for personal promotion, Congressional lobbying, departmental empire building, or for politically partisan purposes. They also fear at times that these activities may threaten the representative system of government in that they will give the Executive branch of the government too much power, and thereby enable the administration to influence, if not undermine, the relationship between legislators and their constituencies. The legislator's influence and ability to advise his constituents will be lessened by increasing information, advice, and propaganda from Executive agencies. The prevailing attitudes and opinions of his constituents may change, and he may be voted out of office!

EXTERNAL RELATIONS

There is another group of public opinion problems that arise out of the external relations of government agencies: relations with Congress and other government agencies, relations with private groups, such as agency publics, and relations with communication media. Some of the problems arising out of relations with Congress have been mentioned, such as Congressional hostility or suspicion of the public opinion function, unwillingness to appropriate adequate funds, and disagreements arising because of agency refusals to disclose particular kinds of information. Another important problem is the problem of control over the public opinion operation. Is budgetary control by Congress, by the Budget Bureau, or control through investigations and hearings the best that can be found? What would be the advantages and disadvantages of making a committee, such as the Moss committee,[25] a permanent, continuous, watchdog committee, continually auditing and advising with respect to over-all government public opinion activities on the domestic, home front? Would a non-Congressional private member advisory committee similar to that for the U. S. Information Agency and public opinion activities abroad, be desirable in place of or as an addition to the Congressional committee?

Each department and agency has several publics with which it is closely related, either because it services them, as the Department of Agriculture services many groups of farmers with information, advice, and training, or it regulates them as, for example, the Interstate Commerce Commission regulates the railroads and the Federal Communications Commission communication agencies, or because it is sponsored by, or depends for much of its support upon them. Labor Unions and the Department of Labor would be a case in point. Often the relationship with a private group comprises all three aspects: service, regulation, and support.

Communication

Finally, many public opinion problems arise, as shown previously, from an agency's relationship with Congress and other government units. Some of the problems arising out of the Congressional relationship have already been discussed, problems of finance, control, sharing information, hostility and suspicion. Similarly, there are problems that arise because of communication failures between and among government bureaus and departments—lack of co-ordination, misunderstandings, contradictions. Various solutions have been suggested, from the setting up of a central clearing house and control agency, to a more informed co-ordination through interdepartmental conferences. During the early days of World War II, the domestic branch of the Office of War Information tried, rather unsuccessfully, to give an impetus to greater uniformity in objectives, publicity content, and procedures. Since then, with more or less success, the Office of the President has served as a clearing house, to give guidance and some semblance of a common purpose to the public opinion activities of the various government departments, bureaus, agencies, and offices.

NOTES FOR CHAPTER 12

Epigraph. Zechariah Chafee, *Government and Mass Communications* (1947) p. 777.
1. See Rourke, F. E., *Secrecy and Publicity: Dilemmas of Democracy* (Baltimore: The Johns Hopkins Press, 1961).
2. See Krock, Arthur, "Mr. Kennedy's Management of the News," *Fortune Magazine,* Vol. 67 (March, 1963), pp. 82ff. Presidential press secretary, Pierre Salinger, vigorously denied news management charges, claiming that the nation's newspaper, television, and radio editors determine what their readers will read and what their listeners and viewers will hear." *Washington Post,* March 24, 1962.
3. This was concretely and dramatically illustrated in the fight over Medicare. See Kelley, Stanley, *Professional Public Relations and Political Power, op. cit.*
4. See Mott, Frank Luther, *American Journalism, op. cit.*
5. Amos Kendall, editor of the Kentucky *Argus of the Western World*; Isaac Hill, editor of the New Hampshire *Patriot*; and Francis P. Blair, editor of the *Washington Globe*. See "Kitchen Cabinet Portraits," chap. 6 in Bowers, Claude G., *The Party Battles of the Jackson Period* (Boston: Houghton Mifflin Co., 1922).
6. *Niles' Weekly Register* (1811-49), published in Baltimore, Md.

7. In 1862, the newly created U. S. Department of Agriculture was instructed by Congress "to acquire and diffuse information" and in 1867, the U. S. Office of Education was instructed to give "information regarding the organization and management of schools."

8. See McCamy, James L., *Government Publicity* (Chicago: University of Chicago Press, 1939).

9. 38 U. S. Stat. 212 (Oct. 22, 1913).

10. See Creel, George, *How We Advertised America* (New York: Harper and Brothers, 1920).

11. "Almost every city, hamlet, and village in the United States has been organized by its leading citizens, and an army of a million and a half volunteer workers is either now in the field or ready to take the field to insure the success of the President's reemployment campaign." See "Pointed Paragraphs for Speakers," The Blue Eagle Drive, Speakers' Division, Bureau of Public Relations, Washington, 1933.

12. See Childs, Harwood L., "Public Information and Opinion," Sec. 5 in "American Government in Wartime: The First Year," *American Political Science Review,* Vol. 37 (February, 1943), pp. 56-68, and in the following chapter 13.

13. See Dizard, Wilson P., *The Strategy of Truth: The Story of the USIS* (Washington, Public Affairs Press, 1961).

14. See Kolbe, Richard, "Public Relations and American Administration," (Unpublished Ph.D. Thesis, Dept. of Politics, Princeton University, 1962).

15. See Harding, T. S., "Informational Techniques of the Department of Agriculture," *Public Opinion Quarterly,* Vol. 1 (January, 1937), pp. 83-96.

16. *Government Publicity, op. cit.*

17. From time to time the Secretary of State holds press conferences, and the outpouring of press releases is prodigious. But such efforts are feeble in comparison with the needs of the situation, and with the requisites of a well-developed, informational policy. See Cohen, Bernard C., *The Press and Foreign Policy* (Princeton, N. J.: Princeton University Press, 1963).

18. See Rourke, F. E., *Secrecy and Publicity: Dilemmas of Democracy* (Baltimore: Johns Hopkins Press, 1961), and Summers, R. E. (Comp.), *Federal Information Controls in Peacetime* (New York: H. W. Wilson Company, 1949).

19. See annual *Proceedings* of the American Society of Newspaper Editors for frequent reports and discussions of the work of ASNE's Freedom of Information Committee.

20. See *Bulletin of the Atomic Scientists,* especially during 1949 and 1950. Also, Gilpin, Robert G. Jr., *Scientists and National Policy* (New York: Columbia University Press, 1964).

21. On September 23, 1961, the House Government Information Subcommittee reported on thirty-four cases of what it regarded as unwarranted restriction of public information, concluding that "a thin veneer of new leadership, superimposed on the massive bureaucracy, is not enough to prevent secrecy-minded career officials from equating secrecy with good government." *New York Times,* September 24, 1961.

22. See U. S. Congress, House, Committee on Expenditures in Executive Departments, *Investigation of War Department Publicity and Propaganda in Relation to U. M. T.,* 1947.

23. See Catlin, G. E. E., "Propaganda as a Function of Democratic Govern-

ment," *Propaganda and Dictatorship,* ed. Harwood L. Childs, chap. VI (Princeton, N. J.: Princeton University Press, 1936), pp. 125-45.
24. See Campbell, H. C., "N. Y.'s Public Information Council," *State Government,* Vol. 23 (October, 1950), pp. 224-25.
25. U. S. Congress, House, Subcommittee of the Committee on Government Operations, 84th Congress, 1st and 2nd Sess., 1955-56; 85th Congress, 1st and 2nd Sess., 1956-57; 86th Congress, 1st Session, 1958.

SUPPLEMENTARY READING

ALPERT, HARRY. "Opinion and Attitude Surveys in the U. S. Government," *Public Opinion Quarterly,* Vol. 16 (Spring, 1952), pp. 33-41.
ALPERT, HARRY, and others. "Congressional Use of Polls: A Symposium," *Public Opinion Quarterly,* Vol. 18 (Summer, 1954), pp. 121-42.
CARROLL, GORDON. "Dr. Roosevelt's Propaganda Trust," *American Mercury,* Vol. 42 (Sept., 1937), pp. 1-31; Vol. 42 (Oct., 1937), pp. 194-213; Vol. 42 (Nov., 1937), pp. 319-36.
CATLIN, GEORGE E. E. "Propaganda as a Function of Democratic Government," in *Propaganda and Dictatorships.* Edited by Harwood L. Childs. Princeton, N. J.: Princeton University Press, 1936.
CHAFEE, Z. *Government and Mass Communications.* 2 vols. Chicago: University of Chicago Press, 1947.
CORNWELL, ELMER E., JR. "Wilson, Creel, and the Presidency," *Public Opinion Quarterly,* Vol. 23 (Summer, 1959), pp. 189-202.
GRAVES, W. B. "Public Reporting in the American States," *Public Opinion Quarterly,* Vol. 2 (April, 1938), pp. 211-28.
HARDING, T. S. "Informational Techniques of the Department of Agriculture," *Public Opinion Quarterly,* Vol. 1 (Jan., 1937), pp. 83-96.
INKELES, ALEX. *Public Opinion in Soviet Russia.* Cambridge, Mass.: Harvard University Press, 1958.
KROCK, ARTHUR. "Mr. Kennedy's Management of the News," *Fortune,* Vol. 67 (March, 1963), pp. 82ff.
LAROCHE, CHESTER J. *et al.* "Should the Government Advertise?" *Public Opinion Quarterly,* Vol. 6 (Winter, 1942), pp. 511-36.
MCCAMY, JAMES L. *Government Publicity.* Chicago: University of Chicago Press, 1939.
MIMMO, DAN D. *News Gathering in Washington.* New York: Atherton Press, 1964.
PFIFFNER, JOHN M. *Public Administration.* Part V. New York: The Ronald Press Company, 1935.
PIMLOTT, J. A. R. *Public Relations and American Democracy.* Princeton, N. J.: Princeton University Press, 1951.
POLLARD, JAMES E. *The Presidents and the Press.* New York: The Macmillan Co., 1947.
POLLARD, JAMES E. "The White House News Conference as a Channel of Communication," *Public Opinion Quarterly,* Vol. 15 (Winter, 1951-52), pp. 663-78.
ROURKE, F. E. *Secrecy and Publicity: Dilemmas of Democracy.* Baltimore: Johns Hopkins Press, 1961.
RUBIN, BERNARD. *Public Relations in The Empire State.* New Brunswick, N. J.: Rutgers University Press, 1958.

SHILS, EDWARD A. *The Torment of Secrecy*. Chicago: The Free Press of Glencoe, Ill., 1956.

STANLEY, EDWARD, and SULLIVAN, LAWRENCE. *Report on the Information Services in the Executive Branch of the Government*. A report to the Commission on Organization of the Executive Branch of the Government, Washington, D. C., 1948.

SUMMERS, R. E. (Comp.). *Federal Information Controls in Peacetime*. New York: H. W. Wilson Co., 1949.

U. S. Congress, House Committee on Expenditures in the Executive Departments. *Hearings: Investigation of War Department Publicity and Propaganda in Relation to Universal Military Training*. 80th Congress, 2nd Sess., Jan. 14, 1948.

XIII · Public Opinion
and Public Policy

*The sharp definition of the role of public opinion as it affects different
kinds of policies under different types of situations presents an analytical
problem of extraordinary difficulty.*

—V. O. KEY, JR.

MANY YEARS AGO Jeremy Bentham wrote that the principal problem of public opinion was not to find out what it is but to maximize
the rectitude of the decisions by it. Our great educational system, public
and private, is supposedly dedicated to this task of enlightenment. Starting
with some conception of rectitude, it disseminates knowledge, seeks new
facts and truths, and imparts skills.

For those who believe in democracy, it is also important to find out what
public opinion is, that it may be translated into public policy, if not directly,
at least indirectly. Today in the United States, few believe that many (if
any) public questions should be referred directly to the voters for decision,
though some states permit this procedure to a limited extent. There does
seem to be a general feeling that public opinion should influence public
policy indirectly, through chosen representatives of the people, but a surprising and increasing number of students of government, in company
with Walter Lippmann, question the wisdom of giving mass opinion any
role in the determination of public policy. Democracy, in the sense of rule
by public opinion, seems to be facing not only external, military dangers,
but internal threats to its self-confidence from various types of elitists,
aristocrats, and authoritarians. Before popular government, government by
public opinion, is allowed to go by default, it seems prudent to try and
reassess the role of public opinion, both from the point of view of what
it actually is today, what it should be in the light of its changed competence,
and the kind of issues it is capable of deciding. This chapter contains com-

ment on the first part of this question—what is the relationship between public opinion, in the sense of the collective opinions of the American voters, and public policy in the United States today?

For more than twenty-five years polling agencies have been making nation-wide surveys of public opinion, and a wealth of opinion data has been collected regarding the views of the American people on issues of domestic and foreign policy. The question arises to what extent, if at all, public opinion actually influences public policy. There has been much theoretical speculation regarding the answer but very few hard facts. To obtain the facts some students have been making case studies of specific public policies and the relation of public opinion to them.[1] It is difficult to separate the influence of public opinion itself from other influences, and it is not easy to trace the influence of public opinion from the voters to the decision-makers. Conclusions, therefore, are very tentative. They may suggest, however, pertinent questions for those accustomed to dealing in generalities.

INFLUENCE OF PUBLIC OPINION ON PUBLIC POLICY

References will now be made to six of these case studies: those dealing with nuclear testing policy, the Kennedy-Steel dispute, federal aid to education, Cuba, Medicare, and military expenditures. In each case a definite time period was designated, and an effort was made, with the data available, to show the relationship between trends in public opinion and changes in public policy.

Nuclear Testing

In the case of nuclear testing the period selected was from March, 1954, to December, 1962.[2] The major United States policy decisions during this period were: (1) a decision announced on August 22, 1958, to suspend tests on a year by year basis starting October 31, 1958; (2) an announcement on December 29, 1959, refusing to extend the ban on tests during 1960; (3) announcement on September 5, 1961, of the resumption of underground tests and tests in laboratories; (4) announcement on March 2, 1962, of an intention to resume atmospheric tests. Public opinion during this period was in favor of tests until the latter part of 1958; it then became strongly favorable to a ban on tests until 1962, when it again favored tests. During 1962, however, the sentiment in favor of tests tended to weaken slightly.

The study of the interrelationship of public opinion and public policy in this case seemed to indicate that:

(a) Public opinion played a minor and subordinate role in influencing policy decisions partly because of the need for official secrecy; and the obvious complexity and technical nature of the problem, as well as the exigencies of relations with other countries. In at least two instances, important decisions were made affecting testing without majority support; namely, President Kennedy's last two decisions regarding the resumption of testing.

(b) The study showed that policy decisions themselves often had a decisive influence on public opinion, instead of the other way round. Also, specific events at home and abroad and the content of mass media often had a simultaneous effect on both public opinion and the decision-maker.

(c) The study suggested that perhaps the principal functions of public opinion were: (1) to delineate the general direction of policy and to isolate certain basic objectives; (2) to determine the outer limits of permissible government action; and (3) to decide certain crucial issues which government experts or elites avoid until public opinion has crystallized.

The Kennedy-Steel Controversy

The second case study concerned the Kennedy-Steel controversy in April, 1962.[3] Following collective bargaining negotiations which began on February 15th of that year, new contracts were signed on April 7. On April 10, United States Steel announced an increase in the price of steel a few hours after President Kennedy had been told of the intention to do so. The President's reaction was quick and angry. Steps were taken at once to induce United States Steel to rescind its action, including appeals to the public, launching government investigations of steel practices in setting prices, and direct pressures on steel company officials. On April 13, Inland Steel announced that it would not follow United States Steel and raise its prices. In a short time other companies made similar announcements or rescinded previously announced price raises. Finally, United States Steel capitulated, and the crisis was over.

Since the crisis and President Kennedy's actions could not have been foreseen by the pollsters, the only polls dealing directly with the issue came afterward. On May 19, the Gallup poll reported that of the 76 million adults (7 out of 10) who were familiar with the President's moves in the dispute, 58 per cent approved, 22 per cent disapproved, 5 per cent were mixed in their feelings, and the remaining 15 per cent had no opinion. The "blue collar" workers were much more favorable to the President (67 per cent) than business and professional people (34 per cent and 45 per cent). Some light is thrown on the public opinion impact of President Kennedy's decisions by trends in his popularity during this period: the monthly popularity index which had been 77, 78, 79, 77 in January through April dropped to 73 in May following the crisis.

What conclusions can be drawn in this case regarding the interrelationships of public opinion and public policy?

(a) This is quite definitely a case where public opinion had very little if any direct impact on the formation of public policy. The President's reaction to Roger Blough's announcement of United States Steel's intention to raise prices was immediate. There was no time to take a poll, and there is no evidence that Kennedy was guided by previous, anticipatory surveys. This is not to say that public opinion had no influence, since the President undoubtedly knew or thought he knew, from experience and numerous clues, how large segments of the population would respond if they were polled.

(b) In this case events, especially government actions and decisions, had a profound effect on public opinion. It underscored the role played by leadership, especially that of the President of the United States, in molding public opinion. It is estimated that more than 65 million people were tuned in to President Kennedy's press conference on April 8 when he explained and undertook to justify the government's actions in the controversy. In making decisions the policy-maker not only tries to predict what the public's reaction will be, but he also tries to estimate how successful he will be in molding a public opinion that will approve the decisions.

(c) In addition to the nation-wide Gallup poll mentioned earlier, there were other cruder indices of the public's reactions to this dispute, such as newspaper polls, industry-wide surveys, letters to the editor and to the participant parties, newspaper editorials, even stock market prices, and the election returns in the November Congressional elections. These indices point to two things: (1) those who write letters to newspapers or the participants tend to be unrepresentative of the general public and to have very strong feelings about the issue; and (2) the over-all, average opinion of the public may conceal wide differences of opinion between subgroups and individuals. As might be expected business opinion was more favorable to increases in the price of steel and less favorable to President Kennedy's actions than other groups were.

Federal Aid to Education

The study of public opinion in relation to government policy on federal aid to education served to confirm the findings of other case studies and to suggest additional aspects of the relationship.[4] The period covered in this case was from 1949 to 1961. The question of federal aid to education came to the fore during the thirties under the New Deal, and resumed after World War II. In 1949, some legislative progress was made in Congress until stopped by House action. In 1950, the so-called "impacted area" law was passed providing aid to areas where new United States government installations brought sudden increases in population and created over-taxed school facilities. This law was extended from time to time. In 1956, a rider denying aid to segregated areas was defeated in the House, 224 to 194. In 1958, partly due to Russian satellite successes, Congress passed the National Defense Education Act (NDEA) containing special aid provisions. In 1960, two different aid bills passed the House and Senate, only to fail because the House Rules Committee would not allow the House bill to go to Conference Committee. President Kennedy had come out strongly for federal aid to education in his 1960 campaign, and soon after his inauguration a special task force report brought the whole issue forcibly to public and Congressional attention. The religious side of the issue was debated vehemently. Again, the House Rules Committee brought the drive for a comprehensive federal aid program to a halt by refusing eight to seven to send the bill to the floor.

Throughout the period nation-wide polls of public opinion on the issue were taken, revealing general approval of federal aid in principle, down to 1960. In February, 1956, for example, 67 per cent approved federal aid generally for school construction; in February, 1957, the percentage rose to 76 and dropped to 65 in 1960. Breakdowns of the poll data revealed that some segments changed their opinions during this period, notably the independent voters who moved from the lowest degree of support to first place. Throughout the period the Democrats were more in favor than the Republicans, and Catholics supported federal aid, even if private schools would be denied such aid. The opinions of Southern voters were definitely affected by whether or not segregated areas were to be granted or denied aid. The last nation-wide poll taken before the defeat of the Kennedy program in July, 1961, was more specific than previous ones and revealed that on the public versus private school issue 57 per cent favored aid to public schools only, 36 per cent to both. Only 23 per cent favored aid to integrated schools only, 68 per cent to both.

This study disclosed certain aspects of the relationship between public opinion and public policy not mentioned before.

(a) Public opinion may not always be translated into public policy quickly and without distortion, because of blocks in the channels between public opinion and public policy, notably in Congress. On at least two occasions the Rules Committee of the House was able to halt legislative progress, apparently contrary to the majority opinion of the public and Congress as a whole. There are many other built-in obstacles to a speedy and truly representative translation of public opinion into public policy, such as the committee system in Congress, certain formal parliamentary procedures, the unrepresentative composition of the Senate, and to some extent of the House.

(b) This study also demonstrates that a public which approves a policy in principle may change its views considerably after discussion reveals more clearly particular implications of that policy, or unforeseen consequences.

(c) The study also shows that as discussion of a policy becomes protracted and pressure groups enter the fray, they exert considerable influence on both public opinion, the decision-makers, and the channels connecting the two.

Cuba

The case of Cuba well illustrates the point that the relationship between public opinion and public policy can be quite varied and flexible, and also that it is generally a two-way relationship, cyclical, and dynamic.[5] The period covered in this study was from January 7, 1959, when the United States formally recognized the Cuban Revolutionary government under Fidel Castro through November 9, 1962, when President Kennedy announced that Russian missiles had been removed from Cuba. For the sake of convenience, each of the four years will be considered separately, and the relationship of public opinion and public policy discussed accordingly.

During 1959, public opinion, partly because of its lack of certainty and unity, had very little, if any, effect on United States policy toward Cuba. Similarly, public policy, because of indecisiveness and possibly complacency, seems to have had little impact on public opinion, in developing a trend. This uncertainty of public opinion was revealed in a poll taken in mid-August showing that 20 per cent of the American people were favorable to Castro, 48 per cent unfavorable, and 32 per cent uncertain.

During the early part of 1960 the mounting hostility of the American people toward the Castro regime seems to have had an influence on policy. In May the Mutual Security Act was passed, barring aid to Cuba except when the President believed such aid would be in the national interest, and it granted the President the power to reduce sugar quotas, which he did to the vanishing point by the end of the year. By mid-August 81 per cent of the American people were opposed to the Cuban leader. Public opinion influenced policy, and policy, together with events especially in Cuba, influenced public opinion.

The year 1961 illustrated still further the variety of relationships which may exist between public opinion and public policy. Early in January, weeks before leaving office, President Eisenhower broke off diplomatic relations with Cuba—a policy decision made without consulting public opinion, but one undoubtedly supported by it. The Bay of Pigs episode showed what may happen when, for reasons of national security, the public cannot be consulted. Differences of opinion within the Administration, plus uncertainty regarding the state of public opinion, prevented the formation and pursuance of a strong, positive policy. Although this episode turned out badly, a subsequent poll showed that 61 per cent of the people said they approved the Administration's handling of the situation. This points up another significant aspect of the relationship between public opinion and public policy—the marked tendency of the public to fall in line to support a policy or decision once it has become a *fait accompli*.

The tractors-for-prisoners-trade proposed by Castro on May 17 aroused a flood of protests, and a Gallup poll, reported July 7, showed 67 per cent opposing the deal. In this instance, public opinion may well have caused the Administration to veto the idea. The airplane hijackings in May, July, and August also caused much resentment, and early in August, Congress provided drastic penalties, including the death penalty, for piracy of civil aircraft in flight.

The Russian buildup in Cuba during 1962 caused the public to demand positive intervention. Congress finally adopted a resolution on October 3 authorizing President Kennedy to decide when an offensive threat justified the use of force. A Gallup poll released on October 14 indicated that 63 per cent of the American people opposed the use of United States troops to invade Cuba. When asked what action the United States should take 25 per cent did not know, 26 per cent said something short of war, 10 per cent favored some belligerent act such as bombing or invading, 13 per cent suggested trade embargoes, and 22 per cent favored a hands-off policy. It is clear that only a very small percentage at this time were in favor of going to war with Cuba. To what extent President Kennedy was aware of this state of public opinion and was guided by it is not known. In any case, when he proclaimed the blockade of Cuba and ordered reserves mobilized on October 23, 84 per cent of the American people endorsed the decision.

To summarize: During the four years of the Cuban crisis many policy decisions had to be made by the United States government. The role of public opinion varied from decision to decision. On some decisions its influence seemed to be great and direct; on others, remote and indirect. Public opinion tended to favor policies, once they became official, more strongly than before. Public opinion was at times basically formed after the fact, yet the relationship was often two-way, interacting and cyclical. In some instances policy remained constant and opinion changed; in others, the reverse. When public opinion was sharply divided or uncertain it had little effect. Policy-makers showed some reluctance to commit the nation when public opinion regarding a policy was in doubt. In the final analysis, a state of public opinion, known or assumed, seems to set the outer limits of governmental action, within which public officials exercise much discretion. The Cuban crisis revealed a public policy being gradually, but decisively, molded by public opinion.

Medicare

Two case studies remain to be considered: Medicare and military expenditures. In the case of Medicare, the period covered was from 1957 when the Forand bill was first introduced, to July 17, 1962, when the Senate defeated the Kennedy supported King-Anderson bill by the narrow margin of 52 to 48.[6] Hearings were held on the earlier Forand bill in 1959, but in 1960 the Committee on Ways and Means by a vote of 17 to 7 refused to send the bill to the floor. Meanwhile, the opposition proposed a counter measure, the Kerr-Miller bill. The platform of the Democratic party in the 1960 campaign gave top priority to Medicare, but again the Administration measure failed to pass the Senate by a vote of 51 to 44. In his message to Congress early in 1961, President Kennedy stressed the importance of Medicare, but an intensive drive for legislation was postponed until 1962. As noted above, the Medicare proposal was defeated once more after an unusually intensive battle.

One of the first nation-wide polls on Medicare was taken in late May, 1961, and showed that 67 per cent of the people favored Medicare. However, the first Gallup poll in March, 1962, showed that only 55 per cent favored financing medical care through Social Security, and 34 per cent favored private financing. By May, the respective figures were 48 per cent and 41 per cent, and in August, after the defeat of the King-Anderson bill, they were 44 to 40. At all times the majority of the American people who had an opinion on the issue were in favor of the Administration measure with its Social Security provisions, but the margin of approval declined.

This study underscored several aspects of the relationship between public opinion and public policy: (a) As other studies demonstrate, Congress does not always respond quickly to public opinion, although it may be somewhat more responsive in an election year; (b) As the public becomes better informed about the nature of proposed policies and their implications, it becomes more cautious and discriminating; (c) Finally, this case shows, not only the great influence that minority pressure groups have, but also that this influence affects the opinions of the people, as much, if not more than the attitudes of Congressmen.

Military Expenditures

The last case study deals with the relationship of public opinion to public policy regarding government expenditures for military purposes.[7] On the policy side, the period from 1935 to the present has been one of steadily growing military budgets, war or no war. Annual military outlays today now exceed the total expenditures for military purposes throughout the nation's history prior to World War II. Since 1935, when Gallup began his nation-wide surveys of public opinion, repeated polls have been taken to probe public attitudes regarding the military establishment and its costs. Invariably, the public supports the enlarged programs and the mounting costs. It seems to accept without question what the defense establishment says it needs.

In 1935, the polls revealed that the American public was already in favor of large military budgets. In 1937, it held that the last place to attempt to reduce the budget was in the area of military expenditures. Two months later 74 per cent of the voters endorsed a larger naval program. In the latter part of 1938, about 90 per cent expressed a "desire for bigger armed defenses." From December 25, 1942, to January 25, 1956, 16 polls were taken on the question of Universal Military Training, and these surveys showed anywhere from 63 per cent to 77 per cent in favor of UMT. In November, 1949, the public wanted a tax cut, but no cut in military expenses. After the explosion of the first Russian bomb and the fear of war rose, the trend in favor of larger military expenditures moved rapidly upward. At the time of the outbreak of the Korean conflict the $42 billion budget received the support of 73 per cent, and this overwhelming support for large military budgets continued after the cessation of hostilities. Following the launching of the first Russian sputnik, the public strongly supported more defense expenditures to close the gap between United States and Russian military progress. Ever since then the public seems to have been quite well satisfied with whatever defense expenditures government and the military recommend.

This case study seemed to show that public opinion tends to follow and approve rather than lead or directly influence the official policy regarding military expenditures. In fact, there seems to be virtually no public opinion check on the upward trend of such expenditures, since the public wants all defense needs met, and apparently it has full confidence in the definition of those needs by the executive and legislative officials of the government.

This study also shows how difficult it is for public opinion to influence public policy when that policy is favored by a gigantic executive department of the government, when it involves complicated, technical issues beyond the knowledge of the public, when powerful, private interest groups support it, and when opposition to it can so easily be interpreted as endangering national security. This case also shows how difficult it is for the public to pass intelligently upon issues of policy when many crucial facts are hidden, when much of the deliberation and discussion is carried on behind closed doors, and when one side of the debate outweighs the other to the extent that the so-called military complex outweighs whatever countervailing representatives of the public may exist.

CONCLUSIONS

What conclusions may be drawn from these six studies?

(1) In the first place, it is apparent that the relationship between public opinion and public policy varies greatly from issue to issue. The influence of public opinion on policy varies from virtually no influence to enormous influence. Influence may be exerted quickly or slowly, it may change over time or remain constant, and its impact may be direct or indirect.

(2) It is also clear that the extent of the influence depends on a great many different factors such as: the degree of agreement within the public, the intensity with which the opinions are held, the nature and extent of organized support for and against the public position, the degree to which obstacles exist to the facile channeling of public opinion to the government decision-makers, the power structure in the government, the vigor of government and private leadership, the time available for discussion, the nature of the question, and the clarity and simplicity of the issues.

(3) The studies also suggest some of the difficulties and obstacles to the easy translation of public opinion into public policy. These include the difficulty of finding out what public opinion really is on a specific issue, not only within the competence of the public, but in such a form and at such a time to be useful to policy-makers. These obstacles also include such things as a biased press, special groups and interests that strive to make their voices appear the voices of the majority of the people. Also, public opinion, before it finally reaches the ultimate decision-maker may have to be filtered through more or less unrepresentative legislative bodies and administrative agencies which have built in rules and procedures to check the free, effective flow of public opinion.

(4) Notwithstanding these obstacles and conditioning factors, public opinion does seem to influence public policy on most issues in at least two ways. First, it usually sets limits to government decisions and policy-making by reason of a rather widespread knowledge of its tolerances, and secondly, officials are generally reluctant to take a stand in the face of probable widespread, popular disapproval. Public opinion seldom acts positively to promote a new policy, but it often acts negatively to demonstrate its dissatisfaction with existing policies. It may be a powerful instrument of control after, rather than before, the fact.

(5) Again, the relationship between public opinion and public policy is two-way, cyclical, and dynamic. Public opinion not only influences policy, but policy influences opinion. As was noted in several of the cases cited, once a policy decision was made, there was a tendency for public opinion to accept it. As general policies become more specific and the

implications of the policies become clearer, public opinion often changes.

(6) Finally, in almost all the cases reviewed, the government itself, the President or some government department, was often able to influence public opinion considerably through information, propaganda, and official actions, however, there was no proof that government officials could press public opinion into a rubber-stamp or feedback, of official opinion management. In most of the cases cited, public opinion was sometimes very responsive to official leadership, but it was also influenced by many other factors such as significant events, private interest group propaganda, and the content of the mass media.

To find out more precisely how public opinion influences public policy decisions does not, of course, answer the question of what influence it should have. It may put to rest some of the fears of those, like Walter Lippmann, who assert that public opinion has altogether too much influence and that it is largely responsible for the mistakes of our policymakers in the past, especially in the realm of foreign policy. Facts regarding the relationship between public opinion and policy may also temper the optimism of those who believe that this is truly the wisest of all governments because it is a government of, for, and by the people. Actually, the influence opinion varies greatly from issue to issue.

NOTES FOR CHAPTER 13

Epigraph. V. O. Key, Jr., *Public Opinion and American Democracy* (1961) p. 7.

1. These students, Princeton, Class of 1965, were: Robert Snedeker, James Gildea, Jr., Mark Baskir, Hugh Lynch, Richard M. Jacobson, Robert D. Huxley, and Barry R. Fischer.
2. Snedeker, Robert, "Public Opinion and Nuclear Weapons Testing: A Chronological Survey, 1954-62." See also Gilpin, Robert, "American Scientists and Nuclear Weapons Policy," *op. cit.*
3. Barry R. Fischer, "The Public's Verdict: Kennedy vs. Steel. April, 1962"; Hooper, Roy, "The Steel Crisis," *Day,* 1963; McConnell, Grant, *Steel and the Presidency, 1962* (New York: W. W. Norton, 1963).
4. Gildea, James, Jr., "Public Opinion and Federal Aid to Education"; Munger, Frank, Jr., and Richard F. Fenno, Jr., *National Politics and Federal Aid to Education* (Syracuse, N. Y.: Syracuse University Press, 1962).
5. Baskir, Mark, "American Public Policy Towards Cuba and the American Public Reaction"; Lynch, Hugh, "The Relationship Between Public Opinion and Public Policy with Respect to Cuba"; Alsop, Stewart and Bartlett, Charles, "In Time of Crisis," *Saturday Evening Post,* December, 1962, pp. 235ff.; Larson, David L., *The Cuban Crisis of 1962: Selected Documents and Chronology* (Boston: Houghton-Mifflin Co., 1963).
6. Robert D. Huxley, "Influence of Politics, Lobbies, and Public Opinion on the Medicare Bill."
7. Jacobson, Richard M., "Public Opinion and Military Expenditures."

SUPPLEMENTARY READING

ALMOND, GABRIEL A. *The American People and Foreign Policy.* New York: Harcourt, Brace & Co., 1950.

ALMOND, GABRIEL A. "Public Opinion and the Development of Space Technology," *Public Opinion Quarterly,* Vol. 24 (Winter, 1960), pp. 553-72.

BAILEY, THOMAS ANDREW. *The Man in the Street.* New York: The Macmillan Co., 1948.

BASSETT, REGINALD. *Democracy and Foreign Policy.* London: Longmans, 1952.

BAUER, RAYMOND A., POOL, ITHIEL DE SOLA, and DEXTER, LEWIS ANTHONY. *American Business and Public Policy: The Politics of Foreign Trade.* Englewood Cliffs, N. J.: Atherton Press, 1963.

BELOFF, MAX. *Foreign Policy and the Democratic Process.* Baltimore: Johns Hopkins Press, 1955.

CANTWELL, FRANK V. "Public Opinion and the Legislative Process," *American Political Science Review,* Vol. 40 (October, 1946), pp. 924-35.

CARTER, LAUNAR F. "Survey Results and Public Policy Decisions," *Public Opinion Quarterly,* Vol. 27 (Winter, 1963), pp. 549-57.

CHANDLER, G. "American Opinion and Foreign Policy," *International Affairs,* Vol. 31 (Oct., 1955), p. 477.

CORY, ROBERT H. "The Role of Public Opinion in United States Policies Toward the UN," *International Organization,* Vol. 11 (1957), pp. 230-37.

DAHL, ROBERT A. *Congress and Foreign Policy.* New York: Harcourt, Brace, & Co., 1950.

DICEY, A. V. *Lectures on the Relation Between Law and Public Opinion in England During the Nineteenth Century.* New York: The Macmillan Co., 1905.

ELDER, ROBERT ELLSWORTH. *The Policy Machine: The Department of State and American Foreign Policy.* Syracuse, N. Y.: Syracuse University Press, 1960. (Especially Part III).

FINKLE, JASON L. *The President Makes a Decision: A Study of Dixon-Yates.* Governmental Studies No. 39. Institute of Public Administration. Ann Arbor: University of Michigan, 1960.

GALLUP, GEORGE. "Absorption Rate of Ideas," *Public Opinion Quarterly,* Vol. 19 (Fall, 1955), pp. 234-42.

GLEASON, JOHN H. *The Genesis of Russophobia in Great Britain: A Study of the Interaction of Policy and Opinion.* Cambridge, Mass.: Harvard University Press, 1950.

IRISH, MARION D. "Public Opinion and American Foreign Policy: The Quemoy Crisis of 1958," *Political Quarterly,* Vol. 31 (April-June, 1960), pp. 151-62.

JORDAN, ELIJAH. *Theory of Legislation: An Essay on the Dynamics of the Public Mind.* Indianapolis, Ind.: Progress Publishing Co., 1930.

KATZ, DANIEL, et al. *Public Opinion and Propaganda.* New York: Dryden Press, 1954.

LARSON, DAVID L. (ed.). *The 'Cuban Crisis' of 1962.* Boston: Houghton Mifflin Co., 1963.

LOWI, THEODORE J. *Legislative Politics, U.S.A.: Congress and the Forces that Shape It.* Boston: Little, Brown & Co., 1962.

MARKEL, LESTER, et al. *Public Opinion and Foreign Policy.* New York: Harper & Bros., 1949.

McCONNELL, GRANT. *Steel and the Presidency, 1962.* New York: W. W. Norton & Co., 1963.

MICHAEL, DONALD N. "The Beginning of the Space Age and American Public Opinion," *Public Opinion Quarterly,* Vol. 24 (Winter, 1960), pp. 573-82.

PADOVER, SAUL K. *U. S. Foreign Policy and Public Opinion.* New York: Foreign Policy Association, 1958.

ROSENAU, JAMES N. *National Leadership and Foreign Policy.* Princeton, N. J.: Princeton University Press, 1963.

"The U.S.A. and the World: A Special Survey." *United Nations World,* Vol. 6 (July, 1952), pp. 13-59.

WIEBE, G. D. "Public Opinion Between Elections," *Public Opinion Quarterly,* Vol. 21 (Summer, 1957), pp. 229-36.

XIV · International Propaganda

Most of that which formerly could be done by violence and intimidation must now be done by argument and persuasion. Democracy has proclaimed the dictatorship of palaver, and the technique of dictating to the dictator is named propaganda.

—HAROLD D. LASSWELL

IN RECENT YEARS international propaganda has become an increasingly significant item in the array of factors which make public opinion what it is in the United States and abroad. The word "propaganda" is used to denote conscious efforts to spread ideas. It is a very general term and comprises various methods and techniques and an almost infinite variety of ideas, programs, and doctrines. To propagandize is to propagate, to cause to spread, to disseminate thoughts, views, beliefs, and notions. The word was certainly in use by the middle of the seventeenth century, and probably much earlier, because the Roman Catholic Church used it in the name of its great missionary organization for the "propagation of the faith." Then, at least in the minds of anti-Catholics, the word had an insidious connotation, and it came to be associated with Roman Catholicism itself.

HISTORY AND DEVELOPMENT

Propaganda between and among nations has existed throughout history as rulers, sovereigns, and national governments competed for control over land and national resources, for control over the minds and emotions of men, for favorable alliances, concessions of one kind or another, and for prestige and renown. Whenever and wherever nations try to win support or favor from other countries, there propaganda exists. Over the years the ideas propagated have changed, as well as the methods used and the

322

tools employed. The strategies of argument, persuasion, organization, and publicity have been the same and as prevalent yesterday as today. Earlier rulers might have had to depend on personal emissaries, private messages, displays of force, manifestations of friendliness or hostility, but the objectives, basic procedures, and over-all problems were much the same as today.[1]

Many developments have shaped the evolution of international propaganda: from the introduction of printing by means of movable type in western Europe during the fifteenth century, and the gradual emergence of the newspaper press, to the advent of motion pictures, radio, and television during the early decades of the twentieth century. Too great an emphasis can be placed on these and other communication agencies, including point-to-point communication by telephone, telegraph, and cable. Improvements in transportation, the Industrial Revolution with its rise in standards of living, the spread of education with its rapid expansion of intellectual horizons and concomitant rise in human desires and expectations—all of these change the appearances, if not the basic nature, of international propaganda.

Propaganda has always increased in volume during periods of tension and conflict; this seems to be true internationally as well as domestically. Also, periods of rapid social change, scientific and technological progress, exploration and discovery, and intellectual ferment, usually generate new ideas, reform programs, new hopes, desires, and new propagandas. From the fifteenth century in the western world there have been a succession of these explosive, germinating periods which seem to become more frequent, and sustained, to the point of being continuous. Wars and rumors of war have usually increased the volume and intensity of international propaganda—this was definitely the case during the American Revolution. The writings and speeches of James Otis, Patrick Henry, Thomas Paine, and Samuel Adams did much to foment the revolutionary spirit in the colonies and to create sympathy abroad.[2] Emissaries were sent abroad to France and other countries to win support, and at home committees of correspondence helped to strengthen and unify the efforts of the colonies. There were no international wire services, radio, or telephone to take the case of the colonies abroad, but there were mails to take letters, newspapers, and pamphlets, and ships to take Benjamin Franklin and Thomas Jefferson to France.

This is not the place to trace the history of international propaganda, either in war or peace. It is sufficient to note that the wars of nations during the nineteenth century were wars of propaganda words, pictures, deeds as well as wars of arms and violent conflicts. This was true of the Napoleonic Wars, the Mexican War, the Franco-Prussian War, the Crimean struggle, the Spanish-American War, the Russo-Japanese War, and others.[3] The belligerents in each struggle used the strategies of argument, persuasion, publicity, and organization to win allies, to gain the support of neutrals, to build up morale at home, and to engender defeatism in the ranks of the enemy. Napoleon Bonaparte, the Duke of Wellington, Prince Otto von Bismarck, and other belligerent leaders capably used the printed word, deeds, and symbols. The newspaper press became a telling ally of whichever side it supported. In fact, the Spanish-American War of 1898 was influenced so much in its initiation, continuation, and results by the newspapers, especially the Hearst press, that the label "newspaper war" would not be inappropriate.[4]

International propaganda by governments was by no means the only type of international propaganda which developed following the Renaissance and the establishment of movable type in the West. Mention has already been made of propagation of the faith by the Roman Catholic Church. Gradually, the various Protestant and non-conformist denominations began to disseminate their doctrines abroad until by the nineteenth century most of the larger religious organizations were supporting far-flung missionary activities in many parts of the world. Also, during the late eighteenth and early nineteenth centuries a number of reform movements reached out beyond national borders to promote such causes as anti-slavery, peace, and temperance. Marxism was by no means the first political ideology to enter the streams of international communication—for the spread of democracy itself in various parts of the world, notably in English-speaking countries, had been phenomenal. The doctrines of Karl Marx and Friedrich Engels, during the middle of the nineteenth century proved to be a captivating dogma for millions of workers and intellectuals throughout the world. Marxism and its derivative Russian or Stalinist socialism became, after the Russian Revolution of 1917, the principal antagonist of liberal democracy in the international propaganda arena. Marxism was not only an ideology, but also a method, and it recognized from the beginning the potentialities and requisites of propaganda.

World War I was a landmark in the development of international propaganda, mainly because of the size and scope of government propaganda. Before the end of hostilities, Germany, France, Austria, Italy, Japan, and the United States had created propaganda organizations and facilities of unprecedented proportions. The story of the American Creel Committee has been reviewed many times.[5] It harnessed the existing media of mass communication to the Wilsonian war aims with skill and vigor. It enlisted on a voluntary basis the co-operation of newspapers and other publications, of artists and advertisers, of business, the professions, labor, and agriculture. It used thousands of "minute men" to deliver frequent pep talks to theater-goers and religious audiences, and it sent abroad to neutral, as well as allied, countries special agents to co-ordinate, explain, woo, and win support for the Allied cause. Newspapers, books, pamphlets, and a few motion pictures were the main instruments of mass communication, both at home and abroad. Many of Creel's associates on the Committee on Information subsequently confessed that this experience really opened their eyes to the potentialities of propaganda as an instrument of foreign policy. Perhaps because of this evidence of the power of propaganda or perhaps for other reasons, Congress quickly when the war ended dismantled the apparatus which Creel had established.

The period between the two World Wars saw the rapid rise of totalitarian propagandas; first, that of Soviet Russia, then Mussolini's Fascist propaganda, and, finally after the Nazi seizure of power in 1933, that of Goebbels and Hitler. The democracies were slow to respond, although Great Britain and France certainly recognized the need for counter-action by the late twenties and early thirties. The development of radio broadcasting after World War I led to the emergence of short-wave broadcasting across national boundaries.[6] The Nazis and Fascists were quick to exploit the use of these facilities of international propaganda, and England and France, too, began to use them to speak to their colonials and then to other countries. The United States government, however, remained aloof from these activities, until disturbing reports, especially from Latin America, and the actions of foreign agents in the United States itself[7] pointed the need for defensive action. As the war clouds in Europe darkened and the activities of Mussolini and Hitler became more menacing, steps were taken to register foreign agents in the United States, to uncover subversion, and to counter totalitarian propaganda in Latin America. It was not, however, until after Pearl Harbor, December 7, 1941, that vigorous action in the international propaganda field was taken with the establishment of the Office of Censorship, the Office of Strategic Services, and the Office of War Information.

PROPAGANDA IN TWO WORLD WARS

When the United States entered the war in 1941, those previously involved had elaborate propaganda machines already, notably Germany, Italy, Great Britain, France, Japan, and Russia. Despite the work of the Creel Committee in World War I, the outpouring of propaganda and public opinion studies during the years following, the public relations and publicity activities of American economic groups and New Deal government agencies, as well as the constant threat of foreign propaganda, United States officials were at first reluctant to set up a highly centralized, comprehensive propaganda machine. However, it was not long before doubts were resolved, once the United States declared war. In a number of important respects, however, the United States propaganda efforts in World War II differed from those in World War I.

In the first place, notwithstanding a reluctance to make propaganda an instrument of foreign policy, officials and the public generally were far more cognizant of and sophisticated about propaganda, public relations, and psychological warfare as practiced abroad than they were in 1913. Secondly, they decided at the outset to separate censorship from information activities and established offices for each, in contrast to what was done in World War I. Also white (overt) propaganda was segregated at an early date from black (cloak and dagger) operations which were placed under the Office of Strategic Services, and the decentralization process was furthered by keeping propaganda and cultural operations in Latin America in a separate organization.

A third, important difference between the two World War propaganda operations was the far greater emphasis in World War II upon propaganda activities abroad. To be sure, the Office of War Information, at first, laid considerable emphasis upon its Domestic Branch, seeking through it to co-ordinate federal government information activities at home, to assist departments and agencies in their particular information jobs, and to carry on independently certain major domestic information programs. In a few months, however, the Overseas Branch, in money and staff, began to assume a dominating position in OWI, and before the war's end the activities of the Domestic Branch had atrophied. During the war the OWI experienced a few major and several minor reorganizations, but throughout, it was organized on a basic two-fold plan, by geography and by media. The three major geographical divisions were (1) the enemy powers, (2) the allies, and (3) the neutrals. Within each broad area, special desks for individual states were staffed with people to draft propaganda directives, maintain contacts with corresponding desks in the Department of State, the War, Navy, and other departments, and supervise the carrying out of directives at home, and in the outposts abroad. During most of the war period the policy-making staff for the divisions remained in Washinton, D. C. Along with the geographical structure of the Overseas Branch there were several media divisions which served all geographical areas, including press and publications, motion pictures, and radio broadcasting. The last was often referred to as the "Voice of America." [8] The media operating staffs were in New York City.

In the fourth place, one may discern quite a significant difference in the propaganda objectives of the two World Wars. Whereas the war aims, as forcefully stated in 1918, seemed to raise the level of participation to that of a glorious struggle to make the world safe for democracy, by 1941 a disillusioned American people were doggedly but somewhat cynically enlisted in a fight to defend themselves from catastrophe. In many respects, the war aims of 1918 were clearer, more positive, and more inspiring than in World War II and thus made the propaganda job of Wilson and Creel much easier. The second war, necessary as it was from the United States' viewpoint, lacked the inspiration of glittering promises. Not only did the promises of the aftermath lack glitter, but they emanated from so many contradictory motives that only unresolved confusion seemed inevitable. Peace was almost certain to bring Allied disunity, economic and political disorganization, toil, and trouble. Under the competent leadership of Elmer Davis the OWI could play up Allied determination and resources to win the war, but they could say little that was convincing about the future of Europe, Germany, Austria or about much of anything for that matter. Even the pronouncement that winning the war meant unconditional surrender by the enemy was objectionable to those who seemed to prefer a negotiated end to hostilities. In many respects, therefore, the substantive job of United States and Allied propaganda was much more difficult from 1941 to 1945 than it was in 1917 and 1918.

In any comparison of the international propagandas of the two wars consideration must also be given to the much wider scope of the second war, its longer duration, and the improvements made in the communication media, especially in radio broadcasting. Nearly all the belligerents in World War II made extensive use of radio, including medium and short-wave broadcasting, for projecting their propaganda messages. Television, although available in a very limited and crude form, was not yet practical. Almost no one had television receiving sets to view programs had they been telecast. United States participation in World War I lasted less than two years; World War II was twice that long. Instead of being restricted mainly to Europe, the high seas and the Middle East, this war spread out to the Far East and Africa as well. This fact greatly enlarged the scope of the propaganda problems of all propagandizing nations. It meant that a greater concern than ever before had to be exercised regarding national objectives and aspirations, that great care had to be taken to avoid conflicting and contradictory statements, and that many cultures had to be studied as well as many foreign languages.

The end of World War II did not bring the sudden demise of the Allies' official propaganda that the end of World War I had. The wartime battles for military victory were succeeded by struggles for economic, political, and other objectives. The war had left a tangled maze of issues, problems, tensions, and aspirations. In the United States careful consideration and study were given to the future of propaganda as an official instrument of foreign policy.[9] The OWI, as such, was reduced in size and transferred to the Department of State, where it functioned somewhat as an orphan until it was accorded a statutory basis by the passage of the Smith-Mundt

Act in January, 1948. By this time congressmen as well as others began to see the need for a propaganda instrument to explain the objectives, plans, and policies of the United States and to counter Russian and other forms of anti-American propaganda, as well as to help the United States in its newly acquired position of world leadership. Already, in 1947, the international propaganda organization of the Communist party, the Comintern (later Cominform), had been recreated, misunderstandings regarding American plans and intentions were rampant, and to committees of Congress traveling in Europe during the summer of 1947, the danger of losing the peace became very real.

THE UNITED STATES INFORMATION AGENCY

The development of the United States Information Agency through its numerous reorganizations, its changes in directors and personnel, its relations with the Department of State, the military establishment, and the executive offices of the President, its yearly bouts with Congress for appropriations, to say nothing of its internal problems of staffing, and formulating of propaganda policy—all constitute a truly fascinating, if also frustrating, story of propaganda as an instrument of foreign policy gradually finding its accepted place in the great American bureaucracy.[10] Since August 31, 1945, when overseas information activities were transferred from the OWI to the Interim International Information Service in the Department of State, there have been eleven directors of this activity.

The changes in policy, objectives, organization, and activities have been as numerous, if not more so, than the shifts in directors. At various times one or more of the following aims have been paramount: to promote peace by creating a better understanding of the United States, its people, policies, intentions, and activities; to win friends and prestige for the United States throughout the world, either by trying to give a "full and fair picture," or by presenting a "showcase" image of the United States; to focus primarily on the job of explaining, interpreting, and advocating the foreign policies of the United States; and finally, to counter and combat Russian communist propaganda, and other types of international communication hostile or inimical to the United States. As the years have passed emphasis has been placed more and more on implementing specific foreign policies, explaining them and trying to show that they are in accord with the interests of other countries as well as those of the United States. In a sense, however, all of the above aims find a place in over-all propaganda policy. As it operates today the USIA seeks to further United States foreign policy, to project a strong, dynamic America, to advise the President regarding the reactions of people abroad, to prepare a propaganda plan for each target country by taking established propaganda objectives and eliminating those not applicable to the particular country. More and more emphasis is being placed on reaching specific, influential audiences in each country, such as the military, party leaders, labor, youth, and so on. Among the themes recently emphasized have been man's desire to choose his own future, the need for effective disarmament, the United States position on Berlin, the value of the United Nations organization, the need for helping undeveloped countries. In addition to such long term objectives the USIA must take a stand on day to day developments such as the Cuban crisis, atomic testing, space exploration, to play them up or down, to treat them blandly or tersely or to spell them out, to explain or interpret them. Like a great newspaper or wire service, the organization is disseminating news, but with a selection, emphasis, treatment, and display that reflects and supports the interests and objectives of the United States. It is not engaged in news gathering, selection, treatment, presentation, and distribution for profit, nor merely for the sake of information, enlightenment, and truth for their own sakes, but primarily for the purpose of implementing foreign policy and the objectives previously mentioned.

The organization and activities of USIA have become fairly stable, although some changes in structure, personnel, and activities go on at all times. The annual budget is usually between 110 and 125 million dollars. The agency employs about 11,000 people, of whom nearly 6,000 are local, native employees overseas, 3,300 are Americans in the United States, and 1,500 Americans overseas.[11] The structure of the organization reflects that of its predecessor, the OWI. The broad regions of the world —Far East, Africa, Near East and South Asia, Latin America, Western Europe, the Soviet Union and Eastern Europe—are all target areas. There are special, operational and policy-making units for the individual countries in each area. The principal media services are press and publications, motion pictures, broadcasting, television, and information centers. In addition, there are administrative services, units concerned with program direction and appraisal, co-operative programs with private organizations, and research and reference work. Almost one half of the total spent for media services went for radio broadcasting in 1962. As sets for receiving television programs increase in number in the target areas, the use of this important medium will expand.[12] The geographical distribution of emphasis has shown more and more attention being given to Africa and Latin America, and perhaps some slight de-emphasis in western Europe.

It should be remembered that Radio Free Europe, with its broadcasting operations centered largely in Munich, and Radio Liberty, based in France, concentrated their propaganda activities on the satellite countries in eastern Europe, and on Soviet Russia respectively.[13] Radio Free Europe came into existence at the close of World War II, with the encouragement if not the assistance of the U. S. Department of State. Manned to a large extent by exiles from these satellite nations, it sought by psychological means to do what it could to free those countries from Soviet Russian domination. As the hope of doing so has dimmed, at least for the immediate future, Radio Free Europe has tried to find other propaganda themes with which it can serve the interests of these people.

United States Information Service

The United States Information Service (USIS), as the USIA overseas operation is called, had 229 posts in 103 countries abroad in 1962, figures which have since grown larger, especially in Africa. The USIS unit in each country is an integral part of the United States diplomatic mission to that country, and it is also responsible to the appropriate area director of the USIA in Washington. In each country, the Service engages in many different activities. It produces programs for local radio and television stations or supplies material from those produced by the Broadcasting Service of USIA. It may also produce programs locally for the "Voice of America" and promote that medium. It produces and distributes locally —or supplies them from the USIA—magazines, newspapers, wall newspapers, bulletins, pamphlets, books, and special displays. It undertakes to place in native publications various articles, pictorial material, reports, and other types of printed matter. In each country, film libraries are maintained, and motion pictures are produced, exhibited, and distributed through local commercial outlets, private organizations, and the government, or shown by mobile units. A very important undertaking is the operation of information centers where reading rooms with a sizable assortment of American books and magazines are provided. The USIS promotes the translation, production, and distribution of many books by American and foreign authors, presents books and subscriptions to American magazines and newspapers to key opinion leaders, and promotes the teaching of English through classes and seminars.

The eagerness of foreign nationals to learn English and to take advantage of these information centers is clearly shown by the number of visitors to them and by the large number of students in the language classes. In some areas, particularly in Latin America, support is given in cash, personnel, and materials to so-called binational centers: "a non-political, non-profit, non-sectarian cultural institution dedicated to the principle of strengthening understanding between the United States and the host country." They are operated by joint boards of local nationals and American residents of the area. Every effort is made by the foreign missions of the USIS to present many aspects of American life and culture through conferences, shows, art exhibitions, American studies programs in foreign universities, and exchange programs. In carrying out its work co-operation is given, not only to other United States governmental programs in the country, such as foreign aid, technical assistance, exchange of persons, and Peace Corps programs, but also to relevant programs of the United Nations, private foundations, business corporations, and other such enterprises.

The general outline of USIS activities abroad has been depicted, but each country and each post has its peculiar problems. In the Far East, for example, there is intensive competition from the Chinese Communists, and considerable effort must be given to counter their attacks. Special efforts are made to reach the future leaders in government, education, and the military. In Africa, because of widespread illiteracy, special emphasis is placed on the use of films, and the teaching of English. In the Near East and South Asia, long range programs are stressed, radio and television are quite effective, binational centers are growing in number, and mobile exhibits have met with success. In Latin America, USIS activities have been oriented largely to the binational centers previously mentioned. In Brazil, for example, these centers have a membership of over 10,000, over 300,000 people attended functions of the centers in 1960, and more than 35,000 students were studying English in Center classes. In western Europe, the primary aim is to show that United States interests in Europe are based on enlightened self-interest, and that ties are enduring. In general, the treatment of current topics and issues is quite sophisticated. In eastern Europe the only countries receiving a full USIS program are West Germany and Yugoslavia, although the "Voice of America," Russian and Polish editions of *Amerika,* and Radio In the American Sector[14] (RIAS), as well as unofficial Radio Free Europe and Radio Liberty, penetrate the Iron Curtain.

It is by no means easy to describe briefly the manifold, world-wide activities of this tremendous information and propaganda agency of the United States. However, a few additional details regarding the media services may be illuminating.

PRESS AND PUBLICATION SERVICE. This is a service that supplies materials to local missions from Washington and from service and printing centers in Mexico City, Manila, and Beirut; it also maintains a wireless file and a world-wide radio teletype communications network servicing local posts. The local missions distribute the materials received to local media, particular audiences and select groups, together with materials produced locally, including magazines, newspaper supplements, wall newspapers, newsletters, bulletins, articles, news, and features.[15] The Service publishes four magazines, three entirely in the United States—*America Illustrated* in Russian, *America Illustrated* in Polish, and *Problems of Communism* in English. The fourth, *Life in America,* is prepared in Washington for translation and printed at Beirut in Arabic.

THE MOTION PICTURE SERVICE. The Motion Picture Service adapts for use by posts in the field films produced or acquired in the United States. Documentary films, newsreels, and special coverages are also produced locally for exhibition there. Films are distributed and exhibited by means of mobile units and local commercial outlets, and through private organizations and government channels. Among the subject areas to be emphasized in 1964 are: "Progress Through Freedom—the U. S. Social Scene," "Films for Labor," "American Youth," "Results of Communism," "U. S. Race Relations Reports in Perspective," "Freedom to Choose," "The U. S. Position—Test Ban and Disarmament," and "Modernization." As of February 1, 1963, the list of films in the USIA program comprised 867 original productions, of which 811 were in foreign languages, and 696 acquired films, of which 643 were in foreign languages.

INFORMATION CENTER SERVICE. The principal activities of the Information Center Service are (1) information center support, (2) low-priced books program, (3) exhibits program, (4) English-teaching promotion, (5) binational center support, (6) non-profit publishing, (7) presentations program, and (8) music program. In its appearance before the Appropriations Subcommittee of the House in 1963 the Service stated:

> The Information Center Service is the principal cultural arm of the U. S. Information Agency. It makes extensive and varied use of books, periodicals, and other publications by supplying the libraries of information centers and binational centers; by placing loan collections with foreign schools, universities, and other institutions; by presentations to key individuals and organizations; by translation of books into local languages; and by encouraging the distribution and sale of American books abroad through regular commercial channels. The Service also promotes the teaching of English, encourages the performance of American music, and produces exhibits which portray American life and achievements.[16]

For 1964, the USIA estimated that it would be supporting 188 Information Centers: Far East (46), Africa (60), Near East and South Asia (32), Latin America (11), West Europe (36), and Special European Program (3). The figure for Latin America is low because of the importance of binational centers. The budget estimate for 1964 provided for 268,790 books, 28,412 magazine subscriptions, 570 newspaper subscriptions, 14,422 government publications, and 104,913 other publications. In 1963, the budget provided for the publication and distribution of 3,628,-000 copies of American books, 2,294,000 in foreign language translations. It also contained provisions for 18 circulating exhibits dealing with science, fine and applied arts, government, and several special subjects. Since the establishment of a USIA supported, non-profit publishing corporation in 1952, it has published directly or assisted in the publication of 1,298 editions in six foreign languages totaling over 5,300,000 books. To insure that important American books and periodicals reach key people abroad, selected items are given to libraries, schools, and opinion leaders in the professions, industry, labor, government and journalism. In 1962, for example, over 46,000 books, 5,000 magazine subscriptions, 69 newspaper subscriptions, 10,000 government publications, and many other publications were given away for this purpose.

THE BROADCASTING SERVICE. The Broadcasting Service spends almost as much as all other USIA media combined. In fiscal 1962, the actual expenditures were $19,811,539, and for the other media: Press and Publications $10,105,834, Motion Pictures $6,501,230, Information Centers $5,668,826, and Television $2,144,324. This Service, commonly known as the Voice of America (VOA), has a centralized program service which produces news shows, news analyses, and features; language desks which edit and translate these programs into foreign languages, produce programs of their own, and prepare recorded material for foreign stations. The VOA, in addition to studios in Washington, maintains subsidiary program centers in New York, Miami, Munich, Cairo, Bangkok, Rhodes, and various African cities where programs are produced for particular geographical areas. In his report to the House Appropriations Subcommittee in 1963, the Director of the Broadcasting Service made several illuminating points. He stated that during the fiscal year 1962 broadcasts to Africa were doubled, broadcasts in three Southeast Asian languages were initiated, the total power of VOA's short-wave transmitters was doubled, the Cuban crisis brought an expansion of Spanish-language broadcasts to 24 hour a day service, and ten private radio stations agreed to relay VOA Spanish programs to Cuba. During the height of the Cuban crisis, VOA European transmitters staged a saturation broadcast of the President's speech clearly audible throughout Russia. In addition to direct broadcasts, 14,000 hours of programs per week were placed on local stations, the major increases being in Latin America and Africa. "Although the United States dominates the field in placement of programs on friendly foreign radio stations, the Voice is facing increasing competition in direct international broadcasting —the only method of reaching an audience without the consent of the foreign government. Last year [fiscal 1962] total international broadcasting increased about 2,000 hours per week to a total of 17,000 hours per week —an increase of 10 per cent. Moscow rose 200 hours per week to a total of 1,200, almost twice as much as the Voice's 766 hours per week." Voice of America still ranks third in total program time among international broadcasters, with Moscow first, and Peking second.

THE TELEVISION SERVICE. The Television Service is the fastest growing of the USIA media services. From December, 1961, to December, 1962, the number of television transmitting stations in the free world, exclusive of the United States and Canada, increased about 18 per cent to almost 2,000, and receivers in the above mentioned free world increased 13 per cent to almost 50,000,000. By the end of the calendar year 1962, a total of 10,610 hours of local television time were devoted to USIA materials, an increase of 317 per cent over the previous calendar year. In 1962 a program, "Let's Learn English" was seen by millions in 33 countries. Other programs are especially designed for young people to explain U. S. foreign policy objectives, to support the Alliance for Progress in Latin America, to compare life in Communist and free countries, and so on. Communication satellites will continue to increase the transmission of television programs to audiences around the world.

Finally, a brief word regarding non-media services: The Office of Private Cooperation stimulates and co-ordinates "people to people" activities, encourages participation by civic, business, professional, and other groups, donations of books and magazines, affiliations between cities and universities here and abroad, travel in the United States, and many other relationships and activities to promote better international understanding. The Office of Program Direction and Appraisal drafts over-all plans for the USIA, obtains information and policy guidance from the Department of State, the National Security Council and other government agencies, and advises these agencies regarding public opinion abroad. This advice is based on public opinion surveys and analyses conducted in the various target countries overseas.

CONTRAST IN PROPAGANDAS: IDEOLOGICAL PROBLEMS

How does this machine differ essentially from the international propaganda programs and procedures of other countries, especially those of Soviet Russia and the Communist nations? A few, only, of the salient contrasts may be underscored. In the first place, its objectives, its aims, are very general and somewhat vague. It lacks the systematic, doctrinaire, definitive, totalitarian ideology of the Marxists. To be sure, the philosophy of USIA is grounded in beliefs in democracy and freedom, justice and the worth of human beings, but nowhere is the over-all credo spelled out systematically and related to current events and developments, except in terms of various, pragmatic themes. The Communists have their bible; whereas the liberals, capitalists, and other believers in democracy possess only an array of theories, a maze of generalizations, and wide divergencies of opinion. This fact makes the propaganda task of the USIA much more difficult than that of the Communists. To be sure, important, ideological differences may exist among the Communists—between Soviet Russia, Communist China and Yugoslavia, for example—but by and large the strategy of Communist argument, in all Communist countries has a unity, coherence, and singleness of purpose, at least on the surface, which the democracies lack.[17]

Closely related to this contrasting feature of United States and Communist propagandas, is the difficulty democratic countries, and especially the United States, face in trying to create and maintain a united propaganda front before the outside world. The commitment of the United States to freedom of speech and press means that the USIA is only one of many voices inside the United States projecting images of the United States. The conflicting views of employer and employee, businessman and farmer, colored and white are freely exposed to the world through our media of communication. Within as well as between branches and agencies of government conflicts arise and are often made public. Strenuous efforts by the President and department heads to avoid this have never been wholly successful. The constitution and government of the United States are fundamentally based on the necessity for and the efficiency of this freedom, and few would have it otherwise, but it does mean that the official information and propaganda of the USIA has to compete, not only with foreign, but often with domestic propaganda, official and private.

Another aspect of the contrast between democratic and totalitarian propagandas is the much closer relationship in totalitarian countries between all official policies and propaganda policy.[18] In Soviet Russia, for example, the totalitarian nature of the regime means that efforts are made to co-ordinate at all times political, military, economic, and propaganda policy. There seems to be a fuller and more widespread appreciation of propaganda among all government and party officials in Russia and Communist China than in the United States, and this makes it easier for these regimes, more natural perhaps, for them to take public opinion and propaganda into their foreign policy considerations. Since domestic public opinion is always a very important element of foreign policy, the totalitarian domination of its citizens' opinions makes possible even greater unity before the world. This tight regimentation of opinion behind foreign policy, while it may give certain advantages to the international propagandist, narrows considerably the base of policy-making which may entail some very real risks which more democratic and liberal procedures would avoid.

When it comes to methods of, and organization for international propaganda, the differences between countries are mainly of degree rather than kind. To the extent that their budgets permit, all use radio, television, motion pictures, press and publications of all kinds, cultural exchanges and exchanges of persons, exhibitions, and various other kinds of communication. They all use the strategies of organization, argument, persuasion, and publicity. The Communist countries operate directly, and indirectly through their international organization, the Cominform, in practically all countries. Usually the local embassies serve as area headquarters, out of which control and direction in the field are exercised. One important respect in which they have an organizational advantage over the democracies is that local Communist parties are usually closely affiliated with each other and to the Communist states themselves. None of the democracies have such closely affiliated party organizations in other countries to promote their ideologies and aims. To be sure, some of the Roman Catholic parties and socialist parties might be regarded, in some instances, as local representatives or agents of the Vatican or the international socialist ideology, but in this respect they are usually far behind the local Communist parties in effectiveness.

To what extent are the methods of Communist international propaganda more or less reprehensible than those of other countries? Here one enters the difficult zone of judgment and values. Even though totalitarian regimes are more tightly knit, more closely integrated, possibly a distinction should be drawn between overt propaganda and information, covert, black, cloak-and-dagger operations, and military activities. Possibly totalitarianism is more committed to the notion that the end justifies the means, in times of peace or in cold war at least, than democracies are. Certainly, it would seem that the Communist countries have in the past relied more on covert, subversive acts than other countries, particularly the United States, although hard facts regarding the extent and nature of these black operations are few. In the arena of overt international propaganda the competitive struggles of nations for success inevitably lead them closer and closer to the same techniques and strategies. The problems of the effective use of radio, television, books, magazines, and other media are largely the same for Communists as non-Communists. Perhaps the former make greater use of editorial than news material, classical music instead of jazz, documentary films than entertaining features, exhibits and fairs than discussions. In any case, it is more a difference in degree than kind. The Russian Communists have been particularly effective, it would seem, in the use of cultural exchanges, in alternating threats with promises, and in promoting international organizations for various interests, such as those of labor, the professions, artists, and sports as well as organizations intended solely to lead and disseminate propaganda.[19]

Mention should also be made of the efforts of most Communist countries to wall out objectionable external communications. Foreign broadcasts are "jammed" with determination and considerable effectiveness. Emigration and immigration are carefully controlled. Books, motion pictures, newspapers and magazines are rigorously screened. Foreign correspondents from abroad are censored and restricted in what they can say or do.

VALUE OF PROPAGANDAS

What may now be validly said regarding the effectiveness, the success of particular national propagandas? Success may be measured in many different ways: by the rise and fall of general public popularity, prestige, and esteem in foreign countries, by the extent to which diplomatic goals are won or lost, or by the degrees to which international tensions are mitigated. Each nation has, of course, a variety of diplomatic goals: security, peace, profitable trade with other countries, just treatment, access to natural resources, freedom to travel. Very often the attainment of these and other objectives, even some of them, may seem far more important than world-wide popularity or even the removal of tensions. In any case, many factors, other than propaganda, are usually involved in trying to reach them—economic, political, diplomatic, even military. In other words, it is usually extremely difficult to isolate and measure the effectiveness and the effects of international propaganda. Can propaganda alone solve the Berlin and Cuban crises? Can propaganda alone curb the ambitious designs of Communist China? Or can propaganda alone alter to any great extent the aims of De Gaulle and Khrushchev? Propaganda may help, but the outcome of most of the major moves on the international chess board is nearly always the result of the interplay of innumerable factors. Every year representatives of the USIA appear before committees of Congress to explain and try to justify their requests for appropriations. Invariably, they are asked to show, to prove, that they have spent wisely in the past and that they can point to real accomplishments. They can, of course, point to the number of employees they have, the number of radio programs, books, and pictures distributed, the reports of surveys, of panels of emigrees, and of the responses of opponents, but in the final analysis they simply cannot say with precision just what the effect of their propaganda really was. To what extent was the Cuban crisis, the Congo disturbances, the Chinese Communists' attacks on India, the anti-American attacks in Canada, the developments in Vietnam and Indonesia, due to the failures or the successes of USIA? No one will ever know. Undoubtedly, American, French, Russian, English—all national propagandas—have their special appeals. One may suspect that the United States is particularly adept in combining words with money, propaganda with economic blandishments, whereas the Communists seem to combine rather adroitly their propagandas with threats of violence. It is doubtful whether the Communists owe very much to the persuasive power of words alone, although studies of the appeals of Communism seem to show that words do win acceptance for certain types of people, at particular times, and under special circumstances.[20] Nevertheless, real limits to the effectiveness of international propaganda are frequently set by the military and economic position of the country, as well as its aims, alliances, and international involvements.

The activities of the United States in the international information and propaganda arena have always been criticized. The charges are numerous and varied. It is claimed that the funds available for this work are inadequate, that more emphasis should be placed on the successful advertising methods used for selling soap and automobiles, that more use should be made of psychological warfare techniques instead of relying altogether on truth and facts, that the targets as a rule should be opinion leaders and influentials, not mass publics.[21] These are only a few of the many allegations made. They come from advertisers who imply, if they do not state explicitly, that advertisers should direct the propaganda operation, or from journalists, public relations people, educators, psychologists, military personnel, media executives, and opinion leaders—each group confident that it knows how the job should be done. The several directors of USIA since its beginning have had varied backgrounds such as advertising and education (Benton), journalism (Barrett), government (Allen), and radio-TV (Murrow). Certainly knowledge of and experience in these fields are most useful, but there are other requisites, not the least of which are administrative competence, ability to obtain adequate funds from Congress, integrity, good judgment, vision, knowledge of foreign countries, and some understanding of the foreign policies of the United States and foreign countries and the history of international relations, at least in recent times.

OBSTACLES TO AMERICAN PROPAGANDA ABROAD

What are some of the principal obstacles and some of the main opportunities and advantages now confronting the USIA and the use of information and propaganda as an instrument of foreign policy. A few of the obstacles have already been mentioned earlier, especially the lack of a united front, the inability to speak with one voice, the democratic traditions of freedom of press and opinion. In the second place, government actions not infrequently belie official words, due in part to the failure to carry out policies because of shifts in party control, because of the operations of constitutional checks and balances, and even because of changes in public opinion. Perhaps the most notable case in point was Woodrow Wilson's inability to persuade the public and Congress of the United States to join the League of Nations after World War I. Each change in administration brings policy modifications and changes, as well as failures to do the expected if not the promised thing. To a certain extent this is inevitable, but none the less a hindrance to effective propaganda and information work.

Another obstacle has been the Foreign Service of the United States, although much less obstructive today than formerly. The Foreign Service approach in the past seemed to lack a dynamic, public opinion, public relations sense. It tended to be opportunistic, legalistic, and businesslike. It was too ready to rely on force. Emphasizing a kind of crisis approach, it failed to plan adequately. Moreover, the Foreign Service was often guilty of using poor, narrowly based, even misleading intelligence from abroad.

Its representatives overseas moved in rather limited, elite, perhaps purely diplomatic circles, oblivious of basic public opinion trends and significant group developments. Intelligence reporting has improved in recent years, but serious gaps are still left in some areas.

In the fourth place, the lack of public understanding of foreign policy issues and problems in the past has been a serious handicap, due in part to official secrecy and traditional aloofness in these matters. In matters of foreign policy, the public-be-damned attitude held by the business world during the latter part of the nineteenth century seemed to pervade the official agencies of government, especially the Department of State, until the present day. Even today the distribution of foreign affairs information through press releases and occasional press conferences, but mainly through private media, is far from adequate.

Mention has already been made of the fact that the United States, in contrast to the Communists, does not have organized political parties in foreign countries to further its causes, but many private groups in the United States, such as churches, labor organizations, business, and professional groups are members of international organizations with affiliates in foreign countries. These formations may, however, impede as well as facilitate the work of USIA abroad, as also might such organizations as the United Nations, NATO, SEATO, and the Organization of American States. Although sponsored and supported by the United States, these regional and world-wide organizations are in no sense information and propaganda organizations for the United States and its policies.

Finally, mention should be made of an obstacle which is especially important—the failure to appreciate the real nature of the cold war and its historical climate, and to understand that it encompasses to a considerable extent a tremendous economic and social revolution sweeping over the Far East, Middle East, Africa and South America. Even Europe and the United States have not been wholly unaffected by it. World Wars, expansion of mass media, speedier transportation, increased mobility, mass education—all have brought the peoples of the earth closer together and have given the developing nations new perspectives, new hopes, and new desires. The world-wide struggle, the cold war, may be in part an ideological struggle between various kinds of Marxists and the non-Marxists, but it is also a striving of previously enchained, suppressed, poor people for better food, clothing, housing—for a higher standard of living. The earlier, dim and distorted picture of the true nature of the climate of the cold war did divert information and propaganda into the wrong channels toward goals less meaningful to the peoples of the underdeveloped world. So long as this failure to understand the true nature of the social, economic, and political upheavals abroad persists, USIA and international propaganda, will continue failing to meet the critical issues of our time.

FAVORABLE RECEPTION OF AMERICAN PROPAGANDA

These are some of the obstacles our information and propaganda activities abroad have encountered, but there have been many favorable factors and numerous facilitating circumstances. One, of course, is the enormous prestige the United States enjoys throughout the world, coupled with respect, and at times popularity. The United States has been severely criticized at times for past mistakes and for individual policies. In some areas it has been envied, scorned, and hated. But underneath all the flamboyant, anti-American propaganda there seems to be a considerable amount of respect for the good will, strength, and accomplishments of the United States. To be sure, this respect is sometimes debased by envy and a lively eagerness to exploit to the full whatever mistakes are made, but the physical, military, technological, know-how resources of the United States are remembered. This attitude not only gives a certain amount of credibility and force to what American propaganda says, but it helps to bring conviction.

The United States has also been fortunate in having an exceptional record of concern for other peoples, a record of willingness to help with foreign aid, technical assistance, and military strength. No country, probably, has done more to promote the health and well being of peoples of other lands, no country has been more zealous in spreading its spiritual, political, and humanitarian values; and no country has been in a position to do as much in recent decades to promote international organizations to serve the interests of international peace and welfare. Today the United States can point with pride to the contributions it has made to the United Nations, UNESCO, the Peace Corps, and through private as well as public grants for humanitarian purposes. The people of other countries may see in these endeavors merely enlightened self-interest; they may criticize the United States for its business civilization, its drive, its mistakes, its tactlessness, perhaps. They may shout "Yankee Imperialism," but many more are aware of the fundamentally unselfish motivations, integrity, lack of any territorial ambitions, real desire to help the world obtain a just and lasting peace. There are, naturally, less high-minded and world-minded groups in the United States. Some American businessmen have exploited, ravished, and sacrificed principle for profit; so have some politicians, labor leaders, farmers, and professional people. All in all the USIA and the Voice of America gain much credence and persuasive strength because of what the United States government and the religious and philanthropic organizations have done and are doing to promote the welfare of all peoples, not merely those in the United States. This may sound smug, immodest, and distorted, but it is safe to say that no country has ever done more in terms of money spent and people sent to reconstruct, to remove poverty, to restore health, to educate, to free, than the United States. Most of the world leaders know this and applaud. This greatly enhances the voice of the United States when it speaks.

The United States also speaks through exceptional facilities of communication. With its newspapers, magazines, books, motion pictures, radio, and television, to say nothing of its hordes of tourists, students, businessmen, and professional people, it can reach almost any person anywhere with its messages. In the arena of world propaganda today the United States enjoys whatever communication facilities are needed. It took the lead long ago in advertising, marketing research, motion pictures, and television. There is really no dearth of communication talent, tools, or know-how. It should excel in publicity, persuasion, possibly organization. As the authority appealed to moves away from philosophy, religion, even law, to science, it remains to be seen whether U. S. propaganda is able to compete effectively for world-wide acceptance with scientific methods as it was with lawyers' brief, theologians' exegetics, or philosophers' logic.

Democratic international propaganda as exemplified by the USIA has other advantages. Subjected to criticism and proposals for improvement on many sides, compelled to justify annually its work before committees of Congress, and moving in an open arena of competition and even conflict with private media, it becomes of necessity more adaptable, more sensitive to new methods and possibilities. There is always the pressure to improve, and improvements there have been in probing and understanding the attitudes, desires, and basic traits of peoples in foreign countries, in differentiating between mass publics and important, specialized publics, in defining objectives, in harmonizing information policy with foreign policy, and in controlling output and evaluating effects. Progress is also being made in co-ordinating words and deeds, in bringing understanding of the purposes, potentialities, and need for this work to members of Congress, other government agencies (especially the Foreign Service), and opinion leaders, and to the public at large. All in all the information and propaganda resources of USIA are many. The propaganda machines of the Communist world, in spite of their authoritarian procedures, are by no means awesome competitors of the free world. What they seem to gain from monopoly, centralization, and unity they may and often do lose in rigidity, lack of initiative, boring uniformity and standardization. If democracies suffer from too much freedom, from too much disorder, initiative, experimentation, waste, and lack of direction, authoritarian governments tend to let their propaganda machines fossilize, stagnate, and ultimately fail to mesh with the needs of a dynamic world society.

PRINCIPLES OF INTERNATIONAL PROPAGANDA

What are the requisites for a sound, overseas information and propaganda program for the United States? Since the end of World War II and even before many prominent people in addition to the directors of USIA have attempted to give the answer.[22] Among these have been public relations and advertising executives, scientists and army officers, educators and publishers. No attempt will be made here to review or appraise their proposals. It may be of use to state, however, what seem to be, at least in the minds of some, a few of the salient principles that should characterize our policy.

(1) It should be recognized that the basis of sound information policy is sound foreign policies: constructive, positive, satisfying policies. It is not the proper job of a propaganda agency to make foreign policy, although it may be very advisable to hear such an agency's advice when such policies are made. This is not the place, were it possible to do so, to stipulate the requirements of the United States' Cuban, Berlin, Canadian, Congo, or Vietnamese policies. It is sufficient to emphasize that propaganda policy can really never be better than the basic decisions of policymakers themselves.

(2) Closely related to this point is the importance of co-ordinating words and deeds. This is not always easy as administrations and officials change, as circumstances and world conditions and relationships vary, as new perspectives appear. Perfect consistency is not possible, but prudence and restraint may help to avoid the more salient divergencies.

(3) More attention should be given to the viewpoints and questions of peoples abroad, the vital questions they are asking, the needs that are closest to their hearts as well as their minds. This requires more careful studies, research, and surveys. It means that the agency must develop an international point of view, must understand the real reasons for dissatisfaction, tension, and hate where they exist abroad. Progress is being and has been made, but all too frequently stress is placed on what the agency thinks foreign peoples should hear, not on what problems and issues are vital to peoples abroad.

(4) There is probably no justification for the use by an information and propaganda agency of the government, especially in peacetime, of hate, subversive, or slanderous propaganda against foreign countries and their peoples.[23] If psychological warfare techniques seem justified in wartime, or during cold war periods, they should be clearly divorced from the procedures of an agency such as the USIA and placed within the jurisdiction of the military. Not only are these techniques more or less reprehensible in themselves and justified only by the defensive needs of war,

but their effectiveness is usually short-lived and greatly overrated. To employ them in peacetime not only engenders international tension, but it also undermines the confidence of the people who use them abroad in what the country says or does. The USIA must use every means possible to maintain the credibility of its information and propaganda output and avoid purely psychological warfare methods.

(5) The main emphasis of an information and propaganda agency which serves as an instrument of foreign policy for a democracy should be on information and interpretation. It is seriously questionable whether much time and money need be spent merely trying to entertain the people of foreign countries with cultural exchange programs. In many cases local, private agencies abroad can do this better, and whatever good will is created by such programs will likely be ephemeral. The people of foreign countries are entitled to read, see, and hear about the policies of the United States, the reasons and motives for them, and any other news and information about the United States which cannot be readily and adequately obtained from their own private and unofficial sources.

(6) It is extremely important to maintain the credibility of the information agency. This can best be done, not by tricks of advertising, boasting, distortions, and deceptions, but by sincere, honest, illuminating reporting. It is preferable for such an agency to have a reputation for sincerity and accuracy than to be known for its propaganda slickness, deviousness, and cleverness. Strategies and techniques are never as important as substantive content, evidence, and logic.

(7) The relations with private media are important too. In the years immediately after World War II, fears were expressed that newspapers, news agencies, radio and other mass media would be subjected to a kind of unfair competition if the government continued its world-wide press, news, and radio services. However unrealistic these fears were, they were very real, and they accounted in part for the opposition of many media officials to government activities in the international, as well as the domestic, information field. It is clear that a government information agency must supplement, not supplant private media. The presumption always is that when and where the private media can do the better job it should do it. When gaps exist, when the people of foreign countries are not getting the adequate, unbiased news needed to preserve a favorable view of U. S. government action and policies, then the government must step in. At present many remote areas are not served as well as they should be, partly because it is too expensive to do so. This is an opportunity for the government, if it is clear that these areas of ignorance really should be penetrated.

(8) Every effort should be made to co-operate with existing private international organizations, that they may help in the tremendous job of spreading enlightenment. Mention has been made previously of the world-

wide propaganda effectiveness of religious groups, business organizations, trade unions, sports and professional associations. With certain publics abroad these are perhaps the most effective educational and propaganda channels which exist. The "People-to-People" program was planned with these opportunities in mind, but it has not been vigorously and persistently pursued.

(9) Finally, the Information Agency should think of itself as the public relations arm of the government in the highest and best sense. It must forever be concerned with improving relations between the United States and foreign countries. This is not merely a crisis job; it is a continuous, everlasting one. As indicated in a previous chapter, the job entails the persistent study and survey of the relations between countries, and the analysis of bad situations where they exist to determine why they are bad. Finally, it may involve recommendations to remedy those bad situations, steps that may involve changes and improvements in information policy, modifications of public policy, or negotiation, arbitration, judicial settlement. The role of democratic, international propaganda, as an instrument of foreign policy, finds its greatest justification in the part it plays in creating greater international understanding, mollifying tensions, adjusting and accommodating conflicting national interests to the end of international peace.

NOTES FOR CHAPTER 14

Epigraph. Harold D. Lasswell, "The Theory of Political Propaganda," in *American Political Science Review,* Vol. 21 (1927), p. 627.

1. Lumley, F. E., *The Propaganda Menace* (The Century Company, 1933) though more than thirty years old and concerned with reprehensible propaganda, nevertheless is useful because of its historical and world-wide sweep.
2. See Davidson, Philip G., *Propaganda and the American Revolution* (Chapel Hill: University of North Carolina Press, 1941).
3. See Mathews, Joseph J., *Reporting the Wars* (Minneapolis: The University of Minnesota Press, 1957).
4. See Wilkerson, Marcus M., *Public Opinion and the Spanish-American War: A Study in War Propaganda* (Baton Rouge: Louisiana State University, 1932).
5. See Mock, James R., and Cedric Larson, *Words That Won the War: The Story of the Committee on Public Information, 1917-1919* (Princeton, N. J.: Princeton University Press, 1939).
6. See Childs, H. L., and J. B. Whitton (eds.), *Propaganda By Short Wave* (Princeton, N. J.: Princeton University Press, 1942).
7. See Smith, Bruce L., "Democratic Control of Propaganda Through Registration and Disclosure," *Public Opinion Quarterly,* Vol. 6 (Spring, 1942), pp. 27-40, and Vol. 7 (Winter, 1943), pp. 707-19.
8. See Thomson, C. A. H., *Overseas Information Service of the United States Government* (Washington, D. C.: The Brookings Institution, 1948).

9. See MacMahon, Arthur W., *Memorandum on the Postwar International Program of the United States,* Department of State Publication, 2438 (Washington: U. S. Government Printing Office, 1945).

10. Much of the story of USIA may be found in the *Hearings* of the Appropriation Committees of Congress. See also Dizard, Wilson P., *The Strategy of Truth;* Dyer, Murray, *The Weapon on the Wall;* Stephens, Oren, *Facts to a Candid World;* Barrett, Edward W., *Truth Is Our Weapon.*

11. See *Hearings,* Committee on Appropriations, House of Representatives, 88th Congress, 1st Sess., April, 1963, p. 30.

12. *Idem.,* p. 497.

13. See Holt, Robert T., *Radio Free Europe* (Minneapolis: University of Minnesota Press, 1958).

14. On January 25, 1964, the United States announced that it would suspend its most powerful radio propaganda transmission into East Germany, February 1, 1964. "The cessation of seven hours of the long-wave broadcasts of RIAS, the United States radio station in West Berlin, represents half of an unwritten bargain struck last summer between the United States and the Soviet Union. The Soviet concession, which went into effect last June 19, was suspension of the jamming of Voice of America short-wave and medium-wave broadcasts beamed into the Soviet Union." *New York Times,* January 26, 1964, p. 1.

15. Much of the information regarding USIA activities is taken from *Hearings* before the Appropriations Committee of the House of Representatives, 98th Congress, 1st Sess., April, 1963.

16. *Idem.,* p. 402.

17. See Barghoorn, Frederick C., *Soviet Foreign Propaganda* (Princeton, N. J.: Princeton University Press, 1964), and Kirkpatrick, E. M., *Target: The World: Communist Propaganda Activities in 1955* (New York: The Macmillan Co., 1956).

18. See Hazard, John N., *The Soviet System of Government* (3rd ed.; Chicago: University of Chicago Press, 1964), and Inkeles, Alex, *Public Opinion in Soviet Russia* (Cambridge, Mass.: Harvard University Press, 1958).

19. See Barghoorn, Frederick C., *Soviet Foreign Propaganda,* as well as his *The Soviet Cultural Offensive: The Role of Cultural Diplomacy in Soviet Foreign Policy* (Princeton, N. J.: Princeton University Press, 1960).

20. See Almond, Gabriel A., *The Appeals of Communism* (Princeton, N. J.: Princeton University Press, 1954).

21. See Holt, R. T., and Van de Velde, Robert W., *Strategic Psychological Operations and American Foreign Policy* (Chicago: University of Chicago Press, 1960); also *Sprague Committee Reports to Ike re United States Activities Abroad,* Department of State Bulletin, Vol. 44 (February 6, 1961), pp. 82-195.

22. Many of the authors previously cited have made proposals for reform of USIA such as Wilson P. Dizard, Murray Dyer, C. A. H. Thomson, R. T. Holt, R. W. Van de Velde. See also Goodfriend, Arthur, *The Twisted Image* (1963); and the suggestions of James P. Warburg, *Unwritten Treaty* (1946); Wallace Carroll, *Persuade or Perish* (1948). *The New York Times* carried suggestions from many prominent people in 1950: Arthur Compton (Jan. 18); Senator Brien McMahon (Feb. 2); Dean Acheson (April 2); Bernard Baruch (July 7); Arthur Krock (August 5); George Gallup (Nov. 22); William Benton (June 1); David Sarnoff (July 7); Dwight Eisenhower (Sept. 6).

23. See Whitton, John B. (ed.) *Propaganda and the Cold War* (Washington, D. C.: Public Affairs Press, 1963); Martin, Leslie J., *International Propaganda: Its Legal and Diplomatic Control* (Minneapolis: University of Minnesota Press, 1958).

SUPPLEMENTARY READING

ALLEN, GEORGE W. "Are the Soviets Winning the Propaganda War?" *Annals of the American Academy of Political and Social Science,* Vol. 336 (July, 1961), pp. 1-11.

Anon., *Sprague Committee Reports to Ike re United States Information Activities Abroad.* Department of State Bulletin, Vol. 44 (Feb. 6, 1961), pp. 182-95.

BARGHOORN, FREDERICK C. *Soviet Foreign Propaganda.* Princeton, N. J.: Princeton University Press, 1963.

BARRETT, EDWARD W. *Truth Is Our Weapon.* New York: Funk-Wagnalls, 1953.

BOGART, LEO. "Measuring the Effectiveness of an Overseas Information Campaign: A Case History," *Public Opinion Quarterly,* Vol. 21 (Winter, 1957-58), pp. 475-98.

CARROLL, WALLACE. *Persuade or Perish.* Boston: Houghton Mifflin Co., 1948.

CHILDS, HARWOOD L., and WHITTON, J. B. (eds.). *Propaganda by Short Wave.* Princeton, N. J.: Princeton University Press, 1942.

CHILDS, HARWOOD L. (ed.). *Propaganda and Dictatorship.* Princeton, N. J.: Princeton University Press, 1936.

CHILDS, HARWOOD L. (ed.). "Office of War Information," *Public Opinion Quarterly,* Vol. 7 (Spring, 1943). Entire issue devoted to O.W.I.

DAUGHERTY, W. E., and JANOWITZ, MORRIS. *A Psychological Warfare Casebook.* Baltimore: Johns Hopkins University Press, 1958.

DAVISON, W. PHILLIPS. *The Berlin Blockade: A Study in Cold War Politics.* Princeton, N. J.: Princeton University Press, 1958.

DIZARD, WILSON P. *The Strategy of Truth: The Story of the USIS.* Washington, D. C.: Public Affairs Press, 1961.

DYER, MURRAY. *The Weapon on the Wall: Rethinking Psychological Warfare.* Baltimore: Johns Hopkins University Press, 1959.

EVANS, FRANK BOWEN (ed.). *World-wide Communist Propaganda Activities.* New York: The Macmillan Co., 1955.

GROTHE, PETER. *To Win the Minds of Men: The Story of the Communist Propaganda War in East Germany.* Palo Alto, California: Pacific Books, 1958.

HOLT, ROBERT T. *Radio Free Europe.* Minneapolis: The University of Minnesota Press, 1958.

HOLT, ROBERT T., and VAN DE VELDE, ROBERT W. *Strategic Psychological Operations and American Foreign Policy.* Chicago: University of Chicago Press, 1960.

INKELES, ALEX, et al. "Propaganda in World Politics," *Columbia Journal of International Affairs,* Vol. 5, No. 2 (Spring, 1951).

JANOWITZ, MORRIS. "Mass Persuasion and International Relations," *Public Opinion Quarterly,* Vol. 25 (Winter, 1961), pp. 560-70.

JOYCE, WALTER. *The Propaganda Gap.* New York and Evanston: Harper and Row, 1963.

KAMINS, BERNARD FRANCIS. *Basic Propaganda.* Los Angeles: Houlgate House, 1951.

KIRKPATRICK, EVAN MAURICE. *Target: The World. Communist Propaganda Activities in 1955.* New York: The Macmillan Co., 1956.

KLAPPER, JOSEPH T., and LOWENTHAL, LEO. "The Contributions of Opinion Research to the Evaluation of Psychological Warfare," *Public Opinion Quarterly,* Vol. 15 (Winter, 1951-52), pp. 651-62.

LINEBARGER, PAUL M. A. *Psychological Warfare.* Washington: Infantry Journal Press, 1954.

LUMLEY, F. E. *The Propaganda Menace.* New York: The Century Co., 1933.

MACMAHON, ARTHUR W. *Memorandum on the Postwar International Information Program of the United States.* Department of State, U. S. Government Printing Office, 1945.

MARKEL, LESTER, *et al. Public Opinion and Foreign Policy.* New York: Harper & Bros., 1949.

MARTIN, LESLIE JOHN. *International Propaganda: Its Legal and Diplomatic Control.* Minneapolis: University of Minnesota Press, 1958.

MOCK, JAMES R., and LARSON, CEDRIC. *Words That Won the War.* Princeton, N. J.: Princeton University Press, 1939.

PADOVER, SAUL KUSSIEL. *Psychological Warfare.* New York: Foreign Policy Association, 1951.

SCHNEIDER, MAARTEN. "International Propaganda in Recent Decades," *Gazette,* Vol. 7. (No. 2, 1961), pp. 199-210.

SPEIER, HANS. "The Future of Psychological Warfare," *Public Opinion Quarterly,* Vol. 12 (Spring, 1948), pp. 5-18.

STEPHENS, OREN. *Facts to a Candid World.* Palo Alto, Calif.: Stanford University Press, 1955.

THOMSON, CHARLES A., and LAVES, WALTER H. C. *Cultural Relations and U. S. Foreign Policy.* Bloomington: Indiana University Press, 1962.

THOMSON, CHARLES A. H. *Overseas Information Service of the United States Government.* Washington, D. C.: Brookings Institution, 1948.

U. S. Departments of State, Justice, and Commerce, the Judiciary, and Related Agencies Appropriations for 1963. *Hearings before the Subcommittee of the Committee on Appropriations, House of Representatives,* 87th Congress, 2nd Sess. pp. 1-767. (U. S. Information Agency and eight others included.)

WARBURG, JAMES P. *Unwritten Treaty.* New York: Harcourt Brace, & Co., 1946.

WHEELER, G. E. "Propaganda and Counterpropaganda in Asia," *Royal Central Asia Society Journal,* Vol. 48 (July, 1961), pp. 264-73.

WHITAKER, URBAN G. *Propaganda and International Relations.* San Francisco, Calif.: Howard Chandler (1960).

WHITTON, JOHN B. (ed.). *Propaganda and the Cold War.* (Washington, D. C.: Public Affairs Press, 1963.)

XV · The Role of
Public Opinion

The excellence of popular government lies not so much in its wisdom—
for it is apt to err as other kinds of government—as in its strength.
—JAMES BRYCE

IT IS ONE THING to try and discover what role public opinion is playing in policy-making and quite another to decide what role it should play. There are, of course, those who argue that social scientists should not be concerned with what ought to be, but solely with what is, but to strip them of values and ideals is to leave them naked indeed. Neither politicians nor students of politics have been able, since the times of Plato and Aristotle, to avoid entirely the role of philosopher, amateur or professional. The framers of the American Constitution of 1787 were deeply concerned with the issue of what role "the people" should play in policy-making, and this question has persisted to the present. Walter Lippmann, for example, takes a very dim view of the public's role in policy-making.[1] In contrast, George Gallup and many other modern pollsters are very optimistic. Others, however, take what may be called a more discriminating attitude.

THE ROLE OF PUBLIC OPINION

An answer to the question of what the role of public opinion should be will be determined in large part by (1) the definition of the term "public opinion" itself, and (2) by the general philosophical outlook within which it is defined. Ever since the term "public opinion" came into widespread use during the latter part of the eighteenth century, it has meant different things to different people. The only point on which all agree is that the

348

term refers to the opinions of a number of people. From there on almost an infinite variety of interpretations appear as indicated in Chapter 2. These differences of interpretation usually relate to differences of opinion regarding the particular group of people constituting the "public," the degree of agreement necessary, the extent to which the opinions must be formed in a particular way, the subject matter of the opinions and their intensity and stability, as well as their influence. Most of the differences in definition can be explained by attempts to restrict the meaning of the term to collections of opinions in one or more of the above respects.

It is obvious that a person's view of the role of public opinion will be profoundly affected by whether the public he is thinking of is the totality of the electorate in the United States, those paying attention to the issue, those whose opinions the government will pay attention to, or some other group. Similarly, his conception of the role of public opinion will be determined in part by whether he limits the meaning to opinions formed rationally and based on information necessary for an intelligent decision, or includes all opinions regardless of their method of formation, their quality, or their effectiveness. If public opinion means majority opinion, its role may be defined quite differently from what it would be if restricted to a much higher degree of agreement, even consensus. The point is clear: definitions of public opinion differ and consequently opinions regarding the role of public opinion will differ.

Views regarding the role of public opinion will also differ because of differences in philosophical outlook, in social, economic, political, and religious beliefs. What are the chief ends of the state—survival, justice, the good life? Why should the people—however you define them—be consulted? Is it because they are all wise, wise in some matters, because consulting the people is expedient, or because it is just? What is justice? Is it to be found in some higher, transcendental moral order, or here and now in the decisions of the majority? What about science? If the only path to truth, justice, and the public interest is the scientific one, is there really any logical role for public opinion to follow except the scientific expert?

The point of all this is not to suggest that there are definitive answers but to indicate that our views on these and other profound philosophical questions do have and inevitably must have a very important influence on the role we think public opinion should play in public policy decisions.

Now we turn specifically to the problem of what the role of public opinion should be in the United States today. My definition of public opinion is very general and very simple; it is merely "any collection of individual opinions," thereby leaving open the question of what group and what aspects of opinions to consider at a particular time. For the purposes of this discussion, however, the public will be defined as the American electorate, and the opinions of interest will be its opinions regarding major foreign and domestic policies.

WHY CONSULT PUBLIC OPINION?

Why should the opinions of this public be consulted, and to what extent should these opinions be binding? In the first place, because it is expedient. As Lord Bryce said many years ago, "The excellence of popular government lies not so much in its wisdom . . . as in its strength." [2] A government which is founded on consent, whose major policies, personnel, and procedures have the explicit or implicit support of the generality of the people, is less subject to violent overthrow and sudden change. It is also expedient in a negative sense, in that it is difficult, if not impossible, to identify a smaller group more competent than the general public to decide certain kinds of questions.

In the second place, it seems only just that those who are affected by major policy decisions should be consulted about them or have some share in their making. Finally, it may be argued, and with much force, that public opinion, as defined above, is wiser on some matters than the opinion of any other smaller group. It is to this last point that I want to give special consideration.

On what kinds of questions, if any, is the general public especially competent? As indicated earlier, political philosophers have wrestled with this question for centuries. Their answers vary from those who believe that the voice of the people is the Voice of God to those who say it is the Voice of the Devil. It is necessary, however, to take a more discriminating view and to differentiate questions such as those concerning the ends of policy from the means of attaining it, general from specific questions, technical from non-technical questions, those within from those outside the experience of the voter, voting for men from voting on measures, choosing a party from deciding an issue, financial questions from non-financial, voicing grievances from choosing remedies, assessing the results of government action from formulating new proposals. Many would argue, therefore, that the general public is especially competent, probably more competent than any other group—elitist, expert, or otherwise—to determine the basic ends of public policy, to choose top policy-makers, to appraise the results of public policy, and to say what, in the final analysis is fair, just, and moral. On the other hand, the general public is not competent to determine the best means for attaining specific goals, to answer technical questions, to prescribe remedies for political, social, and economic ills, and to deal with specialized issues far removed from the everyday experience and understanding of the people in general.

UNDERMINING FORCES

Now, it is my thesis that every effort should be made to preserve, and if possible expand, the role of public opinion in its special areas of competence. I say preserve, because many forces seem to be at work curtailing and undermining the role of public opinion as we have known it in the past. I shall mention only a few—the growth in executive power, the speed of social change, the growing complexity and technical nature of public issues, and the oligarchic, bureaucratic, centralizing tendencies within parties, pressure groups, mass media, and other channels through which the influence of public opinion is brought to bear on public officials. Representative bodies are becoming less representative, and elections, although they indicate the preferred candidate, often give only a nebulous indication of the public's attitudes on policies.

How has the growth of executive power affected the role of public opinion? It has meant that the President and his advisers have assumed more and more responsibility for the formulation and initiation of legislative policies, that they have been able to bring new and powerful pressures on Congress to enact legislation, and that the role of Congress as the basic, constitutional channel for translating public opinion into public policy has lost much of its effectiveness. The growth in executive power has also meant a tremendous increase in the role of the President and the executive branch as leaders of public opinion and in the skillful use of publicity, propaganda, and censorship to mold public opinion. An increasingly large number of public policy decisions of the greatest importance are made by the President and his staff without the direct participation of the legislative branch, to say nothing of public opinion, as for example in the recent steel crisis and the Cuban affair. On several occasions President Kennedy sought to justify this exercise of power on the ground that he alone could represent the public interest in these matters. What we are actually witnessing, I believe, is a marked transition from public opinion influencing government to government influencing public opinion. This trend may be inevitable, and, under present circumstances, possibly desirable to a certain extent, but it modifies considerably the traditional role of public opinion in the United States and the theory of government responsibility.

The speed of social change has tended to restrict the role of public opinion. It is not only jet planes that move with the speed of sound, but political, economic, social, and technological developments as well. It is not only difficult for people to keep up-to-date in their information on these changes, but it is well-nigh impossible for them to bring their collective judgment to bear at the right place, at the right time, and in a useful, helpful way. In many areas of public policy, particularly domestic, problems and the decisions which have to be made in consequence of them do not have to be resolved suddenly, and they can be anticipated. An ever increasing number of crises, especially in the international field, arise overnight. On these issues public opinion cannot make its influence felt.

Closely related to the above trend is the growing complexity and technical nature of public issues. Whether one turns to the issues of national security, public finance, agricultural policy, or public health and education, this complexity is evident. The scientific aspects of many of these questions loom so large that sometimes the non-scientific aspects, aspects well within the competence of the layman and not the expert, are lost sight of.

Finally, what tendencies or trends may be discerned in the functioning of those channels between public opinion and government through which the influence of public opinion presumably flows? As pointed out earlier, public opinion seldom brings its influence to bear directly on public officials. Rather, this influence is mediated through political parties and pressure groups of all kinds, through representative bodies, by elections, and by the mass media—to mention the more important. Now these channels function in a three-fold capacity. They serve to transmit the opinions of the people to government, to transmit government opinions down to the people, and they also serve as independent molders and controllers of both government and public opinion. Many changes are taking place in the three-fold functions of these channels. It would take us too far afield to attempt to discuss separately even a few of the many developments in the mass media, in the arena of political parties and pressure groups, in elections and legislative bodies—all of which are significant. Possibly a few generalizations can be made which will apply to all channels: (1) None of these mediating links, not even elections, reflect public opinion precisely, and very frequently the distortions and discrepancies are great. (2) In the political party and pressure group sector, and to some extent in the mass media, centralization and bureaucratization even more than formerly are obstructing the free flow of public opinion to the seats of power and authority. (3) There is an increasing emphasis by government, groups, and media alike on the use of propaganda, publicity, and public relations techniques to direct and control public opinion.

EXPANDING THE ROLE OF PUBLIC OPINION

In view of all these developments what may be done to preserve, and possibly to expand, the participation of public opinion in policy-making? I am assuming that it is expedient and just for public officials to consult the people and that, on certain types of questions, the people may be wiser than other more select groups. For the sake of convenience, suggestions for preserving and expanding the role of public opinion may be considered with specific reference to the particular developments mentioned above.

In the first place, what does the growth of executive power suggest? More specifically, how can responsible government, in the sense of government responsible to the people, be preserved in the face of ever-increasing executive power and control over public opinion? There is no simple solution. The problem will need to be attacked along many different lines. Only a few of these avenues can be suggested.

In the first place, machinery could be devised and utilized for ascertaining more quickly and accurately the state of public opinion on crucial issues for use by executive authority. Not only would such machinery have to be geared to questions which the public is peculiarly competent to answer, but crises would have to be anticipated, issues formulated, and questions asked before the crises actually reached the decision stage. In view of the fact that a survey agency would need to work in close association with executive authorities and be fully informed of developments, negotiations, and relevant data, it is questionable whether a non-governmental agency would be satisfactory.

It would seem that the time has come to set up, possibly in collaboration with state governments, an official survey agency. Such an agency would supplement, not supplant, private polling agencies, and it could help to maintain and increase the desirable role of public opinion in policy-making. In the framing of questions it could be guided solely by its judgment of the importance, priority, and public significance of issues. It could take special pains to differentiate between those questions within and those outside the competence of the public. Working in close co-operation with the proper officials it could try and anticipate crises, foresee to some extent the crucial issues which might arise and lie within the competence of the masses, thus giving the people a chance to influence public policy even in a day of very rapid social change. This anticipatory function is very important in view of the virtual impossibility of public opinion to participate in policy decisions, especially in foreign policy decisions, in this day of sudden, speedy movement. Such a government survey agency could help to solve the public opinion problems which arise because of the technical, complicated nature of so many public policies. Although it is true that major issues of public policy do have an increasing scientific and technological complexity, nevertheless most of them also have their normative, value laden, moral aspects. It is toward the solution of these aspects that the public could make a worthwhile contribution. A government survey agency would be able, in many instances, to separate these aspects from the others and give public opinion an opportunity to participate meaningfully.

In advocating the participation of public opinion in policy-making, I do not mean to suggest that public opinion is all-wise or that the public interest is always what public opinion says it is on all kinds of questions. There has been much discussion of the term "public interest": what it is, how it may be ascertained. The basic clash in opinions stems from differing views regarding the nature, force, and relationship between God-made and man-made law; the higher, moral, or natural law and the lower, man-made law. For those who believe in the existence of the former, the public interest in the final analysis is whatever is in tune with the higher, natural or God-made law. For the "unbelievers" the public interest must be what is constitutional, legal, and statutory. What is in the public interest at this level will always be determined and conditioned by the form of government, its procedures, and the constitutional principles underlying it. In the United States the process of law-making from constitution, to statute, to local ordinance is a complicated one. Numerous groups play a part in it, formally and informally, from the general public, pressure groups, mass media, representative bodies, administrative agencies, to the judicial tribunals. The public interest at the lower, mundane level is, in the United States at least, what emerges as law or legal principle. The public interest at any higher level will vary with one's conception of higher law.

Some have argued that the influence of public opinion on government in the United States reached its peak several decades ago and that since then so-called "free public opinion" is being progressively enslaved by government management, censorship, and propaganda.[3] The notion of a "free public opinion" is a slippery one, since opinions are never really "free" from the influences that mold them. If what is meant is a public opinion free from government attempts to manage it, the fact is that governments have always tried to mold public opinion and win public support. One may agree, perhaps, that governments in the United States, especially during the last thirty years, have used the mass media and other communication agencies with zeal, skill, and more vigor than before, but the difference is essentially one of degree. To see the matter in perspective, however, one should remember that not only governments, but pressure groups, including political parties, economic and professional groups, churches, and educators, to say nothing of the wielders of mass media themselves, are continually trying to curb this "free public opinion." The real question is not, should government influence be curtailed, and the influence of some other group be enhanced, but what is the way best calculated to preserve the most desirable balance among these competing influences? As stated previously, under certain conditions, and these conditions are extremely important, the most satisfactory balances will be found in an arena of open competition in which the government as well as private groups compete. The rules of competition must be enforced, in order that the competition may serve the intended purpose, that is public enlightenment. The task of rule-making is unending, and much progress has been made in outlawing libels, slander, false advertising, and many other means and devices for defeating the purposes of the competition. The pressure for improvements must continue. Among other things a clearer differentiation between the roles of electorate, legislature, executive, and expert must be spelled out and put to work. The line between what the government should and should not do as a propagandist must be more tightly drawn. Rules must be drafted and used to deflate the influence of money and material resources and to elevate the power of evidence, information, logic, and public virtues.

The Cuban crisis in the fall of 1962, a crisis that brought the world to the brink of a third world war, demonstrated in an awesome way how fateful a responsibility did rest, and could rest again, on the President of the United States himself and a few hand-picked advisors. Not even Congress or the President's Cabinet (much less public opinion) really participated directly and significantly in the crucial decision. This is not to imply that either Congress or public opinion should have participated directly, but it does suggest that methods need to be found to make the voice of the people and their elected representatives count when the chips are down if democracy in any real sense is to work. The constitutional requirement that only Congress can declare war has long since been outdated, and more explicit and realistic procedures must be installed to avoid the withering away of the democratic ideal.

A second major development, not unrelated to what has just been discussed, is the accelerating tempo of social change. How could Congress, much less public opinion, participate in the President's decisions on Cuba, in view of the race against time precipitated by the rapidly mounting bomb installations in Cuba? Isn't the speed of social change, particularly technological, political, and economic so rapid and the necessity for quick decisions so paramount that democracy, in the sense of rule by public opinion, must default in many matters in the realm of foreign policy? There are, of course, many times when democratically made decisions must give precedence to the decisions of one or a few, but this is not the ideal procedure from the liberal viewpoint, when the decision is one involving a problem peculiarly within the competence of the electorate. In order that democracy may keep pace with the rapidly changing scene, greater emphasis must be given to study developments, to anticipate crises, to consider alternative ways of dealing with them, and to get the public's reaction to these alternatives and to other questions within its competence where feasible.

Regarding some of the critical areas of the world today—Berlin, the Near East, Vietnam, Taiwan, Cuba—no one knows when these powder kegs may explode or at what time the United States may have to make quick, tragic decisions. Each case will involve questions for the experts, questions for the President and his advisors, questions for Congress, and, if our previous considerations of the competence of the electorate are valid, perhaps a question or two regarding ends, values, national purpose, which preferably the voters as a whole should decide. To get the answers from the voting public during the heat of the crisis would be undesirable, and probably impossible. Now government agencies are looking ahead, identifying contingencies, working out alternate solutions. This is true of the civilian as well as the military agencies of government. What is not done, in any significant way, is to select from the many questions considered, the few on which public opinion is more competent to answer than any other group, and to obtain the public reactions to them. Unless this is done, the influence of public opinion on public policy will dwindle, and democracy in the sense of rule by public opinion, will atrophy. This may be what some Platonists, elitists, or authoritarians desire, to deprecate the masses and their opinions. For those, however, who believe that superior wisdom on some questions (perhaps a very few) does lie with the masses, it is necessary through planning, foresight, and anticipatory action to give the people a say before it is too late. One of the crucial tasks will be to distill from the bewildering maze of technical–non-technical, ends and means questions, the fundamental, core queries for the mass public. This is a job for philosophers as well as scientists, for those who see deeply, broadly, and clearly.

A third trend, in addition to the growth of executive powers, and the acceleration of social change, has been the multiplication of technical questions, and questions involving to a large extent complicated, scientific aspects. Scientific advances have affected substantially farm problems and questions of public health, transportation, and urbanization, also in problems of disarmament, nuclear testing, space exploration, to say nothing of defense contracts, supplies, and construction. The advice of scientists is required in practically all areas of public policy. This would seem, at first blush, to remove most public issues from the purview of mass public opinion, and it undoubtedly will unless the purely technical issues are separated from the non-technical, and the questions of means from those of ends and goals. The problem of rendering unto experts the questions for experts and unto citizens the questions for public opinion is one that must be solved if democracy is to keep pace with technological development. Who should perform this task? He who has the authority to frame the question for the public or for the experts may practically determine the issue. Many sources should be encouraged to do this: the President and his advisors, Congressmen, political party and group leaders, scholars, philosophers, educators. Undoubtedly, in a great many cases, there will be substantial agreement regarding what question or questions are for the public. Where there is not, further study, analysis, and discussion is needed before polling the public. There should be some official body, executive, legislative, or independent, to identify the questions on which there seems to be general agreement that they are suitable for the public and to see that the public's opinion is obtained.

Not only does the public need guidance regarding the questions appropriate for it, but there is a desperate need for more orderly public discussion of some of the great national issues. Legislative bodies, as well as the courts, have developed over the years rules of procedure to promote more orderly discussion, deliberation, and final decision-making. In the public arena, there is chaos. All kinds of issues are being discussed at the same time; newspaper readers are confronted with the views of numerous columnists on a variety of topics in a single edition; television programming is similarly confusing; and throughout the court of public opinion the lack of orderliness promotes confusion, befuddlement, disgust, and very often indifference. There is no pat remedy for this situation. Perhaps one may detect, since the revival of the great debates in the Presidential campaign of 1960, a movement in the direction of better focus, but the detector would have to be very sensitive indeed. Progress will have to be made slowly, step by step. Above all, political leaders, government officials, and media executives will have to take the lead, work out an agenda for public discussion of issues for the electorate, and then co-operate in focusing on those issues at the agreed upon times. If, for example, an effort were made by leading newspaper, radio, and television executives on the one hand, and the President and Congressional leaders on the other to select one different public issue for emphasis each month during the coming year, and then advocates pro and con and on all sides were encouraged to discuss that issue during the month stipulated, it would undoubtedly contribute to public enlightenment. Such an improvement would only be in emphasis. It could only underscore an issue each month in an orderly manner; one could hardly expect other issues to be removed from the arena, as well as other distractions.

Finally, what may be done to alleviate the centralizing tendencies in all organized groups to obstruct the impact of public opinion on public policy? Here again, one encounters the argument that public opinion is not competent to pass on any questions of public policy, or any aspects of the questions; that public opinion must always be filtered through and colored by the opinions of leaders of organized groups and legislative representatives. Those who accept this argument are not much perturbed by centralizing tendencies. They say that democracy is realized, not by democracy within groups, but between groups, and so long as there are two or more political parties, for example, competing for votes, there is no reason for concern about anti-democratic tendencies within the parties. The absurdity of this argument is revealed if it is applied to the international scene. It would approve, apparently, of national dictatorships, since competition among them would best preserve democracy. Believers in democracy cannot accept this line of reasoning. If public opinion has a role to play in the national life of states, it has a role to play in the groups within those states. From the largest groups to the smallest, there are questions for the members as a whole, as well as for the leaders and experts, not only on the grounds of justice or of expediency, but because the general public is the most competent public to decide particular questions.

If one accepts this democratic position, then efforts should be made to implement it by democratizing as far as possible the groups that make up society. This means carefully discriminating between and among the roles and functions of leaders and followers, experts and amateurs, officials and members. The role of public opinion, in the sense of the collective opinions of its members, must be defined in terms of its competence, and it must be continually redefined as conditions change and competence rises or lowers. Machinery and procedures must be devised for enabling members to express opinions and participate in policy-making to the extent of their capabilities, and every effort must be made to raise the capabilities through information and education.

There are many, many problems of public opinion, problems of finding out what it is, problems of improving its quality and making it what it ought to be. There are also problems of reconciling conflicts of opinion between states, groups, and individuals. There is the problem of the role of public opinion, the problem of according to the masses, the adult electorate, the part it should play in the public affairs of the town, city, state, nation, even the world. Not to discriminate carefully between what it can and cannot do may well encourage pessimism regarding the prospects of democracy, or unwarranted optimism. To ask the masses the wrong questions, questions for which they have little or no competence, may be as disastrous to the cause of democracy as not asking any questions at all, for democracy must be redefined continually in terms of the capacities of public opinion.

NOTES FOR CHAPTER 15

Epigraph. James Bryce, *The American Commonwealth,* Chapter 77, Vol. 2, p. 263.
1. "Where mass opinion dominates the government, there is a morbid derangement of the true functions of power. The derangement brings about the enfeeblement, verging on paralysis of the capacity to govern." *The Public Philosophy* (Boston: Little, Brown and Co., Mentor Book ed., 1956), p. 19.
2. *The American Commonwealth* (The Macmillan Co., 1924 edition), ch. 77, Vol. II, p. 263.

3. See Wilson, Francis Graham, *A Theory of Public Opinion* (Chicago: Henry Regnery Co., 1962).

SUPPLEMENTARY READING

ANGELL, NORMAN. *The Public Mind.* New York: The Macmillan Co., 1927.
BARNETT, J. D. *The Operation of the Initiative, Referendum, and Recall in Oregon.* New York: The Macmillan Co., 1915.
BERELSON, BERNARD. "Democratic Theory and Public Opinion," *Public Opinion Quarterly,* Vol. 16 (Fall, 1952), pp. 313-30.
BRYCE, JAMES. *The American Commonwealth.* Vol. II, pp. 261-403. (1889 edition)
BRYCE, JAMES. *Modern Democracies.* New York: The Macmillan, Co., 1921.
CHILDS, HARWOOD L. "Rule by Public Opinion," *The Atlantic Monthly,* Vol. 157 (June, 1936), pp. 735-64.
COTTRELL, EDWIN A. "Twenty-five years of Direct Legislation in California," *Public Opinion Quarterly,* Vol. 3 (Jan., 1939), pp. 30-45.
DAHL, ROBERT ALAN. *A Preface to Democratic Theory.* Chicago: University of Chicago Press, 1955.
DEWEY, JOHN. *The Public and Its Problems.* Chicago: The Macmillan Co., 1927.
ERNST, MORRIS LEOPOLD. *The People Know Best.* Washington, D. C.: Public Affairs Press, 1949.
FRIEDRICH, CARL. *The New Belief in the Common Man.* Boston: Little, Brown & Co., 1942.
GOSNELL, H. F. and SCHMIDT, M. J. "Popular Law-Making in the United States, 1924-1936," in *Problems Relating to Legislative Organization and Powers.* New York State Constitutional Convention Committee, 1938, pp. 314-35.
GRIFFITH, ERNEST S. *The Impasse of Democracy.* New York: Harrison-Hilton Books, 1939.
HALL, A. B. *Popular Government.* New York: The Macmillan Co., 1923.
HOOK, SIDNEY. "Do the People Rule, and Can They?" Review of Rossiter, Clinton, and Lare, James, *The Essential Lippmann* (Random House, 1963), in *N. Y. Times* Book Review, July 14, 1963, p. 1ff.
KORNHAUSER, WILLIAM. *The Politics of Mass Society.* Chicago: The Free Press of Glencoe Ill., 1959.
JANOWITZ, MORRIS, and MARVICK, DWAINE. "Competitive Pressure and Democratic Consent: An Interpretation of the 1952 Presidential Election," *Public Opinion Quarterly,* Vol. 19 (Winter, 1955-56), pp. 381-400.
LANE, ROBERT E. *Public Opinion and Ideology.* New York: Prentice-Hall Inc., 1963.
LASSWELL, H. D. *Democracy Through Public Opinion.* Menasha, Wis.: George Banta Publishing Co., 1941.
LIKERT, RENSIS. "Opinion Studies and Government Policy," *Proceedings of American Philosophical Society,* Vol. 92, No. 5 (Nov. 12, 1948), pp. 341-50.
LIPPMANN, WALTER. *Essays in The Public Philosophy.* Boston: Little, Brown & Co., 1955.
LIPPMANN, WALTER. *The Phantom Public.* New York: Harcourt, Brace, & Co., 1925.
LIPSET, SEYMOUR MARTIN. *Political Man: Where, How, and Why Democracy*

Works in the Modern World. Garden City, N. Y.: Doubleday & Co., 1960.

LIVINGSTON, JOHN C., and THOMPSON, R. G. *The Consent of the Governed.* New York: The Macmillan Co., 1963.

LOWELL, ABBOTT L. *Public Opinion and Popular Government.* New York: Longmans, Green, 1921.

LOWELL, ABBOTT L. *Public Opinion in War and Peace.* Cambridge, Mass.: Harvard University Press, 1923.

National Municipal League. *Democracy Must Think.* The League: 1939.

RIKER, WILLIAM H. *Democracy in the United States.* New York: The Macmillan Co., 1953.

SCHUBERT, GLENDON. *The Public Interest.* Chicago: The Free Press of Glencoe, Ill., 1960.

• Index of Names •

· Index of Subjects ·

367

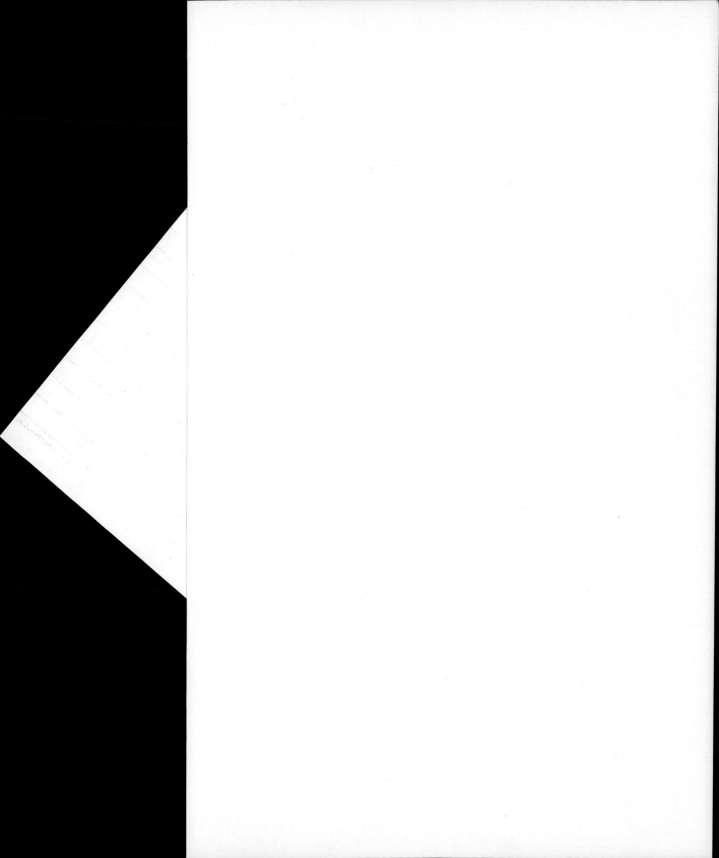

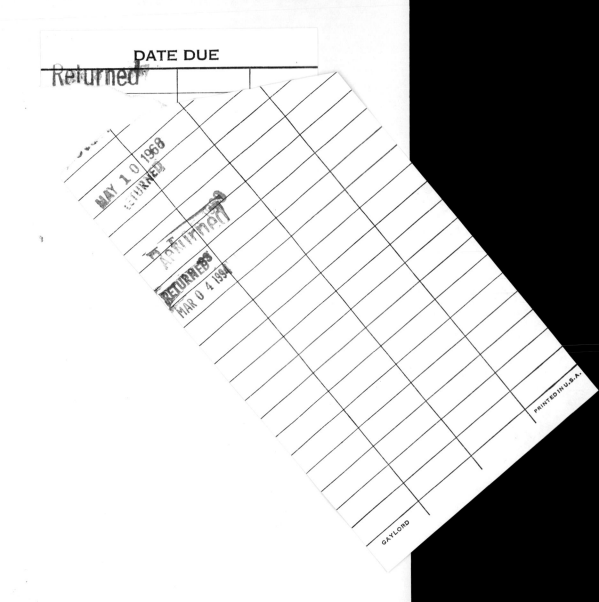